American Indians

HISTORICAL TO CONTEMPORARY PERSPECTIVES

Sebastian Braun | Grant Christensen | Birgit Hans

Kendall Hunt
publishing company

Cover images © Shutterstock.com

Kendall Hunt
publishing company

www.kendallhunt.com
Send all inquiries to:
4050 Westmark Drive
Dubuque, IA 52004-1840

Copyright © 2017 by Kendall Hunt Publishing Company

ISBN 978-1-5249-3560-3

Published in the United States of America

Contents

Appendix   **199**

Key Concepts in American Indian Studies

Grant Christensen

Every serious academic discipline has its own vocabulary. American Indian Studies is no exception. No matter what class or topic you are addressing within an American Indian/Native American curriculum, there are certain foundational ideas and events that every student needs to be familiar with. This section is intended to give readers that familiarity. Below you will find 12 topics that underlie many core concepts within our discipline. You may need to refer back to these topics with some regularity, and all students are encouraged to use these definitions as a jumping off point for further discussion.

Tribal Sovereignty

The formal status afforded to Indian tribes is that they are "domestic dependent nations" – they maintain an independence from the various States in which they sit but are still ultimately subject to the laws of the United States. The "domestic" part of this terminology prevents tribes from raising their own armies or going to war, creating embassies in foreign capitals, or joining international bodies like the United Nations. However tribes retain the status as 'nations' capable of independent self-government within lands set aside for them by treaty or other arrangement. This makes Indian tribes 'sovereign' – capable of maintaining an independent government.

One of the most important corollaries to tribal sovereignty is that most of the laws and rules of the states in which tribal land sits are not enforceable in Indian Country. While tribes are free to negotiate compacts with state law enforcement to ensure a seamless criminal justice system, often join with states for the purpose of sharing tax revenue, create consistent zoning ordinances in cooperation with state authority, and will sometimes join their state counterparts in promoting environmental protection – they are seldom required to do so. Instead tribes act as their own states creating and enforcing their own laws and customs.

Interestingly, tribal sovereignty also means that the U.S. Constitution does not apply on the reservation in the same way that it applies elsewhere in the United States. The Constitution is an agreement signed by the various sister states of the Union. Tribes have never ratified the document and therefore while they are inside the United States they are not bound by the Constitution in the same way as federal, state, and local governments. However, because they are 'dependent,' while not bound by the Constitution Indian tribes are subject to all federal laws passed by Congress. Accordingly, Congress has required Indian tribes to comply with most parts of the Constitution under the Indian Civil Rights Act of 1968. There are some notable exceptions. Tribes are not required to use 18 as their legal voting age, they are allowed to establish an official governmental religion, there is no second amendment right to bear arms, no requirement that the tribe ensure a republican form of government, etc.

Tribal sovereignty extends to business dealings made by the tribe. Under a common law tradition where an individual is not allowed to sue the king Indian tribes can raise the issue of tribal sovereignty to avoid being sued. This unique status of tribal sovereignty can be used to avoid all lawsuits except where the federal Congress has specifically allowed tribes to be sued or where tribes have waived their right to exercise their sovereign immunity.

Justice Elena Kagan's majority opinion in the 2014 case of *Michigan v. Bay Mills Indian Community* provides an excellent overview of what tribal sovereignty means in the context of the complicated relationship between Indian tribes and the states with which they regularly conduct business:

> Among the core aspects of sovereignty that tribes possess—subject, again, to congressional action—is the 'common-law immunity from suit traditionally enjoyed by sovereign powers.' *Santa Clara Pueblo*, 436 U. S., at 58. That immunity, we have explained, is 'a necessary corollary to Indian sovereignty and self-governance.' *Three Affiliated Tribes of Fort Berthold Reservation v. Wold Engineering, P. C.*, 476 U. S. 877, 890 (1986) . . . In doing so, we have held that tribal immunity applies no less to suits brought by States (including in their own courts) than to those by individuals. First in *Puyallup Tribe, Inc. v. Department of Game of Wash.*, and then again in *Potawatomi*, we barred a State seeking to enforce its laws from filing suit against a tribe, rejecting arguments grounded in the State's own sovereignty. In each case, we said a State must resort to other remedies, even if they would be less 'efficient.' That is because, as we have often stated tribal immunity 'is a matter of federal law and is not subject to diminution by the States.' Or as we elsewhere explained: While each State at the Constitutional Convention surrendered its immunity from suit by sister States, 'it would be absurd to suggest that the tribes'—at a conference 'to which they were not even parties'—similarly ceded their immunity against state-initiated suits. (Some internal citations omitted). *Michigan v. Bay Mills Indian Community*, 134 S. Ct. 2024 (2014)

Today, tribal sovereignty ensures that tribes are acting as formal and independent governments free to make their own laws and rules to govern the actions and activities of their members and the events that occur on their reservations. In most instances, states are not allowed to prevent tribes from creating their own rules. Accordingly, tribes have their own vehicle license bureaus, tax brackets, catch limits, hunting seasons, water and air quality standards, etc. This exercise of tribal sovereignty permits tribes to promote their own economic development with minimal state interference.

Bureau of Indian Affairs/Indian Agents

The Bureau of Indian Affairs (commonly called the BIA) was created by Secretary of War John C. Calhoun in 1824 and was formally approved and funded by Congress in 1832. It has been in continued existence since then, although its responsibilities have changed substantially since its creation. In 1849, responsibility for the Bureau was transferred from the Department of War to the Department of Interior where it has remained. The department has been the primary government body responsible for policies affecting American Indians which have included the negotiation and enforcement of Indian treaties, attempts to assimilate Indians and to terminate their status with the federal government, policies surrounding the distribution of land on reservations and at times its use and sale to non-Indians, education, health care, environmental and resource management, assistance with tribal self-government, and the formal agency responsible for the government-to-government relationship which exists between federally recognized tribes and the United States.

To help direct and carry out this work, the BIA has long employed "Superintendents" of Indian affairs responsible for various regions of the country and "Indian Agents" responsible for a single or small group of reservations/tribes. Today the nation's federally recognized tribes are divided among 12 BIA regions, each with a central office and a superintendent.

Historically, the Indian Agent possessed substantial control over the life of those living on the reservation. The Agent was responsible for securing and distributing rations of food and materials needed to live, accounting for funds expended by the government on behalf of the tribe, securing medical care, monitoring the work of missionaries and other non-members who lived on or near the reservation, resolving disputes and delivering punishment, etc. Many agents abused their power or were simply incompetent, resulting in a breakdown of civility or worse the unchecked spread of disease and starvation. Other Indian Agents were overzealous in their enforcement of Indian policy, resulting in the expedited loss of territory, encouraging non-Indian settlement on tribal lands, removing Indian children from their families and assigning them to boarding schools, and even advocating for the termination of a tribe's political relationship with the United States. Still others used the position for self-enrichment, often stealing money designated for the use or the benefit of the tribe or contracting for the provision of resources and services with personal connections without regard to the quality actually delivered to the reservation. Given this varied and pockmarked history, different tribes have markedly different relations and impressions of their Indian Agents.

Today, Indian Agents play a much different role in Indian Country. While they are still charged with being the representative of the United States on the reservation, many agents are themselves members of federally recognized Indian tribes. Additionally, tribes have taken over the provision of many services formerly assigned to the Indian Agents with the BIA paying for the services but providing minimal direct oversight. Every year tribes are changing their own laws to minimize the role BIA agents play in their daily operations. The role of an Indian Agent now is generally focused on promoting the self-governance of tribes in Indian Country, and in many places continuing to monitor law enforcement, land use and resource preservation, and tribal compliance with federal law as required by various federal statutes and agency directives.

The United States maintains a 'trust relationship' with its constituent tribes. The Indian Agent is the embodiment of the United States in each of the 12 regions and ultimately is responsible for maintaining this relationship. Federal law gives the agents the responsibility for control and supervision of tribal lands. Various laws ensure this control extends to timber resources, mineral extraction, Indian traders, and even some law enforcement responsibilities. The BIA meanwhile administers federal programs, from scholarship assistance to low-interest loans to promote tribally owned businesses, which are designed to benefit all Indian people regardless of whether they reside in Indian Country.

Treaty Rights

While it is commonly recognized that the United States has breached or abrogated virtually all of the treaties it has made with American Indians, rights granted in those treaties are enforceable today. "Abrogated" is a legal term that means that Congress has replaced the obligations conferred in a treaty or has expressly indicated that the treaty is no longer applicable. Article VI of the United States Constitution makes clear that treaties entered into by the United States are the supreme law of the land:

> This Constitution, and the laws of the United States which shall be made in pursuance thereof; and all treaties made, or which shall be made, under the authority of the United States, shall be the supreme law of the land; and the judges in every state shall be bound thereby, anything in the Constitution or laws of any State to the contrary notwithstanding.

It has long been settled that a treaty with an Indian tribe is no different than a treaty made with any other foreign government. Accordingly, it does not matter how long ago the treaty was signed if the United States has not clearly and expressly abrogated the treaty it is still binding and enforceable. The United States can ask an Indian signatory to honor its obligations under the treaty and the tribe may force the United States to honor its obligations through litigation if necessary.

The only limits on the rights a treaty may confer upon a tribe are that the rights granted cannot otherwise violate the Constitution. There are a number of interesting Indian treaty rights that are still enforced even if they may more generally now contradict a common public policy of the United States. For example, the Makah in Washington State secured the right to "whale" in the Treaty of Neah Bay. The United States is a member of the International Whaling Commission and has banned the killing of whales in American waters. However, to honor its treaty commitment, the United States secured a small quota of grey whales under the cultural subsistence exception of the treaty creating the Commission. Today the Makah are legally allowed to hunt grey whales in keeping with their culture and tradition, a right established by treaty, even though virtually all other Americans are prohibited from doing so.

Fourteen tribes in the Pacific Northwest secured a treaty that guaranteed: "the right of taking fish, at all usual and accustomed grounds and stations, is further secured to said Indians, in common with all citizens of the territory, and of erecting temporary houses for the purpose of curing. . . ." In *United States v. State of Washington* the district court held that treaty rights should be read as the Indians would have understood them at the time they were entered into, and that because of the disparate levels of bargaining power any ambiguities in treaties should be read in favor of the Indians. In trying to give meaning to the treaty right Judge Boldt held:

> There is no record of English having been spoken at the treaty councils, but it is probable that there were Indians at each council who would have spoken or understood some English. One Snohomish Indian who understood English helped translate the Point Elliott treaty. Since, however, the vast majority of Indians at the treaty councils did not speak or understand English, the treaty provisions and the remarks of the treaty commissioners were interpreted by Colonel Shaw to the Indians in the Chinook jargon and then translated into native languages by Indian interpreters. Chinook jargon, a trade medium of limited vocabulary and simple grammar, was inadequate to express precisely the legal effects of the treaties, although the general meaning of treaty language could be explained. Many of those present, however, did not understand Chinook jargon. There is no record of the Chinook jargon phrase that was actually used in the treaty negotiations to interpret the provision "The right of taking fish, at all usual and accustomed grounds and stations, is further secured to said Indians, in common with all citizens of the Territory." A dictionary of the Chinook jargon, prepared by George Gibbs, indicates that the jargon contains no words or expressions that would describe any limiting interpretation on the right of taking fish.
>
> The treaty language "in common with all citizens of the Territory" was probably introduced by George Gibbs, who was a lawyer and advisor to Governor Stevens. There is no discussion of the phrase in the minutes of the treaty councils, in the instructions to Stevens or to the treaty negotiators, or in Stevens' letters of transmittal of the treaties. There appears to be no phrase in the Chinook jargon that would interpret the term in any exact legal sense. . . .
>
> The Indians who negotiated the treaties probably understood the concept of common ownership interest which could have been conveyed in Chinook jargon. The clause "usual and accustomed [fishing] grounds and stations" was all-inclusive and intended by all parties to the treaty to include reservation and off-reservation areas. The words "usual and accustomed" were probably used in their restrictive sense, not intending to include areas where use was occasional or incidental. The restrictive sense of the term "usual and accustomed" could have been conveyed in Chinook jargon.

As a consequence of the Indians likely understanding that sharing the fish 'in common' meant that there was common ownership, Judge Boldt held that the 14 tribes in the Pacific Northwest were entitled to 50% of all of the Salmon in the Columbia River Basin. The tribes could harvest or not harvest their share of the salmon every year, but non-Indian owners could take only half of the number of salmon provided by state fisheries laws and federal environmental quotas.

Indian treaties commonly contained unique provisions that were especially relevant to the specific tribe or tribes with which the treaty was made. They also commonly gave the tribe either shared or exclusive use over resources that were important for the tribe ranging from whales to the right to collect wild rice. Some treaties guaranteed land, often they contained a promise of annual payments from the United States for a terms of years, they could provide rations to support a transition to reservation life, and commonly contained provisions to encourage Indians to take up farming. For an example of a treaty that still touches the lives of tens of thousands of Native Americans, the Fort Laramie Treaty of 1851 and the Treaty of Fort Laramie of 1868 are reproduced in the appendix.

Rations

Many Indian treaties required that the federal government provide 'rations' to Indian tribes in exchange for the tribe laying down its weapons or ceding some of its land. The rations were meant to take the place of the nomadic tradition of following the buffalo or foraging for food. The Act of 1883 explained that rations would ensure that Indians "may live after the manner of white men." When Indians, who had never previously be forced to remain sedentary instead of roaming the land following the seasons and the abundance of game, were confined to a reservation they required some assistance for basic survival. The ration cards issued by the government to these Indians indicated the ability of the bearer of the card to take beef, salt, corn, flour, beans and sometimes cloth, tobacco, sugar, soap, coffee, etc. for their families. The food and goods were often of poor quality and sometimes spoilt or rotten.

Many Indians, their previous way of life interrupted by the explosion of settlers and their confinement to the reservations, came to rely on these rations for their survival. However, the federal government did not always guarantee sufficient rations for a tribe's continued existence. For example, during the winter of 1884 a majority of the Blackfeet people suffered from severe malnutrition due to the poor quality and relative scarcity of the rations provided. A quarter of the tribe died of starvation. While an appalling breach of their treaty right to sufficient rations, little was done to compensate the tribe for its massive losses.

To the frustration of many Indians, the United States often played games with the rations after a treaty was signed and the tribe was either no longer a military threat to new settlers or the tribe had finished ceding its territory. Common games included the deduction of financial assistance to tribes and the use of rations to force accommodation with American policy goals that often severely injured the effected Indians.

Treaties often specified that in addition to rations the United States would pay a fixed sum annually for a period of years. However, the United States would deduct the cost of the rations from the annual payment even when such deductions were not included in the text of the treaty. Additionally, the value of the rations deducted would sometimes be many times the actual fair market value of the goods supplied, with no discount for the quality of the goods or for supplies that were rotten or never reached the Indians. In 1946, the United States Congress established the Indians Claims Commission where tribes could bring claims against the United States for, among other things, violations of treaty rights. Multiple claims were lodged surrounding the mishandling and improper accounting for rations ultimately costing the federal government millions of dollars.

Some treaties allowed the United States to deny rations to any family that refused to send their children to school. (See Treaty with Pawnees 1857, Treaty with the Poncas 1858). The requirement to send children to school could then be extended not to a local school but the forced removal of children from their families to be placed in Indian boarding schools. Parents who resisted the removal of their children were then denied the basic rations necessary to live. Some Indian families were forced to choose between starvation and the forced removal of their children.

In other instances, the United States threatened to withhold rations unless tribal leaders would sign subsequent treaties giving up more land without any additional compensation. For example, in 1868, the Sioux Nation signed the Treaty of Fort Laramie which among other provisions provided for one pound of meat and one pound of flour per person per day. Six years later, in 1874, a military expedition led by General Custer claimed to have found gold and other wealth in the Black Hills which were part of the lands held by the Sioux under the Treaty of Fort Laramie. A Commissioner of Indian Affairs was sent to negotiate a new agreement for the cession of land. In order to attempt to secure the support of the Sioux, the Commissioner threatened to withdraw the rations unless the Sioux ceded these new lands for $6 million. The Sioux, understanding the value of the land, demanded no less than $70 million. Negotiations broke down, but the United States sought a pretext to take the lands by force. The United States Supreme Court in *United States v. Sioux Nation of Indians* described what happened next:

> In August, 1876, Congress enacted an appropriations bill providing that "hereafter there shall be no appropriation made for the subsistence" of the Sioux, unless they first relinquished their rights to the hunting grounds outside the reservation, ceded the Black Hills to the United States, and reached some accommodation with the Government that would be calculated to enable them to become self-supporting. Act of Aug. 15, 1876, 19 Stat. 176. Toward this end, Congress requested the President to appoint another commission to negotiate with the Sioux for the cession of the Black Hills.
>
> This commission, headed by George Manypenny, arrived in the Sioux country in early September and commenced meetings with the head men of the various tribes. The members of the commission impressed upon the Indians that the United States no longer had any obligation to provide them with subsistence rations. The commissioners brought with them the text of a treaty that had been prepared in advance. The principal provisions of this treaty were that the Sioux would relinquish their rights to the Black Hills and other lands west of the one hundred and third meridian, and their rights to hunt in the unceded territories to the north, in exchange for subsistence rations for as long as they would be needed to ensure the Sioux' survival. In setting out to obtain the tribes' agreement to this treaty, the commission ignored the stipulation of the Fort Laramie Treaty that any cession of the lands contained within the Great Sioux Reservation would have to be joined in by three-fourths of the adult males. Instead, the treaty was presented just to Sioux chiefs and their leading men. It was signed by only 10 of the adult male Sioux population.

Despite the fact that their nation was facing starvation, a majority of Sioux chiefs refused to sign away their land. This situation was not unique to the Sioux. Rations were used by the federal government repeatedly to force tribes to give up their claims to land and to accept payment of terms which were far from equitable. Despite the fact that only 10 Sioux signed the new agreement in 1876, Congress ratified it in 1877 permanently removing the Black Hills from their status as Indian lands and depriving the Sioux of land that was critically important to their tradition and cultural practice.

Today the memory of rations is still pervasive in parts of Indian Country. The heavy emphasis on flour and fats as part of rations has helped solidify fry bread as a tribal staple in many communities. The physical paper coupons which could be redeemed for rations have become historical artifacts. The memory of rations and often the starvation and loss of independence that the rations represent is an ever-present backdrop to the relationship between the United States and Indian tribes.

Tribal Membership

Who is an Indian? There is not one commonly accepted definition of who qualifies to be an Indian. The context of the discussion will determine the parameters of membership. For example the U.S. census does not require any "proof" of membership, all individuals can self-identify their race. In contrast, federal benefits under the Indian Health Service require Indians to produce some form of tribal identification in order to qualify for and receive benefits.

So can anyone claim to be an Indian? The United States government and the individual Indian tribes may have different definitions for who is an Indian. The United States has long struggled with this question – as many laws apply differently to Indians and to non-Indians, and thus require some formal way to determine tribal membership. In 1846, in an attempt to avoid federal prosecution a white man named William Rodgers claimed to be an Indian because he had lived among the Cherokee. The Supreme Court rejected this argument, holding that the term "Indian" should be reserved for persons who can claim descent from native peoples who were present before the arrival of Europeans:

> [W]e think it very clear, that a white man who at mature age is adopted in an Indian tribe does not thereby become an Indian, and was not intended to be embraced in the exception above mentioned. He may by such adoption become entitled to certain privileges in the tribe, and make himself amenable to their laws and usages. Yet he is not an Indian; and the exception is confined to those who by the usages and customs of the Indians are regarded as belonging to their race. It does not speak of members of a tribe, but of the race generally,– of the family of Indians; and it intended to leave them both, as regarded their own tribe, and other tribes also, to be governed by Indian usages and customs. And it would perhaps be found difficult to preserve peace among them, if white men of every description might at pleasure settle among them, and, by procuring an adoption by one of the tribes, throw off all responsibility to the laws of the United States, and claim to be treated by the government and its officers as if they were Indians born. It can hardly be supposed that Congress intended to grant such exemptions, especially to men of that class who are most likely to become Indians by adoption, and who will generally be found the most mischievous and dangerous inhabitants of the Indian country. *United States v. Rodgers*, 45 U.S. 567 (1846)

From *Rodgers* has evolved the modern understanding of who qualifies as an Indian. While Indian tribes, exercising their inherent sovereignty, are permitted to determine for themselves who is a member, the United States will officially recognize only those individuals who (1) are recognized as members by their tribe AND (2) can trace their ancestry to a documented Indian person. It is common for Indian tribes to issue tribal identification cards that essentially show both that the individual named on the card is an enrolled member and list the member's degree of Indian descent.

Today tribes have developed many different qualifications for membership which are often codified in tribal Constitutions or articles of incorporation and overseen by tribal enrollment officers. Some require individuals to actually live on the reservation or maintain continued contact with the tribe, others require a specific level of blood quantum (i.e. you must be 1/4 or 1/8 or 1/16 Indian by blood). Still others have adopted a lineal descent standard where anyone who is descended from a member is eligible for membership. As a result of these various metrics, an individual who is 1/8 Indian by blood and lives in New York City may or may not qualify for membership depending on the specific rules of their tribe.

As examples of the various membership criteria among tribes consider the following tribal requirements:

The Turtle Mountain Band of Chippewa

Section 1. The membership in the Turtle Mountain Band of Chippewa Indians shall consist of:

(a) All persons whose names appear on the roll prepared pursuant to Section 2 of the Act of May 24, 1940 (54 Stat. 219), and approved by the Secretary of the Interior on March 15, 1943.
(b) All descendants of persons whose names appear on the roll defined in Section 1 (a) of this Article, provided that such descendants possess one-fourth or more Indian blood, and provided further that such descendants are not domiciled in Canada.

The Cherokee Nation of Oklahoma

Section 1. All citizens of the Cherokee Nation must be original enrollees or descendants of original enrollees listed on the Dawes Commission Rolls, including the Delaware Cherokees of Article II of the Delaware Agreement dated the 8th day of May, 1867, and the Shawnee Cherokees of Article III of the Shawnee Agreement dated the 9th day of June, 1869, and/or their descendants. The Cherokee Nation recognizes the basic rights retained by all distinct People and groups affiliated with the Cherokee Nation, retained from time immemorial, to remain a separate and distinct People. Nothing in this Constitution shall be construed to prohibit the Cherokee-Shawnee or Delaware–Cherokee from pursuing their inherent right to govern themselves, provided that it does not diminish the boundaries or jurisdiction of the Cherokee Nation or conflict with Cherokee law.

The Confederated Tribes of the Colville Reservation

Section 1 – Membership: The membership of the Confederated Tribes of the Colville Reservation shall consist of the following:

(a) All persons of Indian blood whose names appear as members of the Confederated Tribes on the official census of the Indians of the Colville Reservation as of January 1, 1937, provided that, subject to the approval of the Secretary of the Interior corrections may be made in said roll within two (2) years from the adoption and approval of this amendment.

(b) All children possessing one-fourth (1/4) or more Indian blood, born after January 1, 1937, to any member of the Confederated Tribes of the Colville Reservation maintaining a permanent residence on the Colville Indian Reservation.

(c) All children possessing one-fourth (1/4) or more Indian blood, born after January 1, 1937, to any member of the Confederated Tribes of the Colville Reservation maintaining residence elsewhere in the continental United States, provided that the parent or guardian of the child indicate a willingness to maintain tribal relations and to participate in tribal affairs. To indicate such willingness to maintain tribal affiliation, the parent or guardian shall, within six (6) months after the birth of the child submit a written application to have the child enrolled. The application shall be accompanied by the child's birth certificate together with any other evidence as to the eligibility of the child for enrollment in the Confederated Tribes of the Colville Reservation. If the certificate and application are not filed within the designated time, the child will not be enrolled.

The tribal definitions of membership can be changed by tribes by following the rules laid down in the tribal Constitution or tribal law. Tribes have regularly changed their requirements to meet evolving circumstances. Where many members of a tribe marry out, the tribe may be encouraged by its members to lower blood quantum requirements so that member's children and grandchild can also enroll. Other tribes have amended their membership criteria on the basis of history or economic circumstance. The Cherokee Nation of Oklahoma is engaged in a protracted battle regarding whether or not descendants of freed and escaped slaves ('freedmen') should remain members of the tribe. Gaming tribes sometimes increase the required blood quantum so as it limit membership. With fewer members, the existing members each share a larger return of casino revenue.

There is such variance among tribal membership criteria that it is difficult to generalize about membership rules. Perhaps it is most important to remember that it is the tribes themselves that are able to determine who is and who is not a member and great deference is given to tribal decisions on these matters.

Federal Recognition

How many Indian tribes are there? The question appears simple, but has a very complicated answer and often depends on who you are asking. Many students are surprised to learn that some Indian tribes are gaining recognition even in the twenty-first century. By far the largest group of American Indian tribes are those that are 'federally recognized.' This means that the United States federal government officially recognizes the tribal government as sovereign and that the tribe and the United States share a 'government-to-government' relationship. Federal recognition brings with it the ability to have land taken into trust, i.e. protected from state regulation, and it permits the tribe the authority to establish its own tribal government and justice system which will be recognized by the United States.

So how does a tribe become federally recognized? The most common way is for Congress to pass a resolution affirming a tribe's official status as an Indian tribe. Treaties between the United States and various Indian tribes have often served as the legal basis to affirm that a tribe has been formally recognized. In 1978, Congress required the Department of Interior to publish annually a list of all federally recognized tribes and created a procedure under which unrecognized tribes could petition the United States for recognition. The rules and guidelines were published at 25 CFR 83, and accordingly petitions made under these scheme are often termed section 83 applications.

As of 2017, there are 567 federally recognized Indian tribes, including 229 tribes composed of Alaska Natives. Since 1978, Congress has recognized about 30 Indian tribes directly by resolution, and the Department of Interior has granted federal recognition to 18 tribes but denied more than 34 applications through its Office of Federal Acknowledgment (OFA). In July 2015, the Department of the Interior extended government-to-government federal recognition to the Pamunkey Tribe of Virginia – making it the 567th federally recognized tribe.

The Section 83 application process has not worked as well as intended. Some tribes were left waiting decades after submitting their application for a yes/no answer from the Department. Between 1978 and 2015 more than 140 applications had been made, and only 51 cases were resolved by Interior. The process has justly been widely criticized:

> Some members of Congress, such as Chairman John Barrasso of the Senate Committee on Indian Affairs, have stated that the process simply takes too long. S. Hrg. 112–684 (July 12, 2012). Previous Chairs of the Senate Committee on Indian Affairs, such as Byron Dorgan, have raised similar critiques. S. Hrg. 110–189 (September 19, 2007). Congressional leaders in the House have raised other concerns. For example, Congressman Tom Cole has said that the process is "complex," "controversial," and "frankly, has not worked well." H. Hrg. No. 110–47 (October 3, 2007). Chairman Don Young has said that "reforms to expedite the

process and to upgrade the fairness, consistency, and transparency are warranted." H. Hrg. No. 110–47 (October 3, 2007). *Federal Acknowledgement of American Indian Tribes* 80 Fed. Reg. 126 (July 1, 2015).

In response, the Department of Interior issued new guidelines under Section 83 that are designed to speed up and to simplify the review process.

In order for the Department of Interior to grant a prospective tribe's petition for federal recognition the tribe must show (a) that it has been identified as an American Indian entity continuously since 1900, (b) that it comprises a distinct community and has continuously existed and acted as a community from 1900 until the present, (c) that it has maintained political influence or authority over its members as an autonomous entity from 1900 to present, (d) it must provide its government document or a written statement detailing its membership criteria and current governing procedures, (e) that its members descend from a historic Indian tribe, (f) a majority of its members are not members of a currently recognized Indian tribe, and (g) that the tribe and its members never had their political relationship terminated by Congress nor has Congress passed a law prohibiting federal recognition of the candidate tribe and its members. After the Office of Federal Acknowledgement receives documented proof of the seven criteria, it will publish all of the relevant material in the Federal Registrar and allow any member of the public to provide comments on the submitted material. After the period for public comments is closed, the OFA will give the applicant tribe 90 days to respond to the comments. It will proceed to then review each application as it is completed and as resources allow. The review will occur in two phases: the first to determine whether all documents have been provided and the second to evaluate the merits of the tribe's petition for recognition. The guidelines require the OFA to come to a decision within 6 months of beginning each phase. It is widely hoped by both prospective tribes and by the Department of Interior that the new process will more easily and fairly facilitate the recognition of Indian tribes.

Even if a tribe is not federally recognized, it could still be recognized by a state. As of 2017, more than 60 tribes were recognized by the state in which they claimed traditional lands but were not federally recognized. Among the largest of these tribes – the Lumbee of North Carolina have more than 55,000 enrolled members. These state recognized tribes do not formally share the government-to-government relationship with the United States, and therefore their lands are generally subject to taxation by the state and their courts and elected governments serve under the auspices of the state in which they are incorporated. State recognized tribes are typically not eligible for federal programs designed to benefit Indians and they cannot operate casinos under the Indian Gaming Regulatory Act nor protect their children under the special rules provided by the Indian Child Welfare Act. However, state recognition does convey some benefits. By virtue of their status as a state recognized tribe members may have some protection from state taxation, may be eligible for special state government programs including scholarship assistance and aid to minority-owned business, and the tribes are given some measure of self-governance with the ability to draft laws and enforce them on lands recognized by the state as long as the activity of the tribe does not otherwise violate federal law.

"Indian Country" and the Modern Reservation

While American Indians live throughout the United States, generally tribal law and policies apply only within lands designated as "Indian Country" regardless of whether the land is owned by tribal members or even the tribe itself. Land located outside of "Indian County" is subject to the laws of the state in which it is located, and Indian people are likewise subject to state laws when located off of Indian lands.

By far the most common land in "Indian Country" is land that is part of an Indian reservation. There are 326 reservations in the United States created by treaty, executive order, or statute. The word reservation itself is fairly all encompassing and tends to refer to any time land has been taken by the United States and held for the benefit and use of an Indian tribe. However not all such lands are termed 'reservations.' For example, many tribes in New Mexico refer to their 'reservations' as pueblos (i.e. Laguna Pueblo and Pueblo of the Acoma), whereas in California it is common for the reservations to be called rancherias (i.e. Big Bend Rancheria, Roaring Creek Rancheria). Other terms are less common and often stem from historical usage. Colony is fairly common among Nevada tribes while "Community," "Village," and "Trust Land" are also formally used in official reservation names.

The reservations vary tremendously in size. Twelve reservations are each larger than the state of Rhode Island. The Navajo Nation is more than 16-million acres, making it larger than 11 states. In contrast, the smallest reservation is a 1.32-acre plot of land constituting a cemetery of the Pit River Tribe.

The term "reservation" should not be confused with Indian tribes. Reservations refer to the land held in trust by the United States for the benefit of various tribes. As of 2016, there are 567 federally recognized tribes. Some tribes share a reservation. For example, there are both Shoshone and Arapahoe on the Wind River Reservation in Wyoming and the Mandan, Hidatsa, and Arikara tribes share the Fort Berthold Reservation in North Dakota, an arrangement that is commonly termed the "Three Affiliated Tribes." Other tribes may be spread across several reservations. For example, the Pit River Tribe is the beneficiary of land on six different reservations in California.

Additionally, not all Indian tribes have a reservation. Having a land base is a separate issue from whether a group of Indians can form and constitute a tribe capable of maintaining relations with the United States. While the federal government can take additional land into trust and create new reservations through a process requiring public comment and giving nearby landowners the opportunity to appeal – it is not required to ensure that every tribe has a reservation. For example, in 2016, a dozen tribes in California remain landless. They have a formal governance structure, even pass laws to govern the conduct of members and are able to create courts to resolve questions of family law or child custody, but they have no formal land base on which to live or run tribal operations.

Historically, reservations have been most commonly created by treaty approved by Congress. Until 1871, the United States often sent agents to various tribes to negotiate treaties. Treaties were used as a tool both to purchase land and to end hostilities between the government and Indian tribes. Typically a treaty involved the United States recognizing an Indian tribe's claim to a set of lands (sometimes millions of acres) and in exchange the tribe released its claim on all other lands. The land set aside for the tribe became its "reservation" and on this land the tribe typically retains control of law and policy. In 1871, Congress passed a law prohibiting the negotiation of new treaties with Indian tribes, and so since 1871 there have not been any new Indian treaties. However, the Bureau of Indian Affairs and an Indian tribe can negotiate an "Agreement" that gets approved by both chambers of Congress and signed by the President. These Agreements can add land to existing reservations or create new reservations. More common in recent decades, tribes lobby Congress directly to pass legislation that takes public land held by the United States and reserves it for the use of one or more Indian tribes. Essentially Congress can just pass a law creating a new Indian reservation if the land is already part of the public lands of the United States.

Until 1919, the President of the United States could, by executive order, create an Indian reservation by reserving public lands held by the federal government for the exclusive use of an Indian tribe or set of tribes. An executive order is a written directive from the President of the United States to tell the executive branch of government to act or refrain from acting in order to execute the laws. More than 23 million acres of land were set aside in this way by presidents in the late nineteenth and early twentieth centuries before Congress passed a law banning the practice. Much of the land granted was in the west, particularly in Arizona and New Mexico. It was senators from these states that urged the 1919 legislation. In exchange for prohibiting the further use of an executive order to expand Indian lands, Congress recognized the right of reservation Indians to the mineral wealth under their lands.

Finally, there are several regulations that allow the Department of Interior, without separate approval from any other branch of government, to take land into trust for the benefit of one or more Indian tribes. Essentially the United States, the tribe, or one of its members buys land in or near an existing reservation or the traditional lands of the tribe. The purchase is made on the open market and a fair market value price is typically paid. Then the owner of the land asks the Department of Interior to take the land into trust. The decision to take the land into trust creates "Indian Country" and typically gives jurisdiction and control of the land over to the tribe. This comes at the expense of state and local government control. For example, after the land has been taken into trust, the state can no longer tax it and commonly loses the authority to zone it or control what activity occurs on the land. Before a final decision is made upon whether to take the land into trust, the state and local governments as well as local property owners can voice their concerns during a formal notice and comment period and often challenge a favorable decision to take the land into trust. Notwithstanding these challenges, the Department of Interior may proceed to take the land into trust despite the objections. When an official decision is reached, it is announced by the Department, and the land is removed from state tax rolls.

Alaska and Hawaii are typically excluded from "Indian Country." Of the 229 tribes in Alaska only one, the Metlakatla Indian Community, has a reservation because it opted out of the Alaska Native Claims Settlement Act in 1971. The remaining Alaska tribes are divided among 13 regional corporations which manage land reserved by that statute on behalf of their members. The United States still does not recognize the sovereignty of Native Hawaiian people. There are lands set side by the Hawaiian constitution to preserve traditional cultural spaces and to be used for the benefit of Native Hawaiian people, but there is no federal recognition of a special status of these lands.

The statute formally defining "Indian Country" is codified at 25 U.S.C. § 1151. The statute is reproduced here:

§ 1151. Indian country defined
Except as otherwise provided in sections 1154 and 1156 of this title, the term "Indian country", as used in this chapter, means

(a) all land within the limits of any Indian reservation under the jurisdiction of the United States Government, notwithstanding the issuance of any patent, and, including rights-of-way running through the reservation,
(b) all dependent Indian communities within the borders of the United States whether within the original or subsequently acquired territory thereof, and whether within or without the limits of a state, and
(c) all Indian allotments, the Indian titles to which have not been extinguished, including rights-of-way running through the same.

The statute clearly includes "any Indian reservation" but goes on to include "dependent Indian communities" and "all Indian allotments." Dependent Indian communities include all land set aside for Indian use and over which the United States maintains control and supervision but which may not formally be considered a 'reservation.' This includes land held by the BIA for all Indians, and may include Indian schools or BIA detention facilities which support tribal courts as well as tribal villages or cultural spaces.

While the definition is broad and fragmented, an understanding of the extent of "Indian Country" is important for anyone working with tribes for it sets the boundary between state and tribal authority. Too often "Indian Country" is viewed only as 'reservation' lands, but the actual extent of tribal control is wider and encompassing all lands set aside for tribal use.

Tribal Government

No two tribal governance structures are exactly alike. Tribal governments today take on many forms and while some look very similar to the structure of states – with three branches of government and a written Constitution – others reflect the unique cultural or traditional values of their members.

Early tribal governments had a variety of structures, from those that were highly complex to decentralized bands who acted together only rarely for a common cause. Felix Cohen's Handbook of Federal Indian Law describes some of these early structures:

> The Iroquois or Haudenosaunee Confederacy, for example, joined six warring nations together in peace, making decisions according to an elaborate system of checks and balances. Under the terms of its "Great Binding Law" or constitution, member nations selected chiefs to serve on a Council of Fifty, which met annually to resolve important issues. Although women were ineligible to serve on this Council, they wielded considerable power through the clan mothers, who nominated representatives to the Council of Fifty and who had the authority to dismiss leaders guilty of misconduct. The Cheyenne were governed by a civil council of forty-four chiefs, which was led by five priestly chiefs. Chiefs were responsible for mediating disputes, even by paying restitution themselves in order to restore harmony within the band. In times of war, moving camp, and the buffalo hunt, the people took orders from members of six men's societies, who were themselves governed by a council of twenty-four war chiefs.
>
> Many tribes were in fact largely independent villages or bands that would come together for collective purposes, but otherwise were bound only by common culture and kinship ties. One elaborate outgrowth of such a system was the Creek or Muscogee confederacy, which joined together up to eighty self-governing towns, representing six language groups. The towns were divided into white towns, which governed matters of peace, and red towns, which governed matters of war. The white towns were responsible for jointly enacting laws and regulations, and regulating internal affairs of the confederation, while the red towns conducted foreign relations and military campaigns. Underlying these government structures was a basic system of matriarchal and matrilocal clans.
>
> Despite their differences, many pre-contact systems of government shared common features. Political actions were often informed by spiritual guidance and directed toward spiritual as well as material fulfillment. Kinship groups and clan relationships usually had great social, economic, and political significance. And the values that most often animated traditional tribal governments were those of responsibility to the community, leading to more emphasis on consensus and conflict resolution than present in the American system. *Cohen's Handbook of Federal Indian Law* LexisNexis Publishing (Nell Jessup Newton Ed. 2012)

Even today, tribal governments vary considerably in their structure. In 1934, Congress enacted the Indian Reorganization Act or IRA. The IRA directed tribes to create formal government structures and adopt a Constitution. A boiler-plate constitution was created by the Indian Office as a model and many tribes adopted it without any changes. The boiler-plate constitutions were modeled on business charters and typically attempted to separate some government functions between a chairperson/executive officers and a committee or council in a basic attempt to encourage checks and balances in government. In total, 181 tribes voted to accept the terms of the IRA and constitute their governments accordingly while 77 tribes rejected it. Most tribes that adopted the IRA model have subsequently amended their constitutions to better reflect tribal demographics, to remove the role of the Department of Interior from tribal governance, and/or to better reflect traditional tribal custom and culture.

Regardless of whether they accepted or rejected powers under the IRA, most tribal governments have adopted some form of checks and balances within their government. The Navajo Nation for example never adopted the IRA and today runs a sophisticated government that includes a directly elected President, the Navajo Nation Council consisting of 24 delegates representing the 110 chapters of the Nation, and a Navajo Nation Supreme Court hearing appeals from the 10 district courts.

However, not all tribal governments allow for popularly elected leaders or create a system with tribal institutions designed to create a series of checks and balances on the use of governmental power. The United States Constitution, in Article IV section 4, guarantees to each citizen a republican form of government: "[t]he United States shall guarantee to every state in this union a republican form of government. . . ." In this way, representative democracy is required in every state, and American citizens elect their representatives to established terms for the purpose of making laws to govern society. However, the Constitution is binding upon states because it is a document each state has ratified. Essentially prior to admittance into the Union each state assembles a convention or takes a vote of the people agreeing to be bound by the Constitution. Indian tribes have never ratified the Constitution and accordingly the Constitution does not apply to their governments. Congress has passed laws that incorporate much of the Constitution against tribal governments anyway. For example, the Indian Civil Rights Act of 1968 requires tribes to provide for freedom of speech and freedom of the press, prevents tribes from handing down cruel and unusual punishments, requires tribes to give their citizens due process and recognize the equal protection of laws, etc. However, no law requires tribes to give their citizens a republican form of government and accordingly tribal governments run the gamut in their form and structure.

Some tribes continue to use a clan-based structure giving seats in their legislative bodies and the right to exercise political power to different clans. Other tribes have adopted religious governance with a headman or headwoman leading the tribe for life. This position may be hereditary with the tribal leadership passing down through a clan or kinship network. For example, the Acoma Pueblo has a "cacique" or a community religious leader. The cacique is a hereditary position that is always awarded to a member of the Antelope clan. While traditionally a religious role, the cacique is the ultimate authority in community matters.

The Catawba Indian Nation does have a Constitution but instead of an elected legislative branch the tribe employs a general council in which every adult member participates directly. The general counsel elects an executive committee with the power to enforce the laws. Under the Catawba Constitution, the general council is the only entity that can negotiate with the state or federal government; it can veto the sale of tribal lands, and pass tribal ordinances.

Tribal sovereignty means that each tribe can decide for itself the appropriate form of government. Tribes have very different numbers of members, different land bases, and different cultural views on leadership and governance. There is clearly not one form of government that works for every tribe. There continues to be an ongoing debate between the importance of a system of checks and balances set against traditional roles for elders and hereditary clan leaders. The government system used by each tribe is a reflection of the choices its members have made regarding how they want to collectively be governed.

Taxation

There is a common misconception that Indians do not pay taxes. The United States Constitution, in the apportionment clause that determines how many seats in the House of Representatives each state is allotted, claims to exclude "Indians not taxed." In the early days of the United States, Indians were not considered American citizens but instead they were recognized as citizens of their own distinct political communities. Eventually, these communities were given the status of 'domestic dependent nations.' Because Indians were not American citizens, the general laws of the United States including laws related to taxation did not extend to Indian people nor Indian lands.

In 1924, Congress enacted the Indian Citizenship Act extending American citizenship to the various American Indian communities. One of the duties of citizens is an obligation to pay federal taxes and since 1924 Indian people have been required to pay federal income taxes indistinguishably from all other American citizens. However, tribal members who live on an Indian reservation and earn money on the Indian reservation do not pay state income taxes. Tribes are sovereign in a similar way that states are sovereign. A tribe may choose to levy its own income taxes on all income earned on the reservation regardless of whether it is earned by a member of the tribe or even a non-Indian. States have the authority to levy an income tax against their own citizens and against income earned in the state – but an Indian living on the reservation and earning their income on the reservation is outside the jurisdiction of the state. This also means that states cannot tax the profits earned by tribal governments or tribal businesses operating on the reservation.

Taxation gets more complicated when it moves from income taxes to excise or sales taxes. A number of tribes have claimed that they do not have to collect and remit the state sales tax on products like gasoline, alcohol, or cigarettes. This has encouraged some tribes to create profitable businesses selling these products either without any tax or with a tax levied directly by the tribe that is lower than the tax that would be collected by the state. This tax advantage encouraged economic development and allowed some tribes to derive a majority of tribal revenues from these industries.

However this tax advantaged status did not go unchallenged. In the 1980s and 1990s, state and local governments who saw large decreases in revenue challenged the tax-exempt status of tribal businesses. While even today not all parts of tribal tax law are clearly established, several principles have emerged. First, the state has no right to collect a sales tax paid by a tribal member making a purchase on the reservation. Because tribes are sovereign, the states cannot interfere in a transaction involving a tribal member on tribal land. Second, tribes are not allowed to simply market a tax exemption for non-members. The courts have held that when the tribe is doing nothing more than creating a new market for itself by marketing a tax exemption that the state has a sufficient interest to require that its taxes be collected and remitted to state government even for goods sold on the reservation. Third, the general principle that the state can tax transactions involving non-members on the reservation does not apply when the tribe takes some action to add value while the product is on the reservation. This third principle has been used by tribes to help build new industries from growing tobacco to building oil refineries on tribal land in order to add value on tribal land and thus remove the sale of the product from the category of transactions which the state is legally able to tax.

Casinos

W hy are Indians allowed to operate casinos? Today more than 200 tribes operate casinos or other gaming facilities that collect more than $35 billion in revenue. Indian tribes are allowed to operate casinos on land that has been taken into trust by the United States for the use of the Indian tribe because of tribal sovereignty. Essentially, since the 1830s, the United States Supreme Court has held that a state cannot regulate what happens on Indian land. In 1987, the Supreme Court extended this principle to gambling in the landmark case of *California v. Cabazon Band of Mission Indians*.

In *Cabazon*, the Cabazon Band of Mission Indians was operating a bingo parlor where a majority of the patrons were not tribal members. Some of the bingo games were 'high stakes' such that the winner would take away more than $250. California had passed a law that allowed bingo and other card games but only if the profits went to charity and the prize did not exceed $250 per game. When California tried to shut down the bingo parlor on the Cabazon reservation, the Indian tribe appealed all the way to the Supreme Court.

The Supreme Court reasoned that because California did not prohibit all gambling, merely regulated how much could be earned, that the state could not object if the tribe wanted to create its own different regulations for gambling that occurred on tribal lands. In response to the Supreme Court's ruling, Congress enacted the Indian Gaming Regulatory Act or IGRA which essentially applied the Supreme Court's reasoning to all Indian tribes. It divided games into three classes.

Class I gaming includes traditional tribal games and social games with minimal prizes. These games are governed exclusively by the tribe and neither the state nor the federal government regulates them.

Class II games include games of chance like bingo and card games where you play exclusively against other players (like most kinds of poker). As long as the state in which the tribe sits permits some kind of Class II gaming, then the tribe is permitted to regulate its own Class II gaming. Because even a basic lottery falls into this category as a game of chance virtually all tribes are permitted to operate Class II gaming facilities. Only Hawaii and Utah continue to ban all forms of gaming. In these states, tribes are not permitted to engage in any gaming activity without state approval. Utah continues to deny such approval while Hawaii has no federally recognized Indian tribes.

Class III games are virtually everything else, specifically including slot machines, roulette, craps, and card games played against the house like blackjack. In order to operate a facility where Class III gaming takes place the state in which the tribal facility sits must allow that kind of gaming, the facility must be approved by the Chairperson of the Indian Gaming Commission, and the tribe and the state need to have signed a compact specifying the terms of the gaming operation including which entity is responsible for law enforcement at the facility and how proceeds from the facility will be taxed.

In response to IGRA, some states have offered tribes a monopoly on gaming in exchange for a larger share of the revenues. In other words, the state will prohibit any non-Indian from operating a competing casino or gaming facility anywhere in the state in exchange for the tribe paying a larger share of revenue to the state. States like California have been particularly successful with tribes paying 25% of revenue in exchange for the virtual monopoly on gaming enterprises.

IGRA also contains a provision that allows tribes to distribute some of their casino gaming revenue directly to their members under an allocation plan that must be approved by the Secretary of Interior. These payments are known as "per caps" because the sum is divided equally among all eligible members of the tribe; that is, the revenue is distributed per capita. Some, but not all, tribes elect to make these distributions which can range from a few hundred dollars for large tribes with little revenue to well into the six-figures for tribes with fewer members and particularly profitable gaming enterprises.

Despite the advent of casino gaming, poverty among American Indians has remained high. The United States Census Bureau reported that in 2014, 28.3% of single race American Indians and Native Alaskans were living in poverty. This is the highest rate of any reported racial group and almost twice as high as the national average of 15.5%. The fact that casino gaming has not noticeably reduced poverty among American Indians is largely attributed to the asymmetry between the size of the Indian nation and its proximity to large dense population centers. Because of settlement patterns, the largest groups of Indians often live in the most remote parts of the country. Building a casino in the middle of South Dakota is considerably less profitable than building on land immediately off a highway between New York City and Boston. Accordingly while the Pine Ridge Indian reservation in South Dakota with its more than 20,000 members regularly reports an 80% unemployment rate and is one of the poorest places in the United States, the Mashantucket Pequot in Connecticut with only about 1000 members are comparatively well off as the owners of Foxwoods – the largest single gaming facility in the United States.

Indian Child Welfare Act (ICWA)

The history of the relationship between the United States federal government and Indian children is not a happy one. By the late 1800s, the government adopted a policy of boarding schools where Indian children were sometimes forcibly removed from their families and educated for years away from their family at schools administered by the Bureau of Indian Affairs. Ultimately more than 20 schools were organized and funded by the federal government spread across 15 states. There is ample documentation of abuse and neglect within these schools. Children were often used as cheap or even free labor, beaten for using their native language or expressing their tribal custom, forced to wear "modern" clothing, and were the victims of physical and emotional abuse.

The boarding school era waned in the first half of the twentieth century, but after the Second World War states stepped in with their own policies toward Indian children. By the 1960s, in some states between 25% and 35% of all Indian children were removed from their parents by state social workers, a rate up to 20x greater than that of non-Indian children. Often the result of prejudice or stereotyping, Indian children were removed for causes which could include leaving a grandparent in charge of the child or even the presence of unopened alcohol in the home. Courts upheld the majority of these removals on the basis of the "best interest of the child." It was unlikely a coincidence that more than 85% of Indian children removed from their home were ultimately placed with non-Indian families.

The loss of so many Indian children was devastating to the tribes affected. Some faced the prospect of losing an entire future generation of tribal leaders. Advocates for Indian tribes and Indian children argued vociferously for the adoption of a federal law to legally protect a tribe's interest in its children. At the same time, social scientists found that Indian children who had been removed from their reservation families and placed with non-Indian parents were more likely to commit suicide, to report depression or feelings of alienation, and to be unemployed than similarly situated unremoved Indian children, even if the removed children were placed in families with better education and resources.

As a result of these competing pressures, Congress enacted the Indian Child Welfare Act (or ICWA) in 1978. ICWA requires that tribal courts are the sole judicial entities capable of making custody decisions of Indian children located in Indian Country. Additionally, before any state court can make a custody decision regarding the placement of any child it is required to determine whether the child may be governed by ICWA. If Indian parentage is identified all state proceedings must stop while the relevant tribe or tribes are notified. Tribes have the ability to ask the case to be transferred from a state into tribal court and can even appear in court directly to assert parental rights. The presumption written into the law is that state courts must transfer the case if requested by the tribe absent 'good cause' to the contrary. Subsequent regulations have interpreted 'good cause' very narrowly.

ICWA also includes placement preferences. It specifically directs courts reviewing the placement of an Indian child to take into account the cultural importance of being a part of an Indian family. This has been interpreted as requiring a "best interest of the *Indian* child" standard in which placement decisions are made by explicitly accounting for the child's connection to Indian culture. Accordingly ICWA includes preferences for placement with an Indian family member, even a grandparent who may ordinarily be viewed as too old to be eligible or with an extended family member even if the family has less resources than a prospective non-Indian adoptive parent.

Importantly, an eligible 'Indian Child' includes any child eligible for enrollment in a federally recognized Indian tribe whether or not that child is actually enrolled. Eligibility also explicitly does not take into account whether the child was born on or grew up near the reservation or the extent of prior connection with tribal culture. That means that in courts of every state there are Indian children subject to the act. For example, in 2013, the nation was captivated by the case of *Adoptive Couple v. Baby Girl* where the Indian Child in question was 3/256ths Oklahoma Cherokee but born in South Carolina. Throughout the litigation all parties agreed that baby Veronica was an Indian Child, the disagreement was about whether her biological Indian father constituted an Indian parent.

In *Adoptive Couple*, baby Veronica was originally adopted out to a non-Indian couple after her non-Indian mother and Cherokee father had given up parental rights. The Indian father claimed he did not know that when he was giving up his rights that his daughter would be adopted, believing instead that the birth mother would raise the child and he would be able to see her regularly. Immediately after learning about the adoption, the Cherokee father set about seeking custody of his daughter.

The Supreme Court of South Carolina recognized that the Indian father had given up his parental rights under South Carolina law but held that ICWA permitted an Indian parent who had given up rights to reverse that decision and seek custody since there is an expressed preference for placement with an Indian family. Accordingly South Carolina ordered baby Veronica, now 2 years old, to be removed from the non-Indian adoptive family and returned to her Cherokee father.

Two years later, in 2013, the United States Supreme Court reversed. In a 5-4 opinion Justice Alito wrote that since the Indian father gave up custody before the birth of his daughter, and provided no support to the biological mother during her pregnancy, he never actually had custody of the child and therefore the more generous preferences under ICWA did not apply. Essentially Justice Alito concluded that while an enrolled member of the Cherokee tribe and the biological father of baby Veronica, the father did not constitute an "Indian parent" under the act. Justice Scalia, writing for the dissent, would have held ICWA applies because the man seeking custody was both the child's father and an Indian and therefore was an "Indian parent". Following the decision, baby Veronica, now almost four, was forcibly removed from her biological father in Oklahoma and returned to the non-Indian adoptive couple.

The case of baby Veronica is just one of the many complicated examples of how ICWA affects the legal decisions over Indian children. Indians who have experienced family court will all be familiar with the unique preferences and procedures laid down by the law which treat Indian children differently from others. Policy makers working in Indian Country need to be generally aware of the legacy of government-Indian child relations and conscience of past traumas and current tribal preferences which now exist under the law.

Violence Against Women Act (VAWA)

American Indian women are the demographic group most likely to be victims of violent crime, with the Department of Justice and Bureau of Justice Statistics reporting that native women are 2.5x more likely to be victims of violent crime than any other racial group. More than one in three Indian women report being the victim of rape during their lifetime. Moreover, this violence against native women is not equally spread throughout Indian Country. There are some Indian communities where violence is rare and others in which violence is truly endemic.

This problem has been compounded by jurisdictional constraints. In 1978, the Supreme Court decided that tribal courts lack the authority to criminally prosecute non-Indian persons. Instead, the Court held that the criminal jurisdiction of tribal courts could not be extended to non-Indian persons because it was inconsistent with the tribe's status as a 'domestic dependent nation.' Moreover, most states lack the authority to criminally prosecute non-Indians who commit crimes against Indians in Indian Country because, as sovereign entities, the state's authority ends at the tribal border.

This jurisdictional quagmire left only the federal government capable of prosecuting crimes by non-Indians against Indians that occurred in Indian Country. However, federal prosecutors are not used to involving themselves in domestic violence. Even when prosecutors are interested in bringing cases forward, many Indian victims and witnesses are unwilling to work with, or even talk to, non-Indian representatives from the Department of Justice. This reticence stems from a legacy of distrust between the United States and Indian people. Accordingly, comparatively few non-Indians are ever prosecuted or convicted of domestic violence occurring in Indian Country.

Congress recognized this problem and in 2013 added a historic provision to the Violence Against Women Act (VAWA). VAWA must be regularly reauthorized by Congress and during the 2013 reauthorization a new provision was added that grants tribes the ability to criminally prosecute non-Indians for acts of (1) domestic violence, (2) dating violence, or (3) violation of a protective order that occurs in Indian Country. Notably the VAWA expansion does not include sexual assault that does not occur within domestic or dating violence nor does it include offenses occurring in Indian Country if the victim is not an Indian or if the perpetrator does not have sufficient ties to the reservation. Sufficient ties can include living or working on or near the reservation.

Before tribes can accept this greater authority they must ensure that non-Indian defendants are given the same due process rights as would be afforded the criminally accused under the Constitution of the United States, including access to effective assistance of legal counsel. Judges presiding over criminal prosecutions against non-Indians under VAWA must have "sufficient legal training" and the court is obligated to make its rules of evidence and criminal procedure publicly available.

In order to ensure that tribes had time to adjust their legal systems and procedural practices to comply with the enhanced VAWA authority the statute delayed full implementation until March 7, 2015. Even after that date tribes must specifically opt in to the enhanced jurisdiction by adopting a tribal law implementing VAWA. Five tribes were given permission to adopt the rules early as part of a pilot program: the Pascua Yaqui Tribe of Arizona, the Tulalip Tribes of Washington, the Umatilla Tribes of Oregon, the Assiniboine and Sioux Tribes of the Fork Peck Indian Reservation in Montana, and the Sisseton Wahpeton Oyate of the Lake Traverse Reservation in South and North Dakota. Under the pilot program, tribes have both convicted and acquitted persons accused under the law which has helped build confidence that tribal courts will treat non-Indians accused of violent acts against tribal members fairly.

It is still comparatively early in the implementation and adoption of VAWA to know what effect the enhanced jurisdictional rules will have in reducing or preventing domestic violence in Indian Country. As more tribes take advantage of the expanded powers VAWA provides they will collectively begin to establish an effective deterrent to domestic violence in Indian Country. Tribes are already looking to expand VAWA jurisdiction in the future to cover crimes beyond just domestic violence, dating violence, or the enforcement of a protection order and are seeking additional criminal authority over non-Indians even when a member of the tribe is not involved in the dispute or when the accused has minimal connection to the reservation.

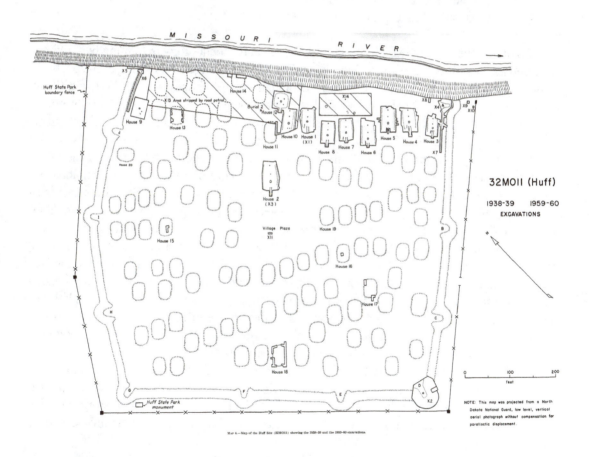

MISSOURI RIVER

32MOII (Huff)

1938-39   1959-60
EXCAVATIONS

0   100   200
                 feet

NOTE: This map was projected from a North
Dakota National Guard, low level, vertical
aerial photograph without compensation for
parallactic displacement.

Map 4.—Map of the Huff Site (32MOII) showing the 1938-39 and the 1959-60 excavations.

Oral Traditions
Birgit Hans

When the Huff Archaeological Site was nominated as a National Historic Landmark in 1997, the application listed four characteristics of the excavation as important to our understanding of fifteenth-century prehistoric Mandan culture:

(1) the rectangular fortification system with bastions,
(2) the dense occupation of the village,
(3) the arrangement of the houses in rows, and
(4) the types and relative quantities of types of artifacts.[1]

A visitor to the site can learn important things about the technology of hunting by looking at spear and arrow points, the way the Mandan built their earthlodges by looking at the postholes of the houses, the protection the prehistoric Mandan deemed important for their families by looking at the way the village was fortified, and their material culture in the shape of pottery shards and a Thunderbird effigy. The trash-filled storage pits provide information about the foods that people in the Huff village ate. The corn cobs, remains of sunflower seeds, as well as berries and squash remains found in them permit the archaeologists to draw conclusions about the gardens the people cultivated. The remains of wild plums, wild cherries, and other harvested foodstuffs indicate how people used the environment surrounding them. A visitor to the Huff site will leave with a sense of what everyday life might have been like for these prehistoric Mandan people and what resources and technologies they could draw on.

However, the information provided by the archaeological excavation does not provide any insights into the belief systems, the social organization, or the history of the people in the Huff village. What is the meaning of the Thunderbird effigy? What were the social rules that made it possible for so many people to live together in a confined space? What had happened between them and their neighbors that made fortifications, both a wooden wall with bastions for crossfire and a ditch in front of the wall, necessary? What happened in the big ceremonial lodge that was excavated? Archaeology can only give very general answers to these questions. Obviously, these prehistoric Mandan people had highly developed social and ceremonial structures, but what exactly these structures were used for remains speculation. Since there is no direct or indirect written information about the people living at the Huff site, hence prehistoric Mandan, we have to go to the ethnographic record of the historic Mandan to get some answers to the questions about prehistoric Mandan life.

The ethnographic record of a people would also include the stories they tell about themselves, their culture, and their history. However, these stories are not static and can adjust to changing cultural realities. For example, the Arikara origin story revolves around Mother Corn who leads the people west to the Heart River where they settle down and grow corn. However, corn which came from Mesoamerica did not appear on the northern Plain until 1000 A.D. The origin story goes back to times immemorial though. Through the archaeological record, we know when the Arikara started to cultivate corn and in general how important it was to them, but through the oral tradition we know in which ways the corn shaped Mandan spiritual thinking. The fact that the archaeological record disagrees with the Arikara origin story does not devalue the oral narrative. Stories cannot be considered historical accounts, but they illustrate how the Arikara perceived and conceptualized the world around them, their relationships with other people, and their spiritual values.

Oral tradition includes all knowledge, sacred, and secular, that people want to pass on to the generations after them. At the same time, some of this knowledge, especially sacred knowledge, was restricted to certain families, clans, societies, or village groups. Someone was usually designated the keeper of this knowledge, i.e. the stories, songs, prayers, etc. that were part of it; and he, in turn, designated his successor or successors and taught him or them whatever he knew. Many people from non-Native cultures that hand down their stories primarily in writing have doubted that the knowledge was handed down accurately. Studies have shown however that the human mind has an incredible ability to memorize, an ability that we rarely bother to develop anymore in cultures dependent on writing. In fact, before European and EuroAmericans became so dependent on external storage, such as writing and computers, our culturally important texts, for example the Bible, the Iliad, the Odyssey, and many other iconic cultural texts, were oral texts as well. It is not unusual in American Indian cultures to find versions of the same narrative in different villages or bands. Stories adjust to the cultural changes of the group that tells them and remain important in everyday life. In cultures that value literacy, stories fixed in text may lose their immediacy and may become removed from everyday life.

Origin Stories

The most sacred narratives within all cultures are the origin stories that usually explain how people came to be, why they are where they are, and why they value what they do. Origin stories can be divided into three groups: creation stories, emergence stories, and or migration stories. All origin stories fit into one or more of these groups. For example, the Christian origin story, Genesis, is one of creation with elements of migration through the Lost Tribes of Israel. God created the world and everything in it in six days and rested on the seventh day. The Lakota have a creation and emergence story. At the beginning of the origin story, Rock creates the universe from his blood and various sacred beings, such as the four winds and the sun, come into being. Double Faced Woman is then tricked into leading the Lakota onto the earth's surface. One of the three Hidatsa groups believes that they emerged from under Devil's Lake, but that many of their people did not make it out because a pregnant woman got stuck in the reed through which they climbed out. The Ojibwa's origin story narrates their migration from the Atlantic Ocean to the Great Lakes area. Each of these stories is equally important to the culture that tells it, and each must be met with the respect that it deserves and that we demand for our own origin story.

Since Europeans and EuroAmericans intended to Christianize American Indians, they often dismissed their origin stories as mere superstitions. If they saw similarities to the Christian origin story, they merely assumed that these events were added after contact and showed the Christian influence. One example would be the destruction of the world by water, an element that is also part of the Lakota and Ojibwa origin stories for example. Christians simply assumed that the floods mentioned in American Indian stories were influenced by the story of Noah in the bible. However, how many ways were there for a supernatural being to destroy the world? At the same time, it is very likely that human beings will anger or disappoint a supernatural being who will wish to correct the mistakes of an earlier creation. Hence, the use of the water's destructive force. In contrast to Christianity, American Indian origin stories do not advocate conversion of others to their spiritual ideas; American Indian people are taught to respect other ideas of origin. It is essential to accept origin stories as unique cultural expressions.

By the way, it is not unusual to have several versions of a story, even of the origin stories. The Hopi of northern Arizona traditionally reside on three mesas, and each mesa has a different version of the origin story. Such variations are caused by geographic distance, environmental differences, and differing needs of communities. The fact that there are versions does not devalue the origin stories and their meaning to American Indian communities. The concept of versions is shared by other cultures as well. A prominent and well-known example are the fairytales recorded by the brothers Jacob and Wilhelm Grimm at the beginning of the nineteenth century. They have been translated and re-written for the last 200 years, and the Disney versions on film have added another layer of complexity. The original Grimm fairytales have been sanitized to meet the changing sensibilities of their readers, especially the readers' changing perception of childhood. For example, the fact that in the Grimms' versions the wicked stepmother had to dance in red hot iron shoes until she died at the wedding of the hero or heroine is not considered appropriate reading for children today. Sometimes the fairytales even carry a different message than they did in the Grimms' version. At the same time, it needs to be acknowledged that the Grimm brothers recorded ancient narratives, and these narratives had undergone changes before they were ever recorded. There is absolutely no telling what the original narratives were like, but it is likely that the early storytellers of those fairytales would not recognize the fairytales as theirs today. That does not make contemporary fairytales inauthentic, and they certainly still have a purpose today. The same thing happened to American Indian stories. From their earliest encounters with American Indians in the fifteenth century, Europeans recorded the stories they were told. Missionaries used the oral tradition to illustrate what they saw as the superstitions of American Indian peoples and to argue that they had to be converted to Christianity. Travelers, government officials, ethnographers and many others recorded American Indian stories that were told to them for a variety of reasons. In most cases, the stories were seen as evidence that American Indian peoples needed to be civilized, i.e. they needed to be Christians and farmers. From their own ethnocentric perspectives, very few non-Native collectors recognized the intrinsic value of American Indian oral traditions as cultural documents and evidence of ongoing and complex cultures. However, they did address the differences in cultural sensibilities. For example, when a narrative described bodily functions, the collectors often followed their own cultural taboos. Often the offending words or passages were translated into Latin which made them inaccessible to the common reader or they were edited out completely. Some stories that are reprinted today have a Latin to English vocabulary list so that the reader can re-translate the Latin. Unfortunately, the omitted passages cannot be recovered. Another common problem in many of these recordings is that the stories are mere summaries rather than the entire oral text. The written version of the story may be entirely different from the one that is still part of the oral tradition which has gone through different changes.

The Arikara origin story below, an emergence and migration story, was told to James Murie, a Skidi Pawnee, by the Arikara elder Hand in 1903; the excerpts included below are from one of several versions included in Dorsey's *Traditions of the Arikara.*

There were large people living upon the earth long ago, who were so strong that they were not afraid of anybody, but they did not have good judgment. They made fun of all the gods in the heaven.

Nesaru looked down upon them, and was angry. Nesaru said: "I made them too strong. I will not keep them. They think that they are like myself. I shall destroy them, but I shall put away my people that I like and that are smaller."

So the animals were made to assist some people to turn into corn and they were taken under ground into a cave, which was so large that animals and people lived down there together. The large people were killed by the flood. The people who were taken in under the ground knew nothing of the flood, for they were not people; they were grains of corn.

Nesaru in the heavens planted corn in the heavens, to remind him that his people were put under ground. As soon as the corn in the heavens had matured, Nesaru took from the field an ear of corn. This corn he turned into a woman and Nesaru said, "You must go down to the earth and bring my people from the earth." She went down to the earth and she roamed over the land for many, many years, not knowing where to find the people. At last the thunders sounded in the east. She followed the sound, and she found the people underground in the east. By the power of Nesaru himself, this woman was taken under ground, and when the people and the animals saw her they rejoiced. They knew her, for she was the Mother-Corn. The people and the animals also knew that she had the consent of all the gods to take them out.

Mother-Corn then called upon the gods to assist her to lead her people out of the earth. There was none who could assist her. She turned around to the people, and said: "We must leave this place, this darkness; there is light above the earth. Who will come to help me take my people out of the earth?" The Badger came forth, and said, "Mother, I will help." A Mole also stood up, and said, "I will assist the Badger to dig through the ground, that we may see the light." The long-nosed Mouse came, and said, "I will assist these other two to dig through."

The Badger began to dig upward. He became tired, and said, "Mother, I am tired." Then the Mole began to dig. The Mole became tired. Then the long-nosed Mouse came and dug until it became tired. It came back. The long-nosed Mouse said, "Mother, I am tired." The Badger began to dig upward. When he became tired the Mole went up. The Mole said, "I was just about to go through when I became tired." The long-nosed Mouse then ran up, and said, "I will try."

* * *

The Mole was so glad that it tried again. It went up to the hole, dug through the hole, and went through. The sun had come up from the east. It was so bright that it blinded the

Mole. The Mole ran back, and said: "Mother, I have been blinded by the brightness of that sun. I can not live upon the earth any more. I must make my home under the earth. All the people who wish to be with me will be blind, so that they can not see in the daytime, but they can see in the night. They shall stay under the ground in the daytime." The Mother-Corn said, "Very well."

* * *

The Mother-Corn then led the way and the Mole followed, going out of the hole; but, as they were about to go out from the hole, there was a noise from the east, and thunder, which shook the earth, so that the earth opened. The people were put upon the top of the earth. There was wailing and crying, and, at the same time, the people were rejoicing that they were now out upon the open land. As the people stood upon the earth, the Mother-Corn said, "My people will now journey west. Before we start, any who wish to remain here, as Badgers, long-nosed Mice, or Moles, may remain." This was then done. Some of the people turned back to the holes of the earth and turned into animals, whichever kind they wanted to be.

* * *

Again the people journeyed, and again they came to an obstacle. The obstacle was the timber. The timber was somewhere near the sun. Mother-Corn turned to the gods and asked for help, for the timber before them was very thick. There were thorns all over the timber, so that even animals could not go through. The gods in the heavens had agreed to help Mother-Corn. They gave power to the Owl to clear a way through the timber for the people. The Owl came and stood before Mother-Corn and said, "Mother, I will help to make a pathway for your people to go through this timber. Any of the people who wish to remain with me may become as I am, and we shall remain in this timber forever." The Owl then flew up through the timber. As it waved its wings it removed the timber to one side, so that when it flew through the timber there was a pathway, so that the people could go through. Mother-Corn then led the people through the timber and passed onward.

* * *

At this place, Mother-Corn brought the people together and said, "I am Mother-Corn; you shall have my corn to plant, so that you, by eating it, will grow and also multiply." Then Mother-Corn also said, "I will have to divide up things among you people," for here at this place they had had their village for some time.

* * *

Mother-Corn then made a bundle, made songs, made the ritual, and gave the people the ceremonies. The medicine-men were instructed by the man, and also were taught sleight-of-hand, and were told to make a village.

* * *

After this was done, Nesaru had gathered in from his garden the crop of corn he had planted. Nesaru then gave three things to the people – Mother-Corn, the office of chief, and the medicine-men. Then Mother-Corn said, "The gods in the heavens are the four world-quarters, for they are jealous. If you forget to give smoke to them they will get mad and send storms." Then she said, "Give smoke to me last. The Cedar-Tree that shall stand in front of your lodge shall be myself. I shall turn into a Cedar-Tree, to remind you that I am Mother-Corn, who gave you your life. It was I, Mother-Corn, who brought you from the east. I must become a Cedar-Tree to be with you. The stone that is placed at the right of the Cedar-Tree is the man who came and gave you order and established the office of chief. It is Nesaru, who still exists all the time, and is watching over you. It will keep you together and give you long life."[2]

As in other tribes' sacred and secular narratives, things happen in multiples; there are three animals digging to the earth's surface – Mole, Badger, and Mouse – and three occasions when animals help the travelers through geographic obstacles – Owl through the timber, Loon through a lake, and Kingfisher through the crevice, thereby creating all birds, animals, and aquatic creatures. Nesaru gives the Arikara people three things – Mother-Corn, the village chief, and the medicine-men. It is unusual that the multiples are three in this case; usually, they are four, since four is a sacred number on the northern Plains. There is reference to the "four world-quarters" though whose sacredness needs to be acknowledged with tobacco smoke. Multiples re-inforce the importance of the event. The number four is also used, however, to indicate an indefinite amount of time in many tribal stories. The statement that an event took four days simply indicates that it took some time; for example, in the Navajo origin story children matured into adults in four days.

The Arikara origin story is a complex one that organizes the spiritual as well as physical world of the Arikara people. There is an all powerful sacred being, Nesaru, who holds the power over life and death, provides the rules by which humans will live, gives support when needed, and must be recognized as the supreme being. Contrary to the Christian origin story where humans are created in the image of the creator and, therefore, enjoy a special status, they are merely a part of creation in the Arikara universe. There is no hierarchy that places human beings above all other animate and inanimate beings in the universe. In fact, humans are entirely dependent on others for their survival, as we see when Nesaru transforms those humans he wishes to save into corn and stores them in an underground cave and when the owl makes it possible for humans to pass through the timber. The distinction between species is fluid, metamorpheses are quite common, and the Arikara are literally related to the animals; some people choose to stay with Mole, Badger, and Mouse underground and others become birds, animals, water creatures; it is not quite clear from the story when humans actually resume their human form after having been transformed into corn kernels and later animals. These stories place little emphasis on anthropomorphism.

At the same time, the Arikara origin story sets out the rudimentary rules of their spiritual beliefs and societal order: Nesaru is not the only supreme being, but there are also other "gods," tobacco is sacred and is used to honor the spiritual beings, the Arikara have sacred bundles that hold spiritual power, they have ceremonies given to them by Mother-Corn, medicine-men are responsible for health in a holistic sense, one of their important spiritual symbols is the cedar tree, the Arikara are to grow corn, which is sacred, for their food, and people would live in villages that are to be guided by the chief. Having received these gifts and guidelines from Mother Corn marks the moment when the people in the story become Arikara. The ethnological literature about the Arikara confirms that these directives in the origin story were indeed the foundation of traditional Arikara culture. Needless to say, the above guidelines only provide a very general outline of Arikara spirituality. To give just one example, the origin story mentions medicine-men, but, actually, the Arikara distinguished between priests and doctors; both of them were religious practitioners. The doctors, in turn, were divided into two groups depending on whether they belonged to established societies or simply had medicine to cure certain diseases. Both groups participated in the ceremonies taking place in August, some of which were public while others were not. However, during these ceremonies, the sleights-of-hand, mentioned in the origin story and belonging to various societies, were performed. The Arikara were well-known for these performances in the northern Plains.[3] Another example would be the importance of corn in Arikara society. As the origin story dictated, the Arikara became horticulturalists who grew 11 varieties of corn, had the sacred bundle whose content was associated with corn and that needed to be renewed yearly. Their gardens were not exclusively dedicated to corn though. They probably grew different varieties of squash, beans, and sunflowers as well as tobacco. Corn was an important food source for survival and trade, along with the buffalo, and the Arikara conducted various ceremonies related to corn to ensure a bountiful harvest.[4] Other narratives continue to fill in the details of Arikara culture. However, it must also be acknowledged that not every Arikara had the right to know, for example, the details of sacred prayers and herbal mixtures for healing. Some knowledge was specialized and shared only by those who were members of a particular group.

Finally, the Arikara origin story clearly indicates that the people migrated. During the prehistoric period, i.e. the late fifteenth century, the ancestors of the Arikara lived on the Loup River in what is now Kansas. Many years later, the Arikara moved from the Loup to the Missouri and eventually moved up the Missouri to present-day North Dakota.[5] During the early eighteenth century European traders and travelers began to visit the Missouri area for trade purposes and, along with the other tribes that they encounter there, mention the Arikara. Etienne de Veniard, Sieur de Bourgmont reports three of their villages located on the Missouri and numerous others further north on the river in 1714.[6] The origin story may not provide specific places the Arikara migrated to and from, but it does indicate that the Arikara were a mobile group that took advantage of what the land offered them and that responded to changing relationships with other groups. It does not provide historic evidence, but it indicates why and in what general area the Arikara were migrating.

Trickster Stories

While the tribal origin stories are vital in defining the culture of tribal groups, there are other categories of narratives as well. What these categories are exactly depends on the tribal group. However, one group of stories that all tribes share are trickster stories. The trickster takes different forms, the most common of which is coyote. Even in North Dakota though, the trickster is conceptualized in a number of different ways. The Mandan, Hidatsa, and Arikara tell tales about coyote; the Ojibwa about Manabozho, a spirit being; and the Dakota and Lakota about Iktomi, the spider. In addition, the Turtle Mountain Chippewa created a new trickster, the Rugaroo, when Ojibwa spirituality encountered Catholicism. The Rugaroo is only visible to people who break the rules of lent; this trickster either assumes the form of a handsome young man with a cloven hoof and tail or that of a big, black dog. In other parts of the United States, the trickster can be a raven, a hare, a fox, etc. It is important to realize that the trickster is not limited to American Indian cultures. For instance, Brer Rabbit fulfills a similar trickster role in African American culture, and EuroAmericans have fox.

The trickster can be a creator and a destroyer in American Indian cultures. This dual role permits him to explore the limits of acceptable human behavior and of the geographic space that he dwells in. Ella Deloria, a Dakota anthropologist, wrote down a story titled "Iktomi Marries His Daughter."[7] In the story Iktomi prepares his wife for his death and tells her to give their beautiful daughter to the young man who would come to their tipi after his death. Then he seemingly dies, is painted by his wife, and buried on a scaffold. However, he returns as a young man and marries his daughter. His wife finally understands his deception and kills him. Iktomi is known as a shape shifter who can change his appearance at will; however, some physical characteristic usually gives him away. In this particular story, his wife recognizes his yellow thighs. His behavior makes clear that incest will not be tolerated in Dakota culture. The storyteller indicates his outsider role from the beginning by locating Iktomi's tipi outside the camp circle, indicating that his actions do not have cultural sanction. Iktomi's death is a common element of trickster stories as well; usually, the trickster will come back to life though. At the same time, Iktomi also has positive characteristics and follows cultural norms. He provides for his large family before he supposedly dies, he instructs his wife in proper burial preparations, and his wife talks about the importance of the "making relatives" ceremony. The complexity of the story reflects trickster's complex character. Often trickster is involved in the creation of the world or at least part of it. It is Manabozhoo in the Ojibway origin story who creates the present-day earth on the back of Turtle after the previous world had been destroyed by water. At other times trickster stories are told to explain the physical appearance of people, animals, and things. For example, an Ojibway story tells of coyote tricking the ducks into dancing with closed eyes so that he can kill them one by one. One duck opens the eyes and warns the others. Because Duck violated the rule of closed eyes, ducks' eyes will be forever red. The EuroAmerican trickster fox is much less complex than American Indian tricksters and falls into this last category of explaining physical appearances. The trickster is a carnal being, and many of the trickster narratives have to do with food, sex, and bodily functions. However, the trickster is also a culture hero who explores what Barbara Babcock calls the "tolerated margin of mess."[8]

Depending on how tribes are counted, the federal government still recognizes 562 tribal groups; of course, there are also numerous groups that still struggle to achieve federal recognition. All of these groups have distinct and complex oral traditions. Oral tradition can be defined as sacred and/or secular knowledge handed down from generation to generation by word of mouth. Common misconceptions about oral traditions are that only American Indian peoples have them in North America and that they are static. Every cultural group in the United States has oral tradition and none of them are static. It is too simplistic to assume that oral traditions only include the handing down of the spiritual beliefs of a people or the stories of their historic encounters with others. Just as cultures continuously change, so do their oral traditions. An American Indian student attending college and telling stories about his or her experiences adds to the oral tradition of his or her people. The same is true for a non-Native student who may be recounting his or her experiences in a rural or urban community. The tales being told can be of ordinary things; there is no rule that they have to be heroic or life changing. Families of all cultures define themselves and their expectations by the stories that they tell about the members of various generations. Ultimately, everyone is a member of an oral tradition.

Contemporary Oral Tradition

In 1879, Congress established the Bureau of American Ethnology (BAE). The rapid population decline of American Indian peoples, caused mainly by disease and warfare, created the stereotype of the Vanishing Indian. The charge of the BAE was to record as much of the cultures of the American Indian peoples as they could and, thereby, to preserve as much knowledge as possible for future generations. This salvage ethnology was conducted by well-known scholars, such as for example Franz Boas, Frances Densmore, James Mooney, and Robert Lowie. Their important contributions also contain sections on the oral traditions of the people they studied, often in sections titled "Myths", "Legends", "Tales", "Folklore", or "Superstitions." Today these narratives are often treated as monolithic, as representative of a particular culture through time. The problem with this assumption is that it denies that cultures change through time, and some people use these recorded stories to measure culture loss; in other words, they assume that, if the contemporary stories do not match the recorded ones, then, obviously, at least some of the group's traditional culture has been lost. In truth, the recording of the stories happens at an arbitrary point in the group's history, and the stories changed before and after. Leslie Marmon Silko, the celebrated writer from Laguna Pueblo in New Mexico, said that she studied the Laguna stories, recorded by Elsie Clews Parson, in the publications of the BAE in 1917, but they did not seem alive to her.[9] However, she does use Laguna oral tradition extensively in her fiction and other writings. There is certainly a strong oral tradition in Laguna today, even though these narratives may be very different from those monolithic stories in the BAE. The stories still deal with the mythic past, the historic past, and contemporary life, just as the stories did when Elsie Clews Parson recorded them. Considering that almost a hundred years have passed since the Laguna stories were recorded, the changes should not be surprising. One of the important points that Silko makes in her writing, however, is that the oral tradition is as meaningful as ever to contemporary Laguna people.

Leslie Marmon Silko is not the only American Indian writer to use oral tradition in her fiction. Storytelling has become an important way of connecting or re-connecting a protagonist to his or her culture. It is usually connected with the main character's search for identity. There were certainly American Indian writers who published before the 1930's; however, Mourning Dove's *Cogewea, the Half-Blood* (1929), John Joseph Mathew's *Sundown* (1934), and D'Arcy McNickle's *The Surrounded* (1936) are the first better known novels by American Indian writers. These novels use but do not integrate the oral tradition very successfully into the text, and these writers use the stories that are reminiscent of the monolithic ones in the BAE. The reader of these earlier works of fiction must remember though that the federal government had been discouraging all aspects of Native cultures since the 1880s in an attempt to assimilate all American Indians into the EuroAmerican mainstream culture. By the 1920s and 1930s, many young people had grown up without any knowledge of their communities' oral traditions. It was not until 1934 that the federal government encouraged American Indian peoples to acculturate rather than assimilate when Congress passed the Indian Reorganization Act as part of the New Deal for all Americans. American Indians were told that their cultures and languages had value and that they should maintain them. For some younger American Indians, it was too late. One example would be William D'Arcy NcNickle (1904–1977), a mixed-blood member of the Salish Kootenai Confederated Tribes (Flathead) from Montana, who had grown up during the assimilation phase. The educational system in the form of public schools, federal boarding school, and the University of Montana and his family and his social environment had all advocated assimilation. By the 1930s, McNickle was very much aware of his cultural loss, but he never had the opportunity to return to the reservation and learn about the culture of his people. His knowledge of the oral tradition mainly stemmed from published collections of stories. In his novel, *The Surrounded*, he uses a separate chapter to tell the Flathead stories rather than integrate them into the text throughout. The stories are definitely pertinent to the development of the plot, but, unconnected to the main text as they are, they seem extraneous at first glance. McNickle was more successful in integrating the story of the Flathead EuroAmerican encounter into the text by employing excerpts from the Jesuit character's, Father Grepilloux' history.

No novels were published by American Indian novelists in the 30 years between 1936 and 1968. However, the publication of N. Scott Momaday's Pulitzer Prize novel *House Made of Dawn* in 1968 was quickly followed by numerous other novels which have received many prestigious awards. American Indian novelists have been experimenting with the genre and have found innovative ways to integrate oral traditions into their writings. Louise Erdrich (born 1954), the Ojibwa (Chippewa) writer from North Dakota, is one of the most successful practitioners. Unlike McNickle, Erdrich uses traditional and contemporary oral tradition in her fiction. Even though Louise Erdrich grew up in Wahpeton, North Dakota, she is closely connected to the Turtle Mountain Reservation in the same state and the Chippewa culture that she learned while growing up on her visits to the reservation. In fact, oral tradition weaves in and out of the plot in a way that makes it difficult to separate the two sometimes. Two of her earliest and most successful novels are *Love Medicine* (1984) and *Tracks* (1988).

The northern Plains have a rich tradition of contemporary fiction published by American Indian writers who use the oral traditions of their people in their fiction. McNickle's and Erdrich's novels are joined by Ella Deloria's *Waterlily* (1988), a novel describing Dakota life during early contact times; James Welsh's novels about Blackfeet life, for example *Fools Crow* (1986) and *Indian Lawyer* (1990); and Susan Power's novel *Grass Dancer* (1995) and collection of stories *Roof Walker* (2004) about Lakota life on Standing Rock. There are many other American Indian writers on the northern Plains who use oral tradition in their fiction as well as poetry. Many of the writers have received prestigious awards for their writings.

We do not know what stories the people inhabiting the lodges at the Huff site told, but we can be certain that they did tell stories and that these stories helped to define and reinforce their culture. The earliest recorded Mandan stories give an inkling of what these stories might have been, but they changed through the centuries to help define and reinforce a changing culture. Today the oral traditions of American Indian cultures remain very much alive.

Endnotes

1. National Park Service, www.nps.gov/nhl/designations/samples/nd/Huff.pdf
2. George Dorsey.1904. *Traditions of the Arikara.* Carnegie Institution of Wshington Publications 17. Washington, DC: Carnegie Foundation, pp. 12-17.
3. Douglas R. Parks. 2001. "Arikara" in *Handbook of North American Indians*, Vol. 13, Part 1. Washington: Smithsonian Institution, pp. 381-383.
4. Douglas R. Parks. 2001. "Arikara" in *Handbook of North American Indians*, Vol. 13, Part 1. Washington: Smithsonian Institution, pp. 369-370.
5. Mary Jane Schneider. 2002. *Cultural Affiliations of Native American Groups within North and South Dakota: An Ethnohistorical Overview.* U.S. Bureau of Reclamation, Bismarck, ND, pp. 5-8.
6. Douglas R. Parks. 2001. "Arikara" in *Handbook of North American Indians*, Vol. 13, Part 1. Washington: Smithsonian Institution, p. 366.
7. Ella Deloria. 19. . . *Dakota Texts.*
8. Franchot Ballinger. 2004. *Living Sideways: Tricksters in American Indian Oral Traditions.* Norman: University of Oklahoma Press, p. 134.
9. Leslie Marmon Silko. 1978. "Running on the Edge of the Rainbow," *Words and Place: Literature from the American Southwest*, 1978. National Endowment for the Humanities, video series.

Modernization and Race
Sebastian F. Braun

Introduction

In order to hold the following conversations, some key terms need to be defined first, since these terms are often misunderstood and confused with each other. In contemporary American society, people often use culture, ethnicity, race, nationality, and society as if they carried the same meaning. However, in social science, these terms mean very different things. First, we need to define these terms, then, and think about their similarities and differences.

Nationality simply denotes citizenship in a state. Thus, American citizens share American nationality, regardless of how else they define themselves culturally, religiously, ethnically, or socially. A **society** is a group of people that cooperates, shares institutions, rules or laws, common social, political, economic, or other interests, and is bound together by social relationships. As the term is used here, a society refers to a politically relatively autonomous body. Every society establishes rules on how to relate to others; these rules and norms are expressed through kinship relations. In a society that is relatively alienated, like most industrialized societies, kinship is often taken to only influence how we relate to our closest relatives. Cultural meanings of social relations are usually very similar for norms of behavior between structurally similar actors. The same rules and norms govern our relations to relatives as our spiritual and environmental relations. Such relationships can be impersonal, as in a large society, where the minority of people actually know each other. If the relations are personal, the society is a community. However, every society needs to create the sense of its members being related, needs to construct itself at least theoretically as a community. A society can therefore create or imagine social ties, if needed across cultural and ethnic boundaries. Large states like to create so-called imagined communities. This is especially important in countries that need to hold together different cultural, linguistic, and ethnic groups, such as China, Russia, Nigeria, Canada, Switzerland, Belgium, or the United States. Through real or imagined continued interaction and cooperation, as well as common institutions and interests, a society probably develops certain values that most members hold in common: a society usually develops a shared **culture**. For example, although there are many subcultures present within the United States, an American culture has been developed, based on a set of values that are American values, and organized by American social behavior. However, societies can integrate several different cultures as long as they are compatible with the institutions and interests that govern it. This was the model, for example, used to integrate different ethnic nations into the Soviet Union. Also, a society can share cultural values with other societies. For example, although Canada, France, Switzerland, and Cote d'Ivoire are different societies, certain people within each one of these societies all belong to the cultural sphere of the "francophonie."

Culture means all values, meanings, institutions, arts, artifacts, and behavior patterns that a group of people holds in common and that are shared among them. A culture is, then, that group of people that holds them in common. A culture can be a society, but it can also be a part of a society or a society can be a part of a larger culture. Culture is **learned** and **structured**; it depends on systematic thought and expresses a largely systematic, logical order. Culture is **mutually constructed** and **continuously changes** as it integrates new thought and artifacts and rejects old ones. Because culture is learned, no part of culture is inherited from those by whom a person is enculturated. Since it is usually assumed (at least in the dominant American culture) that these are one's parents, children often seem to inherit cultural values, such as language. This is all the more so because the process of enculturation is unconscious. While everybody is enculturated within a culture, it is possible to consciously learn other culture values, and sometimes even to switch cultures. This long and arduous process is probably never perfect, but because cultural values vary slightly between individuals anyway, residual cultural differences, especially if they concern relatively unimportant values, can be overlooked. People can be bicultural, perhaps even tricultural; they cannot be transcultural, however. Much of the structure that expresses the meaning of culture is symbolic and arbitrary: cultural meaning is never reflecting a "natural order" of things, but is to the contrary a construction. This last statement is only possible from a distance. For people within a cultural system, its order and structure are "natural" and are not questioned: they are unconsciously internalized and taken-for-granted as "common sense." For example, most people cannot explain the grammar of their own language without thinking about it, yet they use it every day. It is when we learn another language that our own grammar becomes much more apparent to us. Similarly, most people simply use the grammar of their culture without having conscious knowledge of it: values of morality, relation, beauty, law, religion, taste, engineering, or health. It is when cultures interact that the common-sensical quality of these concepts becomes questioned and the relative value of such concepts is discovered.

The fact that culture is learned and constructed means that somebody from the outside of any given culture can gain insights to the cultural values. Because it is disconcerting that outsiders understand one's culture and because knowledge is power and needs to be controlled, societies sometimes deny this possibility. Outsiders, because they consciously learn a culture, constantly compare and question the information they receive. They are not threatened in their own identity by this practice and can therefore use a very analytical view of a given culture, one that does not always agree with the view of one's own culture from the inside. These issues often become very obvious and important in discussions between an academic and a cultural view of history, identity, and values.

Every human being is integrated into a culture; somebody without culture would not be recognizable as human. However, there cannot be anything like a personal culture. No person can have an absolutely unique culture; having a culture that is not shared is the same as having no culture at all, since it cannot be made understood. Somebody who holds values that cannot be understood by others within the same group is held to be either criminal or insane. While culture is always shared, no two people within a culture share all aspects of their culture in the exact same way. Individuals interpret cultural meanings in slightly different ways; culture is an inclusive concept. People often simply ignore unimportant differences to make communication possible, until the differences become too large or too important to ignore; then, either communication breaks down or negotiations about cultural meanings are necessary. Culture is therefore an inclusive concept: we know when somebody is not from our own culture, but it is impossible to define who does and who does not belong to our culture. Attempts to define, for example, who is and is not Lakota, Zulu, Thai, or Basler must rely on a standard – but such a standard does not exist naturally. It needs to be constructed. There are Cheyenne lawyers, ranchers, ballet dancers, and construction workers; rich and poor, highly educated and illiterate, deeply spiritual and agnostic people. Sometimes divisions are imagined between traditional and assimilated or mixed-blood and full-blood Klamath; beyond a description of specific characteristics, however, such labels cannot serve to describe culture as a whole. Frequently, urban Mohawk lawyers working everyday in highrise offices, driving luxury cars, wearing expensive suits, and belonging to Bahai, Christian, or Universalist congregations hold traditional cultural values, sometimes more so than Ponca who very visibly identify with Native cultures. Once culture is used to exclude people from belonging, the concept turns into ethnicity.

Ethnicity is the superficial, political, exclusive expression of culture, and very often involves a discourse about belonging. The political is the division of anything into distinct, oppositional entities. Ethnicity marks membership in a specific society, defined according to a defined list of cultural criteria, such as language, clothes, behavior patterns, food, hairstyle, or any other. Ethnic groups are exclusive because of the definitional character of the selected criteria. For example, the believe that "real" or "authentic" Comanche hold certain beliefs, speak a certain language, or behave in certain ways does not define Comanche culture, but Comanche ethnicity, especially if it is used to exclude all others from being accepted as Comanche. In contrast to culture, which makes it possible to accept individuals who do not necessarily conform to all cultural values, ethnic groups only accept people who conform to all selected criteria.

Ethnicity makes very clear that identity is not simply a matter of personal choice. Ethnic identity needs to be acknowledged by other members of a culture or ethnic group. This means that my chosen identity as a member of a group can fail. It is easier to forget about this when one is not in direct contact with members of a group of whom one thinks as being a member. For example, living in North Dakota makes it easy to think of oneself as Norwegian; however, when going to Norway, one might discover that Norwegians do not accept that identity. That identity, then, cannot be upheld while in Norway. Insistence on it will be taken as arrogance or appropriation. Standards for ethnicity are often defined by other, dominant groups, which makes ethnicity prescribed. Resource allocations, upward social mobility, employment, or, in the extreme, survival might be dependent upon how one is classified, and on fitting in with a certain ethnic group. Being seen as Hispanic, Irish, Appalachian, Dixie, Yankee, or American Indian leads to consequences, either positive or negative. Simply by being able to fit in with privileged groups, individuals become themselves privileged; being classified with an ethnicity that is seen negatively leads to disadvantages, and in extreme cases to death. Being African American in the early twentieth century, being Catholic in Belfast in the 1960s, being Hutu or Tutsi in Rwanda in the 1990s, being American Indian in reservation bordertowns all carry their own, but very concrete and real consequences.

It is a simple fact that the so-called modern societies are culturally diverse. In fact, **diversity** can be seen in "modern" societies far back into prehistory. This fact, however, does not say anything about the values attached to and emotions evoked by this diversity. We can celebrate this simple fact of diversity; as long as we do not investigate what consequences it has – for all that are affected by it – this is an extremely shallow celebration, perhaps akin to a celebration of the fact that 2+2=4. Every society is bounded into groups determined by class, status, wealth, and power. There are those who are on the inside and those who are on the outside of privilege. If ethnicity confers privilege and status, it gets included within this power dynamic. In societies that rhetorically uphold values of extreme social mobility, becoming powerful cannot be tied to inherited privilege, however. Therefore, those aspects of ethnicity are denied by those who control the discourse. Because those who are privileged enough not to be negatively affected by their ethnic classification often do not notice any ethnic consequences, the dominant discourse of ethnicity in the United States is often one in which ethnicity is somewhat of a hobby. In this discourse, ethnicity does not carry real consequences or define the reality of one's life. It is volitional, a personal choice. This ties in with ideas of the American melting pot, the post-racial society, and infinite possibilities open to all. It does not take into account that for most people, ethnicity is not a choice, nor does it confer privilege or status. In fact, it most often defines their place in society because it ties in with issues of access to education, power, wealth, and status.

Ethnic identity itself is often assigned through a categorization that makes clear the simultaneous hierarchies of ethnicities. What stores, businesses, restaurants or neighborhoods are classified as "ethnic"? Jan Nederveen Pieterse has pointed out that not all ethnicities are seen as "ethnic;" the classification depends on their perceptional distance from the mainstream, and thus from the center of power. American Indians and African Americans, for example, are still ethnic, although Irish or Scandinavian people are not. Within the perception of Native people, however, ethnic refers especially to those attributes that are visibly different and un-assimilated. Assimilation strips people of their otherness, a potential threat, and simultaneously of their ethnic-ness. In popular discourse, ethnicity often denotes something ancestral, tribal, and exotic. Ethnicity is therefore ambiguously picturesque: it is not only a threat, but also rather attractive. The modern attraction to the ethnic and to ethnicity is not only visible in revitalization or invention of ethnicities and their superficial celebration, again, mostly by those who have the privilege to live volitional and optional ethnicities, but also in the commercialization of ethnicity. A superficial notion of culture and ethnicity focuses on the most superficial aspects: eating foods, wearing clothes and jewelry, listening to music, or participating in activities that have been commodified and comfortably separated from their connections to cultural meanings. Eating Italian thus can be seen as an expression of ethnicity that does not involve speaking Italian, engaging in Italian kinship rules, or living any other aspects of Italian culture.

Most cultures classify people according to arbitrary standards such as language, wealth, behavior patterns, or visible traits. **Race** is the idea that people can be classified according to selective criteria of biological descent or inheritance. It is the combination of biological and cultural traits, the assumption that one influences the other. Because these criteria are narrowly selective, race is a social construction that cannot actually reflect biological or cultural difference. Inherited, biological difference varies more widely between people classified as being of the same race than between people classified as belonging to different races. Because all humans have a common origin, any attempt to divide races need to start with an artificial, assumed point of origin of "pure" races. In other words, racists need to select a time zero from where they can identify races. In reality, both before and after that arbitrary point in time, however, people from all societies have intermarried, adopted others into their societies and otherwise mixed their biological characteristics. Race is a concept that has no use in a description of reality except as a social construction. Thus, while people are killed every day because of their racial classification, that classification is purely a cultural standard. This can also be seen because racial classifications are arbitrary and change between cultures. For example, in the United States, anybody who has any "African American blood" – whatever this means in reality – is seen as African American. However, if this person flies across the Atlantic to Africa, the racial classification applied, if any is applied, might be the exact opposite. Race exists where a society invents it and believes in it. When race is a prescribed standard, it has become so because of specific historic developments, usually ideas used to enforce social hierarchies through racism.

Racism is thought or action that forms or uses opinions of people because of their alleged racial classification. The attachment of values, such as intellect, wealth, work ethic, religion, value to society, beauty, or behavior patterns, to classifications of race is racist. The performance of such categorical value attachments is racist. Finally, acting on such racist categorizations is racist. Racism can take many forms and is not always obvious to those who think along its lines; many racist categories have become so ingrained in the cultural constructions of the world that they are taken-for-granted "facts." Racism can be obvious or it can be covert or silent; it can be intended or stem from habitual ignorance.

Privilege and Perspectives

The ability to define others, historically, socially, culturally, ethnically, or racially, is called privilege. Privilege translates into power and the ability to bestow power upon selected others. It does not have to be intended or conscious; in fact, most people who are in a position of privilege do not even think about themselves in such a way, which leads to unconscious uses and abuses of privilege. In social interactions, for example, the position of a referee or arbiter is a privileged, not a neutral position, although few people in these positions and those who make use of their services are conscious of that fact.

Privilege can consist of expertise; those to whom others turn for expertise are privileged because they determine the prevalent discourse. This is why knowledge is power, and why gaining an education and continue to learn is important: both so one can influence the discourse and so one can critically deconstruct it. In social or cultural contact situations, those who can translate meaning, or are assumed to be able to do so, are privileged because they can direct and control the discourse. In these situations, it is often those who have lived marginal lives, on the edges of a given society, who have amassed that expertise; this is why cultural contact sometimes leads to upheaval within the power structures of a given group. For example, when it became clear that Native peoples would have no choice but to conduct negotiations with the federal government within the American discourse of cultural values, behavior, and language, those young American Indians who had been to school often achieved positions of status despite historic value systems that denied power to young, traditionally inexperienced people.

Because those who enjoy privilege do not want to lose it, the construction of discourses about others often shifts responsibility for their relatively unprivileged position to them. Others – economically, politically, religiously, "racially", and culturally others – are often portrayed as lacking certain essential requirements to achieve the goals that are set by one's own values. For example, over the history of the United States, Irish, Italians, Native peoples, Catholics, and others have at various times been portrayed to lack sufficient work ethics, values, language, laws, norms, or social cohesion to be as successful as those who were in positions of power. The notion that somebody or a group of people are lacking in terms of culture is only possible by making a comparative judgment in which one's own society is taken to be the measuring stick against which all others are held, and, because they are different, found to be lacking. Such definitions of others by judging them against one's own values are called ethnocentrism. **Ethnocentrism** is the tendency to see one's own culture as the one that makes sense. It is carrying the right values, having the right political organization, the right religion, etc. By implication, and sometimes quite explicitly, other cultures are therefore seen as wrong, or at least as less valid. They can be seen as not simply without the right law, religion, culture, etc., but, if one's own culture is seen to be the only true culture, without any law, religion, social organization, etc. Once that conclusion is reached, others are perceived as "savages" or "primitives" because they live in a presumed state of nature instead of in a cultural or civilized environment. Such judgments have consequences.

If one's own culture is seen as the only valid existence, then ethnocentrism can lead to an attempt of convincing others – whether by force or not – to accept these values. This can take the form of forced assimilation, an entitlement to colonialism, or simply the devaluation of other cultures and alternative values. For example, the notions that everybody needs to assimilate and participate in the global market and the primacy of economic "development" are ethnocentric assumptions. The fact that most people in the world seem to agree might not so much be connected to the supreme logic behind these notions as to the fact that this is the "common sense" held by those people who are currently the most privileged and powerful. Because others are dependent on them, they can privilege and enforce their own cultural values over alternative ones.

If ethnocentrism is the act of judging other cultures by one's own cultural standards, **cultural relativism** holds that cultural values are of the same value, even though they differ between cultures. No comparative moral judgments of other cultures are possible under this tenet. Cultural relativism only applies to the comparison of cultures; within each culture, values are not relative, but absolute. Extreme cultural relativism cannot make judgments of other cultures unless they violate rights or values that are postulated as universal, such as human rights, for example. Cultural relativism does not inhibit comparisons between cultures. It simply does not allow moral judgments to be passed on other cultures.

Judging other societies by comparison to one's own cultural values prohibits a full understanding because unfamiliar events or values are constantly explained by preconceived notions. In learning about different societies, one must therefore withhold judgment as far as possible, and attempt to temporarily rid oneself of preconceived assumptions and cultural common sense. When indigenous peoples study American culture, for example, they can note the American kinship system, the religious values, the actual policies, laws, economy, and ecology of American culture. They can point out contradictions between American rhetoric and practice, or between religious values and actual behavior. Approaching American culture from a position of cultural relativism, however, they cannot judge American culture by a measure of their own. For example, they cannot say that American society is most primitive or backward because their own kinship systems are much more evolved.

Historical Perspectives of Native Societies

During the nineteenth century, American perspectives of Native Americans were guided by three tendencies, all of which are tellingly somewhat contradictory of each other: strong pushes for assimilation and the abolishment of sovereignty, a growing sympathetic activism coupled with a romantic and nostalgic perspective, and the beginnings of a scientific study of indigenous societies. All of these trends are consequences of an expanding role of the liberal state and the integration of indigenous societies into this political system, that is, they are all concerned with, and a consequence of modernization.

Some Native societies, such as those of the Iroquois, Cherokee, and Creek confederacies, had been engaged in direct contact activities with the European societies for a long time, whereas others, such as those of the western plains or the Great Basin, were only now experiencing intensive contact situations. The United States was developing into an expansive and colonial nation of its own with an exploding population, and was facing several identity crises and a rapid, global, technological industrialization. Native societies, too, facing an increasingly unified, militarily powerful and populous state intent on settling the continent from sea to sea, adapted to and tried to shape as fast and best as they could their natural, political, and social environments. The policies extended toward American Indian societies as well as the potential for resistance against these policies therefore changed throughout the century, depending on the political situation, available civil and military technologies, and interests for resources.

Many communities "on the frontier" were ethnically mixed; Native communities integrated Americans, and American communities integrated American Indians. Interactions between the involved societies were therefore often cooperative, although misunderstanding of behavior because of cultural differences and enforcement of power hierarchies could easily lead to fear or aggression. For example, American Indians often peeked through the windows of houses because they were curious; personal privacy rules vary between cultures. Another cultural difference that raised misunderstandings was an expectation of generosity which for Americans raised suspicions of beggary. American rules for generosity, on the other hand, bordered on greediness from the American Indian perspective. The historian Matthew Restall has pointed out that the term "conquest" to describe the events that lead to the political and social dominance of Spain over Central and South America is somewhat misleading, because it implies a total Spanish victory. A similar argument could be made about the "frontier." The frontier implies the transformation of indigenous environments and cultures into American society. This is misleading, not only because there was never such a line but also because this process was never completed – and still is not completed.

The nature of the relationships between Native societies and the United States became increasingly uniform as the nineteenth century wore on and the indigenous nations lost more and more opportunities to be seen as unique nations. For a long time, however, despite efforts by the federal government to apply one general and uniform Indian policy to all Native nations, American Indian societies as sovereign nations were defining their own diplomatic strategies and relationships. Actual relations on the "frontier," that is, between those from Native and American societies who were living in direct contact with each other, were defined as much by personal interactions as by official policies. Often these social relations took precedence and defused harmful ideologies and policies to some degree. The potential for abuse of power relations, however, was always present. From the removals in the east in the 1830s to the genocidal practices in California after 1850, from the abrogation of the treaty process in 1871 to allotment and unilateral, patriarchal, and ethnocidal assimilation policies at the end of the nineteenth century, state violence was always an option; that violence, by individuals, communities, bands, states, or nations, occurred often against the background of cooperation, and sometimes simultaneously. The building of a unified liberal state was not always orderly, but often complex, chaotic, and paradoxical. In order to erase political paradoxes, the actors often took refuge in violence.

American Indian cultures of the eighteenth and nineteenth century were in constant flux; many plains cultures, for example, had just begun to either develop or flourish when American colonization started to threaten them. Many of the most obvious elements of traditional culture no longer exist, but most tribes have retained some aspects of their language, their kinship system and their traditional religious beliefs and practices. The current attitude of educators and government officials is to encourage Natives to recall and revive as much of the ancient culture as is practical for these times. Such preservation and revitalization must also be an exercise in interpretation, because these historic cultures would be absolutely foreign to contemporary people. All of these cultures were impacted by the powerful forces of acculturation and assimilation. The idea that "others" need to acculturate or assimilate, on the other hand, came out of specific ideas about the relative values and uses of cultures as well as their places in a modernized world.

Missionaries, American Indians, and Cultural Analysis

From the start of the conquest of the Americas, Christian missionaries held ambiguous positions in regard to indigenous cultures. Just like the various colonial governments tried to integrate Native societies into their states and, therefore, to change or eradicate political organizations and allegiances, their purpose was to change or eradicate religious and other cultural beliefs deemed incompatible with Christian religion. Both colonial projects, however, the political and the religious, necessitate at least a basic understanding of indigenous practices. Therefore, both engaged in the gathering of information about and documentation of American Indian cultures. The state could rely on the collection of abstract data by missionaries and traders; while these data were centrally analyzed, collected, and protected, the states initially sent very few government agents into the field. At the same time that missionaries worked toward the destruction of parts of the indigenous cultures, however, they had to personally gain an understanding of these societies.

Especially in the early Spanish colonies, but not only there, missionaries destroyed sacred sites, ceremonial objects, and Native documentations of religion. However, their own works documented the cultures for generations to come and their presence and activities indirectly served to empower indigenous peoples to resist the colonial state. In order to carry out their mission, agents of the churches had to live within Native communities. In a few instances, especially in New England and in the Spanish colonies, the people were brought to the missionaries by building model Christian communities and missions for converted or converting Native peoples. Congregations built model Christian communities and missions for converted or converting Native peoples. These communities were often interethnic and attracted Christian Native peoples from different cultures. Brotherton, for example, was built in Oneida territory, but also attracted Algonquian speakers. Sometimes these communities assumed new collective identities. Most often, however, missionaries went to live with the people they were trying to convert. Many missionaries thus became fluent in Native languages and cultural knowledge. This knowledge had to be documented in order to pass it on to the next generation of missionaries, and thus became collected in vast volumes describing the languages and cultures of indigenous peoples all across the Americas. Much of this knowledge was collected by Jesuits, who became the first writers of dictionaries and ethnographic reports.

In North America, French Jesuits collected invaluable knowledge especially about Algonquian speaking societies around the Great Lakes. One of these Jesuits, Joseph Francois Lafiteau, went one step further and wrote an analytical work of comparison between Algonquian and European culture, the first ethnological work (1724, *Moeurs des sauvages amériquains comparées aux moeurs des premiers temps*). While his conclusions were wrong – he thought that American Indians are descendants of pre-Hellenic cultures – his analysis pointed out that indigenous cultures had social organization and religion, even though these did not follow European models. It was the missionaries who established that, while American Indian cultures were different, they were still cultures and had to be recognized on their own.

The realization that cultural understanding is relative, that Chinese or Iroquois people find Europeans just as strange as vice versa, made a large impact in Europe, especially in France. Together with ethnographic reports on American Indian peoples, it opened the possibility of an alternative society. Since French society lived under an absolute monarchy, and because of the influence of the growing Romantic movement, what interested French philosophers most were those aspects of American Indian society that emphasized or invented their closeness to nature, simple life, and absence of absolute political powers. In the imagination of eighteenth-century French philosophers La Hontan, Rousseau, Voltaire, and others, American Indian cultures became a model of Romantic and democratic life: noble children of nature that could serve as models against the negative consequences of increasingly alienating civilization. The nostalgia for a simpler life merged with the exotic romanticism of ethnographic reports and a newly discovered, if limited, cultural relativism to form the idea of the "Noble Savage." This is not an oxymoron, as the word savage or "sauvage" simply denoted a person who lived intimately with nature and had, at the time, no prejudicial connotations.

This idea could perhaps only form because relations between the French and Indians were, generally speaking, and as much as possible in a colonial situation, relatively good. At the same time that the general concept of the nobility of perceived simple or primitive culture developed, another stream of thought held on to the image of American Indian societies as lawless, pagan, and unproductive. Thus, two contrasting images of indigenous societies came to be. Both saw indigenous peoples as aspects of the landscape or nature: one saw "wild" nature as a positive influence, the other as dangerous. Unfortunately, of course, both of these perspectives, although influencing policies, laws, and perspectives still today, are stereotypical and not realistic.

While the growing Romantic image of American Indians grew in the cities of the east during the nineteenth century, the prevailing image on the "frontier" was that of Indians as dangerous, wild, and part of a landscape that had to be tamed and civilized. The growing sympathy toward Native peoples came out of the cities, and was based on the illusionary Romantic portrayal; it was as such based just as much on ignorance as was the continuing hostility on the frontier. This is an important point. It explains why later on, when reformers gained influence over federal Indian policies, their projects, such as allotment, although well intended, mostly caused disastrous consequences for those they were intended to help.

Lafiteau and a few other writers on American Indians stand out among travel writers and journal keepers. Many fur traders, explorers, and agents kept detailed notes on the cultures they encountered. These recordings, from John Lederer to Lewis and Clark, from de Tocqueville to Prince Maximilian and Catlin, are extremely valuable as they describe, and often depict, historical details. While they constitute ethnographic accounts, they mostly do not provide, however, an ethnological analysis. The true understanding of American Indian cultures needed a comparative perspective. One of the first scholars to engage in this undertaking was, in hindsight fittingly enough for the subject, a lawyer interested in kinship: Lewis Henry Morgan.

Historical Evolution

When European scientists started to question the way things were around them, they inquired into the history and the development, or in short the evolution of their societies. Many tried to trace back the historical evolution of society from a point zero, a time in which society did not exist. This they called the natural state of man, as opposed to the cultural state in which their contemporaries lived. The natural state was characterized by an absence of the state, of social organization, of language, of religion, and so on. Thomas Hobbes saw this natural state as a negative that had to be overcome; Jean-Jacques Rousseau saw it as a simpler time that had been lost. The progression of civilization was imagined as developing from individuals to families, from families to bands, from bands to larger social units, and so on, until the state evolved. Along the way, moral and social rules developed, were codified into laws, which began to be written down, and evolved into social contracts and constitutions. It is easy to see how, once these rhetorical imaginations were taken literally, American Indians, who were perceived to have rudimentary political authorities at best, had no writing system and, therefore, were assumed to have no laws, would be seen representing a stage of history that European societies had passed.

John Lederer and Lafiteau, among others, had discovered that in some American Indian societies, family descent was not traced through the father, but through the mother. The same was subsequently reported from other societies around the globe. In conjunction with historical evolution, Bachofen (1861, *Das Mutterrecht*) and McLennnan (1865, *Primitive Marriage*) explained this trait, which seemed peculiar to Europeans, by assuming a state of nature in which fathers could not with certainty be known. They assumed, in other words, an original state of general promiscuity in which the institution of marriage did not exist. Both Bachofen and McLennan based their theories on general abstractions and comparisons to ancient Greece. In contrast to them, Morgan would investigate the problem based on a comparison of contemporary societies.

Henry Lewis Morgan was a lawyer in upstate New York when he became interested in Iroquois societies; he explicitly set out to do ethnographic research and write a book on them (1851, *The League of the Ho-de'-no-sau-nee or Iroquois*). He noticed their matrilineal kinship system and realized that it was expressed in kinship terminology – the terms with which relatives address or talk about each other. A few years later, he came across the kinship system of the Ojibwa, which followed the same structure. Since the two nations had different cultures and were of different linguistic families, Morgan assumed that all American Indians might have the same kinship system. However, he wanted to test this assumption. While Morgan went on travels up the Missouri to collect kinship terminologies himself, he also sent out questionnaires, asking traders, colonial officials, and missionaries all over the world to send him kinship terminologies of the people they were working with. Only after he had amassed a large collection of kinship terminologies did he analyze his data (1871, *Systems of Consanguinity and Affinity of the Human Family*). In order to explain the differences in kinship systems that became obvious, Morgan constructed a history of mankind, using the kinship data as the proof for this history. His history is based on the assumption of unilinear evolution – that all peoples originated from the same, uniform society and gradually changed their cultures from there, but all along the same path.

Morgan was not unsympathetic to Indians. He was interested not just in kinship, but also in all matters of Native cultures and societies, and he often critiqued the government policies under which they lived. Although Morgan was interested in defending Indian rights, sharing civilization was a one-way street. Defending the rights of Native peoples and acknowledging that they were intelligent could not keep Morgan from insisting that American culture was still slightly better, and Americans still slightly more intelligent. When Morgan is at Fort Berthold in 1862, he describes in detail religious ceremonies of the Hidatsa, among them the Naxpike, a ceremony not unlike the plains Sun Dance. He describes how young men drag buffalo skulls attached to their skin until the skin breaks. After his description, he concludes that, "The government ought to prohibit these cruel usages, as well as the cutting off of the fingers among the Crows." Cruel to Morgan and most people at his time was what his culture defined as cruel: nobody had to ask the Hidatsa or the Crow what they thought of their practices. His detailed, specific observations do not overcome Morgan's ethnocentrism.

In *Systems*, very basically, Morgan came up with stages of history that matched the stages of kinship systems he perceived from his studies and surveys. Humanity, he concluded, had evolved through consecutive stages of promiscuity, communal families, pair marriage, polygamy, patriarchic family, and finally the "civilized" family. From this constructed history, Morgan developed a more refined version of the general history of human social evolution in *Ancient Society* (1877). Here, he delineated three periods of human history – Savagery, Barbarism, and Civilization – each subdivided into three stages classified as lower, middle and upper. What separated these stages and periods were technological inventions.

Obviously, Morgan was not alone in investigating theories of historical evolution in the nineteenth century: while he focused on ethnographic data, Charles Darwin and Alfred Russell Wallace constructed theories of biological evolution, and Karl Marx worked on theories of economic and political evolution. Marx and later Engels used Morgan's ideas to think through their own ideas of social development; like Marx before him, Morgan also based his perspective of history on a materialistic approach, so that their views of history coincided. Focusing on economic relationships, Marx and Engels expanded Morgan's technological stages into stages of history characterized by the control of means of production. The connection between biology and society – the creation of "social Darwinism" – was left, however, to Herbert Spencer, who generalized Darwin's theory of natural selection through the term "survival of the fittest" and applied it to human cultures. Morgan's theory of historical stages thus came to be abused to identify who was fitter than others by using technological complexity as the standard. The name "social Darwinism" is an absolute misnomer, as Darwin himself never supported the theory that a process of natural selection could be applied to human societies.

The Struggles with Social Darwinism

Both Darwin and Wallace saw "savages" as largely inferior to "civilized" man. Wallace wrote that "such races as the Andaman Islanders, the Australians, and the Tasmanians, the Digger Indians of North America, or the Natives of Fuegia" did not showcase much more intellect than animals. He compares their hunting to that of wolves and jaguars, their thought of future needs to monkeys, antelopes, and field mice, and asks the rhetorical question, "What is there in the life of the savage, but the satisfying of appetite in the simplest and easiest way?" Yet, Wallace repeatedly underlines that these "savages" have a much higher sense of morality than the "civilized" people around him. He recounts a story of prisoners of war, who voluntarily, "with money in their girdles, walked thirty miles back to prison rather than break their word!" Cultural developments, like mathematics, music or art, Wallace finds, cannot be a product of natural selection: "As with the mathematical, so with the musical faculty, it is impossible to trace any connection between its possession and survival in the struggle for existence. It seems to have been arisen as a *result* of social and intellectual advancement, not as a *cause*." Wallace thinks that among "lower savages music, as we understand it, hardly exists, though they all delight in rude musical sounds, as of drums, tom-toms, or gongs; and they also sing in monotonous chants."[10] He beliefs then, in stages of social and intellectual development. However, once people can be brought to broaden the definition of "music, as we understand it" to music as it is understood by the people who create it, that is, once ethnocentrism can be replaced by cultural relativism, Wallace's argument opens the possibility to think about *cultural*, not *human* differences.

It should not be surprising, then, that when Wallace looks at social progress, he discovers problems: there is "no such continuous rise of the high-water mark of humanity" - despite technological advances, humans are not continuously improving. At least implicitly, any ideas about a connection between technological proficiency and higher intellect or superior quality of being are thus denied. "Our modern steam engines and locomotives far surpass those of Watts and Robert Stephenson," Wallace points out, "but of the hundreds who have labored to improve them perhaps none have surpassed those great men in mechanical genius." By implication, technological advance can actually simply be the result of constant improvements, yet simultaneous to intellectual decline. While Wallace himself cannot admit this, Spencer's idea is thus wrong. It is also wrong because, as Wallace points out, the children of two brothers, one a city clerk and one a rural postman, do not inherit the physical and mental characteristics their fathers acquire because of their different lifestyles. If people do not inherit "the results of education and training," Wallace asks, how can society improve? His answer is the liberation of women:

> When such changes have been effected that no woman will be compelled, either by hunger, isolation, or social compulsion, to sell herself whether in or out of wedlock, and when all women alike shall feel the refining influence of a true humanizing education, of beautiful and elevating surroundings, and of a public opinion which shall be founded on the highest aspirations of their age and country, the result will be a form of human selection that will bring about a continuous advance in the average status of the race.

Perhaps this relates more directly to the development of feminism; but feminism - the liberation of women - and the liberation of indigenous societies are connected. Just replace the word "woman" with "indigenous person" in the above quote. The position of Wallace's "savage" is caused, just like that of women in his time, not by biological disadvantages, but by a lack of education, healthy environment and positive public opinion, which forces people to sell themselves to others. In other words, even though the thought does not occur to Wallace, yet, because his own cultural education and training does not allow it, what separates "savages" from "civilization" is equal opportunity and political, social, and economic freedom.

Although his political vocabulary could not include indigenous liberation, Wallace saw very clearly that natural selection can only work in natural environments, that is, as long as adaptation to changing environment is an absolute necessity and its results are biologically passed on to next generations. Only in these circumstances does the difference in biological adaptation create an advantage or disadvantage for survival or reproduction. Human beings, in contrast, being cultural animals, can and do choose a different strategy: they can either change their environments or adapt culturally. Surviving in the Arctic or in the Sahara is not dependent on biological differences, but on technological innovation and cultural imagination:

> [I]n two distinct ways has man escaped the influence of those laws which have produced unceasing change in the animal world. 1. By his superior intellect he is enabled to provide himself with clothing and weapons, and by cultivating the soil to obtain a constant supply of congenial

food.... 2. By his superior sympathetic and moral feelings, he becomes fitted for the social
state; he ceases to plunder the weak...; he shares the game...; he saves the sick and wounded....

Thus, human adaptation is primarily cultural. Instead of adapting to nature, humans, through culture, build their own natural environments – clothes, lodgings, fire, logging, damming, irrigation, weeding and planting are only a few examples. Since culture is learned, moreover, it is not passed on biologically. Thus, the principles of natural selection cannot be applied to cultural evolution. Humans have positioned themselves largely outside natural selection.

Impact

Despite such criticisms, Social Darwinism became the dominant paradigm of the late nineteenth century – the accepted truth through which societies could be known and compared – perhaps because it provided a legitimization of power hierarchies, in business as well as in politics. The hierarchies it created were transformed with growing ideas of separate "races" of humankind to construct a hierarchy and scientific theory of race. Those people lower on the scale were presumed to simply not be intelligent enough to comprehend the complexities of the "modern" world; they were "stuck in the stone age" to use a common and still current (but absolutely false) stereotypical phrase. In the eyes of racists, since these peoples were not going to survive anyway, as they were not fit enough, their subjugation and even, in the extreme, their extermination was actually to the benefit of mankind, as the stronger race, i.e., northern Europeans and Americans, would not be mixed, and thus made weaker, by the less worthy genetic materials of those exterminated. Those who were fitter and stronger now supposedly were simply working out "a law of nature and a law of God", as John D. Rockefeller put it once to a Sunday school class. Henry R. Schoolcraft, an Indian agent, had the following to say:

> [A]nd, as in all conflicts of a superior with an inferior condition, the latter must in the end succumb. The higher type must wield the sceptre.... The prophet announces that the nation and kingdom that will not serve the Lord shall perish. It is a useless expenditure of senti-mental philanthropy to attribute the decadence of the Indian race to anything else. When the fiat had been uttered, "Thou shalt live by the sweat of thy brow," the question was settled. We sympathize with him, truly, but we do so with our eyes open.

Social Darwinism was extended on the individual level through eugenics, a theory of genetic group health. Because it was wrongly assumed that all characteristics of human beings were inherited, if one wanted to keep the gene pool healthy, those people with tainted genetics could not be allowed to reproduce. If, according to social Darwinism, the "races" on the lower spectrum of social evolution were not going to survive anyway, then any investment in them was a waste of money. This racist discussion became most visible in arguments about the education of freedmen:

> A native of Africa and a savage a few generations ago, then a slave for several generations afterwards; this is the man and the race upon whom the high responsibilities of freedom were thrust.

From such false historical accounts, it appeared that "uncivilized" people were simply not ready for civilization. "A classical education for a negro whose proper vocation is raising rice or cotton or garden truck, is as much out of place as a piano in a Hottentot's tent," wrote another author. Education would place other races into an "unnatural state:"

> [I]t is reasonable to think that, since Anglo-Saxon civilization is... the culmination of a series of steps, all the steps must be taken before it can safely be reached. To suddenly introduce another race, therefore, to any steps in the series, and then to attempt to hurry it over the other steps in the hope of having it reach and occupy the culminating one, must be a hopeless undertaking.... [M]ore - does not the history of races show that the effort on the part of a superior people to lift up inferiors at a single stroke not only fail but established conditions which lead to the actual destruction of the weaker race.

Education of American Indians had to be approached very carefully, because in contrast to "the sturdy Anglo-Saxons," they did not possess the principles of "self-determination and self-development." The civilization of the Anglo-Saxon was therefore:

> strange and new to the uncultured mind of the native of the forest, and he who attempts to solve the problem of Indian education... must recognize that the circumstances surrounding the Indians are so different from those surrounding our own race that the two races may not be placed in the same category. The social, political and industrial conditions of the two races are so widely different as to demand for the Indian special and separate treatment.

When the federal government got directly involved in the education of both African Americans and American Indians, then, it was on the experimental hope that they could be taught. They were not to be overstimulated, of course: the most one could hope for was vocational education. The government's hope was that American Indians could assure their survival through assimilation: that they might be intelligent enough to become competent. In order to do so, however, they had to shed everything that might hold them "back." Thus, Richard Henry Pratt's infamous credo of Indian education, "to kill the Indian and save the man" was a rather progressive notion for his times. "The great problem," wrote one author:

> is to take members of a savage or barbarous race, little acquainted with the arts and industries of modern life, and less inclined to follow them, and to familiarize them with these, at the same time planting within them a desire for improvement.... The older members of the tribe may be past systematic education, past a decided reform, but there can be aroused in them a sentiment for something better and higher for their children.

Indians would die off: the human could be saved if, and only if, it could be extracted from Native cultures and formed in the image of civilization.

Social Darwinism and eugenics, developed by Spencer and his American student John Fiske, were extremely popular in the early twentieth century in the United States. State fairs often had eugenics education exhibitions and sponsored contests determining "Fitter Families" and "Better Babies." The theories solidified support for involuntary sterilization of alcoholics, criminals, and physically and mentally challenged people, as well as for miscegenation and racial segregation laws.

It was applied in policies to limit the immigration of southern European and Irish people, and in the end lay the foundation for Auschwitz and the Nazi Holocaust. The idea of natural racial hierarchies was applied to American Indians and others well into the 1970s, with involuntary sterilizations of Native and minority women and the preferential adoption of native children by non-Native parents. Much of racist thought, and indeed the idea underlying all racism, namely that different races of mankind exist, is based on the concepts that were developed in the late nineteenth century. Unfortunately, although long since proven to be worthless and wrong in any way, these ideas have been so ingrained in some cultures that they still persist. Just like in the early twentieth century, when supporters of eugenics called for the sterilization of poor people to eradicate poverty, for example, there are still people who favor mandated birth control or sterilization for the recipients of welfare benefits.

Armed with the religious idea of Manifest Destiny, which had crystallized in the early nineteenth century, and the evolving ideas which were to become the scientific concept of Social Darwinism, the United States went to work. After the removal of indigenous societies from eastern parts, and their concentration in Indian Territory, and the purchase of Louisiana Territory, it conquered the Southwest from Mexico in 1848. From 1812 to the 1860s, American Indians became increasingly perceived simply an obstacle to the rightful progress of civilization and the possession of the Promised Land. Those indigenous nations that still resisted American dominance were defeated in the 1870s using the military strategies and technologies developed in the Civil War.

Until the end of the nineteenth century, when social Darwinism developed its full impact, American Indians had never been truly segregated from American society, and perhaps because of this historical experience, they never were. There had been too much intermarriage and contact on an equal footing to simply dismiss Native societies and peoples as fundamentally less evolved. While racism and discrimination were obvious, the army never established segregated units for those American Indians fighting with it. Experienced officers, although using all means at their disposal to defeat Native resistance, including massacres of civilians and a strategy of burnt earth, respected American Indian intellect and capabilities. While assimilation was a necessity for those indigenous peoples who wanted to be successful in the dominant society, the fact that many were successful shows that racial attitudes toward American Indians were never as clear as those toward Chinese immigrants or African Americans.

Modernization and the State

All through the nineteenth century, American Indian societies responded to and shaped new challenges and opportunities that an expanding United States and increased contact with American individuals brought. The southeastern confederations successfully built their own nation states, education systems and economies that followed the models of their non-Indian neighbors. At the same time, the dominant societies were pushing for an expansion of the monetary economy.

Communities, and within them individuals, were facing fundamental choices and, increasingly, their choices were made for them. This fit with the increasing development of the United States as a liberal, modern state. The Civil War marked the definite territorial extent of the state as well as the absolute imposition of federal law. Special exceptions for certain groups within the state could no longer be tolerated. During the 1860s, the federal government also set the stage for the future for the settlement of those regions not yet under its control. In 1862, plans for the trans-continental railroad were finalized; the railroad would be funded by land-grants along the line; settlers would be attracted by the Homestead Act; the agricultural settlement of the West would be supported by the land-grant universities made possible through the Morrill Land-Grant Act; and agriculture in general was to be supported by the newly founded Department of Agriculture. After the Civil War, the pieces for settlement of the West were in place, apart from the fact that American Indian nations still lived on these lands. However, the army had been built up during the war, military technology and strategy had been advanced, and this resource was ready to be deployed against Native peoples.

While many processes of culture change – trade, education, religious conversion – had been ongoing since the first contacts, the nineteenth century showed a marked interest by the state in controlling and guiding these processes. It is one of the characteristics of developing European nation states to increase the cultural and linguistic homogenization of their citizens. The liberal state increased government's role in building direct, individual loyalties through direct control of education programs and indirect control of religious activities. With a redefinition of politics as reaching into all aspects of life, the state had to create institutions to administer or at least control or regulate them.[16]

The accepted way to regulate and homogenize relations with indigenous nations had been through treaties. The process became more and more refined and reached both its highest refinement and its end on the plains in the late 1860s. Two sets of treaties stand out in this context, the Medicine Lodge Creek Treaty of 1867 with the Comanche, and Kiowa and the treaties of 1868 with the Lakota, Northern Cheyenne and Northern Arapaho. In both instances, on the southern and the northern plains, the treaties were designed to bring a final peace, yet, in both cases, the treaties were the preliminaries for a final war.

During most of the nineteenth century, however, American Indian societies responded to both opportunities and challenges as sovereign nations, just like they had responded to changes for time immemorial. While some decided that it was in their best interest to resist American political and economic expansion, as well as pressure to assimilate militarily, others decided that it was in their best interests to build alliances with the United States. Contrary to stereotypical notions of history, many American Indian nations never fought against the federal government; quite a few actually fought with it. This is an extremely important point. Many people hold a sentiment that the United States simply "conquered" American Indian societies or "won the war." The historical reality of the nineteenth century could not be more different. Even though the increasing American military power and the political will to use it left Native societies with fewer and fewer real alternatives, relations were based on treaties until 1871, when the federal government ended the treaty process. Legally, Native nations were still sovereign, but in practice, their sovereignty had become more and more limited. The expansion of the United

States and Canada meant that resources on which American Indian societies depended were increasingly either decimated or appropriated.

Native communities were always aware that the implementation of policies, that the establishment of missions and schools would result in and was geared toward at least partial culture change. Responses to these events therefore depended on whether assimilation was seen in a positive or a negative light. Some communities, who saw formal education as a necessary key for equal footing, asked for schools to be built for their children. This became increasingly true when having a school in a reservation community came to be seen as an advantage over other communities. Other communities, who relied on the strength of their traditional cultures, resisted schools and missionaries. By the turn of the century, half of all American Indian children attended school.

Most American Indians were not citizens of the United States. However, in order to solve the "Indian Problem," the federal government increasingly saw their future, if, indeed, they were to have one at all, as becoming integrated into the state and into American society and culture. They were to be "civilized:" to become agricultural, Christian, self-sustaining citizens. The emancipation of African Americans, especially, but also riots over the treatment of Irish and other minorities showed that the state had to take an active role in this. It was thus the evolution of the liberal state that created federal assimilation policies. Two obstacles had to be overcome: education and land ownership. Both issues were to define the relations between the federal government and American Indians, as well as discussions of assimilation and culture change far into the twentieth century.

Sources and Further Readings

Diversity:
Thomas Hylland Eriksen and Finn Sivert Nielsen. 2001. *A History of Anthropology*.
     London: Pluto Press.
Benedict Anderson. 1991. *Imagined Communities*. New York: Verso.
V.P. Gagnon, Jr. 2004. *The Myth of Ethnic War*. Ithaca: Cornell University Press.
Jan Nederveen Pieterse. 2007. *Ethnicities and Global Multiculture. Pants for an Octopus*.
     Lanham: Rowman & Littlefield.
Vilna Bashi Treitler. 2013. *The Ethnic Project. Transforming Racial Fiction into Ethnic Factions*.
     Stanford: Stanford University Press.

Social Darwinism:
John S. Haller, Jr. 1971. *Outcasts from Evolution. Scientific Attitudes of Racial Inferiority, 1859-1900*.
     Carbondale: Southern Illinois University Press.
John Bellamy Foster. 2000. *Marx's Ecology. Materialism and Nature*. New York: Monthly
     Review Press.
Alfred Russel Wallace. 1869. *The Malay Archipelago: the Land of the Orang-Utan and the Bird of
     Paradise. A Narrative of Travel, with Studies of Man and Nature*. New York: Harper and Brothers.
Alfred Russel Wallace. 1871. *The Action of Natural Selection on Man*. New Haven:
     Charles C. Chatfield and Co.

Alfred Russel Wallace. 1875. "The Limits of Natural Selection as Applied to Man" in: *Contributions to the Theory of Natural Selection. A Series of Essays*. London: Macmillan and Co.

Alfred Russel Wallace. 1889. *Darwinism. An Exposition of the Theory of Natural Selection with Some of Its Applications*. London: Macmillan and Co.

Alfred Russel Wallace. 1900. *Studies Scientific and Social*. London: Macmillan and Co.

Henry Lewis Morgan. 1993 *The Indian Journals, 1859-62*. Mineola: Dover Publications.

Frank W. Blackmar. 1892. "Indian Education," in: *The Annals of the American Academy of Political and Social Science, 2, 813-837.*

History and Modernization:

Matthew Restall. 2003. *Seven Myths of the Spanish Conquest*. Oxford: Oxford University Press.

Tzvetan Todorev. 1984. *The Conquest of America*. New York: Harper and Row.

Ter Ellingson. 2001. *The Myth of the Noble Savage*. Berkeley: University of California Press.

Gregory H. Nobles. 1997. *American Frontiers. Cultural Encounters and Continental Continuity*. New York: Hill and Wang.

Nancy Shoemaker. 2004. *A Strange Likeness. Becoming Red and White in Eighteenth-Century North America*. Oxford: Oxford University Press.

The Marshall Trilogy
Grant Christensen

Introduction

The Supreme Court under Chief Justice John Marshall was the first to provide guidance on an array of legal issues underpinning the creation of a new nation. Among the most pressing issues confronting the new nation was the status of its original inhabitants. In dealing with American Indians, there were few British legal precedents that the Court could follow. Instead the Supreme Court was forced to essentially create what today has become 'federal Indian law.'

Indians are mentioned only twice in the Constitution itself. In Article 1, Section 2 the Constitution provides that, when counting the number of persons resident in each state for the purpose of allocating that state's political representation in Congress, "Indians not-taxed" shall not be included in a state's population. Article 1, Section 8 provides that Congress shall have the power to "regulate commerce. . . with the Indian tribes." From these brief references, the Supreme Court had to extrapolate the basic legal principles creating the relationship between Indian tribes and the other governments of the United States as well as determine the rights Indians had to the land, its resources, and the extent to which the United States would recognize tribes' ability to govern themselves.

Chief Justice Marshall presided over three Indian law cases that collectively have become known as the Marshall Trilogy: *Johnson v. M'Intosh*, *Cherokee Nation v. Georgia*, and *Worcester v. Georgia*. Taken together these three cases established an initial legal framework that carved out the rights, duties, and responsibilities of the three competing sovereigns (Tribes, States, and the United States). An understanding of the trilogy remains indispensable for the study of American Indians as these cases articulate a way of thinking about sovereignty and government that underpin not only modern Indian law and life on the reservation, but also shape the way that legislation and policy is crafted at all levels of government.

The Status of Indian Land

Even before the United States won its independence, The Proclamation of 1763 was issued by King George III of Great Britain upon the British victory in the French and Indian Wars/Seven Years' War. It specially forbade any settlement west of the Appalachian Mountains – reserving those lands for the exclusive use of Indian tribes. It was enacted, in part, because Great Britain did not have the resources to fight multiple tribes on the American frontier while maintaining sufficient defenses from France and Spain back home and simultaneously expanding her empire abroad.

The Proclamation was poorly received by American colonists, who resented the inability to expand west of the Appalachians and generally had little respect for the right of Indians to land that had not been put to a demonstrated economic use like pasturage, agriculture, or manufacturing. Following the Proclamation, many land speculators sent emissaries into the territory closed to settlement and negotiated personally for the sale of large tracts of land directly from the Indians.

On July 5, 1773 one of these emissaries, William Murray, purchased on behalf of himself and other investors a large tract of land from the chief of the Illinois Indian Nation (in modern-day Illinois). On October 18, 1775, another emissary, Louis Viviat, purchased on behalf of himself and other investors a large tract of land from the chief of the Piankeshaw Indian Nation (in modern-day Indiana). Joshua Johnson eventually inherited title to the same lands as a successor in interest to those investors who participated in the Murry and Viviat cessions.

After its independence from Great Britain, the United States later acquired the same land from the local tribes in the Treaty of Greenville (1794) following an American victory in the Battle of Fallen Timbers. Eager to recoup the cost of maintaining an army on the frontier, the United States sold large parcels of this land to private parties. On July 20, 1818, the United States sold to William M'Intosh an 11,560 acre parcel of land containing parcels of land that were originally included in the land patents procured by Murray and Viviat.

This created a legal question of some importance on the American frontier: who properly owned the land? Johnson's claim originated first. It could be traced back to the original purchase from the Indians in 1773 and 1775. M'Intosh's claim came second, but was bolstered by his purchase of the land directly from the United States who claimed title from the Treaty of Greenville in 1794. Johnson brought suit against M'Intosh to force a decision from the federal courts of the United States on land ownership. The case eventually reached the Supreme Court where Chief Justice Marshall issued a landmark ruling which has established the legal basis for how Europeans took title to the lands of North America.

The decision was unanimous. As you read the following opinion consider what legal basis Chief Justice Marshall applied to determine how the United States ultimately claimed a right to the lands of North America. What rights to the land are Indians left with? Do you agree with the legal principles adopted by the Supreme Court?

....

JOHNSON v. M'INTOSH
Supreme Court of the United States (1823) 21 U.S. 543

Syllabus

On the part of the plaintiffs, it was contended, that upon the facts stated in the case, the Piankeshaw Indians were the owners of the lands in dispute, at the time of executing the deed of October 10th, 1775, and had power to sell. But as the United States had purchased the same lands of the same Indians, both parties claim from the same source.

* * * On the part of the defendants, it was insisted, that the uniform understanding and practice of European nations, and the settled law, as laid down

by the tribunals of civilized states, denied the right of the Indians to be considered as independent communities, having a permanent property in the soil, capable of alienation to private individuals. They remain in a state of nature, and have never been admitted into the general society of nations. * * *

* * * The act of Virginia of 1662, forbade purchases from the Indians, and it does not appear that it was ever repealed. The act of 1779 is rather to be regarded as a declaratory act, founded upon what had always been regarded as the settled law. These statutes seem to define sufficiently the nature of the Indian title to lands; a mere right of usufruct and habitation, without power of alienation. By the law of nature, they had not acquired a fixed property capable of being transferred. The measure of property acquired by occupancy is determined, according to the law of nature, by the extent of men's wants, and their capacity of using it to supply them. It is a violation of the rights of others to exclude them from the use of what we do not want, and they have an occasion for. Upon this principle the North American Indians could have acquired no proprietary interest in the vast tracts of territory which they wandered over; and their right to the lands on which they hunted, could not be considered as superior to that which is acquired to the sea by fishing in it. The use in the one case, as well as the other, is not exclusive. According to every theory of property, the Indians had no individual rights to land; nor had they any collectively, or in their national capacity; for the lands occupied by each tribe were not used by them in such a manner as to prevent their being appropriated by a people of cultivators. All the proprietary rights of civilized nations on this continent are founded on this principle. The right derived from discovery and conquest, can rest on no other basis; and all existing titles depend on the fundamental title of the crown by discovery. The title of the crown (as representing the nation) passed to the colonists by charters, which were absolute grants of the soil; and it was a first principle in colonial law, that all titles must be derived from the crown. * * *

CHIEF JUSTICE MARSHALL Delivered the Opinion of the Court

* * * On the discovery of this immense continent, the great nations of Europe were eager to appropriate to themselves so much of it as they could respectively acquire. Its vast extent offered an ample field to the ambition and enterprise of all; and the character and religion of its inhabitants afforded an apology for considering them as a people over whom the superior genius of Europe might claim an ascendency. The potentates of the old world found no difficulty in convincing themselves that they made ample compensation to the inhabitants of the new, by bestowing on them civilization and Christianity, in exchange for unlimited independence. But, as they were all in pursuit of nearly the same object, it was necessary, in order to avoid conflicting settlements, and consequent war with each other, to establish a principle, which all should acknowledge as the law by which

the right of acquisition, which they all asserted, should be regulated as between themselves. This principle was, that discovery gave title to the government by whose subjects, or by whose authority, it was made, against all other European governments, which title might be consummated by possession.

* * * In the establishment of these relations, the rights of the original inhabitants were, in no instance, entirely disregarded; but were necessarily, to a considerable extent, impaired. They were admitted to be the rightful occupants of the soil, with a legal as well as just claim to retain possession of it, and to use it according to their own discretion; but their rights to complete sovereignty, as independent nations, were necessarily diminished, and their power to dispose of the soil at their own will, to whomsoever they pleased, was denied by the original fundamental principle, that discovery gave exclusive title to those who made it.

While the different nations of Europe respected the right of the natives, as occupants, they asserted the ultimate dominion to be in themselves; and claimed and exercised, as a consequence of this ultimate dominion, a power to grant the soil, while yet in possession of the natives. These grants have been understood by all, to convey a title to the grantees, subject only to the Indian right of occupancy.

The history of America, from its discovery to the present day, proves, we think, the universal recognition of these principles.

* * *

No one of the powers of Europe gave its full assent to this principle, more unequivocally than England. The documents upon this subject are ample and complete. So early as the year 1496, her monarch granted a commission to the Cabots, to discover countries then unknown to Christian people, and to take possession of them in the name of the king of England. Two years afterwards, Cabot proceeded on this voyage, and discovered the continent of North America, along which he sailed as far south as Virginia. To this discovery the English trace their title.

In this first effort made by the English government to acquire territory on this continent, we perceive a complete recognition of the principle which has been mentioned. The right of discovery given by this commission, is confined to countries "then unknown to all Christian people;" and of these countries Cabot was empowered to take possession in the name of the king of England. Thus asserting a right to take possession, notwithstanding the occupancy of the natives, who were heathens, and, at the same time, admitting the prior title of any Christian people who may have made a previous discovery.

* * *

By the treaty which concluded the war of our revolution, Great Britain relinquished all claim, not only to the government, but to the "propriety and territorial rights of the United States," whose boundaries were fixed in the second article. By this treaty, the powers of government, and the right to soil, which had previously been in Great Britain, passed definitively to these States. We had before taken possession of them, by declaring independence; but neither the declaration of independence, nor the treaty confirming it, could give us more than that which we before possessed, or to which Great Britain was before entitled. It has never been doubted, that either the United States, or the several States, had a clear title to all the lands within the boundary lines described in the treaty, subject only to the Indian right of occupancy, and that the exclusive power to extinguish that right, was vested in that government which might constitutionally exercise it.

* * *

The United States, then, have unequivocally acceded to that great and broad rule by which its civilized inhabitants now hold this country. They hold, and assert in themselves, the title by which it was acquired. They maintain, as all others have maintained, that discovery gave an exclusive right to extinguish the Indian title of occupancy, either by purchase or by conquest; and gave also a right to such a degree of sovereignty, as the circumstances of the people would allow them to exercise.

* * *

We will not enter into the controversy, whether agriculturists, merchants, and manufacturers, have a right, on abstract principles, to expel hunters from the territory they possess, or to contract their limits. Conquest gives a title which the Courts of the conqueror cannot deny, whatever the private and speculative opinions of individuals may be, respecting the original justice of the claim which has been successfully asserted. The British government, which was then our government, and whose rights have passed to the United States, asserted a title to all the lands occupied by Indians, within the chartered limits of the British colonies. It asserted also a limited sovereignty over them, and the exclusive right of extinguishing the title which occupancy gave to them. These claims have been maintained and established as far west as the river Mississippi, by the sword. The title to a vast portion of the lands we now hold, originates in them. It is not for the Courts of this country to question the validity of this title, or to sustain one which is incompatible with it.

Although we do not mean to engage in the defense of those principles which Europeans have applied to Indian title, they may, we think, find some excuse, if not justification, in the character and habits of the people whose rights have been wrested from them.

* * *

[T]he tribes of Indians inhabiting this country were fierce savages, whose occupation was war, and whose subsistence was drawn chiefly from the forest.

To leave them in possession of their country, was to leave the country a wilderness; to govern them as a distinct people, was impossible, because they were as brave and as high spirited as they were fierce, and were ready to repel by arms every attempt on their independence.

* * *

Frequent and bloody wars, in which the whites were not always the aggressors, unavoidably ensued. European policy, numbers, and skill, prevailed. As the white population advanced, that of the Indians necessarily receded. The country in the immediate neighborhood of agriculturists became unfit for them. The game fled into thicker and more unbroken forests, and the Indians followed. The soil, to which the crown originally claimed title, being no longer occupied by its ancient inhabitants, was parceled out according to the will of the sovereign power, and taken possession of by persons who claimed immediately from the crown, or immediately, through its grantees or deputies.

* * *

This opinion conforms precisely to the principle which has been supposed to be recognized by all European governments, from the first settlement of America. The absolute ultimate title has been considered as acquired by discovery, subject only to the Indian title of occupancy, which title the discoverers possessed the exclusive right of acquiring.

* * *

The person who purchases lands from the Indians, within their territory, incorporates himself with them, so far as respects the property purchased; holds their title under their protection, and subject to their laws. If they annul the grant, we know of no tribunal which can revise and set aside the proceeding. We know of no principle which can distinguish this case from a grant made to a native Indian, authorizing him to hold a particular tract of land in severalty.

As such a grant could not separate the Indian from his nation, nor give a title which our Courts could distinguish from the title of his tribe, as it might still be conquered from, or ceded by his tribe, we can perceive no legal principle which will authorize a court to say, that different consequences are attached to this purchase, because it was made by a stranger. By the treaties concluded between the United States and the Indian nations, whose title the plaintiff's claim, the country comprehending the lands in controversy has been ceded to the United States, without any reservation of their title. These nations had been at war with the United States, and had an unquestionable right to annul any grant they had made to American citizens. Their cession of the country, without a reservation of this land, affords a fair presumption, that they considered it as of no validity. They ceded to the United States this very property, after having used it in common with other lands, as their own, from the date of their deeds to the time of cession; and the attempt now made, is to set up their title against that of the United States.

* * *

It has never been contended, that the Indian title amounted to nothing. Their right of possession has never been questioned. The claim of government extends to the complete ultimate title, charged with this right of possession, and to the exclusive power of acquiring that right.

* * *

After bestowing on this subject a degree of attention which was more required by the magnitude of the interest in litigation, and the able and elaborate arguments of the bar, than by its intrinsic difficulty, the Court is decidedly of opinion, that the plaintiffs do not exhibit a title which can be sustained in the Courts of the United States; and that there is no error in the judgment which was rendered against them in the District Court of Illinois.

Judgment affirmed, with costs.

....

Chief Justice Marshall's opinion in *Johnson v. M'Intosh* laid out several organizing principles for American Indian tribes that are still present and affecting Indian law and policy today; the Doctrine of Discovery, the legal title Indians hold to land and how that title was transferred from tribes to settlers and the United States, and the recognition that Indian tribes had some status as sovereign entities to which the United States was legally able to contract with and who thus retained reciprocal powers of government and protection.

So how did the United States ultimately acquire the territory to North America? By discovery. Justice Marshall reasons that because Indians were hunters and not cultivators of the land they could not claim rights to it. Instead, Indians essentially exchanged their rights to the land for Christianity and civilization. As Chief Justice Marshall wrote: "[t]he potentates of the old world found no difficulty in convincing themselves that they made ample compensation to the inhabitants of the new, by bestowing on them civilization and Christianity, in exchange for unlimited independence." Essentially Indian tribes lost their full rights in land when European states 'discovered' their territory.

So what do Indians have after discovery? Chief Justice Marshall is equally clear that Indians have kept most of their rights to the land. Indians can continue to live upon, to use, to profit from, to tread across, etc. What was lost by discovery was the right to alienate the land. After discovery only the 'civilized' and 'Christian' nation that first discovered the land has the right to procure it from the Indians.

The Doctrine of Discovery

Before *Johnson v. M'Intosh*, there was no clear articulation from the United States regarding how it came by the right to new lands within the territory it controlled. Much of the early

Republic was built on land that had been acquired by Great Britain. The origin of title to most of this property was obtained either by treaty or by conquest. The British fought various Indian tribes in skirmishes and wars too numerous to count, and often ended these hostilities by entering into treaties with clans, bands, groups, and tribes which ended hostilities in exchange for a cession of land. When the United States secured independence, it inherited the claims Britain had to all of these lands.

What about land claimed by Britain, and inherited by the United States, but not subject to a treaty? It was in the Northwest Territories (modern-day Ohio, Indiana, Illinois, Minnesota, Wisconsin, and Michigan) that American settlers encountered and claimed lands occupied by Indians but to which the legal title was never codified by war or treaty. The dispute between Johnson and M'Intosh brought this issue to a head and required the Supreme Court to intervene in order to articulate the status of what would eventually be hundreds of millions of acres of land which were occupied by Indians but ultimately claimed by the United States.

The solution the Supreme Court arrived at was the full scale adoption of the 'Doctrine of Discovery.' Notably, the Doctrine of Discovery was not something invented by Chief Justice Marshall for the purposes of resolving *Johnson v. M'Intosh*; but was instead the formal American adoption of a legal principle that had been established centuries ago for the purpose of ending conflicts between European nations and justifying their wars during the crusades and later their colonization of Africa, Austral-Asia, and the Americas. From the Doctrine of Discovery came the limited right of 'Indian title.' Individual tribes had at the moment of 'discovery' the right to use, to occupy, to be upon, to harvest from, and to use the land, but they lost the right to dispose of the land to anyone but the "discovering" nation. Essentially – the European nation acquired a legal interest in the land (the sole right to acquire it from the Indians).

At the time *Johnson v. M'Intosh* was decided there was nothing mandating that the Doctrine of Discovery be adopted by the United States. Instead of claiming that Indians had lost their full rights to the land, the Supreme Court could have recognized the inherent title of native peoples, or alternatively could have denied Indians any right to the land they occupied. Chief Justice Marshall ultimately adopted this middle ground, where Indians retained their title to the land but lost the right to dispose of the property to anyone but the United States federal government.

In adopting the Doctrine, the Court needed to identify when Indian had been officially 'discovered' by Great Britain. Marshall's opinion makes clear that the British claim can be traced back to Henry Cabot Lodge's first voyage down the east coast of North America, originating in the Canadian Maritimes and traversing as far as modern-day Virginia. Little is known about the interaction between Cabot and any Indians he may have encountered, but the Supreme Court makes clear that in its mind, Cabot's journey claimed for Britain the 'discovery' of all lands from the coast inland as far as the Mississippi river (and perhaps all the way to the Pacific Ocean). The Doctrine of Discovery was thus an incredibly broad tool used to divest tribes that would not meet a European for several more centuries of the full rights to the land that they occupied.

After the Supreme Court's decision, Indian tribes were prohibited from selling their land to anyone but the United States. Understandably, with only one legal buyer tribes have sometimes struggled to convince the United States to pay the fair market value for the property that was taken. Beginning in 1946, an 'Indian Claims Commission' was established to hear claims from tribes regarding compensation for abuses committed by the United States, including a failure to properly value tribal land at the time of taking. By the time the Commission wrapped up its work in 1978, it had paid out more than $818 million dollars to satisfy almost 200 claims, some of them dating back to the founding of America.

Even today *Johnson v. M'Intosh*'s declaration of the Doctrine of Discovery remains the legal principle by which the United States claims title to land from Indians. As recently as 2005, Justice Ginsburg used the Doctrine in determining that Indian tribes had lost the right to tax property that had been ceded to the State of New York but subsequently reacquired by the Oneida Indian Nation. In *City of Sherrill v. Oneida Indian Nation* Justice Ginsburg wrote: "Under the 'doctrine of discovery' fee title to the lands occupied by Indians when the colonists arrived became vested in the sovereign – first the discovering European nation and later the original States and the United States." Accordingly, reasoned the Justice, once the tribe allowed the land to be acquired by non-Indians it lost all interest in the land. Even when the tribe re-purchased the land at market rates, the tribe did not have the right to tax that land restored to the reservation without the consent of the United States.

The Cherokee Cases

The status of tribes and their associated 'Indian title' was challenged directly in the Supreme Court a mere decade after *Johnson v. M'Intosh* was decided. The Cherokee Nation were numerous in number and posed a military threat to the settlers in the early American republic. After the Revolutionary War was concluded the government created by the Articles of Confederation took over from the British the responsibility of policing the western boundary between Indian tribes and white settlers. With the end of hostilities against Britain, many soldiers returned home and then set out westward to clear new lands creating innumerable conflicts with Indian tribes already living there.

The Cherokee Nation was well organized and equipped and was particularly effective at policing its lands, resulting in many violent confrontations between the Cherokee and settlers moving westward from Georgia and the Carolinas. To resolve the conflict, representatives of the United States met and negotiated with Cherokee leaders at Hopewell (in modern-day South Carolina) a treaty that would end the conflict by establishing clear boundaries between Cherokee lands and the United States. Accordingly, in 1785, the Treaty of Hopewell purported to establish clear boundaries between Cherokee lands and the southern states. However, even at the time of the treaty's creation more than 3000 settlers were illegally settled upon lands the treaty gave to the Cherokee.

The boundary created by the Treaty of Hopewell was unsustainable from the beginning. While the treaty gave the Cherokee the right to remove the settlers, in practice the number of settlers increased rapidly and any attempt to remove them was met with violence. Just six years later a new treaty, the Treaty of Holston, was signed in which the Cherokee made additional land cessions in exchange for an agreement from the United States that it would help prevent settlers from entering the now diminished Cherokee lands. Despite these treaties, conflict between white settlers from southern states and the Cherokee continued.

In 1830, a Georgia court convicted a Cherokee named George Tassel of killing another Cherokee on tribal land. Tassel appealed in federal court for a writ of *habeas corpus* (asking to be set free), arguing that the treaties between the United States and the Cherokee Nation gave exclusive jurisdiction to the tribe and therefore his trial in state court was improper. Essentially, he argued that he could be punished only by the laws of the Cherokee Nation and not by the state of Georgia. Chief Justice Marshall granted the writ, which was promptly ignored by the state of Georgia. George Tassel was hanged.

In protest, the Cherokee Nation hired William Wirt, a former United States Attorney under Presidents Monroe and Adams, to take their case to the Supreme Court. Wirt filed an action against the state of Georgia enjoining the enforcement of its laws on Cherokee land on behalf of the Cherokee directly in the United States Supreme Court. In order to start a case in the Supreme Court instead of in a lower court Wirt argued that the Cherokee were a foreign state and thus qualified for the Court's original jurisdiction. The state of Georgia refused to recognize the Cherokee Nation and accordingly did not file a reply nor send a representative when the Court heard the Cherokee's case.

As a preliminary matter, the Supreme Court needed to determine whether it had the authority, or "jurisdiction," to hear the dispute. In *Cherokee Nation v. Georgia*, the Supreme Court was thus asked to determine the status of Indian tribes. Are they foreign governments? Are they sovereign nations? What respect is given to them by the law and the United States? Unlike the decision in *Johnson v. M'Intosh*, this time the Supreme Court was not unanimous in its decision. The fractured opinion was especially uncommon in the early nineteenth century, with four of the six participating justices writing their own answers to these questions. (The Supreme Court at that time had only seven members and one did not participate in the decision). As you read the opinion, see if you can synthesize from the justices what principles might command a majority. Can you explain why Chief Justice Marshall's opinion is commonly referred to as the binding judgment of the Court? What is the settled status of Indian tribes?

....

CHEROKEE NATION v. GEORGIA
Supreme Court of the United States (1831) 30 U.S. 1

CHIEF JUSTICE MARSHALL Delivered the Opinion of the Court. (Joined by Justice McLEAN)

This bill is brought by the Cherokee nation, praying an injunction to restrain the state of Georgia from the execution of certain laws of that state, which, as is alleged, go directly to annihilate the Cherokees as a political society, and to seize, for the use of Georgia, the lands of the nation which have been assured to them by the United States in solemn treaties repeatedly made and still in force.

If courts were permitted to indulge their sympathies, a case better calculated to excite them can scarcely be imagined. A people once numerous, powerful, and truly independent, found by our ancestors in the quiet and uncontrolled possession of an ample domain, gradually sinking beneath our superior policy, our arts and our arms, have yielded their lands by successive treaties, each of which contains a solemn guarantee of the residue, until they retain no more of their formerly extensive territory than is deemed necessary to their comfortable subsistence. To preserve this remnant, the present application is made.

Before we can look into the merits of the case, a preliminary inquiry presents itself. Has this court jurisdiction of the cause?

The third article of the constitution describes the extent of the judicial power. The second section closes an enumeration of the cases to which it is extended, with "controversies" "between a state or the citizens thereof, and foreign states, citizens, or subjects." A subsequent clause of the same section gives the supreme court original jurisdiction in all cases in which a state shall be a party. The party defendant may then unquestionably be sued in this court. May the plaintiff sue in it? Is the Cherokee nation a foreign state in the sense in which that term is used in the constitution?

The counsel for the plaintiffs have maintained the affirmative of this proposition with great earnestness and ability. So much of the argument as was intended to prove the character of the Cherokees as a state, as a distinct political society, separated from others, capable of managing its own affairs and governing itself, has, in the opinion of a majority of the judges, been completely successful. They have been uniformly treated as a state from the settlement of our country. The numerous treaties made with them by the United States recognize them as a people capable of maintaining the relations of peace and war, of being responsible in their political character for any violation of their engagements, or for any aggression committed on the citizens of the United States by any individual of their community. Laws have been enacted in the spirit of these treaties. The acts of our government plainly recognize the Cherokee nation as a state, and the courts are bound by those acts.

A question of much more difficulty remains. Do the Cherokees constitute a foreign state in the sense of the constitution?

* * * The condition of the Indians in relation to the United States is perhaps unlike that of any other two people in existence. In general, nations not owing a common allegiance are foreign to each other. The term foreign nation is, with strict propriety, applicable by either to the other. But the relation of the Indians to the United States is marked by peculiar and cardinal distinctions which exist nowhere else.

The Indian territory is admitted to compose a part of the United States. In all our maps, geographical treatises, histories, and laws, it is so considered. In all our intercourse with foreign nations, in our commercial regulations, in any attempt at intercourse between Indians and foreign nations, they are considered as within the jurisdictional limits of the United States, subject to many of those restraints which are imposed upon our own citizens. They acknowledge themselves in their treaties to be under the protection of the United States; they admit that the United States shall have the sole and exclusive right of regulating the trade with them, and managing all their affairs as they think proper; and the Cherokees in particular were allowed by the treaty of Hopewell, which preceded the constitution, "to send a deputy of their choice, whenever they think fit, to congress." Treaties were made with some tribes by the state of New York, under a then unsettled construction of the confederation, by which they ceded all their lands to that state, taking back a limited grant to themselves, in which they admit their dependence.

Though the Indians are acknowledged to have an unquestionable, and, heretofore, unquestioned right to the lands they occupy, until that right shall be extinguished by a voluntary cession to our government; yet it may well be doubted whether those tribes which reside within the acknowledged boundaries of the United States can, with strict accuracy, be denominated foreign nations. They may, more correctly, perhaps, be denominated domestic dependent nations. They occupy a territory to which we assert a title independent of their will, which must take effect in point of possession when their right of possession ceases. Meanwhile they are in a state of pupilage. Their relation to the United States resembles that of a ward to his guardian.

They look to our government for protection; rely upon its kindness and its power; appeal to it for relief to their wants; and address the president as their great father. They and their country are considered by foreign nations, as well as by ourselves, as being so completely under the sovereignty and dominion of the United States, that any attempt to acquire their lands, or to form a political connection with them, would be considered by all as an invasion of our territory, and an act of hostility.

These considerations go far to support the opinion, that the framers of our constitution had not the Indian tribes in view, when they opened the courts of the union to controversies between a state or the citizens thereof, and foreign states.

In considering this subject, the habits and usages of the Indians, in their intercourse with their white neighbors, ought not to be entirely disregarded. At the time the constitution was framed, the idea of appealing to an American court of justice for an assertion of right or a redress of wrong, had perhaps never entered the mind of an Indian or of his tribe. Their appeal was to the tomahawk, or to the government. This was well understood by the statesmen who framed the constitution of the United States, and might furnish some reason for omitting to enumerate them among the parties who might sue in the courts of the union. Be this as it may, the peculiar relations between the United States and the Indians occupying our territory are such, that we should feel much difficulty in considering them as designated by the term foreign state, were there no other part of the constitution which might shed light on the meaning of these words. But we think that in construing them, considerable aid is furnished by that clause in the eighth section of the third article; which empowers congress to "regulate commerce with foreign nations, and among the several states, and with the Indian tribes."

In this clause they are as clearly contradistinguished by a name appropriate to themselves, from foreign nations, as from the several states composing the union. They are designated by a distinct appellation; and as this appellation can be applied to neither of the others, neither can the appellation distinguishing either of the others be in fair construction applied to them. The objects, to which the power of regulating commerce might be directed, are divided into three distinct classes – foreign nations, the several states, and Indian tribes. When forming this article, the convention considered them as entirely distinct. We cannot assume that the distinction was lost in framing a subsequent article, unless there be something in its language to authorize the assumption.

* * *

The court has bestowed its best attention on this question, and, after mature deliberation, the majority is of opinion that an Indian tribe or nation within the United States is not a foreign state in the sense of the constitution, and cannot maintain an action in the courts of the United States.

* * *

If it be true that the Cherokee nation have rights, this is not the tribunal in which those rights are to be asserted. If it be true that wrongs have been inflicted, and that still greater are to be apprehended, this is not the tribunal which can redress the past or prevent the future. The motion for an injunction is denied.

JUSTICE JOHNSON, Concurring in the Judgment

* * * I cannot but think that there are strong reasons for doubting the applicability of the epithet state, to a people so low in the grade of organized society as our Indian tribes most generally are. I would not here be understood as speaking of the Cherokees under their present form of government; which certainly must be classed among the most approved forms of civil government. Whether it can be yet said to have received the consistency which entitles that people to admission into the family of nations is, I conceive, yet to be determined by the executive of these states. Until then I must think that we cannot recognize it as an existing state, under any other character than that which it has maintained hitherto as one of the Indian tribes or nations.

* * *

In the very treaty of Hopewell, the language or evidence of which is appealed to as the leading proof of the existence of this supposed state, we find the commissioners of the United States expressing themselves in these terms. "The commissioners plenipotentiary of the United States give peace to all the

Cherokees, and receive them into the favor and protection of the United States on the following conditions." This is certainly the language of sovereigns and conquerors, and not the address of equals to equals. And again, when designating the country they are to be confined to, comprising the very territory which is the subject of this bill, they say, "Art. 4. The boundary allotted to the Cherokees for their hunting grounds" shall be as therein described. Certainly this is the language of concession on our part, not theirs; and when the full bearing and effect of those words, "for their hunting grounds," is considered, it is difficult to think that they were then regarded as a state, or even intended to be so regarded. It is clear that it was intended to give them no other rights over the territory than what were needed by a race of hunters; and it is not easy to see how their advancement beyond that state of society could ever have been promoted, or, perhaps, permitted, consistently with the unquestioned rights of the states, or United States, over the territory within their limits. * * * But every advance, from the hunter state to a more fixed state of society, must have a tendency to impair that pre-emptive right, and ultimately to destroy it altogether, both by increasing the Indian population, and by attaching them firmly to the soil. The hunter state bore within itself the promise of vacating the territory, because when game ceased, the hunter would go elsewhere to seek it. But a more fixed state of society would amount to a permanent destruction of the hope, and, of consequence, of the beneficial character of the pre-emptive right.

* * *

Where is the rule to stop? Must every petty kraal of Indians, designating themselves a tribe or nation, and having a few hundred acres of land to hunt on exclusively, be recognized as a state? We should indeed force into the family of nations, a very numerous and very heterogeneous progeny. * * * I vote for rejecting the motion.

JUSTICE BALDWIN, Concurring in the Judgment

* * * I concur in the opinion of the court in dismissing the bill, but not for the reasons assigned. In my opinion there is no plaintiff in this suit; and this opinion precludes any examination into the merits of the bill, or the weight of any minor objections. My judgment stops me at the threshold, and forbids me to examine into the acts complained of.

* * *

There can be no dependence so antinational, or so utterly subversive of national existence as transferring to a foreign government the regulation of its trade, and the management of all their affairs at their pleasure. The nation or state, tribe or village, head men or warriors of the Cherokees, call them by what name we please, call the articles they have signed a definitive treaty or an indenture of servitude; they are not by its force or virtue a foreign state capable of calling into legitimate action the judicial power of this union, by the exercise of the original jurisdiction of this court against a sovereign state, a component part of this nation. Unless the constitution has imparted to the Cherokees a national character never recognized under the confederation; and which if they ever enjoyed was surrendered by the treaty of Hopewell; they cannot be deemed in this court plaintiffs in such a case as this. * * *

JUSTICE THOMPSON, Joined by JUSTICE STORY, Dissenting

* * * That a state of this union may be sued by a foreign state, when a proper case exists and is presented, is too plainly and expressly declared in the constitution to admit of doubt; and the first inquiry is, whether the Cherokee nation is a foreign state within the sense and meaning of the constitution.

The terms state and nation are used in the law of nations, as well as in common parlance, as importing the same thing; and imply a body of men, united together, to procure their mutual safety and advantage by means of their union. * * * Every nation that governs itself, under what form soever, without any dependence on a foreign power, is a sovereign state. * * * Consequently, a weak state, that, in order to provide for its safety, places itself under the protection of a more powerful one, without stripping itself of the right of government and sovereignty, does not cease on this account to be placed among the sovereigns who acknowledge no other power. Tributary and feudatory states do not thereby cease to be sovereign and independent states, so long as self-government, and sovereign and independent authority is left in the administration of the state.

Testing the character and condition of the Cherokee Indians by these rules, it is not perceived how it is possible to escape the conclusion, that they form a sovereign state. They have always been dealt with as such by the government of the United States; both before and since the adoption of the present constitution. They have been admitted and treated as a people governed solely and exclusively by their own laws, usages, and customs within their own territory, claiming and exercising exclusive dominion over the same; yielding up by treaty, from time to time, portions of their land, but still claiming absolute sovereignty and self-government over what remained unsold.

* * *

The progress made in civilization by the Cherokee Indians cannot surely be considered as in any measure destroying their national or foreign character, so long as they are permitted to maintain a separate and distinct government; it is their political condition that constitutes their foreign character, and in that sense must the term foreign, be understood as used in the constitution. It can have no relation to local, geographical, or territorial position. * * * If we look to lexicographers, as well as approved writers, for the use of the term foreign, it may be applied with the strictest propriety to the Cherokee nation. * * *

....

In *Cherokee Nation* the Supreme Court clarified the status of Indian tribes that still prevails today. What is the settled status of Indian tribes? Tribes are appropriately termed 'domestic dependent nations.' The Court's divided opinion was based around the difference between being a 'state' and a 'foreign state.' Combining the opinions together it becomes clear that while a majority of the Court held that tribes are 'states' and therefore sovereign, they are not 'foreign states' and therefore could not begin any complaint directly in the Supreme Court. Instead the Court explains that tribes are 'wards' to which the United States is a 'guardian.'

Domestic Dependent Nations

The justices in *Cherokee Nation v. Georgia* were sharply divided over the status of tribes and whether they are 'states' and if so, whether they are 'foreign states' as those terms are used in the Constitution. The language used by the concurring justices seem to question at times whether Indians have any rights under the Constitution, while the dissenting justices would afford Indian tribes not just the status of a state, but also of a foreign nation capable of maintaining itself against the United States. Counting the opinions a consensus emerges:

	Are Tribes States?	Are Tribes Foreign States?
Marshall (Joined by McLean)	YES	NO
Johnson	NO	NO
Baldwin	NO	NO
Thompson (Joined by Story)	YES	YES

In 1831, the Supreme Court had seven justices instead of the nine that serve today, but Justice Duvall did not participate in the case. In *Cherokee Nation v. Georgia*, four of the six participating justices concluded that the Cherokee Nation, and by extension all Indian tribes, were not 'foreign states' and so they were not able to appear before the Supreme Court using its 'original jurisdiction.' Accordingly the Supreme Court never reached the merits of whether the State of Georgia was allowed to convict and punish George Tassel for a crime committed against another member of the tribe on land belonging to the tribe.

However, there were also a total of four votes for the proposition that Indian tribes, while not 'foreign states' are 'states' – they are functioning and self-governing communities. Accordingly, the term 'domestic dependent nation' has been taken from Chief Justice Marshall's opinion and applied consistently as the legal position tribes hold in the United States even today.

As a result of *Cherokee Nation*, Indian tribes even today are not permitted to maintain their own military, negotiate trade treaties with foreign governments, establish embassies in foreign lands, or apply for membership in international bodies composed of independent countries like the United Nations. However, tribes are permitted to create their own laws and be governed by them – which includes the creation of tribal Constitutions, tribal courts, tribal police departments and detention facilities, tribal rules on the sale of goods, on inheritance, on property ownership etc. It is difficult to overestimate the importance of *Cherokee Nation v. Georgia* on the contours of modern Indian law, for by establishing that tribes constitute sovereign 'states' the Supreme Court in 1831 created a legal foundation for tribal independence and self-governance.

The Cherokee Nation Returns to the Supreme Court

While *Cherokee Nation v. Georgia* created the now eponymous moniker of 'domestic dependent nations' it did nothing to resolve the underlying question of whether a state like Georgia was allowed to enter tribal lands and punish tribal members. Unfortunately the Court in *Cherokee Nation* never determined whether Georgia had the authority to prosecute and execute tribal member George Tassel for crimes committee on Cherokee lands because it had been decided that the Cherokee Nation could not bring a claim directly in the Supreme Court. Accordingly, the tribe needed the assistance of others to raise the issue of state authority on tribal land in a local dispute that could then be appealed to the Supreme Court for review.

The proper test case came just a year later. Georgia had passed a law declaring it illegal to reside upon Cherokee lands without a license from the state and without taking an oath of loyalty to the state of Georgia. A pair of missionaries from Vermont, among them the named plaintiff Samuel Worcester, defied the state law and entered Cherokee lands to live and work as missionaries among the Cherokee people. They were arrested and convicted by the state of Georgia. Both missionaries appealed their conviction to the United States Supreme Court, arguing that the state of Georgia had no authority to enact or enforce its laws on Indian lands.

Justice Marshall again wrote the majority and governing opinion. Finally able to reach the merits and resolve the issue of state authority on Indian land, his reasoning continues to define the boundary between the power of states and tribes and places obligations upon the United States to ensure that tribes are not overwhelmed by their constitute states. As you read the following opinion, consider whether states should be able to make and enforce rules that tribes must follow even on tribal land.

....

WORCESTER v. GEORGIA
Supreme Court of the United States (1832) 31 U.S. 515

CHIEF JUSTICE MARSHALL Delivered the Opinion of the Court

This cause, in every point of view in which it can be placed, is of the deepest interest. The defendant is a state, a member of the union, which has exercised the powers of government over a people who deny its jurisdiction, and are under the protection of the United States.

The plaintiff is a citizen of the state of Vermont, condemned to hard labor for four years in the penitentiary of Georgia; under color of an act which he alleges to be repugnant to the constitution, laws, and treaties of the United States.

* * *

The indictment charges the plaintiff in error, and others, being white persons, with the offence of "residing within the limits of the Cherokee nation without a license," and "without having taken the oath to support and defend the constitution and laws of the state of Georgia."

The defendant in the state court appeared in proper person, and filed the following plea:

"And the said Samuel A. Worcester, in his own proper person, comes and says, * * * that, on the 15th day of July in the year 1831, he was, and still is, a resident in the Cherokee nation; and * * * that he is a citizen of the state of Vermont, one of the United States of America, and that he entered the aforesaid Cherokee nation in the capacity of a duly authorized missionary of the American Board of Commissioners for Foreign Missions" * * *

This plea was overruled by the court. And the prisoner, being arraigned, plead not guilty. The jury found a verdict against him, and the court sentenced him to hard labour, in the penitentiary, for the term of four years.

* * *

America, separated from Europe by a wide ocean, was inhabited by a distinct people, divided into separate nations, independent of each other and of the rest of the world, having institutions of their own, and governing themselves by their own laws. It is difficult to comprehend the proposition, that the inhabitants of either quarter of the globe could have rightful original claims of dominion over the inhabitants of the other, or over the lands they occupied; or that the discovery of either by the other should give the discoverer rights in the country discovered, which annulled the pre-existing rights of its ancient possessors.

After lying concealed for a series of ages, the enterprise of Europe, guided by nautical science, conducted some of her adventurous sons into this western world. They found it in possession of a people who had made small progress in agriculture or manufactures, and whose general employment was war, hunting, and fishing.

Did these adventurers, by sailing along the coast, and occasionally landing on it, acquire for the several governments to whom they belonged, or by whom they were commissioned, a rightful property in the soil, from the Atlantic to the Pacific; or rightful dominion over the numerous people who occupied it? Or has nature, or the great Creator of all things, conferred these rights over hunters and fishermen, on agriculturists and manufacturers?

* * *

During the war of the revolution, the Cherokees took part with the British. After its termination, the United States, though desirous of peace, did not feel its necessity so strongly as while the war continued. Their political situation being changed, they might very well think it advisable to assume a higher tone, and to impress on the Cherokees the same respect for congress which was before felt for the king of Great Britain. This may account for the language of the treaty of Hopewell. There is the more reason for supposing that the Cherokee chiefs were not very critical judges of the language, from the fact that everyone makes his mark; no chief was capable of signing his name. It is probable the treaty was interpreted to them.

The treaty is introduced with the declaration, that "the commissioners plenipotentiary of the United States given peace to all the Cherokees, and receive them into the favour and protection of the United States of America, on the following conditions."

When the United States gave peace, did they not also receive it? Were not both parties desirous of it? If we consult the history of the day, does it not inform us that the United States were at least as anxious to obtain it as the Cherokees? We may ask, further: did the Cherokees come to the seat of the American government to solicit peace; or, did the American commissioners go to them to obtain it? The treaty was made at Hopewell, not at New York. The word "give," then, has no real importance attached to it.

* * *

The fifth article withdraws the protection of the United States from any citizen who has settled, or shall settle, on the lands allotted to the Indians, for their hunting grounds; and stipulates that, if he shall not remove within six months the Indians may punish him.

The sixth and seventh articles stipulate for the punishment of the citizens of either country, who may commit offences on or against the citizens of the other. The only inference to be drawn from them is, that the United States considered the Cherokees as a nation.

The ninth article is in these words: "for the benefit and comfort of the Indians, and for the prevention of injuries or oppressions on the part of the citizens or Indians, the United States, in congress assembled, shall have the sole and exclusive right of regulating the trade with the Indians, and managing all their affairs, as they think proper."

* * *

The treaty of Hopewell seems not to have established a solid peace. To accommodate the differences still existing between the state of Georgia and the Cherokee nation, the treaty of Holston was negotiated in July 1791. The existing constitution of the United States had been then adopted, and the government, having more intrinsic capacity to enforce its just claims, was perhaps less mindful of his sounding expressions, denoting superiority. We hear no more of giving peace to the Cherokees. The mutual desire of establishing permanent peace and friendship, and of removing all causes of war, is honestly avowed, and, in pursuance of this desire, the first article declares, that there shall be perpetual peace and friendship between all the citizens of the United States of America and all the individuals composing the Cherokee nation.

* * *

This treaty, thus explicitly recognizing the national character of the Cherokees, and their right of self-government; thus guarantying their lands; assuming the duty of protection, and of course pledging the faith of the United States for that protection; has been frequently renewed, and is now in full force.

* * *

The Indian nations had always been considered as distinct, independent political communities, retaining their original natural rights, as the undisputed possessors of the soil, from time immemorial, with the single exception of that imposed by irresistible power, which excluded them from intercourse with any other European potentate than the first discoverer of the coast of the particular region claimed: and this was a restriction which those European potentates imposed on themselves, as well as on the Indians. The very term "nation," so generally applied to them, means "a people distinct from others." The constitution, by declaring treaties already made, as well as those to be made, to be the supreme law of the land, has adopted and sanctioned the previous treaties with the Indian nations, and consequently admits their rank among those powers who are capable of making treaties. The words "treaty" and "nation" are words of our own language, selected in our diplomatic and legislative proceedings, by ourselves, having each a definite and well understood meaning. We have applied them to Indians, as we have applied them to the other nations of the earth. They are applied to all in the same sense.

* * *

The Cherokee nation, then, is a distinct community occupying its own territory, with boundaries accurately described, in which the laws of Georgia can have no force, and which the citizens of Georgia have no right to enter, but with the assent of the Cherokees themselves, or in conformity with treaties, and with the acts of congress. The whole intercourse between the United States and this nation, is, by our constitution and laws, vested in the government of the United States.

* * *

It is the opinion of this court that the judgment of the superior court for the county of Gwinnett, in the state of Georgia, condemning Samuel A. Worcester to hard labor, in the penitentiary of the state of Georgia, for four years, was pronounced by that court under color of a law which is void, as being repugnant to the constitution, treaties, and laws of the United States, and ought, therefore, to be reversed and annulled.

JUSTICE MCLEAN, Concurring in the Judgment

* * * If a tribe of Indians shall become so degraded or reduced in numbers, as to lose the power of self-government, the protection of the local law, of necessity, must be extended over them. The point at which this exercise of power by a state would be proper, need not now be considered: if indeed it be a judicial question. Such a question does not seem to arise in this case. So long as treaties and laws remain in full force, and apply to Indian nations, exercising the right of self-government, within the limits of a state, the judicial power can exercise no discretion in refusing to give effect to those laws, when questions arise under them, unless they shall be deemed unconstitutional.

The exercise of the power of self-government by the Indians, within a state, is undoubtedly contemplated to be temporary. This is shown by the settled policy of the government, in the extinguishment of their title, and especially by the compact with the state of Georgia. It is a question, not of abstract right, but of public policy. I do not mean to say, that the same moral rule which should regulate the affairs of private life, should not be regarded by communities or nations. But, a sound national policy does require that the Indian tribes within our states should exchange their territories, upon equitable principles, or, eventually, consent to become amalgamated in our political communities.

* * * But, if a contingency shall occur, which shall render the Indians who reside in a state, incapable of self-government, either by moral degradation or a reduction of their numbers, it would undoubtedly be in the power of a state government to extend to them the aegis of its laws. Under such circumstances, the agency of the general government, of necessity, must cease.

* * *

Under the administration of the laws of Georgia, a citizen of the United States has been deprived of his liberty; and, claiming protection under the treaties and laws of the United States, he makes the question, as he has a right to make it, whether the laws of Georgia, under which he is now suffering an ignominious punishment, are not repugnant to the constitution of the United States, and the treaties and laws made under it. This repugnancy has been shown; and it remains only to say, what has before been often said by this tribunal of the local laws of many of the states in this union, that, being repugnant to the constitution of the United States, and to the laws made under it, they can have no force to divest the plaintiff in error of his property or liberty.

JUSTICE BALDWIN Dissented * * *

The opinion of Mr. Justice Baldwin was not delivered to the reporter.

....

Should states be able to pass laws that govern conduct on tribal lands? Chief Justice Marshall's opinion suggests the answer is no. Instead the opinion is commonly understood to establish a strict territorial conception to jurisdiction. The rule that emerges from *Worcester* is fairly simple; the state cannot extend its laws unto tribal land and, reciprocally, a tribe cannot extend its laws unto state land.

After Worcester

In *Worcester v. Georgia*, Chief Justice Marshall made clear that the states lacked the power to enforce their laws on Indian lands and ordered that Samuel Worcester and his fellow missionary Elizur Butler, be immediately freed. Unfortunately however, Georgia did not immediately comply. Instead it refused to recognize the authority of the Supreme Court to limit the applicability of state law unto the Indian reservation. Worcester and Butler remained incarcerated in Georgia. In 1833, the newly reelected governor of Georgia offered to release the missionaries if they agreed to never return to Cherokee lands. Both Worcester and Butler agreed and were finally released.

President Jackson was in the White House when *Worcester* was decided. Jackson was a veteran of Indian wars on the frontier and no friend to tribes. In response to *Worcester v. Georgia* there is a now famous anecdote, probably apocryphal, that upon hearing the Court's ruling Jackson commented: "John Marshall has made his decision, now let him enforce it." It is an important reminder that the judicial branch is charged with interpreting the law while the executive is responsible for enforcing it.

While Worcester and Butler were eventually freed, the Cherokee Nation was not so fortunate. After enduring several more years of hostilities from settlers that the federal government was unable to control, the Cherokee Nation signed the Treaty of New Echota in December of 1835. Under the treaty, the Cherokee Nation ceded its traditional lands in the southeast and agreed to move west of the Mississippi River. In enforcing the treaty, the United States marched the Cherokee and many other eastern tribes to their new lands in modern-day Oklahoma. Thousands of Cherokee died along the way in what is now known as the Trail of Tears.

The Impact of the Marshall Trilogy

The legacy of the Marshall Trilogy cannot be overstated. Both *Johnson v. M'Intosh* and *Worcester v. Georgia* are among the 10 most cited cases decided by the Supreme Court from before the Civil War. Together the cases create a constitutional basis for tribal sovereignty, recognize that Indian tribes hold 'Indian title' to their lands, and create an obligation for the federal government to protect tribes from overzealous state authority.

In *Johnson v. M'Intosh*, the Court adopted the Doctrine of Discovery distilled from earlier European common law. This meant that Indian tribes in the United States had lost the right to sell or give their property to anyone but the United States. However, until the United States took title to the land, Indian tribes retained "Indian title" which included the right to use, to live upon, to harvest from, to exclude, etc. 'Indian title' is commonly called a 'right of occupancy' which has been clarified to include a right to water, mineral resources, timber, and game associated with tribal lands. In subsequent years, when the federal government would take Indian lands without paying the tribe the full value of its 'Indian title,' this title has provided a basis for tribes to seek hundreds of millions of dollars in compensation.

In *Cherokee Nation v. Georgia*, the Court concluded that Indian tribes are 'domestic dependent nations.' The Court recognized the sovereignty of Indian tribes and gave them a Constitutional status as entities distinct from states. As 'domestic dependent nations' tribes are able to exercise a degree of autonomy which has permitted the development of tribal constitutions and tribal courts.

Finally, in *Worcester v. Georgia*, the Court clarified that states have no power to regulate what happens on Indian lands. While the parties struggled with enforcement of the Court's decision, the legal legacy of the *Worcester* opinion has been recognized as providing a bulwark against excessive state interference on the reservation. *Worcester* has helped tribes remain independent from states, adopting laws on the reservation that are meaningfully different from the law of the surrounding state. Accordingly, it forms the legal basis for why tribes are able to operate casinos on tribal lands, helps supplement the argument that tribes should have their own laws to deal with child custody, education, inheritance, business regulation, environmental protection, and has opened to the door to legal claims by tribes against the United States that the federal government has failed to protect tribes from the unlawful encroachment of state power.

The Supreme Court continues to be instrumental in the development of Indian law in ways that are both beneficial and detrimental to tribes. Since the 1960s, the Supreme Court has heard, on average, between two and three Indian law cases a year out of a total caseload that has recently been about 80 cases. However, few of these decisions have been as important to the development of the status of Indian tribes as the Marshall trilogy and virtually all of them continue to rely on the basic tenants and principles laid out by these three cases as the background against which modern decisions are made.

Sources and Further Readings

William Canby, Jr. 2014. *American Indian Law in a Nutshell*. St. Paul: West Academic Publishing.
Felix S. Cohen. 2007. *On the Drafting of Tribal Constitutions*. Norman: Oklahoma University Press.
Vine Deloria, Jr. and Clifford M. Lytle. 1983. *American Indians, American Justice*. Austin: Texas University Press.
Angelique Townsend EagleWoman and Stacy Leeds. 2014. *Mastering American Indian Law*. Durham: Carolina Academic Press.
Matthew L.M. Fletcher. 2006. "The Pedagogy of American Indian Law: The Iron Cold of the Marshall Trilogy." *North Dakota Law Review*, Vol. 82, p. 627.

Nell Jessup Newton and Robert Anderson (Editors). 2012. *Cohen's Handbook of Federal Indian Law*. New Providence: LexisNexis.

Scott R. Lyons. 2011. "Actually Existing Indian Nations: Modernity, Diversity, and the Future of Native American Studies." *American Indian Quarterly*, Vol. 35-3, pp. 294-312.

Robert Miller, Jacinta Ruru, Larissa Behrendt, and Tracey Lindberg. 2012. *Discovering Indigenous Lands: The Doctrine of Discovery in the English Colonies*. Oxford: Oxford University Press.

Robert Miller. 2011. "American Indians, the Doctrine of Discovery, and Manifest Destiny." *Wyoming Law Review*, Vol. 11, p. 329.

Steven L. Pevar. 2012. *The Rights of Indians and Tribes*. Oxford: Oxford University Press.

Rebecca Tsosie. 1994. "Separate Sovereigns, Civil Rights, and the Sacred Text: The Legacy of Justice Thurgood Marshall's Indian Law Jurisprudence." *Arizona State Law Journal*, Vol. 26, p. 495.

Blake Watson. 2012. *Buying America from the Indians: Johnson v. McIntosh and the History of Native Land Rights*. University of Oklahoma Press.

David Wilkins. 1997. *American Indian Sovereignty and the U.S. Supreme Court: The Masking of Justice*. University of Texas Press.

Robert Williams. 1990. *The American Indian in Western Legal Thought: The Discourses of Conquest*. Oxford: Oxford University Press.

A Century of Changing Policy: Indians & Indian Tribes from the New Deal to Present
Grant Christensen

Introduction

The last century has seen a remarkable evolution in Indian policy comprised of at least four distinct eras in Indian affairs. Each of the four eras is distinguished by changing federal policy toward Indians, and with each new policy came changes on the reservation. Perhaps nothing illustrates the difference in objectives in federal policy better than the status of land. In 1900 the federal government was several decades into a policy which actively tried to reduce tribal lands and sell the 'surplus' to non-Indian settlers. It was widely believed by Congress and government officials that Indians should be encouraged to assimilate with the largely European settlers which were fast invading their traditional lands. In contrast, by 2016 the Obama administration met a campaign pledge first articulated in 2008 to return at least 500,000 acres of land to tribal control during his presidency.

The prevailing federal Indian policy at the turn of the last century was Allotment. Beginning in the 1870s the United States ended treaty making and started implementing policies to reclaim tribal land. Federal officials concluded that Indian reservations were too large and individual Indians often irresponsible. The Allotment Era was characterized by the loss of these tribal lands. Agreements were made with Indian tribes to carve up the large reservations and give each individual a set number of acres. The remaining 'surplus' land could then be sold to non-Indian settlers. Prevailing thinking at the time suggested that these non-Indian settlers would provide models of 'civilized' living for their Indian neighbors who would then follow their example. Ultimately the Allotment era was designed to encourage Indians to assimilate into mainstream American culture.

By the 1930s, the federal government began moving away from the allotment of reservations and instead recognized for the first time the importance of tribal government. The New Deal Era, roughly started during the Roosevelt administration, saw the formal recognition of tribal sovereignty long advocated by the courts extended through congressional legislation that for the first time formally recognized Indian rights of citizenship, voting, and self-government. It was during the New Deal that Indian tribes finally found a federal government willing to recognize that past Indian policy had largely been a failure and was responsible for the endemic poverty and many social ills present on the reservation. In order to address these problems, tribal governments were formally recognized by the United States and permitted to adopt their own solutions, taking into account the unique cultural traditions that existed in each tribal community. Hundreds of tribes can date their modern tribal governments as emerging during the New Deal Era.

Many of the positive changes initiated during the New Deal were rolled back during the third period aptly named the Termination Era. Beginning in the early 1950s, the United States again pushed aggressively for the assimilation of Indian people into the larger American society. Unlike the Allotment Era, Termination emphasized relocation away from reservations and cut funding for tribal programs that were designed to combat poverty and encourage education in Indian Country. Reverting to some of the same principles that justified the allotment of reservations, Congress began formally severing its government-to-government relationship with Indian tribes, in some cases denying Indian people access to the programs and policies that were expressly designed to promote tribal development.

Fortunately the termination era was rather brief. By the 1960s, Indian rights were included in the panoply of voices that became collectively known as the civil rights movement. This modern era of Indian policy, commonly called the Self-Determination Era, reaffirmed the rights of Indians to make their own laws and be governed by them. During this modern era, tribes have been increasingly responsible for what occurs on the reservation – taking over many functions previously performed solely by the BIA, other branches of the federal government, or shared with the states. They have found new forms of economic development and tribal revenue, been expressly charged with reducing poverty and unemployment, and given more control over preventing violence and protecting tribal children.

This chapter will take a broad look at the past century of Indian policy. Focusing on major legislative actions and weaving in some important political, cultural, and social events that swept through Indian Country during the last century – this chapter intends to leave the reader with a stronger understanding of the historical developments which underpin life on the modern reservation as well as help the reader understand the current powers of tribal government and introduce some of basic policy developments that have breathed new life into Indian self-determination.

The Allotment Era

Following the end of the Civil War in 1865 westward expansion accelerated quickly. European and American settlers moving west immediately encountered a land that was already populated both by tribes who had connections to the land since time immemorial and tribes who had been relocated west of the Mississippi River just a few decades earlier. As settler numbers increased the pressure to open up the existing reservations that had been created by treaty and executive order before the Civil War grew irresistible. Federal Indian policy in this era recognized that it was no longer possible to keep moving Indian people further west. Instead the federal government's formal policies regarding Indians changed from relocating Indians away from settlers and their growing communities to encouraging Indians to assimilate with the settlers.

After more than a decade of ad hoc policy adjustments, Congress enacted a formal policy to encourage Indians to assimilate with non-Indian settlers while also freeing up tens of millions of acres of land to new settlement. In 1887 Congress passed the General Allotment Act (GAA), also known as the Dawes Act after its chief sponsor Massachusetts Senator Henry Dawes. As the name implies, the Act encouraged that reservations literally be allotted. Sen. Dawes felt strongly that individual land ownership would help Indians develop a sense of pride in their own property and would thus motivate them to improve the land and ultimately earn a living from it. However, many Indian communities were nomadic; others had little cultural or traditional understanding of individual land ownership. Reservations themselves symbolized collective land rights, with land held in trust by the United States for the benefit of the tribes.

The Dawes Act aimed to challenge and ultimately break down collective or group ownership of land. It directed Indian Commissioners to seek to allot out reservation lands. The GAA literally called for reservations to be surveyed and parceled out with a fixed number of acres going to each household, single person, and orphaned child. On virtually all reservations that went through the allotment process the reservation was considerably larger than the amount of land that needed to be allotted out to tribal members. This 'excess' or 'surplus' land was then sold to non-Indians. Accordingly, the Dawes Act strongly encouraged reservations to be broken up and non-Indians to move into Indian Country.

The pattern of Indian allotments scattered among non-Indian's living on the 'surplus' land has yielded the analogy of a checkerboard – with Indian and non-Indian lands sometimes literally alternating in a pattern. The goal of assimilation was to be achieved precisely because non-Indian settlers were to enter the reservation. The Dawes Act contemplated these settlers would provide an example to Indians for how to improve and to live off of their allotments. The arrival of non-Indians would provide good examples to the Indians for how to cultivate the land and profit from its resources. In 1877 Carl Schurz, Secretary of the Interior, justified the policy; "the enjoyment and pride of the individual ownership of property being one of the most effective civilizing agencies."[1]

To ensure that Indians would not just immediately sell their lands, thus reaping short-term profit but losing the ability to provide for themselves or their families in the future, the GAA required that all allotments would be held by the United States in trust for the tribal members for a period of 25 years. However exceptions in the Act permitted Indians to get title to their lands sooner and many did so. Congress recognized that the Allotment Era was permitting too many Indians to lose any access to their traditional or cultural lands. The Dawes Act was amended by the Curtis Act in 1898 and the Burke Act in 1906. Each act prolonged the period in which the United States could retain a trust interest in the land (thus preventing the individual Indian land owners from selling) and also expanded the scope of the Act even to tribes that had been originally exempt.

The Dawes Act was not self-executing. It simply set up a structure for negotiations between Indian commissioners and tribal representatives that showed how an agreement might be made between Indians with large reservations and a federal government eager to open new lands to western settlement. In reality, each tribe had to enter into negotiations and have its own formal allotment act passed by Congress. In theory, this individual tribe-by-tribe approach was designed to ensure that the Allotment Era would be voluntary. In fact, many tribes were subject to allotment acts with fewer than a majority of eligible members participating in the decision.

The Allotment Era and its assimilationist policies are widely considered to be a failure for tribes. Reservations lost their territorial integrity. Of the more than 155 million acres that Indians controlled in 1881 less than 78 million acres remained by 1900. Far from promoting self-sufficiency the policy decimated the land holdings of Indian tribes and often forced the interaction of Indian and non-Indian communities which largely distrusted and even disliked each other.

The New Deal Era

The real impetus to change federal priorities away from allotment's goals of individual land ownership and assimilation, and toward the protection of Indian land rights and strong tribal government, began in 1928 with the publication of the Meriam Report by the Brookings Institute. After visiting 95 jurisdictions (reservations, collections of urban Indians, Indian schools and hospitals, and communities where Indians had migrated), Lewis Meriam issued a scathing report on the failure of the government's Indian policies. The report was rich in detail, with sections on health, education, the status of the family and Indian women, economic development, the work of missionaries, etc. The report attributed the problems of poverty, joblessness, lack of education, low life expectancy, and poor living conditions directly to the current manner in which the Department of Interior and BIA were working with Indians and demanded changes be made immediately.

An abridged copy of the report's summary is reproduced below. The Meriam Report is a remarkable work that has earned an important place in Indian studies. Its value transcends the small piece that can be reproduced below and all students of Indian studies are encouraged to read the original at length.[2]

General Summary of Findings and Recommendations the Problem of Indian Administration

The Conditions Among the Indians. An overwhelming majority of the Indians are poor, even extremely poor, and they are not adjusted to the economic and social system of the dominant white civilization. The poverty of the Indians and their lack of adjustment to the dominant economic and social systems produce the vicious circle ordinarily found among any people under such circumstances. Because of interrelationships, causes cannot be differentiated from effects. The only course is to state briefly the conditions found that are part of this vicious circle of poverty and maladjustment.

Health. The health of the Indians as compared with that of the general population is bad. Although accurate mortality and morbidity statistics are commonly lacking, the existing evidence warrants the statement that both the general death rate and the infant mortality rate are high. Tuberculosis is extremely prevalent. Trachoma a communicable disease which produces blindness, is a major problem because of its great prevalence and the danger of spreading among both the Indians and the whites. * * *

The Causes of Poverty. The economic basis of the primitive culture of the Indians has been largely destroyed by the encroachment of white civilization. The Indians can no longer make a living as they did in the past by hunting, fishing, gathering wild products, and the extremely limited practice of primitive agriculture. The social system that evolved from their past economic life is ill suited to the conditions that now confront them, notably in the matter of the division of labor between the men and the women. They are by no means yet adjusted to the new economic and social conditions that confront them. * * *

Several past policies adopted by the government in dealing with the Indians have been of a type which, if long continued, would tend to pauperize any race. Most notable was the practice of issuing rations to able-bodied Indians. Having moved the Indians from their ancestral lands to restricted reservations as a war measure, the government undertook to feed them and to perform certain services for them which a normal people do for themselves. The Indians at the outset had to accept this aid as a matter of necessity, but promptly they came to regard it as a matter of right, as indeed it was at the time and under the conditions of the inauguration of the ration system. They felt, and many of them still feel, that the government owes them a living, having taken their lands from them, and that they are under no obligation to support themselves. They have thus inevitably developed a pauper point of view. When the government adopted the policy of individual ownership of the land on the reservations, the expectation was that the Indians would become farmers. Part of the plan was to instruct and aid them in agriculture, but this vital part was not pressed with vigor and intelligence. It almost seems as if the government assumed that some magic in individual ownership of property would in itself prove an educational civilizing factor, but unfortunately this policy has for the most part operated in the opposite direction. Individual ownership has in many instances permitted Indians to sell their allotments and to live for a time on the unearned income resulting from the sale. Individual ownership brought promptly all the details of inheritance, and frequently the sale of the property of the deceased Indians to whites so that the estate could be divided among the heirs. To the heirs the sale brought further unearned income, thereby lessening the necessity for self support. Many Indians were not ready to make effective use of their individual allotments. * * *

The Work of the Government in Behalf of the Indians. The work of the government directed toward the education and advancement of the Indian himself, as distinguished from the control and conservation of his property, is largely ineffective. The chief explanation of the deficiency in this work lies in the fact that the government has not appropriated enough funds to permit the Indian Service to employ an adequate personnel properly qualified for the task before it. * * *

Work for the Promotion of Health. The inadequacy of appropriations has prevented the development of an adequate system of public health administration and medical relief work for the Indians. The number of doctors, nurses, and dentists is insufficient. Because of small appropriations the salaries for the personnel in health work are materially below those paid by the government in its other activities concerned with public health and medical relief, specifically the Public Health Service, the Army, the Navy, and the Veterans' Bureau, as well as below those paid, by private organizations for similar services. Since its salaries are sub-standard, the Indian Service has not been able to set reasonably high entrance qualifications and to adhere to them. In the case of doctors the standards set for entrance have been too low. In the case of public health nurses the standards have been reasonable, but it has not been possible to secure at the salary offered a sufficient number of applicants, so that many people have to be employed temporarily who do not possess the required qualifications. Often untrained, inexperienced field matrons are attempting to perform duties which would be fairly difficult for a well-trained, experienced public health nurse. For general nursing positions it has often been necessary to substitute for properly trained nurses, practical nurses, some of whom possess few qualifications for the work.

The hospitals, sanatoria, and sanatorium schools maintained by the Service, despite a few exceptions, must be generally characterized as lacking in personnel, equipment, management, and design. The statement is sometimes made that, since the Indians live according to a low scale, it is not necessary for the government to furnish hospital facilities for them which are comparable with those supplied for poor white people in a progressive community. * * *

Formal Education of Indian Children. For several years the general policy of the Indian Service has been directed away from the boarding school for Indian children and toward the public schools and Indian day schools. More Indian children are now in public schools maintained by the state or local governments than in special Indian schools maintained by the nation. It is, however, still the fact that the boarding school, either reservation or non-reservation, is the dominant characteristic of the school system maintained by the national government for its Indian wards. The survey staff finds itself obliged to say frankly and unequivocally that the provisions for the care of the Indian children in boarding schools are grossly inadequate. * * *

The boarding schools are frankly supported in part by the labor of the students. Those above the fourth grade ordinarily work for half a day and go to school for half a day. A distinction in theory is drawn between industrial work undertaken primarily for the education of the child and production work done primarily for the support of the institution. However, teachers of industrial work undertaken ostensibly for education say that much of it is as a matter of fact production work for the maintenance of the school. The question may very properly be raised as to whether much of the work of Indian children in boarding schools would not be prohibited in many states by the child labor laws, notably the work in the machine laundries. * * *

Although the problem of the returned Indian student has been much discussed, and it is recognized that in many instances the child returns to his home poorly adjusted to conditions that confront him, the Indian Service has lacked the funds to attempt to aid the children when they leave school either to find employment away from the reservation or to return to their homes and work out their salvation there. Having done almost no work of this kind, it has not subjected its schools to the test of having to show how far they have actually fitted the Indian children for life. Such a test would undoubtedly have resulted in a radical revision of the industrial training offered in the schools. * * *

Family and Community Development. The Indian Service has not appreciated the fundamental importance of family life and community activities in the social and economic development of a people. The tendency has been rather toward weakening Indian family life and community activities than toward strengthening them. The long continued policy of removing Indian children from the home and placing them for years in boarding school largely disintegrates the family and interferes with developing normal family life. The belief has apparently been that the shortest road to civilization is to take children away from their parents and insofar as possible to stamp out the old Indian life. The Indian community activities particularly have often been opposed if not suppressed. The fact has been appreciated that both the family life and the community activities have many objectionable features, but the action taken has often been the radical one of attempting to destroy rather than the educational process of gradual modification and development.

The Meriam report was a wakeup call for government and a rallying cry for advocates of Indian rights. It provided the stories and the recommendations upon which reformers could push for change from both the Bureau of Indian Affairs and from Congress more generally.

Taking the report's recommendations to heart, President Hoover's Commission of Indian Affairs, led by Charles Rhoades, pushed for many changes in the government's relationship with Indians and with both the quantity and quality of services the Commission provided. Between 1928 and 1931 many Indian boarding schools were closed as the focus on education returned to day schools near reservations where Indian children could live at home and commute to school during the day. The Bureau of Indian Affairs fought additional loses of tribal property, upgraded the standards for service at the Bureau, increased the number of native employees in both federal and local offices, more than doubled the department's budget, and pushed for an Indian Claims Commission to hear claims by tribes against the United States.

In 1932, the last year of Hoover's term, Congress passed the Leavitt Act which allowed the Secretary of Interior to restructure or discharge debt assigned to Indian tribes for projects which often had very little benefit to the tribe and were undertaken without tribal consultation or consent but were charged to Indian tribes anyway. Many of these projects were originally designed and desired not by tribal members but by non-Indian settlers who had converted the 'surplus' land to agricultural or resource extraction uses and pressured federal agents to develop infrastructure which would benefit their endeavors regardless of the impact it would have on tribal communities. The discharge of this debt under the Leavitt Act came with the understanding that Indian tribes should not be saddled with debt for projects they had no role in procuring and which were not targeted to benefit their members.

The progress in Indian rights made during the Hoover administration was built upon during the Roosevelt administration. President Roosevelt's Commissioner of Indian Affairs, John Collier, aggressively pushed for reform in the context of Indian policy. Upon Collier's appointment as Commissioner of Indian Affairs his department issued a report calling for the preservation of Indian heritage. His most notable achievement came in 1934 when Congress enacted the Indian Reorganization Act (commonly called by its initials; the IRA) which formally ended the process of allotment and for the first time gave formal encouragement to the development of modern tribal governments. In addition to changing the direction of Indian policy on the ground, the IRA's major achievements were reforms of tribal land and tribal government.

By formally ending the allotment process, the IRA preserved the existing territorial integrity of Indian Country and prevented any further loss of land to non-Indian settlement. Additionally, the IRA recognized that the loss of land posed a problem for the development of tribal communities and so authorized, for the first time, a pool of money to be spent by the Department of Interior to reacquire formally allotted lands to restore existing Indian reservations. It also contained provisions allowing existing public lands to be turned into Indian Country and set aside for the use of tribes, created a line of credit tribes could tap to help finance development projects, and formalized the preference for hiring Indian people to serve the department of Indian affairs – a hiring preference that continues to exist today.

Unfortunately Congress seldom provided adequate funding for all of the new programs in the IRA forcing the Commission of Indian Affairs to pick and choose among worthy projects and thus slowing down assistance to Indian Country. Commissioner Collier regularly attributed the lack of federal funding for the new programs as the primary barrier to the development of faster economic development in tribal communities. Despite these challenges the Commissioner did what he could with the resources granted by Congress to meaningfully improve the lives of Indians.

Importantly the IRA also formally recognized the importance of tribal government to tackling problems in Indian Country. During the New Deal federal administrators and congresspersons finally recognized that many of the problems that had been identified on reservations required the assistance of tribal government and the participation of the Indians themselves in order to craft workable resolutions. To this end the IRA established a mechanism whereby tribes were encouraged to adopt tribal Constitutions to create formal government structures that would be officially recognized by the United States. The specific provision authorizing these Constitutions was set forth in section 476:

§ 476 Organization of Indian tribes; constitution and bylaws and amendment thereof; special election . . .

(a) Adoption . . . Any Indian tribe shall have the right to organize for its common welfare, and may adopt an appropriate constitution and bylaws, and any amendments thereto, which shall become effective when,
   (1) ratified by a majority vote of the adult members of the tribe or tribes at a special election authorized and called by the Secretary under such rules and regulations as the Secretary may prescribe; and
   (2) approved by the Secretary pursuant to subsection d) of this section...
(b) Revocation . . . Any constitution or bylaws ratified and approved by the Secretary shall be revocable by an election open to the same voters and conducted in the same manner as provided in subsection a of this section[3]

The IRA did respect the sovereignty of Indian tribes. The IRA did not mandate that all tribes adopt these structures but instead permitted tribes to vote on whether to adopt the governance provisions of the IRA. While ultimately more than 100 tribes have been organized under the IRA, some of the largest tribes (including the Navajo and the Iroquois of New York) promptly exercised their independence and held votes in which a majority of voting members rejected the IRA's governance structure.[4]

Notably, one of the weaknesses of the IRA constitution model is that little to no attempt was made to adapt a tribal constitution to its membership. Several boilerplate constitutions were created and tribes were encouraged to adopt these models without amendment. This resulted in the creation of constitutional rules that did little to take into account the unique history or culture of the tribes that adopted them. Additionally, virtually all of these initial constitutions required the approval of the Secretary of Interior or the Commissioner of Indian Affairs in order to approve any amendments to the constitution and in many cases any legislation enacted by the tribe. While these provisions have largely been amended out of modern tribal constitutions the legacy of federal supervision has clouded the IRA and muddied its legacy.

The New Deal era also saw substantial change in the status of Indians and their formal relationship with the United States. As previously noted, Indians were not originally citizens of the United States because they were perceived to owe their loyalty to the tribe and not to the country. In 1924 Congress enacted the Indian Citizenship Act, also known as the Snyder Act, which recognized that American Indian people born in the United States are also American citizens.

> BE IT ENACTED by the Senate and house of Representatives of the United States of America in Congress assembled, That all non-citizen Indians born within the territorial limits of the United States be, and they are hereby, declared to be citizens of the United States: Provided That the granting of such citizenship shall not in any manner impair or otherwise affect the right of any Indian to tribal or other property." Approved, June 2, 1924.[5]

Prior to the enactment of the Indian Citizenship Act the general presumption was that even though Indian people were born in the United States they were not American citizens. Indians had previously won citizenship on an ad hoc basis – sometimes being granted citizenship in treaties, by serving in the U.S. military, or in exchange for their land. While the Indian Citizenship Act conferred the status of American citizenship on Indians, states were under no obligation to extend a reciprocal recognition of citizenship to Indian people. Throughout the New Deal era Indian reformers worked to force states to recognize Indians as citizens and in 1948 the process was complete when Arizona and New Mexico finally permitted their tribal citizens the right to vote in state elections.

The New Deal Era also brought with it a recognition that previous dealings between the United States and tribes were not always honestly conducted. Following World War II, in 1946 Congress created the Indian Claims Commission or ICC. Indians were not able to enter federal courts as parties until 1875 and even then an Indian tribe required a special waiver of the federal government's sovereign immunity in order to sue the United States for violating tribal rights. Essentially, prior to the ICC an Indian or Indian tribe needed to get Congress to pass a statute giving it permission to sue the United States. This allowed thousands of legitimate claims to remain unheard during the nineteenth and early twentieth centuries. The Commission was the last major advancement of the Indian New Deal Era and provided for a judicial body that was capable of hearing claims from Indian tribes for past harms that had been ignored, often willfully, by the federal government.

The ICC built upon the other major New Deal institutions. Back in 1928 the Meriam report identified the need for a more impartial and speedier mechanism for Indian tribes to bring their grievances forward. Among its recommendations was the creation of a separate judicial institution dedicated only to processing claims brought by Indian tribes. In 1934, the IRA's original draft included provisions for the direct return of Indian land that had been allotted, and ultimately included a provision permitting an allocation of Congressional funds to buy back and restore tribal land that had been lost. Finally in 1946 the Indian Claims Commission was established to provide Indian tribes a judicial forum to bring claims related to the loss of land and breach of treaty promises – but it also included the ability to bring more generalized claims related to the federal government acting in bad faith in its dealings with Indian tribes.

The ICC heard hundreds of claims brought by Indian tribes against the United States. Before it was discharged in 1978 it had distributed more than $818 million in compensation with several hundred cases still on appeal or transferred to other courts for resolution.[6] The legacy of the ICC is controversial. Speaking to its merits – the ICC finally provided a forum for unresolved claims some of which had their origin in the bad faith actors of federal government decades or even a century before its creation. However, the ICC never quite lived up to its potential. Perhaps most obviously the ICC did not provide any mechanism for the return of land that was taken or stolen by non-Indian parties, its remit was instead limited to financial compensation. In addition, many scholars have questioned its structure as being inconsistent with its purpose. Nell Jessup Newton – now Dean of Notre Dame Law School – offers this observation of the ICC:

"The last chair of the Indian Claims Commission, John T. Vance, criticized the Commission for adopting an adversary model, instead of the more cooperative model permitted by the legislation. Congress, for example, included a basis to bring nonlegal claims as well as a provision for the Commission to set up an Investigation Division to "make a complete and thorough search for all evidence affecting claims, utilizing all documents and records in the possession of the Court of Claims and the several government departments, and shall submit such evidence to the Commission." In short, Commissioner Vance argued that the Act did not mandate an adversary system.

Unfortunately, the Commission adopted an adversary model and never established an Investigation Division. Although all the initial commissioners were attorneys, none had experience in Indian law, and only one had experience in claims law. Harvey Rosenthal, the Commission's official historian, posited several reasons the Commission reconstituted itself into a court. The Government certainly feared the Commission might adopt the generous Indian tradition known as the giveaway and simply transfer millions of dollars to undeserving tribes. Additionally, the tribes' Washington attorneys were familiar with the adversary system of the Court of Claims and, no doubt, were opposed to any system that would cut them out of the process. Finally, Rosenthal notes that Indian people themselves demanded an adversary proceeding. If this last point is true, it makes some sense. Indian people have never spoken with one voice and those who come to Congress to testify are often selected by congressional committees to express the appropriate viewpoint. One could imagine why Indian people might be deeply distrustful of congressional agencies that were supposed to act in their interests, but instead handed down edicts without any tribal input. Perhaps they believed an adversary system would, at a minimum, permit them to participate in the decision-making through their attorneys. In other words, viewing their choices as either governmental paternalism or an adversarial model, Indian tribes might well have chosen the latter."[7]

Whatever the final judgment of the ICC's work, the Commission was an achievement well ahead of its time. Canada and Australia waited another 60 years before either began the process of creating specialized courts to hear legal claims by their indigenous populations on the basis of historical bad action. The push by Collier and the Roosevelt administration for the creation of the Commission in 1946 was generally considered a victory for Indian tribes at the time of its enactment and did a great deal to provide at least some compensation to Indian tribes for the bad actions of the United States over the previous century and a half.

Finally, no discussion of New Deal Indian policy is complete without a brief mention of Felix Cohen. Cohen joined the Department of Interior in 1933 – in part to help draft the Indian Reorganization Act. Before his untimely death in 1953 he had also helped to craft the Indian Claims Commission and written the first edition of the Handbook of Federal Indian Law, the first comprehensive guide to the history and legacy of law and policy making regarding Indians. Today Cohen is considered the father of modern Indian law and one of the greatest legal philosophers of the early twentieth century. In his forward to the first edition of the Handbook in 1941 Cohen and Secretary of Interior Harold Ickes wrote:

"That Indians have legal rights is a matter of little practical consequence unless the Indians themselves and those who deal with them are aware of those rights. Such, however, is the complexity of the body of Indian law, based upon more than 4,000 treaties and statutes and upon thousands of judicial decisions and administrative rulings, rendered during a century and a half, that one can well understand the vast ignorance of the subject that prevails even in ordinarily well informed quarters. For more than a century, commissioners of Indian affairs have appealed for aid in reducing this unmanageable mass of materials to some orderly form. Yet during that period none of the attempts to compile a simple manual of the subject was carried to completion.

Ignorance of one's legal rights is always the handmaid of despotism. This Handbook of Federal Indian Law should give to Indians useful weapons in the continual struggle that every minority must wage to maintain its liberties, and at the same time it should give to those who deal with Indians, whether on behalf of the federal or state governments or as private individuals, the understanding which may prevent oppression."[8]

It is unfortunate that barely more than a decade later the Department of Interior and its policy makers would ignore many of the principles articulated by Cohen and instead adopt the last formalized attempt to assimilate Indian communities into the wider body public while simultaneously walking away from legal obligations to Indian tribes. By the early 1950s federal Indian policy was about to enter a nearly two decade long period where the principles espoused by the New Deal – tribal sovereignty, federal protection, and economic development – were largely forgotten in an attempt to relocate and ultimately eliminate the special status of the American Indian in the United States.

The Termination Era

Following World War II, the federal government reactivated a program that later became known as the Voluntary Relocation Program to move Indians off reservations and into larger, more urbanized communities. The program was premised on the commonly held assumption that there were not enough resources on Indian reservations to support the 40-50% of native men of serviceable age who had been deployed in the armed forces or the return to the reservation of the additional 20-30% of American Indians who had been employed in defense contracting.[9]

By the early 1950s, the federal government actively and intentionally began prioritizing tribal resources toward urban relocation programs and away from programs which supported reservation communities. For example, a 1954 BIA report suggested that "in order to concentrate on providing relocation services, placement activities which do not involve relocation have been progressively decreased."[10] Instead the BIA used funds to encourage younger Indians to relocate and resettle in urban areas where jobs were more plentiful and where, it was assumed, the Indians would assimilate into post-War American culture.

Unfortunately, there were never enough jobs for all of the Indians the BIA attempted to relocate. Unemployment, and with it urban poverty, crime, and substance abuse followed for tens of thousands of American Indian veterans and their relatives who had been relocated under the Voluntary Relocation Program. Professor Sarah Krakoff summarized the government's policy during this era as follows:[11]

> The history of federal Indian policies towards tribes shows that Indian people have fared the worst when the federal government has tried to eliminate tribes. * * * Likewise, the effort to eradicate Indian culture left a legacy of broken family structures that to this day creates serious social problems in Indian country. * * * Similarly, as Charles Wilkinson eloquently describes, the termination era of the 1950s, in which the federal government set out to end the federal-tribal relationship with a number of tribes, had devastating effects on the morale and well-being of tribal peoples. "Every terminated tribe floundered.... They made no measurable improvements. Most found themselves poorer, bereft of health care, and suffering a painful psychological loss of community, homeland and self- identify." Without a land-base or a government to call their own, many tribal members left their reservation homes. Many others were deliberately relocated under the auspices of the termination era's urban relocation program. At the ebb of this brief but harrowing policy period, Indian people became all the more committed to ensuring that their sovereignty would be restored. They saw it as the key to addressing the myriad economic and social problems that were eating away at their ability to remain distinct peoples.

Unfortunately, the policy of termination did more than just move Indians from the reservation into urban areas. Tribes like the Menominee and Klamath were faced not just with the loss of their members, but with the termination of their status as Indian tribes.

In keeping with the removal of individual Indians from the reservation into Indian communities, Congress took the next step and formally requested the termination of Indian tribes as unique sovereign political communities. In July 1952, Congress passed a resolution calling for its committee on the Interior and Insular Affairs to conduct a thorough review of the BIA and to formulate plans "designed to promote the earliest practicable termination of all federal supervision and control over Indians."[12] On August 1, 1953 Congress adopted House Concurrent Resolution 108. While not a federal statute, it expressed the goals of Congress and set a direction for both future congressional committee work and policy action on behalf of the Bureau of Indian Affairs. The Concurrent Resolution reads as follows:

> *Resolved by the House of Representatives (the Senate concurring),* That it is declared to be the sense of Congress that, at the earliest possible time, all of the Indian tribes and the individual members thereof located within the States of California, Florida, New York, and Texas, and all of the following named Indian tribes and individual members thereof, should be freed from Federal supervision and control and from all disabilities and limitations specially applicable to Indians: The Flathead Tribe of Montana, the Klamath Tribe of Oregon, the Menominee Tribe of Wisconsin, the Potowatamie Tribe of Kansas and Nebraska, and those members of the Chippewa Tribe who are on the Turtle Mountain Reservation, North Dakota. It is further declared to be the sense of Congress that, upon the release of such tribes and individual members thereof from such disabilities and limitations, all offices of the Bureau of Indian Affairs in the States of California, Florida, New York, and Texas and all other offices of the Bureau of Indian Affairs whose primary purpose was to serve any Indian tribe or individual Indian freed from Federal supervision should be abolished. It is further declared to be the sense of Congress that the Secretary of the Interior should examine all existing legislation dealing with such Indians, and treaties between the Government of the United States and each such tribe, and report to Congress at the earliest practicable date, but not later than January 1, 1954, his recommendations for such legislation as, in his judgment, may be necessary to accomplish the purposes of this resolution.[13]

Acting under the auspices of 'freeing' Indian tribes from any disabilities created by the law, the reality was that tribes that went through the process of termination lost their status as sovereign political entities. Because House Concurrent Resolution 108 did not actually terminate the political relationship with Indians, additional separate legislation was required for each tribe. While some tribes, like Chippewa Tribe of the Turtle Mountain Reservation in North Dakota, escaped a subsequent termination act more than 100 tribes were terminated during the 1950s. (The exact number varies because many bands of California Indians were grouped together within a single termination act with no subsequent accounting of exactly how many 'tribes' these bands constituted. Somewhere between 108 and 130 is probably an accurate number.)

Termination brought with it the immediate resumption of state jurisdiction. Unless the specific termination act expressly forbade the assumption of jurisdiction, states could now tax tribal lands. Indians who could not pay the state property taxes had their property seized and sold. Tribes could no longer create their own hunting and fishing rules and Indians were required to seek state licenses to take part in traditional activities. Many lands of religious or cultural significance were turned over to the states and subsequently developed, exploited for their resource wealth, or opened to general public. Members of terminated tribes were no longer 'Indians' as the federal government understood that term, and so they were no longer eligible for health care provided by Indian Health Services, special tax treatment, affirmative action policies designed to encourage the federal hiring and promotion of native people, housing assistance, or credit and loan programs designed to encourage economic self-sufficiency or promote minority businesses.

At the same time that House Concurrent Resolution 108 was adopted, Congress also passed Public Law-280. Now commonly referred as P.L. 280, the law took away the ability of Indian tribes in five states (California, Oregon, Minnesota, Nebraska, Wisconsin and later Alaska) from enforcing their own criminal laws even on reservation lands. Tribes subject to P.L. 280 lost their tribal court systems and the ability to criminally punish even members of the tribe, thus reversing the sovereignty recognized and restored by the Indian Reorganization Act back in 1934.

Congress did not intend reservations to become lawless. Instead P.L. 280 made states responsible for law enforcement and criminal justice on the reservation. Some tribes lobbied and won exceptions from the law. For example the Menominee Tribe in Wisconsin and the Warm Springs Reservation in Oregon were given explicit statutory exemptions. However P.L. 280 applied to tribes that had not yet had their status terminated in states which were often particularly aggressive in seeking termination. Essentially the act was seen by many at both the state and federal level as an intermediate step on the way to termination.

With few exceptions P.L. 280 destroyed tribal courts and brought state police officers unto the reservation without the consent of the tribes. In addition to the mandatory states, other states were permitted at their discretion, and without the consent of the tribes affected, to assert varying parts of their own jurisdiction on Indian lands. States did so selectively, some selecting just a couple tribes while other states picked areas over which they had a particular interest in regulating like water quality or mineral rights. At first P.L. 280 was embraced by the states as a mechanism to extend their own laws over all reservations located in their states, however it did not authorize the states the ability to tax the tribes to pay for these criminal justice services. Accordingly P.L. 280 functioned like an unfunded mandate. It required states to provide law enforcement, regulatory and judicial services on the reservations without the ability to collect taxes to fund those services. As a result, after assuming jurisdiction in Indian Country for several years many states sharply reduced their presence and maintained only a minimal law enforcement service in Indian Country. Kevin Washburn, former Assistant Secretary of Indian Affairs and Dean at the University of New Mexico School of Law has written about the effects of termination and Public Law 280:

> "When the Termination Era began, the federal government had pervasive control on Indian reservations: the Bureau of Indian Affairs controlled tribal forestry and agriculture, real property leasing and management, law enforcement, education, social services, and numerous other functions and services that are normally handled by local or state governments outside Indian country. Likewise, the Indian Health Service handled Indian hospitals and healthcare. As the federal government gradually withdrew financial support and terminated its relationship with specific tribes, Indians no longer had the federal government or the tribal governments to rely on. Providing education and other services to impoverished American

Indians suddenly became the responsibility of state governments. Cash-strapped states that initially favored increased state authority in Indian country began to see Public Law 280 and the termination acts as unfunded mandates. As a result, Indian people were poorly served, and civil rights issues flared."[14]

This made a bad situation worse. P.L. 280 took away the tribe's ability to create or enforce their criminal laws at the same time that states reduced service because they were unable to pay for the expanded police services. Violent crime, property crime, and drug crime all increased in Indian Country during this era. In recognition of the problems created by P.L. 280 jurisdiction and the failure of the policy to actually protect Indians, in 1968 the Indian Civil Rights Acts limited future expansion of state jurisdiction into Indian Country by requiring tribal consent. It further allowed states to return to the tribes law enforcement and other powers taken under P.L. 280 in order to combat the problems with the unfunded mandate. Since 1968 no tribe has consented to an extension of state jurisdiction unto the reservation and several states have, on a tribe-by-tribe basis, retroceded some or all of the jurisdiction originally taken in 1953.

Terminated tribes eventually received some relief. By the 1960s it was clear that the federal policy of termination had hurt individual Indians and Indian tribes. The United States policy promptly shifted with the election of President Kennedy and the start of the civil rights era. As minority groups began to find a political voice, Indian tribes became more aggressive in demanding the federal government reverse the most damaging parts of the termination era and to formally recognize the sovereign powers held by native nations. President Nixon called directly upon Congress to pass a formal repudiation of the termination era. It never happened. But in 1973 Congress enacted the Menominee Restoration Act, the most prominent of many statutes which formally reestablished government-to-government relations with previously terminated tribes. Beginning in the 1960s, and continuing through the twenty-first century, Indian policy has now embraced an era of self-determination. Today federal institutions and Indian policy generally recognize American Indian tribes as distinct communities with the right to make their own laws and be governed by them free from excessive federal or state interference but supported in their independence by federal programs designed to promote self-government.

The Self-Determination Era

The Indian Self-Determination era finds its origins in several changes in law and policy that coalesced around 1960. In 1959 the United States Supreme Court, in the now famous case of *Williams v. Lee*, articulated that Indian Tribes retained the right to make their own laws and be governed by them. This basic principle was embraced by the Kennedy, Johnson, and Nixon administrations and has manifested itself in federal legislation and BIA policy ever since. It also formed a new basis against which the courts could measure federal and state intervention on Indian reservations. As the civil rights era opened, the Supreme Court began striking down government actions that interfered with a tribal government's right to make its own laws and be governed by them.

In 1961, representatives of 67 tribes gathered in Chicago and adopted the "Declaration of Indian Purpose" – a policy document that expressed the general consensus among Indians that their tribes should have a larger role to play in developing, crafting, and implementing laws to govern life on the reservation and that Indian people had faith in their tribal governments to take a larger role in reservation life.[15] The 1961 Declaration added to voices pressing for change and helped to herald an end to the termination era and mark a shift to federal policy embracing tribal self-determination. Building on the call by Indian people to increase their own self-government, Indian tribes were included in much of President Johnson's anti-poverty programming surrounding his Great Society. In the years since federal policy shifted in the direction of self-determination Congress has taken up the call to aid in tribal self-government.

In 1968, Congress enacted the Indian Civil Rights Act (ICRA). Among its more important provisions was the formal repudiation of Public Law 280, discussed earlier, as well as federal recognition that tribal courts had the authority to hear criminal and civil claims arising between tribal members or occurring on the reservation. Since the adoption of ICRA the number of tribal courts has almost tripled – to more than 220.

Originally, the federal government was highly distrustful of tribal courts, which may or may not have traditional law trained lawyers and judges. To protect against arbitrary or potentially unjust proceedings tribal courts were limited to penalties of no more than $500 per offense and no more than one year in jail. However, as these courts have repeatedly shown to be trusted and generally impartial arbiters of the law and as tribal judges and lawyers have become better trained, tribal courts have been given increasing authority.

In 2010, President Obama signed the Tribal Law and Order Act which provided millions in new funding for tribal courts to increase coordination between the criminal justice systems at the tribal, state, and federal level, to specifically combat domestic violence and substance abuse, and to improve reporting to ensure progress is being made at reducing violence in and around Indian Country. The new law expanded tribal courts' power to issue monetary fines and allowed tribal courts to sentence criminal defendants to up to three years in jail per offense and nine years per event. However, in order to take advantage of these expanded powers tribes needed to secure the availability of a tribally funded public defender to anyone whose offense could result in a penalty exceeding one year incarceration.

An additional victory for tribal courts was achieved in 2013, when Congress reauthorized the Violence Against Women Act (VAWA) with an express jurisdictional provision that allows tribal courts to prosecute non-Indians who are accused of domestic violence in Indian Country. For almost four decades before the tribal VAWA provisions were enacted only the federal government had criminal jurisdiction when a non-Indian was the defendant and the abuse occurred on the reservation. Many tribal members were reluctant to participate in an investigation and prosecution led by the federal government because of a legitimate history of distrust between tribes and federal prosecutors. The situation was made worse because few federal prosecutors were willing to dedicate the resources necessary to going out into Indian Country to collect evidence and prepare to prosecute domestic offenses unless the abuse was acute and severe. As a consequence many known non-Indian domestic violence offenders went unpunished resulting in a disproportionately high level of domestic abuse in tribal communities. The recent expansion of VAWA is in keeping with this era of self-determination where Congress continues to take incremental steps to help Indian tribes manage their own affairs.

The expansion of tribal opportunities during the current era of self-determination is not limited to tribal courts. In 1975 Congress enacted the Indian Self-Determination and Education Assistance Act. Section 450 authorized the Secretary of Interior to enter into self-determination and self-governance funding agreements with Indian tribes and tribal organizations. These tribally run entities would then be in charge of running programs that the BIA would have provided, using the funds the BIA would have spent on them. These self-determination contracts have allowed tribes to take over social assistance, medical provision, law enforcement, tribal policing, education, resource management, etc. Perhaps more than any other federal program, the Indian Self-Determination and Education Assistance Act has given tribes a pool of necessary resources to meet the needs of their communities in a culturally appropriate manner while providing well-paying jobs and opportunities to make a meaningful difference to tribal members.

Not all tribes have entered into these contracts, and new contracts are signed every year. Some tribes started only with social services and then moved into law enforcement. Others have only entered into contracts for the purpose of resource management. Still – the scope of these contracts is hard to understate. In 2014 the BIA transferred $899,793,055 from its budget directly to tribes and tribal organizations for the provision of services under the section 450 self-determination and self-government contracting process.[16] As tribes develop expertise running programs and providing services they are cultivating the skills necessary to move beyond the contracted programs and develop tribally run services without the need for federal support.

To truly be independent tribes need a source of revenue. While section 450 contracts from the BIA provide millions to fund necessary services, the contracts are limited to programs that would be otherwise provided by the BIA. They do not provide tribes with funds to develop their own programs based on tribally identified needs. In 1987 the United States Congress passed the Indian Gaming Regulatory Act (IGRA) which built upon a Supreme Court decision that limited the ability of states to prevent the development of gaming enterprises in Indian Country. IGRA requires the tribe and the state to agree to a 'compact' which lays out rules for operating a gaming enterprise including sharing revenue and clearly defining law enforcement responsibilities. Often these compacts give Indian tribes a monopoly on the operation of casinos in their state in exchange for a share of the profits to help pay for gambling addiction services, increased law enforcement, and infrastructure required to support casinos as entertainment destinations. In 2015 Indian gaming set a record of $29.9 billion in revenue. While the total is large it is not evenly distributed. Not even half of all federally recognized tribes operate a casino or earn gaming revenue and a majority of tribes with a casino earn less than $25 million from its operation. Tribes located near big cities and in states willing to negotiate gaming compacts on generous terms have done well. While the scope of Indian gaming is clearly unevenly spread across Indian Country it has certainly helped assist some tribal communities in achieving a degree of self-determination through economic independence.

Self-determination is not only about monetary independence. In 1978 Congress enacted the Indian Child Welfare Act (or ICWA) which dramatically changed the way Indian children were dealt with by various social service organizations. Congressional hearings revealed that prior to ICWA's enactment 25%–35% of all Indian children were being removed from their families by state social workers and often placed in non-Indian homes.[17] In some states an Indian child was 20 times more likely to be removed from their home than a non-Indian child. Research showed that Indian children were at times being singled out for removal because they had been left in the care of older relatives while parents went to work or because there was alcohol in the home even if there was no evidence of alcohol abuse or drunk and disorderly conduct – justifications that were never used to remove non-Indian children.

Understandably tribes were concerned about the loss of the next generation. Many tribal leaders expressed a real concern that Indian children were not only singled out for removal because they were Indian, but that the removal of Indian children was jeopardizing the continued existence of some tribes by robbing the tribe of its next generation of tribal leaders. Longitudinal studies reinforced the tribes concerns. Indian children placed with non-Indian families reported increased feelings of disorientation during adolescence and were more likely than Indian children who stayed in an Indian family to drop out of school, to abuse drugs and alcohol, and to commit suicide.

The Indian Child Welfare Act aimed to return the ability to protect tribal children to the Indian tribes themselves. It required that the tribe be formally notified before any custody placement decision for an Indian child was made. Additionally, the tribe could request the case be transferred to tribal courts so that the tribal court could formally make the placement decision. ICWA also permitted the Indian tribe to act even if the biological parents objected. It required any placement decision to account for the cultural concerns raised by the tribe. Finally, in the regulations designed to implement ICWA, the Bureau of Indian Affairs established placement criteria which favored placement with an Indian family whenever possible and changed the legal standard of review from "the best interest of the child" to "the best interest of the *Indian* child" – formally recognizing that Indian children had cultural needs that favored placement in Indian families but were often not considered by courts when a wealthier non-Indian placement was also presented as a placement option.

Since 1978 ICWA has helped keep thousands of Indian children in Indian families. It has permitted tribes to favor placement with older grandparents or with extended family that may have been traditionally disfavored by the state court system. In response to ICWA some states tried to limit its application to Indian children who already had some preexisting connection to the tribe or reservation. These states argued that ICWA should contain an exception for Indian children who had no previous affiliation with their Indian family and so their tribes had no right to interfere with the placement of the child with a non-Indian family. However, in 2016 the Bureau of Indian Affairs issued new guidelines that made clear that ICWA applies to any child who is eligible for enrollment in a federally recognized Indian tribe regardless of their connection to the tribe before placement was made. The new guidelines are another example of federal Indian policy moving toward restoring to the tribal government the authority to regulate its members free from state and federal interference.

Finally, in December 2010 President Obama officially committed the United States to the principles enshrined by the United Nations Declaration on the Rights of Indigenous Peoples. The United States was the last nation to remove its objections to the declaration and to fully and firmly embrace both the principles of tribal self-government as well as meaningful consultation with tribal governments and Indian communities on projects which will have an outsized or measurable impact to Indian Country. The declaration expressly articulates protections for tribal language, religion, cultural practice, preservation of tribal land, and consultation over resource development. A portion of the United States' official statement agreeing to abide by the principles of the UN Declaration follows;

> In his Presidential Proclamation last month honoring National Native American Heritage Month, President Obama recommitted —to supporting tribal self-determination, security and prosperity for all Native Americans. He recognized that —[w]hile we cannot erase the scourges or broken promises of our past, we will move ahead together in writing a new, brighter chapter in our joint history.
>
> It is in this spirit that the United States today proudly lends its support to the United Nations Declaration on the Rights of Indigenous Peoples (Declaration). In September 2007, at the United Nations, 143 countries voted in favor of the Declaration. The United States did not. Today, in response to the many calls from Native Americans throughout this country and in order to further U.S. policy on indigenous issues, President Obama announced that the United States has changed its position. The United States supports the Declaration, which—while not legally binding or a statement of current international law—has both moral and political force. It expresses both the aspirations of indigenous peoples around the world and those of States in seeking to improve their relations with indigenous peoples. Most importantly, it expresses aspirations of the United States, aspirations that this country seeks to achieve within the structure of the U.S. Constitution, laws, and international obligations, while also seeking, where appropriate, to improve our laws and policies.
>
> U.S. support for the Declaration goes hand in hand with the U.S. commitment to address the consequences of a history in which, as President Obama recognized, —few have been more marginalized and ignored by Washington for as long as Native Americans—our First Americans. That commitment is reflected in the many policies and programs that are being implemented by U.S. agencies in response to concerns raised by Native Americans, including poverty, unemployment, environmental degradation, health care gaps, violent crime, and discrimination.[18]

No one working in Indian Country will claim that Indian tribes in the United States are fully free to govern their own members and their communities. Many of the rights and ideals enshrined in the UN Declaration are not yet realities in American Indian law and policy. It is undeniable that problems persist in Indian Country, including higher rates of poverty, substance abuse, domestic violence, and unemployment than in the United States at large. While these problems are not universal, in the aggregate American Indian communities are doing their best to recover from a legacy of discrimination where they have, until relatively recently, mostly been unable to proscribe their own solutions to problems that arise even within their own lands. However since the 1960s the federal government has taken small but progressive steps to continue to restore to tribes the power to make their owns laws and be governed by them as free as possible from interference by federal, state, and local government.

Conclusion

The last century has seen a great deal of variance and change in policies toward American Indians. At the turn of the century formal American policy was Allotment. It wanted to divide up reservations and encourage non-Indian families to settle upon traditional tribal lands. Following the First World War and during the New Deal Era the federal government finally started to recognize the independence of Indian tribes and created opportunities for tribal governance to emerge. Following the problems recognized in the Meriam report great advocates for tribal policy, including John Collier and Felix Cohen, created a set of government policies to recognize the basic and inherent rights of Indian people, protect Indian land, and build tribal government.

By the end of the Second World War, and particularly during the Eisenhower administration, federal policy changed. During the Termination Era Indian policies focused on relocating Indians away from the reservation, encouraged their resettlement in cities or their assimilation within traditional suburban America. Federal policy removed the recognition of tribal status from Indian people and government, treating tribal members no differently than any other state citizen and denying tribes the opportunity to enact and enforce their own rules based on tradition, religion, or culture. Fortunately this experiment was recognized for the failures it created and government goals surrounding Indians changed again by the 1960s.

In tandem with the civil rights movement, the Self-Determination Era in Indian policy emerged during the 1960s and 70s and continues today. In this period the federal government finally embraced its government-to-government relationship with Indian tribes and recognized that the best progress could be made when tribal leaders lead reform themselves with minimal government interference. Government policy has consistently moved to enhance the status of tribal courts and the powers of tribal government. While certainly imperfect – today the rights of Indian people are better respected than ever before. With a federal system designed to protect and promote the rights of Indians and tribal governments, advocates today have the tools necessary to hold the government to account and to advocate from a legal, cultural, moral, and policy level for even more protections/rights for Indian communities.

Endnotes

1. D.S. Otis. 2014. *The Dawes Act and the Allotment of Indian Land*. Norman: University of Oklahoma Press.
2. The Meriam Report *The Problem of Indian Administration* 1928. The non-copyrightable parts of the report are collected and reproduced electronically by the Native American Rights Fund at: http://www.narf.org/nill/resources/meriam.html
3. The Indian Reorganization Act. 25 U.S.C. 479.
4. Wilcomb E. Washburn.1984. "A Fifty-Year Perspective on the Indian Reorganization Act." *The American Anthropologist*, Vol. 86-2, pp. 279-289.
5. Indian Citizenship Act of 1924. Act of June 2, 1924. 43 Stat. 253. 8 U.S.C. 1401b.
6. Garrick Alan Bailey and William Sturtevant. 2008. *Handbook of North American Indians*, Vol. 2. Washington: Smithsonian Institution Press.

7. Nell Jessup Newton. 1992. "Indian Claims in the Courts of the Conqueror." *American University Law Review*, Vol. 41-3, pp. 753-854.

8. Felix Cohen. 1942. *Handbook of Federal Indian Law*. United States Department of Interior (Government Printing Office).

9. Nell Jessup Newton and Robert Anderson (eds.). 2012. *Cohen's Handbook of Federal Indian Law*. LexisNexis at 1.06 Termination.

10. Francis Paul Prucha. 2000. *Document of United States Indian Policy*. University of Nebraska Press. (Citing the *Annual Report of the Commission of Indian Affairs 1954* at pg. 238).

11. Sarah Krakoff. 2006. *The Virtues and Vices of Sovereignty*. 38 Conn. L. Rev. 797, 805-06.

12. U.S. Congress. 1952. *Report with Respect to the House Resolution Authorizing the Committee on Interior and Insular Affairs to Conduct an Investigation of the Bureau of Indian Affairs*, H.R. Rep. No. 82-2503.

13. U.S. Congress. *Concurrent Resolution of the Eighty-Third Congress*. August 1, 1953. H. Con. Res. 108. 67 Stat. B122.

14. Kevin Washburn. 2006. "Federal Criminal Law and Tribal Self-Determination." *North Carolina Law Review*, Vol. 84, p. 779.

15. Nell Jessup Newton and Robert Anderson (eds). 2012. *Cohen's Handbook of Federal Indian Law*. LexisNexis at 1.07 Self-Determination. See also *American Indian Chicago Conference,* University of Chicago, June 13-20, 1961, 5-6. For a discussion of the importance of the Declaration *See* Stephen Cornell, The Return of the Native 124-126 (Oxford Univ. Press 1988).

16. United States Department of Interior. *Bureau of Indian Affairs Office of Indian Services and Self-Determination, Fiscal Year 2014 report to Congress*. Available at: http://www.bia.gov/cs/groups/xois/documents/document/idc1-033714.pdf

17. Kirk Albertson. 2005. *Applying 25 years of Experience: The Iowa Indian Child Welfare Act*, 29 Am. Indian L. Rev. 193.

18. The U.S. State Department. *Announcement of Support for the United Nations Declaration on the Rights of Indigenous Peoples: Initatives to Promote the Government-to-Government Relationship & Improve the Lives of Indigenous* Peoples. http://www.achp.gov/docs/US%20Support%20for%20Declaration%2012-10.pdf

Land and Water Rights
Sebastian F. Braun

L and rights have been a prominent aspect of any knowledge about American Indians. There exists a notion that in general, the history of American–Native interactions can be summarized as Americans taking all Indian lands away from Native nations, or pushing all American Indians off their lands, starting in the east and ending in the west. Such notions are too simplistic and do not reflect historical facts.

American Indian nations exist today, sovereign over their own territories. Some nations were indeed removed from their homelands, and their current territories are located far away from their historical lands. Some of these nations, especially in the Ohio River valley and beyond, had to remove and were removed several times. Some nations, such as the Navajo, were removed from their homelands temporarily. Others, however, especially on the Plains, still have communities located on lands that were parts of their historic territories.

Reservations are indicated on most state maps and road atlases, and today on map applications on smartphones. The idea that many people take away from such maps is that everything within these external borders of reservations is Indian land, while everything outside is not. This notion, however, is wrong. This chapter will try to provide some clarity on historical developments of sovereignty and Indian land rights, and look at the contemporary situation of Native land and – increasingly more important – water rights.

Sovereignty

By the nineteenth century, some indigenous societies east of the Mississippi had in practice lost their political and economic status as equals to the newly expanding United States. This was especially true in the Ohio River valley, where continuous warfare and epidemics had weakened indigenous nations that had fought with the French against the British in the French and Indian War and then with the British against the colonists in the American Revolution. At the beginning of the nineteenth century, they were exhausted and not strong enough, anymore, to resist the stream of American settlers flooding over the Appalachians to the fertile lands along the Ohio. After their final resistance under Tecumseh was broken in the War of 1812, nothing could hold back the formation of new states of the Union on their old territories.

While northern states thus made inroads into the Northwest of the United States – the Mississippi was the border of the United States to Spanish and then French Louisiana until 1803 – and into what the British had declared to be Indian country, the southern states were facing American Indian nations that were much stronger. In the southeast, partly because of traditional political organization, partly because of pressures from European colonies, several strong confederacies had formed: the Cherokee, Creek, Chickasaw, and Choctaw nations. The Creek confederacy eventually reached into Spanish Florida, where it developed an identity of its own as the Seminole nation. These confederacies had been successfully trading with the English, French, and Spanish colonies, and had seen a slow but continuous leadership change to descendants of Native women and European traders. The new leadership often combined Native culture, especially leadership skills often dependent on kinship networks, and European formal educational skills. A new elite developed, which built a society that often mirrored the one existing in Georgia and North and South Carolina. Its political and economic power was centered on a plantation economy that, just like its counterpart, used African slaves. Its margins, just like those of the non-Indian societies around them, consisted of hunters and gatherers in the backcountry. The southern states, especially Georgia, were not in a position of strength; the political and economic status of these Native societies was one of equals. The situation changed somewhat after 1812; Andrew Jackson exploited frictions within the Creek confederacy to reduce their powers. At the same time, Georgia was becoming very impatient. In 1802, the state had threatened secession from the United States, and the federal government had promised to buy the lands of the southeastern nations to make room for expansion. However, the federal government refused to simply clear the lands by force – and probably did not have the military power do so until the 1820s.

Under pressure from settlers and the federal government, many Creek, Chickasaw, Choctaw, and Cherokee moved to new territories in Arkansas, but many also stayed. Increasingly, the government played a strategy of passive allowance for trespassers attempting to settle on Indian lands. Federal officials refused to hear the nations' pleas to enforce treaty obligations, or plainly told delegations that the government either could not or had no intention to do so. This left the Native nations the option to either fight the settlers and face certain retribution by the government for doing so, or to remove. The most prominent case of attempting a third option came from the Cherokee.

In 1827, the Cherokee nation gave itself a formal constitution, declaring the Cherokee Republic. The constitution was based on the American constitution and established a government of three branches: a legislative, vested in a General Council divided into a Committee and a Council; an executive, vested in a Principal Chief, elected by the General Council for four years; and a judicial branch. How far the American model was followed by the Cherokee elites who formulated the constitution, both on paper and in some cultural values, might also be seen by the definition of rights:

> Sec. 4. No person shall be eligible to a seat on the General Council, but a free Cherokee Male citizen, who shall have attained to the age of twenty-five years. The descendants of Cherokee men by all free women, except the African race, whose parents may be or have been living together as man and wife, according to the customs and laws of this Nation, shall be entitled to all the rights and privileges of this Nation, as well as the posterity of Cherokee women by all free men. No person who is of negro or mulatto parentage, either by the father or mother side, shall be eligible to hold any office of profit, honor or trust, under this Government.

The adoption of the constitution was the formalization of an independent Cherokee nation, on the same level as any other modern state. As such, it might have been formally recognized as a fellow state by European nations, and this created a potential danger to American claims over the continent. Taking Native sovereignty truly serious was not an option. Colonel Montgomery, the federal agent for the Cherokee, conveyed a message from the president, John Quincy Adams, in 1828. Adams, he said, had asked him to:

> Convene the Chiefs, and inform them, that he wishes them, destinctly [sic] to understand that this act of theirs, cannot be considered in any other light, than as Regulations of purely municipal Character. – And which he wishes them distinctly to understand, will not be Recognized, and Changing any one of the Relations under which they stood to the General Government, prior to the adoption of said Constitution.

Municipal regulations, as Montgomery emphasized, could not take be allowed to interfere with federal laws, and did not exist outside federal laws. In treaties with the United States, the agent further emphasized, the Cherokee had given "up to them, your Sovereign, Independence; and the Right to Regulate all your Intercourse; with Foreign nations, or Individual Foreigners, and with their Citizens. And in Lieu thereof, Received their protection; In life, liberty and property; But in none of your Treatys [sic] with them, do I find that you gave to them, the Right to Regulate your own Intercourse with each other, or to punish your own people for any violation of your own Regulations." The Cherokee constitution, then, for the United States, was simply an internal regulation of a people over which the federal government claimed sovereignty, not unlike a state constitution. Montgomery made it very clear that any other interpretation by the Cherokee was dangerous: "Hold your Great Father the President fast by the hand don't move a single step in any new path, without his Council, and advice. A proper course taken at this time and pursued stadily [sic]; may (with Heavens Blessing) lead you to Greatness and Renown; But one wrong step may be fatal and Remedeless [sic]."

The Cherokee response artfully avoids any dialogue over the exact relationship to the United States, except to emphasize that the Cherokee nation:

> freely & with pleasure coincide, with the Executive in the opinion, that our relation and connection with the General Government, is not changed, but remains the same as it was before the Cherokee Constitution was adopted. That instrument contains a special article, which states, that all lawful treaties between the United States and this Cherokee Nation shall be the supreme law of the land.

The Cherokee thus affirm not only their sovereignty, at the very least over "internal and domestic regulation," but also re-affirm the duties of both the Cherokee and the United States to abode by treaty regulations and therefore the established boundaries. This could not be accepted by Georgia, especially after gold had been found on Cherokee territory. The state enacted a series of laws in December 1828 that, in the eye of the state, basically declared the Cherokee nation to be nonexistent. Georgia extended jurisdiction and sovereignty over territories of the Cherokee within its claimed borders, surveyed and distributed lands to settlers, forgave all debts owed to Cherokee individuals and declared Cherokee unable from giving testimony in court.

The Cherokee nation contested these laws as an unconstitutional act – a state of the union trying to impose its own laws over a sovereign, foreign nation. Within the laws that Georgia had passed, the state also required all non-Indians who wished to live on former Cherokee territory to obtain a license from the state, "to prevent the exercise of assumed and arbitrary power by all persons, under pretext of authority from the Cherokee Indians." Not all Americans were in favor of removal policies. People from New England, especially, took positions in favor of the Cherokee, and some wanted to help them. In 1831, Samuel Worcester, a missionary, was arrested by Georgia for residing, without a permit, in the annexed Cherokee territories and sentenced to four years of hard labor. He appealed his conviction to the Supreme Court, arguing that the laws of Georgia were unconstitutional. These contestations of Georgia's laws – and, by implication, of removal policies overall – led to the Supreme Court decisions of *Cherokee Nation v. Georgia* (1831) and *Worcester v. Georgia* (1832), which defined the legal relationship of American Indians to the United States as domestic-dependent nations and as a relationship resembling that of a ward to a guardian, yet also reiterated their existence as sovereign nations, on whose territories state laws did not have automatic effect.

Ignoring *Worcester v Georgia*, Andrew Jackson, impatient and intent on removing the Cherokee, had a minority faction of Cherokee sign the Treaty of New Echota, agreeing to removal, and his successor, President Van Buren, had the army enforce the removal of the nation in 1836. All of the southeastern nations were eventually removed. Some of the people stayed behind, but they had to assimilate: many denied their identities, even to their children, and lived in constant fear of being removed, too. In Indian Territory, the removed societies continued to integrate many American cultural traits into their own societies. The southeastern nations tried to rebuild their plantation economies, and continued to be governed by their constitutions; the Cherokee printed newspapers and books in their syllabary and established institutions of higher education.

Not only southeastern tribes were removed to Indian Territory, but all nations east of the Mississippi, including tribes from the Northwest Territory, and even the Modoc from the Pacific coast. In all of their adaptations to their new realities, and in their acculturation and sometimes assimilation to American society, Christian denominations were instrumental through their missionary work. Missionaries also exerted pressures on the American consciousness by watching and reporting on federal policies as applied to indigenous peoples. While official policies became more restrictive over time, both in terms of political sovereignty and cultural assimilation, public opinion, at least in the east, grew more sympathetic to American Indians. As indigenous peoples were removed further and further from the larger population centers, people did not feel threatened by them, anymore: this allowed Americans to see them as fellow human beings. In a time that saw an increasing awareness of and sympathy for human plight, especially in regard to slavery, the situation of American Indians could not go unnoticed.

Property Rights

Land holding in most Native communities was historically communal; the community as a whole owned the territory and defended it against others. In many societies, separate parcels of lands were then given to individual families or households to use either for fields, gardens, or as hunting territories. In others, for example the Hopi, clans or larger subgroups owned specific lands and divided them up among the families. Land parcels that were allotted to families were not owned by these families, but they had exclusive usufruct rights over them; they had the exclusive right and responsibility to plant and harvest on them. The plots would be reassigned periodically, based on the needs of the community at that time. Some societies, especially those who primarily engaged in hunting and gathering, kept all of their territory in common, and most societies had commons areas, especially for hunting. As an exception, in some communities, for example some Algonquian nations, families owned individual territories, or perhaps better individual trap lines. It is unclear whether that practice evolved with the increased fur trade after European contact or had been in place before; either way, it was an indigenous development. While individuals did not own lands in most societies, land was owned by societies as a whole and exclusive rights over the national territory were enforced by all societies, but would be customarily waived on appeal by neighbors in need.

The European notion of land ownership had included – and still includes in some areas – the notion of commons or communally held land. However, with the growing control of modern nation states and their elimination of feudalism, the notion of the citizen as an individual landowner came to prominence. When the United States was founded, those who owned land were regarded as full citizens with the right to vote, since they were seen as having an interest in the wellbeing of the nation. In order to expand the nation as a democratic state, Thomas Jefferson imagined a society of yeomen; small-scale farmers who worked their own land, each owning the same amount as the other. Thus, the Land Ordinance of 1785 surveyed newly acquired lands and split them into parcels of quarter sections or 160 acres. This model would be used not only for the Ohio River valley, but also for all subsequent expansions of the United States. The Homestead Act of 1862, and other such acts, like the Pre-emption Law of 1841, the Timber Culture Act of 1873, or the Desert Land Act of 1877, providing incentives for the settlement of the West, followed the same idea, although the amount of acres had to be increased because farmers or ranchers could not make living off a quarter section in arid lands. It was this parcellization of the land that transformed land into a commodity and thus opened it up for speculation.

Following the Jeffersonian ideal, which quickly became one of America's mythical foundations, if American Indians were to be assimilated into American society, they had to be made individual landowners. As such, they would also enter into competition with each other, which would make them, under the false assumptions of social Darwinism, strong enough to survive. Thus, the idea of allotment became a cornerstone of federal Indian policy in the late nineteenth century, and was made general law with the General Allotment Act or Dawes Act of 1887. The act stipulated that:

> in all cases where any tribe or band of Indians has been, or shall hereafter be, located upon
> any reservation created for their use, either by treaty stipulation or by virtue of an act of

Congress or executive order setting apart the same for their use, the President of the United States be, and he hereby is, authorized, whenever in his opinion any reservation or any part therof of such Indians is advantageous for agricultural and grazing purposes, to cause said reservation, or any part thereof, to be surveyed, or resurveyed if necessary, and to allot the lands in said reservation in severalty to any Indian located thereon.

Reservation territories would be surveyed, and American Indians would take ownership of individual parcels of land broken out of their communal land base. Upon receipt of an allotment, American Indians would receive American citizenship. They could choose the lands to be allotted to them: if they had not made a choice after four years, the agent would assign them an allotment. Often, reservations were large enough that even after everybody had an allotment, there was land left. These lands, called surplus lands, could be opened for settlement or homesteading by anyone interested. Because the goal was to make American Indians into individual farmers and ranchers, it could not be allowed that they just sell their allotments. Congress feared they would then just spend the money and would become landless and destitute. To avoid this, and because American Indians were not seen as competent in legal or economic matters, the federal government would hold the title to the lands in trust for the owners. The trust period was set to last for 25 years. While many Native communities were resistant to allotment, once the policy was forcefully applied, it carried huge cultural consequences. An individual landowner has a vested interest in the state, since the state provides protection for his ownership. Those individuals who received titles to their land, and who were simultaneously made citizens of the United States, thus often developed a different attitude toward the federal government and to land than those who, under the conditions of the law, had their allotments held in trust by the federal government. Allotment did not lead to complete assimilation, but it fundamentally changed the cultural landscape in more ways than one. It also created the three different legal types of Indian land ownership that still exist today: individual trust land, tribal trust land, and fee land.

Trust periods were based on the idea that American Indians were "incompetent" in relation to a money economy; if indigenous people were to become farmers, they could not simply sell their land. Increasingly, however, the government saw the administration of trust land as a burden for itself and for the trustees. The specifications of allotment policies were changed, especially by the Burke Act of 1906. The government started to end trust periods, especially for those who were "mixedbloods." Under the racial assumptions of the day, degree of blood was seen as an indicator of culture and of competence. Mixedbloods were often given fee title and subsequently lost their lands, either through sale or through bankruptcy because of additional county and state taxes. The arbitrary standard of degree of blood thus became translated into real social consequences, and in many ways marked the distinction between those who held land and those who did not. This led to internal differences in the early twentieth century. Some tribes restricted council membership to "fullbloods;" after all, landholders have a vested interest in society, the so-called mixedbloods and fullbloods developed diverging political and economic interests.

Impacts

Allotment as a practice was stopped with the Indian Reorganization Act (IRA) of 1934, which stipulated:

> That hereafter no land of any Indian reservation, created or set apart by treaty or agreement with the Indians, Act of Congress, Executive order, purchase, or otherwise, shall be allotted in severalty to any Indian.

Lands that had been declared surplus lands and had not yet been sold to individuals were returned to tribes as tribal lands. Surplus lands that had been sold, however, remained in the possession of their individual owners. While allotment was stopped, however, Congress did not remove trust ownership, but instead legislated that:

> The existing periods of trust placed upon any Indian lands and any restriction on alienation thereof are hereby extended and continued until otherwise directed by Congress.

Thus, any lands held in trust in 1934 are very probably still trust lands – there are ways to remove trust status, but they are rarely applied. The lands restored to tribal ownership were also held in trust; those reservations that were never allotted – the so-called closed reservations, because they were not opened to settlement – are still owned communally, through the tribe. A further section of the IRA authorized the Secretary of the Interior:

> in his discretion, to acquire through purchase, relinquishment, gift, exchange, or assignment, any interest in lands, water rights or surface rights to lands, within or without existing reservations, including trust or otherwise restricted allotments whether the allottee be living or deceased, for the purpose of providing lands for Indians.

The government can thus add to tribal lands and can turn any tribal land purchases into trust lands for Native nations, if it so wishes, wherever those lands might be located. One consequence is that tribal lands are not restricted by reservation boundaries (this was already established by allotment); another consequence of the IRA is that individual and tribal trust lands were created. Of course, individual American Indians could and can also buy lands as citizens of the United States, just like any other citizen. In addition, they can own lands that are no longer in trust status, just like anybody else can own lands that are not held in trust for them. These lands, whose owners hold their titles, are called fee lands. In addition, the IRA made it possible for tribes to incorporate; as corporations, tribes can, of course, buy lands and own lands, and so there are also tribal fee lands. American Indian land ownership thus falls into four basic categories: individual trust lands, individual fee lands, tribal trust lands, and tribal fee lands. The categorization of land ownership and the continued existence of trust lands translate into other consequences.

First, because allotment specified that allotments were not bound to reservation boundaries – if a reservation was too small to provide allotments for all the people eligible for them, allotments could be made outside of reservation boundaries – and because the IRA allowed the Secretary of the Interior to buy any land and turn it into trust land for any tribe, trust lands exist outside of reservations. On the other hand, because reservation lands were declared to be surplus lands and were sold to non-Indians, and because trust periods were ended before 1934, not all lands on reservations are either trust lands or are owned by Native people. In effect, then, exterior boundaries of reservations serve administrative purposes, but they do not actually delineate Indian land ownership or tribal sovereignty. Sovereignty and its consequential duties and obligations – especially jurisdiction – is instead more (but not exclusively) tied to trust lands. Thus, a complex framework is created where checkerboarded and sometimes competing sovereignties lead to claims and counterclaims that need to be resolved in federal court cases.

Second, because the titles to trust lands are held by the federal government as the trustee, and because the federal government does not pay property taxes to states, trust lands do not contribute to state property taxes. American Indians, of course, do pay state property taxes on fee lands, just like anybody else who owns land in fee. The question then, of whether or not somebody pays state property taxes has nothing to do whether or not a person is Native or not, but simply how that person owns land.

Third, the titles to trust lands are not only held in trust by the federal government for their owners, but they are also indivisible. This means that even though there might be several owners to a parcel of land, there can only be one title to it; if land is indeed owned by several people, they do not own separate parcels of land, with their own titles, but they own a part of the one title. Because the one title stays intact, all owners of the title must agree to substantial changes to the property. While this was not a great issue immediately after allotment, because it was usually still close family who co-owned land in this way, over the years, as generation after generation of landowners passed on, more and more descendants own parts of the one, indivisible title. Most American Indians did not draw up wills, and so did not leave the land to one specific descendant, and the lands they owned were divided among legal heirs. These were no longer necessarily close family – many people had moved away from reservations and established families of their own in cities; many people had married outside their communities and lived on other reservations. This process, of smaller and smaller percentages of titles owned by more and more people while the title itself stays indivisible, is called fractionation.

Fractionation has become one of the largest issues for many reservations. In the beginning of the twenty-first century, one property on Lac Courte Oreille Reservation in Wisconsin had 2285 owners. Another property, which had 505 owners, would have paid the one owner with the least rights to it one dollar, every 32,880 years. The smallest ownerships of properties on Standing Rock and Rosebud were 0.000000000%, while on Pine Ridge, it was 0.000000002%, and on the Crow reservation, it was 0.000000005%. One does not need to go to such extremes, however, to understand how fractionation would impact communities. Because titles stay intact, all co-owners of a parcel have to agree on pretty much anything that happens on it. Nobody can farm it unless all others agree. Nobody can build a house on it, unless all others agree. And nobody can take that title and leverage it as a guarantee for a loan, unless all others agree. Imagine how Americans would live if this were true for how everybody owns land; what would happen to the economies of communities in which this were true. It is true for Native communities: imagine what it does to Native economies.

To solve this issue, the federal government tried to pass legislation, with the 1983 Indian Land Consolidation Act and the 2004 American Indian Probate Reform Act. These acts departed from the fact that many shares to titles were very small. By 2008, for example, 85% of all interests in titles were 5% of the whole title or less, and 75% were 2% or less. The federal government thus wanted heirs of small interests to forfeit their ownership in favor of tribal governments so that land ownership would become consolidated as tribal trust lands. However, such legislation was unconstitutional. At the same time, the federal government started a pilot project in Wisconsin, focusing on the Bad River, Lac Courte Oreilles, and Lac du Flambeau reservations in 1999. This pilot project helped found the Indian Land Consolidation Center in 2003, and in 2004 became the permanent Indian Land Consolidation Program (ILCP). The ILCP worked on buying small interests from their owners and then shifting ownership to tribal governments. In 2007, the ILCP bought around 100,000 interests for $34 million; it spent $170 million over eight years. This represented a lot of taxpayer money spent to buy lands from individual Native owners to give that land to tribes. However, the government itself estimated that by spending this money, it saved over $587 million in cost savings and cost avoidance: the bureaucratic effort to keep track of all the divided interest holders alone was an immense expense.

In order to understand current efforts on land consolidation, and lingering consequences from the trust relationship, however, a look at one specific lawsuit is necessary: the Cobell suit.

Cobell

Eloise Cobell was a rancher, treasurer of the Blackfeet Nation, founder of the Blackfeet National Bank, recipient of a MacArthur genius award, and executive director of the Native American Community Development Corporation, among other roles. As treasurer of the Blackfeet Nation in Montana, people used to come to her to find help in getting information on their Individual Indian Money (IIM) accounts. Since the federal government is the trustee and title holder of trust lands, when these lands or rights to natural resources are leased – for grazing, agriculture, timber, gas, or oil – the federal government collects the income and deposits the money into a personal account, an IIM account. Native people found it very hard to access information about their accounts; for a long time, the BIA was not very forthcoming with account balances, and agents often would only provide monies to individuals as they saw fit and useful.

The government knew that there were other issues with IIM accounts. The House Committee on Government Operations released a report in 1992, called "Misplaced Trust: The Bureau of Indian Affairs' Mismanagement of the Indian Trust Fund." Two years later, Congress passed the Indian Trust Fund Management Reform Act. Part of the act reads: "The Secretary [of the Interior] shall account for the daily and annual balance of all funds held in trust by the United States for the benefit of an Indian tribe or an individual Indian that are deposited or invested pursuant to the Act of June 24, 1938." In other words, Congress passed a law attempting to provide IIM account holders the same information that we all expect for our bank accounts – that when we ask the bank how much money we have in our account, and how it changed over the year, the bank gives us that information. Unfortunately, people still came to Eloise Cobell to ask for information they would not get from the BIA, and every time Cobell asked the BIA on their behalf, she could not get the information, either. So, in 1996, she filed a lawsuit. The Cobell lawsuit only covered individuals. Tribes, who also have separate accounts for their trust lands, eventually filed their own lawsuits against the federal government.

The Cobell lawsuit went on for 14 years. During these years, it eventually became clear that the government could not provide information on individuals' accounts, in part because it no longer had the necessary records. It also became clear that the government had taken money out of some accounts to pay for government functions. In 2005, a federal judge came to the following conclusions: "when one strips away the convoluted statutes, the technical legal complexities, the elaborate collateral proceedings, and the layers upon layers of interrelated orders and opinions from this Court and the Court of Appeals, what remains is the raw, shocking, humiliating truth at the bottom: After all these years, our government still treats Native American Indians as if they were somehow less than deserving of the respect that should be afforded to everyone in a society where all people are supposed to be equal." Judge Lamberth continued:

> For those harboring hope that the stories of murder, dispossession, forced marches, as-similationist policy programs, and other incidents of cultural genocide against the Indians are merely the echoes of a horrible, bigoted government-past that has been sanitized by the good deeds of more recent history, this case serves as an appalling reminder of the evils that result when large numbers of the politically powerless are placed at the mercy of institutions engendered and controlled by a politically powerful few. It reminds us that even today our great democratic enterprise remains unfinished. And it reminds us, finally, that the terrible power of government, and the frailty of the restraints on the exercise of that power, are never fully revealed until government turns against the people.

The court noted that the Interior department neither knew the exact number of IIM accounts nor the balances for each, and that although it was giving out balances of accounts to account holders, it really could not back any of them up with data. While the trial had been ongoing, rodents had been destroying trust documents in BIA storage; the Department of the Treasury had also been destroying microfiche documents. When the court appointed a Special Master to ensure that documents needed for historical accounting would be kept safe, he "discovered trust records stored in puddles of water, near bags of fertilizer, and alongside containers of combustible fuels, tires, and debris of various kinds," and "remnants of trust documents that had been shredded." The departments of the Interior and Treasury had lied to the court, and Interior retaliated "against both the Indian beneficiaries and its own employees." The court concluded that: "The entire record in this case tells the dreary story of Interior's degenerate tenure as Trustee-Delegate for the Indian trust – a story shot through with bureaucratic blunders, flubs, goofs and foul-ups, and peppered with scandals, deception, dirty tricks and outright villainy – the end of which is nowhere in sight." In a prophetic statement, the judge wrote: "Real justice for these Indians may still lie in the distant future; it may never come at all. This reality makes a statement about our society and our form of government that we should be unwilling to let stand. But perhaps the best that can be hoped for is that people never forget what the plaintiffs have done here, and that other marginalized people will learn about this case and follow the Indians' example."

Judge Lamberth then ordered that all communications between the Department of Interior or its employees to current or former IIM Trust account holders had to include a statement that, among other things, included the following passage:

> Evidence introduced in the Cobell case shows that any information related to the IIM Trust, IIM Trust lands, or other IIM Trust assets that current and former IIM Trust account holders receive from the Department of the Interior may be unreliable. Current and former IIM Trust account holders should keep in mind the questionable reliability of IIM Trust information received from the Department of the Interior if and when they use such information to make decisions affecting their IIM Trust assets.

In an unprecedented move, the judge was subsequently removed from the case after this opinion and order, because he was seen as biased against the defendants.

In January 2008, his successor, Judge Robertson, found that "the Department of the Interior has not – and cannot – remedy the breach of its fiduciary duty to account for the IIM trust." With accurate accounting impossible, the judge then looked for a reasonable estimate of what the government owed individual landowners. The landowners asked for $46.85 billion, a figure they arrived at by including interest. The government arrived at $159 million, and asserted that its calculations showed that no more than $401 million could be owed. Judge Robertson awarded $455.6 million. In 2009, on appeal, the government asserted that it owed nothing at all to IIM account holders. Faced with an accounting that could go on indefinitely as the documents necessary for it no longer existed, Cobell decided to settle. In December 2009, a settlement for $3.4 billion was announced; $1.4 billion would go for compensation claims and $2 billion would go to address the issue of fractionation of Indian lands. Tribes, in the meantime, had sued individually over the accounting of tribal, not individual trust money accounts. These suits have been settled separately.

Water

While land rights have been in the spotlight of American Indian issues for a long time – and most have been settled – water rights, equally important, are still awaiting settlements in many cases. Access to clean water, or to water in general, is not only an increasing problem for indigenous peoples in the United States, but also for indigenous and non-indigenous peoples the world over. Especially in the western United States, water shortages have become more common. Cities like Denver or Los Angeles are importing water from hundreds of miles away. When reservation communities claim water rights, all the water in the rivers they claim them from is often already allocated, and their claims are seen to cause a disturbance.

Water claims in the western United States depend on "prior appropriation": the person with the oldest water claim has the strongest water claim. If there is a drought, the newer claims have to give up water usage first, and the oldest appropriation claim can use water the longest, as long as it is used for beneficial use. In *Winters v. United States*, the United States Supreme Court held in 1908 that reservations held water rights as an implication of their creation, and that their creation dates to the treaties or proclamations that define them. This creates a problem for many states, because the treaties often precede statehood, so that any water claim filed with the state is automatically younger than the claims by reservations. Indian reserved water rights thus not only carry prior appropriation dates, but theoretically extend to all water that can be reasonably used for the purpose of a reservation.

However, many states claim jurisdiction over all the water within their boundaries, and the federal government does not want to be seen to interfere with growing water demands in these states, as that would be seen as slowing growth. The *Winters* doctrine thus lay dormant for a long time; Native water rights were ignored, in part because irrigation systems off reservation always took precedence in funding and interest by states and the federal government. The federal government also has taken the position, however, that litigation over water rights would not lead to settled allocations, because tribes might not actually need all the water they are entitled to. This argument of course would also apply to any other water user, but it is never made in other contexts. Finally, the federal government has thought that litigation would still not lead to "wet water" for tribes, or to infrastructure improvements like irrigation systems. Therefore, the federal government has been encouraging negotiated settlements between reservations and states. Faced with the apparent unwillingness by the federal government to defend their water rights in court, and simultaneously noting that the federal government is giving states broad freedom to interpret water rights from their own perspective, Indian tribes thus often reach such agreements with states as the best way to ensure some water rights. However, it is important to understand that while such negotiated settlements do guarantee them a quantified amount of water permanently, they also limit the water available to them in the future. In other words, they give up huge amounts of water that theoretically belongs to them in order to secure a smaller amount of "wet water" now.

Water rights issues then follow the same path that the Cobell settlement took. In order to gain some real restitution or guarantees for the future of communities, Native people are giving up what should be rightfully theirs because there is no interest or support from the federal government to truly educate, evaluate, or contemplate past and present wrongs.

None of this is to say that water rights are not a thorny issue. For generations, the federal government, through the Bureau of Reclamation, has sold Americans the idea that deserts should and could be turned into wheat baskets. Farmers and ranchers, and increasingly urban populations, depend on every drop of water they can get. To suddenly tell them that Native communities have the rights to "their" water but that they did not know because everybody had ignored the issue is politically difficult. This is exposed very clearly when courts do protect Native water rights, for example with the Klamath Basin Restoration Agreement. The agreement, signed in 2010, followed a 2002 court decision that tribes' rights to water did indeed precede that of irrigators in the Klamath basin, and provided for the demolishing of several dams. While that lawsuit had been filed in 1975, in 2001, the U.S. Fish and Wildlife Services shut off all except minimum levels of water to irrigators because suckers and coho salmon were dying in the river. The restoration agreement was never signed by Congress, but in 2016, the states and the hydroelectric companies who operate the dams agreed on removing the dams. Tribes in the Klamath basin are still trying to work out issues of water allocation. The lawsuit over whether the federal government can indeed protect fish by shutting off water for irrigators is headed to court in 2017.

Sometimes, the Endangered Species Act is the only hope for tribes who are fighting to get enough water. This was most famously the case with the Pyramid Lake Paiute in Nevada. Here, an irrigation project established in 1905 diverted water from the Truckee River to the Carson River. The Truckee ends up in Pyramid Lake, which is part of the Pyramid Lake reservation, and because of the diversion of water, the lake level lowered 87 feet between 1912 and 1967. In 1983, the U.S. Supreme Court rejected the water rights of the Pyramid Lake Paiute. However, it allocated all the water from one reservoir to the preservation of an endangered species of fish, the cui-ui, only found in Pyramid Lake, taking those waters from supplying Reno area residents. Faced with drought conditions, all water users had the incentives to develop the Truckee-Carson/Pyramid Lake Water Rights Settlement.

One of the most recent water settlements is the Blackfeet Water Rights Settlement, signed into law in 2016. This settlement originated from lawsuits in the 1970s, when the federal government filed water rights cases for all Montana tribes, and the state of Montana responded by filing for water rights adjudication in state courts. In 1984, the Supreme Court decided that the right to determine American Indian water rights lied with the state courts. The Blackfeet Nation initiated negotiations with the state, which took over a decade to complete. The Montana legislature approved the compact in 2009, but it took another seven years to get the approval by the United States Congress. An agreement with the Confederated Salish and Kootenai Tribes in western Montana faced similar challenges. Here, non-tribal water users were concerned with what they saw as a handover of water jurisdiction to the tribe. The tribe owned a 1855 water right over water used for 110,000 acres of irrigation agriculture; while some farmers argued that should the tribe be forced to file suit for their water rights, the irrigators could lose everything, others felt that giving the tribe some powers over "their" water already meant losing everything.

Land and Water Rights and American Indians

What conflicts and agreements over land and water rights – and hunting and fishing rights – often reveal is that contemporary Americans, misinformed or uninformed about the history of settlement, treaties and treaty rights, and Native sovereignty, fear that giving American Indian tribes any rights will take these rights away from them. People often do not reflect upon whether having taken these rights in the first place was not only morally right, but also legal. Assumptions about frontier settlement include that somehow Americans won "the war" against Native people and therefore simply have all the rights to land, water, and natural resources. Alternatively, people assume that because treaties were signed a long time ago, they are no longer relevant, forgetting about the past opens up possibilities to also forget about obligations. Education about those issues is the only way to explore pathways to the future that do not themselves continue or re-establish injustices.

Sources and Further Readings

Indian Rights:

Stephen L. Pevar. 2004. *The Rights of Indians and Tribes. The Authoritative ACLU Guide to Indian and Tribal Rights*. New York: New York University Press.

Joanne Barker. 2011. *Native Acts. Law, Recognition, and Cultural Authenticity*. Durham: Duke University Press.

Removal and Sovereignty:

David S. Heidler and Jeanne T. Heidler. 2006. *Indian Removal*. New York: W.W. Norton.

Cynthia Cumfer. 2007. *Separate Peoples, One Land. The Minds of Cherokees, Blacks, and Whites on the Tennessee Frontier*. Chapel Hill: University of North Carolina Press.

"Constitution of the Cherokee Nation." *Cherokee Phoenix*, 1 (1), Feb. 21, 1828.

"Communications, Cherokee Constitution." *Cherokee Phoenix*, 1 (10), April 24, 1828.

Allotment and Cobell:

Kristin T. Ruppel. 2008. *Unearthing Indian Land. Living with the Legacies of Allotment*. Tucson: University of Arizona Press.

Thomas Biolsi. 1995. The Birth of the Reservation. Making the Modern Individual among the Lakota. *American Ethnologist*, Vol. 22 (1), pp. 28-53.

Mikael Kurkiala. 1997. *Building the Nation Back Up: The Politics of Identity on the Pine Ridge Indian Reservation*. Uppsala: Acta Universitatis Upsaliensis, Uppsala Studies in Cultural Anthropology 22.

Paula Wagoner. 2001. *They Treated Us like Indians. The Worlds of Bennett County*. South Dakota. Lincoln: University of Nebraska Press.

General Accounting Office. 1992. *Profile of Land Ownership at 12 Reservations*. GAO/RCED-92-96BR.

Jake Russ and Thomas Stratmann. 2014. *Creeping Normalcy: Fractionation of Indian Land Ownership*. CESifo Working Paper No.4607.

Jessica A. Shoemaker. 2003. Like Snow in the Spring Time: Allotment, Fractionation, and the Indian Land Tenure Problem. *Wisconsin Law Review*, Vol. 4, pp. 729-788.

Armen H. Merjian. 2010. An Unbroken Chain of Injustice: The Dawes Act, Native American Trusts, and *Cobell v. Salazar. Gonzaga Law Review*, Vol. 46(3), p. 609-658.

Royce C. Lamberth. 2005. *Elouise Pepion Cobell v. Gale Norton*. United States District Court for the District of Columbia. Civil Action No. 96-1285 (RCL). Memorandum Opinion and Order. July 12, 2005.

Water Rights:

Daniel McCool. 2002. *Native Waters. Contemporary Indian Water Settlements and the Second Treaty Era*. Tucson: University of Arizona Press.

Kenichi Matsui. 2009. *Native Peoples and Water Rights. Irrigation, Dams, and the Law in Western Canada*. Montreal: McGill-Queen's University Press.

Roberta Ulrich. 2007. *Empty Nets. Indians, Dams, and the Columbia River*. Corvallis: Oregon State University Press.

History of American Indian Education
Birgit Hans

The treaties that the United States made with American Indian nations usually contained some educational provisions. The Fort Laramie Treaty of 1868 with the Lakota followed a standard pattern which means that the promises and provisions included were those commonly found in agreements between American Indian peoples and the federal government. Both sides made promises; for example, American Indian people agreed to not attack the railroads and forts while the federal government promised American Indians foodstuff to compensate for the declining buffalo numbers and resources, like farmers and blacksmiths, to adjust to their new life on the reservations. It also promised that the federal government would build a school which would provide "the elementary branches of an English education" for every 30 children between the ages of 6 and 16. This provision was to insure that the children of those who entered into the treaty would be civilized (Article VII).

Traditional American Indian Education

Euroamericans thought mistakenly that American Indian children did not receive an education before schools were set up for Native children. They acknowledged that boys were carefully trained to be hunters and warriors and girls were trained in household duties, but they regarded the lack of a formalized educational process as a deficiency in American Indian cultures. They did not care how much effort was expanded on each child in pre-reservation cultures, effort that included the parents as well as the extended family, the clans, and the entire communities. American Indian children definitely did receive an education in addition to their training. Take for example, the autobiographical account of Charles Alexander Eastman (1858-1939) that he gave of his growing up among the Dakota of Canada. He described how his uncle would teach him and his cousin empirical thinking; one day the uncle would ask the boys to deduce from the geography of a lake whether there were fish, and on another occasion, their grandmother asked the boys to give their arguments for their choice of the best mother bird.[1] Other autobiographical accounts furnish similar examples of the educational process.

In American Indian cultures on the northern Plains, boys and girls were brought up together until they reached the age of five or six. Then fathers and other male relatives became responsible for the education of boys, and mothers and female relatives educated the girls. Their education included training for specific tasks as well as education about the community's spiritual beliefs, history, etc. that are contained in the community's oral tradition. If a child had special gifts, he or she received special education to further that gift; if, for example, a child showed a special interest in the oral narratives and had a retentive memory, he might be apprenticed to a keeper of the oral tradition to possibly succeed that person. If a girl wanted to be a quillworker, she would approach a member of the quillworking society and negotiate for admission into the society which had a practical as well as spiritual dimension; this education brought status and economic gain to women and their families.[2]

Many of the accounts which describe encounters between American Indian peoples and Euroamericans note the permissive nature of American Indian child rearing in disapproving tones. While Euroamericans believed in corporal punishment for their children, Native peoples generally did not. Any necessary discipline was not exerted by the children's parents but by their maternal or paternal aunts and uncles, depending on which of the many Native cultures on the northern Plains is being discussed. Occasionally, physical punishment was meted out, but, generally, social control was exerted through teasing and peer pressure. Again, depending on the tribe, there were certain groups of people that could tease you while others could not. In general, Native education was geared toward teaching children self-discipline.

Of course, American Indian peoples did not feel that their education was inferior to European and, later, Euroamerican education. When the Reverend Eleazor Wheelock appealed to the Oneida and Onondaga councils to give him some more of their children to educate in 1772, the councils voiced their opinions in no uncertain terms. They denied his request because they felt that physical punishment was child abuse, that they were exploited as laborers rather than receive the promised education, and that those of their children who returned to them did not have the education to be productive members of their communities. They did offer to educate some of the English youths though.[3] Clearly, the Onondaga and Oneida elders considered their education vastly superior to the one that the English could provide. Needless to say, their generous offer was not accepted by the New England government.

It was not until the federal government provided education on the newly established reservations and the opening of the first federal, off-reservation boarding school, Carlisle Indian Industrial School, in 1879 that the Euroamerican ethnocentric view of education could be enforced uniformly across the country. Early in the educational process, some American Indian parents felt that their children needed both educations in order to succeed in the new social and economic conditions. However, the federal government's assimilationist policy tried to stamp out traditional education and replace it with that of mainstream culture. Unfortunately, the policy of assimilation threatened traditional knowledge and many American Indian children did not learn the spiritual and cultural knowledge that had been handed down in their communities for generation after generation. It was not until Congress passed the Indian Reorganization Act in 1934 that American Indian peoples were urged to teach their children traditional knowledge once more.

Mission Schools

The various Christian denominations were the first to establish schools among American Indian peoples. Missionaries usually learned the languages of the people that they hoped to convert to Christianity. As early as 1570, King Philip of Spain was convinced by Catholic priests working in Mexico to name Nahuatl the official language of Mexico to facilitate the conversion of the Native peoples. And only 34 years later, his son required all Spanish missionaries to learn the languages of the Native peoples with whom they worked.[4] While linguistic competency was never an official requirement for missionaries of any denomination in what was to become the United States and Canada, missionaries recognized that their success would be very limited without knowledge of Native languages.

Bishop Frederic Baraga (1797–1868), for instance, started his work among the Ottawa in 1831 but worked among the Ojibwa of northern Michigan from 1835 on. For many years, he was the only Catholic priest in the Upper Peninsula and served Native people as well as German, French, and English-speaking immigrants to the area. In 1953, his dictionary of the Ojibwa language which also contained a grammar was published; because of its usefulness, the dictionary has been republished several times and is still in print today. Other missionaries used Father Baraga's work to obtain the linguistic skill to minister to the Ojibwa people. The Reverend Stephen Riggs (1812–1883) and his work may serve as another example. He was involved in missionary work among the Dakota and Lakota in South Dakota for more than 40 years and also published a volume containing a grammar and dictionary in 1890 that remains in print today. There are numerous other missionaries whose linguistic skills resulted in publications about American Indian languages.

Missionary schools among American Indian peoples and later on-reservation boarding schools were often taught in the Native languages of the children they sought to educate and convert, at least early on in the educational process. Missionaries felt that children literate in their own languages learned English more easily. However, in the late nineteenth century, the federal government issued the English-only policy which threatened to remove any federal funding from schools that utilized Native languages as a teaching tool. The commissioner of Indian Affairs claimed that it was detrimental to American Indian children to learn the "barbarous dialect" of their parents and ancestors and that English "which is good enough for a white man and a black man, ought to be good enough for the red man."[5] By that time, the federal government had embarked on their assimilation program; Native languages became mere remnants of cultures that were to be wiped out. In reality, the demise of American Indian languages took much longer than expected on many reservations where many people were somewhat bilingual rather than English-only speakers. On the Pine Ridge Reservation in South Dakota, for example, Lakota was still the primary language in the 1930s.

Mission schools were disappearing by 1900, since the government supported public schools rather than provide funds for mission schools. Catholic mission schools were especially hard hit, because of the anti-Catholic feelings that, among other things, questioned the priests' and nuns' ability to make American Indian children into *patriotic* Americans. On the northern Plains, some reservation agents encouraged and sometimes pressured American Indian parents by withholding rations to enroll their children in day or public schools rather than mission schools.[6] Some mission schools exist even today, but they are few and far between and, while they may be important to individual reservations, they do not play an important role on the national level any more.

Canadian Residential Schools

In Canada, the history of boarding schools for Native students also started with missionary efforts. The first boarding school, which operated for only nine years, was opened as early as 1620 by Franciscan brothers in what was New France then. The goal was, just as it had been in colonial America, to educate young Native boys to become missionaries to their people. However, the experiment was not successful and, only when the relationship of Native peoples and the non-Native settlers shifted in the early nineteenth century, did boarding schools, usually referred to as residential schools in Canada, become a force.[7]

The merger of the Hudson's Bay Company and North West Company in 1821 eliminated many jobs for Native people and their mixed-blood descendants; most of the jobs that were eliminated had been related to the fur trade. At the same time, the early nineteenth century saw increased immigration of Europeans which shifted subsistence patterns to agriculture. The position of Native peoples became more and more tenuous in this new environment, since neither their skills nor their knowledge was needed any longer. At the same time, the colonial government and various denominations began to advocate the assimilation of Native peoples. By the middle of the nineteenth century, the three major denominations in Canada – Catholic, Anglican, and Methodists – supported the idea of residential schools and began to establish them by negotiating with the various tribes.

The Canada Act of 1867 clearly stated that the federal government had jurisdiction over Native peoples; its oversight also included day and residential schools. However, the federal government decided to use the denominational residential schools that already existed for the education of Native students. As in America, residential schools were the target of political parties, controversies about the division between state and religions, and the focus of denominational squabbles. Throughout the many decades of their existence, however, residential schools never educated more than one-third of all Native children. The majority of the other two-thirds were educated in day schools; there were also those children that did not receive any education.

By the 1960s, disillusionment with residential school had set in in Canada. The missionaries were acknowledging that they were not achieving their goals, and the federal government was concerned about the cost of schooling. Even those Native communities that had originally supported education for their children felt that residential schools were culturally oppressive and, most importantly, their children were subjected to physical, spiritual, and sexual abuse. Official inquiries into the abuse charges led the various churches to apologize for the abuses suffered by Native peoples in residential schools in the 1990s and to an apology by Canadian Prime Minister Stephen Harper in 2008. In his speech, he outlined the history of residential schools and spoke to the suffering of the children before ending with a plea for reconciliation. Among others, he made the following points about culture loss and personal pain: "We now recognize that it was wrong to separate children from rich and vibrant cultures and traditions, that it created a void in many lives and communities, and we apologize for having done this" and "Not only did you suffer these abuses as children, but as you became parents, you were powerless to protect your own children from suffering the same experience, and for this we are sorry."[8] Instead of "civilizing" Native children, residential schools had led to dysfunctional families and communities.

Day and On-reservation Boarding Schools

The federal government in the United States began to take an active role in the education of American Indian peoples when Congress passed the Civilization Fund Act in 1819 which allocated money to various denominations that were willing to establish schools among Native peoples. When tribes chose to relocate or were forcefully relocated under the Indian Removal Act of 1830, the missionaries had to move their schools as well in order to remain eligible for federal support. At the same time, the federal government continued to make treaties with various American Indian nations, treaties which contained provisions for day schools as the later Fort Laramie Treaty did. These day schools were run either by missionaries or by teachers engaged by the government for that purpose. An additional task for the teachers was to teach Native boys some basic tasks of civilized life like wood cutting and gardening while their wives, officially called housekeepers, were to introduce the girls to some rudimentary tasks like cooking with the ration staples, washing, ironing, and cleaning. The provision that students were to be taught "the elementary branches of an English education" makes clear that the federal government was interested in assimilation and did not recognize American Indian education as a valid and important part of the educational process.

The day schools were not very effective in assimilating children, since they returned to their parents at the end of the day and were able to participate in traditional family life as well as the spirituality of their people. Teachers and housekeepers hoped that they would carry what they had learned to their parents and communities. The goal of the day schools was to establish English as the everyday language, to introduce children to Christianity, and to expose them to industrial pursuits. While these day schools were to be part of the civilizing process, they seem to have been the least intrusive school type.

On-reservation boarding schools, mostly run by various denominations, were only slightly more successful in achieving their goal of assimilation. On the one hand, they managed to separate the children from the influence of their parents; however, on the other hand, children returned to their families and communities during vacations and holidays. Teachers and housekeepers complained that they had to start all over after children returned to schools. Also, because of the proximity of their families and communities, children were more likely to run away from on-reservation boarding schools. The students in the on-reservation boarding schools spent half their day in class acquiring English skills and following a very basic curriculum and half their day in industrial training. Despite its drawbacks in "civilizing" American Indian children, the on-reservation boarding schools educated the majority of American Indian children.

Some of these early on-reservation boarding schools were also run by the federal government, especially if it was too difficult for children to attend day schools regularly or if the social and economic situation of the reservation was unsettled. One example would be the Kiowa–Comanche–Apache reservation in Oklahoma. The Treaty of Medicine Lodge of 1867 provided for educational services, just as the Fort Laramie Treaty did a year later and in exactly the same language. However, the Rainy Mountain boarding school was not opened for Kiowa children until 1893; before that there was hardly any Americanized education for the Kiowa children. In its heyday, the school offered space for 130 students. It was closed in 1920 after having been in operation for only 27 years.[9]

The academic curriculum at the Rainy Mountain boarding school was very poor; the majority of students spent so much time struggling with the English language that they never progressed beyond the introductory classes. The teacher shortage was chronic, and, despite the federal focus on vocational skills, there were few opportunities for students to learn a trade. The physical plant was not kept up, and there was no water at the site at which the buildings were erected; in fact, all the water had to be brought in. Because of the sanitary problems, the very contagious eye disease trachoma was rampant. It is not surprising then that the school consistently received negative evaluations from the federal inspectors in its later years.

Kiowa parents were as aware as anyone else of the problems at the school. However, when the Bureau of Indian Affairs threatened to close the Rainy Mountain boarding school, they lobbied to keep the school open. For them, the on-reservation boarding school kept their children close enough for visits and they realized that children managed to maintain their identity as Kiowa, despite all attempts to "civilize" them. Most of them even maintained their Kiowa language and became bilingual. Opposing the government's decision to close the school, they pointed out the treaty obligations of the federal government and that their children would not be welcomed in public schools by either their white neighbors or people from other tribes. Not surprisingly, their arguments did not prevail.

Among the on-reservation educational institutions, the Cherokee Female Seminary was an anomaly. Even before their removal to Indian Territory, the Cherokee Nation had been interested in education. In 1800, they granted Moravians permission to establish a school with the condition that it would not be a denominational school. Other missionary schools followed. After their removal in the 1830s to what became Oklahoma, the Cherokee Nation established and funded its own public school system.[10]

As part of their educational plan, the Cherokee leaders also established two high schools, one for females and one for males, that would provide education for the upper-class Cherokees. The Cherokee Female Seminary opened its doors in 1851 and had a capacity of 100 students. Unlike the schools funded by the federal government and various denominations, the curriculum emphasized advanced academic studies, including Latin and mathematics, and no industrial labor to prepare the young women to become wives of prominent Cherokees or teachers in the Nation's schools. While contemporary Cherokee politics were emphasized, there was no course in the Cherokee Nation's history. The Seminary definitely worked on the continued assimilation of the Cherokee, especially the upper-class, but the Nation decided on the terms of assimilation. Since the Nation financed its own schools, they could ignore the disapproval of the federal officials who had visualized assimilation in more basic terms. In 1909, the Female Seminary was sold to the state of Oklahoma that took over public education and became Northeastern Normal School, a teachers' college.

While on-reservation boarding schools followed the federal guidelines to assimilate American Indian students into Euroamerican culture, they often had limited success. The students' proximity to their families and communities permitted them to hang on to their cultures to some degree. By 1900, denominational and government on-reservation boarding schools housed 9604 of an overall 26,451 students. The number remained fairly stable but made up a much smaller percentage of students in 1925 when the boarding school era was coming to an end – 10,615 of 65,493 American Indian students; at that point, more than half of the students were attending public schools.[11]

Off-reservation Boarding Schools

In the second half of the nineteenth century, the federal government added another type of school to its educational system: the off-reservation boarding schools. The day schools and on-reservation boarding schools had not achieved the goal that had been set for them – the complete assimilation of American Indian children. All three types of schools – day schools, on-reservation boarding schools, and off-reservation boarding schools – existed side by side.

In 1875, the federal government sent 72 Plains warriors – Cheyenne, Arapaho, Kiowa, Comanche, and Caddo – into exile at Fort Marion in Florida to punish them for recent raids on white settlements. In charge of these prisoners, Richard Henry Pratt (1840–1924), an army officer, embarked on an educational program with them that lasted for most of the three years that they spent in Florida. Several of his former prisoners went on to continue their schooling at Hampton Normal and Industrial Institute for Negroes in Virginia. Pratt had a larger vision to educate American Indian children in off-reservation boarding schools though, since he realized that children who were not yet firmly established within their cultures could be civilized more easily and completely than his adult prisoners. He succeeded in selling his idea to the Bureau of Indian Affairs, and in 1879 he opened Carlisle Indian Industrial School in abandoned army barracks in Carlisle, Pennsylvania, as the first federal off-reservation boarding school. Pratt's motto was: "Kill the Indian in him [American Indian] and save the man."[12] Ultimately, the federal government operated 25 off-reservation boarding schools which included Haskell in Kansas, Chemawa in Oregon, Chilocco in Oklahoma, and Genoa in Nebraska.

In 1877, the anthropologist Lewis Henry Morgan published his thesis on cultural evolution which postulated that all cultures evolved through stages that were associated with various cultural achievements. Not surprisingly, he judged Euroamericans to have achieved the highest stage – civilization – while American Indians were located in the two lower stages – savagery and barbarism. This ethnocentric model was applied to other cultures as well. Morgan said that, since cultures evolved, American Indian peoples had the ability to become civilized. The Eastern reform groups saw it as their responsibility to accelerate the natural development and lead American Indian peoples into civilization, i.e. to introduce them to Christianity, agricultural pursuits, and individualism.

The passage of the General Allotment Act or Dawes Act in 1887 was the federal government's attempt to civilize adult American Indian peoples. The allotment of individual pieces of land would force men to farm to make a living rather than hunt. It would also provide the opportunity to separate extended families on various parcels of land which would force them to work for themselves rather than the community. As Dawes said, it would make them more selfish which was considered a positive trait in nineteenth-century Euroamerican culture. Christianity would be provided by the various churches firmly established on the reservations by that time. Christian American Indian farmers, the Eastern reformers and the federal government believed, would give up their Native cultures and spirituality. At the same time the federal government, urged by Pratt and other reformers, would remove American Indian children from the reservations and subject them to civilizing influences away from their parents before they could learn their peoples' cultures and spiritualities. Off-reservation boarding schools were going to be the answer to the Indian problem.

While Euroamerican educators agreed that the most effective system of teaching American Indian children would be a combination of academics and vocational training, the curriculum in federal schools was not standardized until 1890 when Thomas J. Morgan, commissioner of Indian Affairs, came up with a 3-tiered system. Students would get their first six years of education and vocational training in the on-reservation boarding schools; then they would move into off-reservation boarding schools for five more years of more advanced schooling in academics and vocational skills. Finally, some promising students would be sent to select off-reservation boarding schools for another five years. This tiered system never worked for a number of reasons: students spent much of their time learning English at first, vocational training was not available at the expected level at the two lower tiers, and the teachers were not necessarily qualified enough to teach the children even after the civil service examination became mandatory at the beginning of the twentieth century.

Recruiting American Indian children for off-reservation boarding school proved difficult from the start. Parents were reluctant to entrust their children to the schools. They worried about their health, their treatment, especially after negative stories about students' experiences made it back to the reservations, and their separation from them. During the economically difficult time on reservations in the decade before and after the turn of the century, Indian agents used the threat of withholding the rations that were promised in the treaties to force compliance. Many parents faced the agonizing decision of whether to send one of their children to boarding school or not being able to feed the family. At least children would be fed in the off-reservation boarding schools. Some parents sent their children voluntarily; they sometimes could not support their children, or they were single parents unable to raise the children on their own, or they felt that education was going to be increasingly important for their children in the new world of which they would be a part.

There are dozens of accounts of the children's experiences at the off-reservation boarding schools. They talk about the rigidly structured, military environment, the often harsh discipline that they endured, the food that was often not palatable, the denigration of their tribal cultures, the spiritual and physical abuse they suffered, the physical indignities that they endured, such as having their hair cut and receiving a new name, and their longing for their parents and other relatives. They speak of students' resistance to the assimilation program which took different forms; some student showed passive resistance, others ran away, some set the schools on fire, still others secretly maintained their cultures, and still others defied the rule that they could not speak their languages. Some students adjusted to the life better than others; there are also accounts of students who enjoyed their time in boarding school, especially after the restrictive nature of life at boarding school eased somewhat during the 1920s.[13]

Contrary to stereotypes, not every American Indian attended off-reservation boarding schools. At the turn of the twentieth century, 7430 of 26,451 students attended off-reservation boarding schools, a little more than one-fourth of all students. The number of students in boarding school remained fairly stable throughout the first two decades of the twentieth century. In 1925 only 8542 of 65,493 students attended.[14] The effect on American Indian communities was profound however. Many parents could not or would not teach their children their cultures and languages after their own experiences in boarding schools and, therefore, their children often could not carry on cultural traditions. In many cases, parents felt helpless to protect their children in any other way but silence from what had happened to them at boarding schools. Students often spent many years in boarding schools and never relearned their cultures and languages. Others accepted the ethnocentric ideas that fueled assimilation and rejected anything connected to their tribal cultures.

The 1920s and 1930s saw a renewed interest in American Indian cultures by Euroamericans, and American Indian peoples were encouraged to take back their tribal cultures and languages. The policy of assimilation gave way to acculturation. Many of the off-reservation boarding schools were permanently closed. Not all boarding schools were closed, however, since they started to serve other purposes for American Indian nations. The former Wahpeton Indian School in North Dakota, which was founded as an off-reservation boarding school in 1904, became a full-time academic boarding school in the 1940s. In 1993, its name was changed to Circle of Nations School, and its current mission is "to provide a program, based on an annual written plan, linking clinicians, counselors, and mental health professionals with academic program personnel in a culturally sensitive residential program tailored to the particular needs of Indian students." The Circle of Nations School primarily serves American Indian children from North Dakota, South Dakota, Minnesota, Montana, Nevada, and Wisconsin. A board of governors representing the nations that have children at the boarding school insures that its mission is met.[15] Instead of being subjected to an assimilation program, American Indian children with special needs are introduced to their tribal cultures as part of the educational process.

The Meriam Report of 1928, also known as "The Problem of Indian Administration," addressed education among a number of other things and recommended that American Indian children should not be removed from the care of their parents and communities and the end of the Euroamerican ethnocentric view of the curriculum. These recommendations were certainly reflected in the Indian Reorganization Act of 1934 and the Johnson O'Malley Act of the same year under which the federal government could pay states rather than individual schools for educating American Indian students in public schools. Some of the off-reservation boarding schools that were still operating managed to hang on for another two decades; a few, like the Circle of Nations School, redefined their role in the educational process. American Indian students were going to be educated in the still existing Bureau of Indian Affairs schools, the former day schools, and in public schools from now on. Fifty years of assimilation of Native children came to an end.

Contemporary American Indian Education (1940–2017)

During the 1940s, the attitude of the federal government toward American Indian peoples and their education changed once more. Day schools were judged a failure, and some politicians advocated the renewed use of boarding schools for education and a more culturally sensitive curriculum. However, with Termination and Relocation in 1953 such discussions ended.

Public schools did not always welcome American Indian students. Euroamerican parents objected to their children being taught with American Indian students, there were still language barriers, sometimes the schools lacked the facilities that the Bureau of Indian Affairs considered essential, such as a wood-working shop for example, and budgets were strained. Teaching materials were geared toward the Euroamerican middleclass and had little relevance for American Indian students. Their teachers could usually not compensate for the lack of educational materials, since they had no special training and often lacked cultural sensitivity. Sometimes American Indian students were simply kept in separate classrooms and received little if any educational instruction.[16]

The 1960s saw increased political and social activism on the part of American Indians who also advocated for educational changes as well as self-determination. Some of the issues they were dealing with were high dropout rates, lack of American Indian teachers, lack of sensitivity of Euroamerican teachers, and low self-image and achievement of American Indian students. The findings of two major studies led to the Indian Education Act in 1972 which authorized the development of supporting programs for American Indian students based on culturally sensitive materials and encouraged American Indian parents to become involved in the educational process of their children. At the same time, American Indians were finally given a national voice in regard to their peoples' education; the National Advisory Council on Indian Education consists of 15 American Indian members who are appointed by the president and report to Congress.

The passage of the Indian Self-Determination and Education Assistance Act of 1975 provided opportunities for American Indian tribes to take charge of their own schools. Contracting permits them to run the school and to introduce culturally appropriate materials and activities as well as to encourage tribal languages. However, not all tribal members feel that tribal culture and language are appropriate to be taught in schools. It is an ongoing discussion on many reservations.

From the earliest encounters between American Indians and Europeans and later Americans, Native languages have been judged and found wanting, despite the fact that Native languages are as complex and expressive as the English language. Bilingualism was only rarely considered an option, and the educational efforts of the United States have deliberately tried to exterminate Native languages and cultures. The Native American Languages Act of 1990 makes excellent points as to the value of Native languages but may be too late to truly make a difference in their preservation. It states that "the status of the cultures and languages of Native Americans is unique and the United States has the responsibility to act together with the Native Americans to ensure the survival of these unique cultures and languages" and "to preserve, protect, and promote the rights and freedom of Native Americans to use, practice, and develop Native American languages."[17] However, the predictions as to the viabilities of various American Indian languages are dismal. Valentine estimates that about 175 American Indian languages still exist today and continues: "Kraus makes the following observations on their relative vitality, though: only 20 languages are still being learned by children, and so have a reasonable chance of surviving for several generations; about 30 languages are spoken today only by adults, but are not being learned by children; another 70 languages are spoken only by the elderly; and another 50 or so are spoken by only a very few of the oldest members of communities. This means that within the next generation approximately 25 percent of the surviving languages will be gone; within two generations well over half will disappear."[18]

Despite the positive changes that have taken place in American Indian education in the last couple of decades, there are many important issues that the nations face today. The high school graduation rate of American Indian students has improved somewhat to 69.6% for the academic year 2013–14, but, even though it is up 4.6 percent, it is still significantly lower than that of whites at 87.2%.[19] American Indian students continue to perform poorly on standardized tests which are geared toward the non-Native middleclass. Teacher preparation is not always adequate, and funding for education is diminishing. On the other hand, there are a large number of American Indian teachers today and a greater awareness of culturally sensitive teaching materials. Special programs support American Indian students within the public school system. Nevertheless, much remains to be done to insure that all American Indian students can benefit fully from the educational experience.

Tribal Colleges

It is impossible to talk about American Indian education without mentioning the Tribal Colleges and Universities that have sprung up throughout the United States. Their focus is on the preservation of tribal cultures and languages while also offering various other degree programs. Navajo Community College was the first tribal college to be established in 1968; it was renamed Dine College in 1997 and is located in Tsaile, Arizona, on the Navajo Reservation. In North Dakota, each of the four reservations has its own tribal college and, in addition, United Tribes Technical College is located in Bismarck. The tribal colleges – Sitting Bull College on the Standing Rock Reservation, Turtle Mountain Community College, Fort Berthold Community College, and Cankdeska Cikana Community College on the Spirit Lake Reservation – were founded between 1971 and 1974. United Tribes Technical College originated in 1969. Thirty-seven Tribal Colleges and Universities serve approximately 30,000 American Indian students across the country and award associate's, bachelor's, and master's degrees. There are 358 degree programs at this time.[20]

Tribal colleges are funded through The Tribally Controlled Community College Assistance Act of 1978 which provides Full-time Equivalent (FTE) funding for students. Therefore, funding for tribal colleges depends on enrollment, but federal funding has never been sufficient to cover the actual cost of education in Tribal Colleges and Universities. In addition, tribal colleges receive funding through foundations and federal grants. Like other areas in the educational fields, Native educators expect their appropriations to be significantly cut.

Unemployment rates on the reservations in North Dakota are high, and the tribal colleges attempt to address the problem by providing training for American Indians. For instance, Turtle Mountain Community College has a training program for casino employment. At the same time, the two- and four-year academic programs prepare students for successful careers on the reservations and for transfer to larger institutions of higher learning. In addition, some of the tribal colleges offer degree programs in conjunction with universities and selected graduate degrees.

American Indian education was firmly established by the time Europeans arrived on the American shores. Ethnocentric demands for assimilation finally culminated in the off-reservation boarding school era which seriously affected American Indian languages and attempted unsuccessfully to wipe out American Indian cultures. Once more in charge of their educational system American Indian peoples are trying to heal the wounds left by assimilation.

Endnotes

1. Charles Alexander Eastman. 1972. *Indian Boyhood.* Greenwich: Fawcett Premier Book, pp. 51-52 and pp. 67-69. An excellent description of child rearing can also be found in Ella Deloria. 1988. *Waterlily.* Lincoln: University of Nebraska Press.

2. Mary Jane Schneider. 1983. "Women's Work: An Examination of Women's Roles in Plains Indian Arts and Crafts" in Patricia Albers and Beatrice Medicine, eds. *The Hidden Half: Studies in Plains Indian Women.* Lanham: University Press of America, pp. 101-121.

3. "Speech of the Oneida Headmen" and Speech of the Onondaga Council" in Colin G. Calloway, ed. 1994. *The World Turned Upside Down.* Boston: Bedford Books of St. Martin's Press, pp. 66-70.

4. Jon Reyhner and Jeanne Eder. 2004. *American Indian Education: A History.* Norman: University of Oklahoma Press, pp. 18-19.

5. "Use of English in Indian Schools: Extract from the Annual Report of the Commissioner of Indian Affairs, September 21, 1887" in Francis Paul Prucha, ed. 1975. *Documents of United States Indian Policy.* Lincoln: University of Nebraska Press, p. 176.

6. Irene Mahoney. 2006. *Lady Blackrobes: Missionaries in the Heart of Indian Country.* Golden, Colorado: Fulcrum Publishing contains an interesting account about the Catholic Church's struggle for education funding in the late 19th and 20th century. Interestingly, many reservation mission schools had separate schools for American Indian and AngloAmerican children.

7. J.R. Miller. 1997. *Shingwauk's Vision: A History of Native Residential Schools.* Toronto: University of Toronto Press contains a wealth of information; I draw on Miller's book for all information about Native education in Canada.

8. "Prime Minister Stephen Harper's statement of apology", 11 June 2008, www.cbc/canada /story/2008/06/11/pm-statement.html.

9. Clyde Ellis. 1996. *To Change Them Forever: Education at the Rainy Mountain Boarding School, 1893-1920.* Norman: University of Oklahoma Press gives the history of the Kiowa on-reservation boarding school.

10. Devon A. Mihesuah. 1993. *Cultivating the Rosebuds: The Education of Women at the Cherokee Female Seminary, 1851-1909.* Urbana: University of Illinois Press provides an excellent history of the school.

11. David Wallace Adams. 1995. *Education for Extinction: American Indians and the Boarding School Experience, 1875-1928.* University of Kansas Press, p. 320. The study contains a wealth of information about the American boarding schools. I also used Jon Reyhner and Jeanne Eder. 2004. *American Indian Education: A History.* Norman: University of Oklahoma Press and Jon Reyhner and Jeanne Eder.1989. *A History of American Indian Education.* Billings: Eastern Montana College.

12. David Wallace Adams. 1995. *Education for Extinction: American Indians and the Boarding School Experience, 1875-1928.* University of Kansas Press, p. 52 quotes Pratt's infamous motto.

13. Some excellent examples of boarding school narratives on the northern Plainsare: K. Tsianina Lomawaima. 1994. *They Called It Prairie Light: The Story of Chilocco Indian School.* Lincoln: University of Nebraska Press; Scott Riney. 1999. *The Rapid City Indian School 1898-1933.* Norman: University of Oklahoma Press; and Esther Burnett Horne and Sally McBeth. 1998. *Essie's Story: The Life and Legacy of a Shoshone Teacher.* Lincoln: University of Nebraska Press.

14. David Wallace Adams. 1995. *Education for Extinction: American Indians and the Boarding School Experience, 1875-1928*. University of Kansas Press, p. 320.
15. The history of Wahpeton Indian School can be found at www.cns.bia.edu/history.html
16. Jon Reyhner and Jeanne Eder. 2004. *American Indian Education: A History*. Norman: University of Oklahoma Press and Margaret Connell Szasz. 1999. *Education and the American Indian*. Albuquerque: University of New Mexico Press contain excellent information on American Indian issues during the last part of the twentieth century.
17. Quoted in Jon Reyhner and Jeanne Eder. 2004. *American Indian Education: A History*. Norman: University of Oklahoma Press, p. 309.
18. J. Randolph Valentine, "Linguistics and Languages in Native Studies" in Russell Thornton, ed. 1998. *Studying Native America: Problems and Prospects*. Madison: University of Wisconsin Press, p. 153.
19. U.S. High School Graduation Rate Hits New High, U.S. Department of Education
20. White House Initiative on American Indian and Alaska Native Education, U.S. Department of Education.

Resource Development
Sebastian F. Braun

Two legends that often frame historic accounts of Native lands are that either American Indians were made to move to the most worthless lands or, as a paradoxical twist, that those worthless lands turned out to hold valuable natural resources that kind of constitute a revenge at American politics. As always, there are elements of truth to those legends although neither one is actually true. What is true, though, is that the lands of some American Indian nations do hold valuable natural resources; the extraction of these resources – especially uranium, coal, gas, and oil, but also, often forgotten, water – has sometimes created wealth. Often, however, that wealth itself was predicated on dangerous circumstances, as is often the case with resource extraction. Some of these resources were known at the time that treaties were signed; some were either not known or not important at that time.

Coal, for example, was a resource that had long been valued. Lewis and Clark, going up the Missouri River through the northern plains, for example, noted down the locations and qualities of coal veins with care. Uranium, on the other hand, did not come to play a role as a resource until the Second World War. Oil became important just a few years after the last treaties had been signed, although many oil deposits were not discovered until 40 or 50 years later. However, resource development has played a large role in Native economics, health care, subsistence, diplomacy, and ecologies for a very long time.

Early Resources

While many people assume that natural resource development only becomes important with advanced technology, societies have taken advantage of minerals, for example, for a long time. Native societies are not an exception. Prehistoric societies operated mines for specific lithic materials, for example Knife River Flint or pipestones, as well as metals, for example copper. These resources, together with obsidian and others, were traded throughout the continent. This trade is a good insight in how valued these specific resources must have been. Apart from specific lithic materials and metals, they included other resources like shells and pearls. Of course, early North Americans also used other resources, such as water, soils, and timber. Wood and stones were used for tools, weapons, lodges, and palisades. Wood obviously also served as a fuel for fires. Soils were used not only for horticulture and agriculture, as well as for structures like earthlodges and mounds, but also for pottery. Water was not simply used in its natural environments, but also for irrigation; most famous are the canals along the Gila River around Casa Grande, just to the southeast of today's Phoenix. Apart from these resources, Native peoples of course also used the flora and fauna through hunting, gathering, and agriculture. They manipulated these resources, especially plants. Not only did the peoples of North

America domesticate plants for agriculture, but they also further changed plants domesticated elsewhere. Corn, for example, domesticated in Mesoamerica, was further adapted to northern climate and soils so that it could spread to upstate New York and the northern plains.

Resources such as land, soils, and fauna were probably managed in common by groups, through diverse political and social strategies. Some resources might have been shared between groups – the pipestone quarries in southwestern Minnesota seem to be a late example of this – but some resources were probably owned individually. Grave goods indicate that in certain societies, hierarchies as well as material wealth differences might have been institutionalized at early times. In historic times, resources located on the territories of specific groups could be used by others provided the local group had no shortage and the visiting group asked for permission. In historic agricultural societies, often the group as a whole owned the territory and thus the land, but each family was awarded specific parcels to plant; while they did not own the land, they did own the harvest. Similar arrangements existed for certain animal species. The summer hunt for buffalo, for example, was often tightly regulated, but specific bison killed by individual hunters might belong to individual hunters or their families, although they were often obliged to distribute the meat in prescribed ways to others. Such distribution rules also prevailed in other communal hunts, for example in arctic whale hunts that were carried out by groups under the command of individual whale hunt captains.

Animals and plants as resources became contested with land rights. Even long after treaties had been concluded, however, they remained contentious because states did not necessarily abide by treaty rights. Some treaties, for example those with tribes in the Pacific Northwest and those with the Ojibwe in Wisconsin and Minnesota, guaranteed tribes continued rights of hunting, fishing, trapping, or whaling on territories they were ceding to the United States. In other words, the tribes retained these rights on lands outside reservation boundaries. Those rights, when Native peoples tried to enforce them, were often ignored by states, who were intent to claim all of the resources on their territories for themselves. When federal courts began to side with these treaty rights, such as in the Boldt Decision in 1974 on fishing rights in the northwest, and in the 1983 Voigt decision in Wisconsin, non-Indians sometimes reverted to vigilantism to keep Native people from exerting their rights. Because by treaty, Native people held hunting or fishing rights "in common" with non-Indians, tribes held rights to half of the catchable fish populations, for example, and they could regulate their own seasons and hunting methods. This was not an easy pill to swallow for people who had been able to ignore American Indians. Some of these cases are still contested, for example in Minnesota, where Ojibwe are trying to exert their fishing treaty rights outside of reservation boundaries.

It should not be overlooked that there were resources other than the mentioned physical, natural resources. Songs and ceremonies, for example, were resources, too. They saw different ownership models across the diverse Native cultures. In some, they were owned by individuals, in others by groups such as clans or moieties or simply by the collective whole. They were traded between individuals and between societies, and thus a certain amount of commodification could adhere to some, although by no means to all. Other immaterial resources were exchange networks, which were often used by specific individuals and provided them with status and prestige as well as the ability to look out for others. Early European explorers often mistook the resource management models used by Native societies for communism, a stereotype that has since continued to flourish in assumptions that American Indian groups simply wandered the land, following their hunting resources in an extremely fluid landscape without territories.

In reality, it seems that it was not necessarily the ownership models that were different from European ones. Europe still knew shared resources in the form of commons. More than that, it might have been the prevalence of kinship obligations steering the redistribution of resources that were different, as well as the ways by which individuals could achieve status. Europe was well on the way to concentrate the control of wealth in the hands of a select few who acquired status by showcasing and hoarding resources. North America in general seems to have placed a much higher importance on generosity and redistribution. In the following, this chapter will not so much focus on lands as on minerals, as control of minerals – from gold to coal, from uranium to oil – turned out to be a continuously contested issue in North America.

Gold

Ever since Columbus landed on what he insisted was Asian soils in the Caribbean, gold held a special value for Europeans and Americans. The imagination of Columbus and other travelers looking for the mythical El Dorado, the city of gold, was then heightened by the encounters with the Aztec empire in Mesoamerica and the Inca empire in South America, societies that used gold to a great extent. In South America, the economic value of gold might have been surpassed by silver, which had been mined before Spanish contact. The Spanish mines of Potosi became infamous over decades as a place where the extraction of metals and the exploitation of indigenous labor reached new heights. Gold, however, retained its mystical power over Europeans. The first Spanish expeditions into the interior of North America – De Soto from Florida through the Carolinas to Arkansas and Coronado from New Mexico into Kansas – looked for gold. And while they failed and the real gold mines of North America became the fur trade, any find of gold would set off gold rushes. Gold inspired dreams of instantaneous wealth for centuries, and as is usual for resource booms, those looking for riches ignored property rights, especially those of indigenous peoples.

Gold, therefore, might not be the most important natural resource in North America, but its consequences were and are often devastating for Native peoples. Several remain directly linked to the loss of territories and populations. The gold rush in Cherokee territory contributed to the nation's eventual removal from their lands. The California gold rush had devastating consequences for Native peoples in the newly American territory in the 1850s. The gold rush in Montana in the 1860s led to the building of the Bozeman trail and thus the Red Cloud War, the gold find in the Black Hills led to a rush into the Great Sioux Reservation that at the very least indirectly led to the Lakota wars of the 1870s, and the Klondike gold rush in Alaska and the Yukon appropriated Native lands without treaties. In all of these occasions, the government abandoned its responsibilities to Native peoples in favor of the gold miners. In some cases, as for example in the Black Hills, the government initially tried to defend Native rights to resources. But when push came to shove, the federal government could and would not take the political decision to stand up to its own citizens. Gold rushes thus stand first in line of resource rushes that defined the expansion of the frontier. While they are often famous because they are gold rushes, however, they worked similarly to other resource rushes for more pedestrian resources. Land rushes, beaver rushes, water rushes, buffalo rushes, and timber rushes all shaped the policies of expansion into indigenous territories.

As all booms, gold rushes usually came to a bust after a few years. Many people, unfamiliar with their lasting roles in shaping Native territories and histories, might see their only consequences today in the ghost towns they left behind. Yet, both historic and present gold extraction present another legacy. Too often, when miners left their by then unprofitable operations, they left behind a range of toxic chemicals, many times in rusting barrels. These remains now seep into the groundwater and threaten the water supply for both Native and non-Native rural communities, which often do not have the sophisticated equipment to filter out the pollutants.

Coal

Coal has played an important role for reservations for over a century. In the early twentieth century, it influenced how reservation lands were allotted. Under the 1909 and 1910 Coal Lands Acts, subsurface coal rights were retained by the federal government when surface rights were sold to individual owners. When reservations were newly allotted, subsurface rights to known mineral lands were thus reserved to tribal governments, although sometimes only for a specified time. Thus, whether or not tribal governments or individuals own subsurface rights depends in one part on when the lands were allotted, and under what circumstances. For example, the Osage kept the mineral rights under reservation lands communal property when their reservation was allotted in 1907. In some circumstances, however, neither the federal government nor the tribe knew about existent mineral resources at the time of allotment. Under some circumstances, lands could also be reclassified. For example, in 1915, President Wilson issued the following proclamation about lands on Fort Berthold:

> I, Woodrow Wilson, President of the United States of America, do hereby proclaim that all the lands in the Fort Berthold Indian Reservation, in North Dakota, which on account of their containing coal were reserved from allotment and other disposition under the aforesaid Act of June 1, 1910, and which, under the provisions of the aforesaid Act of August 3, 1914, have been classified as agricultural lands of the first class, agricultural lands of the second class and grazing lands shall be disposed of under the general provisions of the homestead laws and of said Acts of Congress and be opened to settlement and entry and be settled upon, occupied and entered in the following manner and not otherwise: Provided, That patents issued for such lands shall contain a reservation to the United States of any coal that such lands may contain, to be held in trust for the Indians belonging to and having tribal rights on the Fort Berthold Indian Reservation, but any entryman shall have the right at any time before making final proof of his entry, or at the time of making such final proof, to a hearing for the purpose of disproving the classification as coal land of the land imbraced in his entry, and if such land is shown not to be coal land a patent without reservation shall issue: Provided further, That homestead settlers may commute their entries under Section 2301 of the Revised Statutes by paying for the land entered at the appraised price.

When titles to allotments were transferred to individual American Indians in fee, and the subsurface rights had not been reserved to tribes, they also acquired the mineral rights in fee; these rights could then be sold with the surface rights. In some instances, like the above proclamation shows, the government only opened the surface rights of the so-called surplus lands for sale and reserved the mineral rights under those lands for the tribe. This also happened with lands the Crow ceded to the United States in 1904. On the Crow reservation, then, mineral rights are either held by individuals in fee ownership or by the United States in trust for the tribe. On the neighboring Northern Cheyenne tribe, however, the 1926 allotment act reserved mineral rights to the tribe for 50 years. In 1968, that act was amended and reserved mineral rights to the tribe in perpetuity.

One of the most famous – or infamous – cases of coal development is Black Mesa, on Hopi and Navajo lands. Here, a 1962 decision clarified that the Hopi and Navajo tribes shared mineral wealth. In 1966, Peabody Coal proposed a lease to the nations. Without an environmental impact statement or much discussion, the lease was approved. At issue in the dry Southwest was and is not just coal, however, but also water used to transport the coal through a slurry line to power stations. The lease was negotiated by the then Hopi attorney, John Boyden, who at the same time worked for Peabody, and heavily favored Peabody, to the point that the Bureau of Indian Affairs became increasingly worried. However, the energy for powering the developing cities in the Southwest had to come from coal power plants, and the coal for those came from Black Mesa. Coal has played a large part in tribal economics for the Navajo and Hopi over the past four decades. In 2016, the Navajo nation bought the Navajo Mine, which supplies coal to the Four Corners Power Plant. That mine alone had brought $35 million into the nation's general budget in 2015. At the same time, Dine Citizens Against Ruining Our Environment, the Sierra Club, and other organizations sued the BIA, the BLM, and other agencies over a planned enlargement of the mine that would extend its life-span for 25 years. Another power plant, the Navajo Generating Station, employed more than 350 Navajo tribal members in 2017. Its future, however, was in jeopardy as its owners decided to shut it down by 2019 and replace it with a natural gas-powered plant. A closure would also shut down the Kayenta mine that feeds the plant. Together, that would mean the loss of about 850 full-time jobs for Navajo tribal members. It would also mean the loss of $54 million in royalties and water fees for the Navajo and Hopi tribes. On the other hand, the closure of this one plant would mean that 8.6 million tons of CO_2 would no longer be emitted per year, together with mercury, selenium, and arsenic.

Decisions on natural resource development do not only create divisions within tribes, such as the DINE CARE or Hopi traditionalists against their respective tribal councils, but also between tribes. In 2016, for example, the Army Corps of Engineers rejected a permit for the building of a coal shipment port on Pudget Sound in Washington. The Corps did so because of an appeal from the nearby Lummi nation, which feared that the port might jeopardize its fishery, a treaty right. The port had been proposed by Cloud Peak Energy, which wanted to export coal mined on the Crow reservation. Cloud Peak had leased 1.4 billion short tons of coal from Crow in 2013, a deal that paid the poverty-stricken tribe $3.75 million and promised $10 million more. Coal development in Indian country follows the same complex decision making patterns as elsewhere, with the exception that some tribes – and their members – are dependent on coal development, an income that cannot be shifted to another resource in their nation.

Timber

Like coal, timber shaped policies and land ownership. The Supreme Court, in the 1873 decision, United States v Cook, decided that the federal government owned timber from Native lands. That decision also said that Native timber could only be cut to clear lands for agricultural purposes, not for sale alone. The decision was reversed in 1938, but the early intent of federal policy – to turn woodland tribes into farmers – becomes clear. By 1889, the President could authorize Indian tribes to cut and sell dead timber on their lands; other exceptions soon followed, such as an authorization for Ojibwe in Minnesota to sell timber from their allotments in 1904. In Minnesota, timber payed a large role in the allotment process. Under the Nelson Act of 1889, which aimed to resettle all Ojibwe to White Earth and Red Lake, timber lands were not to be allotted, but to be offered for sale. Thus, timber as a valued resource directly influenced the dispossession of Native lands. Timber would play a large role again under Termination, roughly 50 years later. Both the Klamath in Oregon and the Menominee in Wisconsin were affected by the connection of timber to land and sovereignty, although in different ways.

When the Klamath were terminated in 1954, tribal members were given two choices: to choose to withdraw from the tribe, or to remain within a diminished tribe, with a trust relation-ship no longer with the federal government, but the United States National Bank in Portland. Those tribal members that withdrew would have to paid for the loss of their rights, especially their rights to land; their rights to tribal lands would be sold and they would get the cash value. This value was mostly dependent on timber; the reservation owned 750,000 acres of forest lands. Managed by the BIA on a sustainable-yield base, this forest was paying an income of about $2 million per year. However, of the 2133 adult tribal members, 1649 elected to leave the tribe; 74 voted to remain, and the 410 who did not vote were classified with them. The majority of those voting to leave – about 90% of them – elected to do so because it was unclear what kind of "management plan" they would face if they stayed, that is, they preferred sure cash rather than insecurity in the future. In order to pay those leaving the tribe, the federal government sold 617,000 acres of timber lands; 525,680 of those acres, it sold to itself, and created the Winema National Forest. When the remaining tribal members voted against the bank as their trustee in 1969 and in 1971, the federal government and the trustee took this as a vote in favor of terminating the trust altogether, and in 1973 bought the rest of the land from the trustee for $60 million. Ultimately, their resources – the timber lands that sustained them – had proven so valuable that the Klamath were dispossessed of them. The Klamath, however, were at least successful in keeping their treaty rights to hunt, fish, and trap on their former reservation lands in the 1979 Kimball v. Callahan decision.

In the same year that the rest of the Klamath land was dispossessed, 1973, another Native nation, the Menominee of Wisconsin, were restored from termination. The Menominee had also been terminated in 1954, and like the Klamath, their main resource had been timber. In contrast to the Klamath, however, the Menominee assets were not sold off, but converted into Menominee Enterprises, Inc. (MEI), and the former reservation was converted into its own county, Menominee County, entirely owned by MEI. Every one of the 3280 members of the tribe in 1954 received a bond and 100 shares of stock in the company. In 1969, Determina-tion of Rights and Unity for Menominee Stockholders (DRUMS) was founded to take over control of MEI, which was exerted largely by a non-Menominee voting trust representing minor and incompetent stockholders. MEI had been faced with a company that needed investments and repairs to its operations, yet there was no money to inject. The new county had to close the hospital and its own power station, and eventually started to sell lands, most often to non-Menominee. However, because the land had not been sold off to individual owners or the federal government, the Menominee had a land base to return into a reservation upon restoration. Since the restoration of the tribe, the Menominee have used their timber assets to build a successful sustainable forestry program.

Other tribes who manage large timber resources as economic assets, for example Alaska Native Corporations, have come under criticism for practicing clear cutting. Those critiques are often similar to the critique of Native peoples engaging in coal mining; indigenous peoples, when not engaging in practices that can be seen as models for ecological preservation, are sometimes seen as removed from traditional culture and no longer indigenous. Such critiques depart from a romantic view of indigenous peoples and hold them to different standards from those for non-industrial societies. Thus, they are seen as non-modern. Similarly, when the Makah expressed interest in revitalizing whale hunting, and harvested a whale in 1999, one of the responses was that no Native people would hunt whales because indigenous peoples always respected the environment. What "respect" means, however, or "sacred," is a cultural question. Some people have advanced the notion that the Lakota should not kill bison, for example, because traditionally the animals were sacred to them. This is a confusion of the Christian concept of "sacred" and the Lakota concept of "wakan," which has been translated as "sacred" but carries different connotations.

Water

Water is the ultimate natural resource because without water, there is no life. As one of the fundamental bases for human, animal, and plant life, water – and more than that, clean water – is thus an existential resource. Apart from the use of water for drinking water, for numerous daily tasks, and for the sustenance of the whole ecosystem in which humans lived and live, water has been and is used for the extraction and production of other resources. Industrial mining, agriculture, and fisheries depend on water supplies, as does one of the newest technologies of resource extraction, hydraulic fracturing. Water is also uses as a resource to produce electric and mechanical power, and to create recreational spaces. For over a century, the most common way to exploit water as a resource has been to build dams. Many of these dams have impacted Native communities; in the Pacific Northwest, they have disrupted salmon runs, in arid areas, they have often led to the drying up of rivers, and in many places places, they have flooded significant sites and homelands. In a few cases, some of these concerns have been addressed over the past few decades by dam removals. However, arguably nowhere has a systematic use of water affected Native communities on a larger scale than along the upper Missouri River. In the Dakotas and Montana, large-scale dams flooded reservation lands and ruined reservation economies with devastating consequences.

After the early twentieth century had seen a series of floods impacting the growing cities of the lower Missouri River valley, the Bureau of Reclamation and the Corps of Engineers developed the so-called Pick-Sloan Plan to control the river in 1944. The plan was heavily dependent on large mainstream dams, which would be used to create flood control, regulate water flows, produce electricity, and provide recreational opportunities. The plan was heavily influenced by the model of the Tennessee Valley Authority that had been used to modernize Kentucky and Tennessee. The Corps of Engineers had already completed one mainstream dam in 1940, the Fort Peck Dam. As President Roosevelt outlined during his 1934 remarks at the construction site, however, the dam was:

> only a small percentage of the whole dream covering all of the important watersheds of the Nation. One of those watersheds is what we call the watershed of the Missouri River, not only the main stem of the Missouri, but countless tributaries that run into it and countless other tributaries that run into those tributaries. Before American men and women get through with this job, we are going to make every ounce and every gallon of water that falls from the Heaven and the hills count before it makes its way down to the Gulf of Mexico.

The Pick-Sloan dams were to be the fulfillment of that dream. Because dams flood riverbeds, and because on the arid plains, towns were located along rivers, the mainstream dams were planned in a way that would impact the least people, or at least not the people that counted po-litically. The capitols of North and South Dakota, Bismarck and Pierre, were thus to be spared. Instead, the dams were planned in a way that Lewis and Clarke Lake, behind Gavins Point Dam, would begin north of Yankton, Lake Francis Case, behind Fort Randall Dam, would end south of Chamberlain, Lake Sharpe, behind Big Bend Dam, would end south of Pierre, Lake Oahe, behind the Oahe Dam, would begin just north of Pierre, but end south of Bismarck, and Lake Sakakawea, behind the Garrison Dam, would be located north of Bismarck. This had the effect that the flooded areas would affect reservations. Lewis and Clarke Dam flooded parts of the Santee Reservation in Nebraska, and Lake Francis Case flooded parts of the Yankton Reservation in South Dakota, although these lakes predominantly flooded non-Indian lands. Lake Sharpe flooded much of the Crow Creek Reservation and the Lower Brule Reservation; the lands flooded by Lake Oahe include the length of the Cheyenne River and Standing Rock reservations; and Lake Sakakawea cuts right through the Forth Berthold reservation in North Dakota.

While for the federal government, this landscape of flooding had the advantage that much of the affected territory was held in trust and could thus easily be bought from itself, the consequences, especially for the more upstream reservations, were devastating. Not only were the lands along the river the ones most suited for agriculture, they were also the timber lands, providing access to not only trees for wood, but also as shelter in the winter. When the people – and with them their cattle, and their economy – had to move out of the river valley onto the plains uplands, it was not only their homes and significant cultural sites that were destroyed, but also their economies. This had lasting effects. The tribes were also underpaid for their lands, as the federal government basically negotiated with itself, and they did not see any benefits that had been promised, such as cheaper electricity rates or an influx of tourists. Those benefits instead went to the states surrounding them. While non-Indians, too, had to move, these personal hardships did not affect state economies; for the reservations, however, the dream that President Roosevelt had coveted in 1934 turned out to be a nightmare of underdevelopment. Fort Berthold, for example, which had been largely self-sufficient before the building of the Garrison Dam, became dependent on federal assistance. When, 30 to 50 years after the fact, the federal government acknowledged that it had not reimbursed the tribes fairly for the lands it had taken, restitution funds came too late in many cases because while the surrounding communities had been building their economies, the reservations had not been able to do so.

Uranium

Uranium became an extremely valued resource during the Second World War. The federal government tried to become independent from foreign sources of uranium and in 1948 guaranteed not only a price for uranium mined in the United States, but also that it would buy all uranium ore extracted. The government was the only buyer of uranium until 1966. Much of the uranium mined in the following decades came from the southwest, but significant amounts were also mined elsewhere, especially the Hanford area on the Columbia River and, among other places, the northern plains, where Canada, too, extracted uranium. Plans to build new or reopen old uranium mines on the plains are still ongoing, and with those plans come dangers of water contamination and other risks to Native communities or their treaty lands. Because uranium is radioactive, and because some waste products of uranium milling have half-lives of 4.5 billion years, even old mines and mills pose a threat. Both during and after operations, tailing piles, tailing ponds, the burning of uranium-containing coal seams, milling itself, and the loading of materials into trucks and railroad cars can lead to the contamination of large areas by water and air. Old tailing heaps – often tens of thousands of cubic yards – were also used as cheap backfill materials for housing developments and other uses. The focus on impacts on Native communities has been in the southwest, however, especially on the Navajo reservation, where both environmental and working conditions led to massive contamination and exposure during the uranium boom that lasted into the early 1980s. About 75% of the 15,000 abandoned uranium mines in western states that the Environmental Protection Agency (EPA) identified are on federal and tribal lands. They produced over 225 million tons of uranium ore between 1950 and 1989. The Navajo Nation had four uranium mills and over a thousand mines on its lands, where almost 4 million tons or uranium ore were extracted until 1986.

When the uranium boom started, the Navajo Nation was in the middle of several social forces that were exerting pressures on its tribal members to get wage-earning industrial jobs. For those without a higher education who wanted to stay on the reservation, jobs in uranium mines were very attractive in the 1950s. They blasted the rocks, built mine support structures, loaded the materials for transport, and worked in the mills. Few adult Navajos at that time spoke English or had a formal education. They did not know about the dangers of radiation, and often, they had no protective gear. The Public Health Service began a study on the risks of lung cancer for uranium miners in the southwest in 1950, but the only result for the miners were some brochures distributed in 1959. Scientists knew that radon caused lung cancer from data in European uranium mining, but efforts to require ventilation in uranium mines were blocked. When, in the early 1960s, Navajo mine workers, as well workers from other tribes and non-Indians in the area, started to die of lung cancer, it was their widows who started to organize complaints. The Navajo Nation had outlawed unions on the reservation in 1958. Federal standards for radon in uranium mines were finally set in 1969.

Although the last uranium mine in Navajo territory closed in 1986, long-term consequences are evident. In 2007, the EPA, together with the BIA, the IHS, and other agencies, developed a five-year plan to address contamination issues in collaboration with the Navajo Nation. A second five-year plan followed in 2014. These efforts address the most immediate threats and emphasize outreach and education efforts. As the 2014 five-year plan points out, although mining and milling are discontinued:

> the legacy of these activities remains, including more than 500 abandoned uranium mine claims with thousands of mine features such as pits, trenches, holes, etc., and some homes that were built from mine and mill site materials. In addition, there are drinking water sources with elevated levels of uranium, radium, and other metals. Uranium and other elements (selenium, arsenic, etc.) are associated with mine and mill sites, although the same constituents occur naturally at elevated levels in rock, soil, surface water, and groundwater across the Navajo Nation and the broader Four Corners region. Health effects as a result of non-occupational exposure to these elements can include lung cancer and impaired kidney function.

Many communities will have to live with the consequences of uranium mining for decades and centuries to come. Native communities often do not have the money or the visibility to address the lingering issues.

Oil and Gas

Some Native communities have been involved in oil and gas extraction on their lands for a long time. The Osage saw an infamous oil boom in the early twentieth century; the Navajo have been involved in oil and gas extraction for almost a century. For many tribes, early involvement meant to make decisions on leasing. While some Native people worked in the oil industry, tribes themselves were not engaged in the industry. This, however, did not mean that there were no consequences for communities. Tribes like the Osage, whose lands were now recognized to be extremely valuable, saw new threats over land rights and fraud on a large scale by individuals who wanted to get "their" share of the Indians' oil.

In the 1950s, when Canada and the United States began to take a keen interest in the subarctic and arctic regions, oil and gas was discovered in Alaska and the Canadian north. Native communities became the focus of anthropological investigations, often commissioned by the respective governments, often focusing on what was perceived to be a sudden encounter of modernity and insulated indigenous lifeways, In reality, northern peoples had interacted with consecutive modernities for centuries; the fur trade centering around Hudson Bay and the Russian posts along the northwest coast had seen to that. This became clear when Native communities started to protest the consequences of oil and gas development on their lands, especially the building of pipelines across their territories. This was the background for the

Berger Report, Judge Thomas R. Berger's report on the Mackenzie Valley Pipeline Inquiry, published as a book, *Northern Frontier, Northern Homeland*, which has served as a model for engaging indigenous peoples ever since. Berger wrote that:

> I went to the North assuming that the pipeline represented the means of bringing northerners into the mainstream of the Canadian economy. My assumption was shared by most Canadians. But as the hearings went on, I realized that the environmental losses would be severe, the opposition of the native people unyielding, and the issues we faced far more difficult that we had thought. By the time the hearings were concluded, I realized that it would be necessary in my report to recommend against the pipeline.

He pointed out that while the pipeline construction would offer Native people "unprecedented opportunities for wage employment," a majority in the communities was afraid of what the pipeline would bring in addition: "an influx of construction workers, more alcoholism, tearing of the social fabric, injury to the land, and the loss of their identity as a people." In his report, Berger laid the foundation for the current ideal of free, prior, and informed consent by Native peoples for infrastructure and extraction projects on their lands. He predicted that without clear agreements on project size, lands affected, and a settlement of all land rights, projects would inevitably impact communities in negative ways:

> You can sign an agreement or you can impose one; you can proceed with land selection; you can promise the native people that no encroachments will be made upon their lands. Yet you will discover before long that such encroachments are necessary. You can, in an agreement, promise the native people the right to rebuild the native economy. The influx of whites, the divisions created among the native people, the preoccupations of the federal and territorial governments, faced with the problems of pipeline construction and the development of the corridor, would make fulfillment of such a promise impossible.

While the Mackenzie Valley energy corridor was never built, subsequent project developments elsewhere have proven Berger right.

Under the policies of self-determination, tribes in the United States were able to find better ways to exercise their sovereignty. One consequence of that was the 1975 founding of the Council of Energy Resource Tribes (CERT). Peter MacDonald, Navajo tribal chairman and newly elected director of CERT, compared CERT to "a domestic OPEC" in 1977. Two years later, CERT hired the former Iranian deputy minister of economics and oil, Ahmed Kooros, as chief economist. Kooros thought that like OPEC member countries in 1968, Indian tribes were both similarly underdeveloped and had the energy resources to improve their situation. MacDonald's goals included "self-sufficiency for his impoverished, welfare-supported tribe, a strong, stable tribal economy and, in the long run, U.S. commonwealth status for an independent Navajo nation." After the Iranian revolution, CERT abandoned the comparison to OPEC; the image that all Native tribes lived on resource rich lands and thus would no longer need federal moneys, however, became a trope in the Reagan administration. In fact, a BIA report pointed out that fewer than 15% of all Native people lived on reservations where energy resources might someday provide significant enough revenues to improve the economy.

The initial vision of CERT as energy-rich and therefore powerful nations on the level of OPEC has not yet been realized, in part because tribes' sovereignty is limited by the federal government. The discussions on coal and uranium have showed some of the controversies. However, in the decades since 1975, some tribes with oil and gas reserves have gone from offering leases on their mineral rights to owners of exploration and extraction companies. At the forefront of this movement have been the Southern Ute, although the Jicarilla Apache were the first tribe to purchase oil wells. Just as with coal, direct tribal involvement in oil extraction is a highly political decision. It can offer economic profits, but it can also be seen as a break with traditional values toward the environment, and thus a break with traditional culture. While many tribal members need money, quite a few also fear the consequences of accidents, leaks, spills, water consumption, landscape changes, and participation in a global capitalist economy.

In the second decade of the twenty-first century, pipelines once again became the focus point of controversies over energy development. The Keystone XL pipeline raised other issues, such as whether the United States should import oil from tar sands mining that is threatening in itself First Nations communities in Canada. The Sandpiper pipeline in Minnesota thrust into the spotlight issues of tribal sovereignty. And the Dakota Access pipeline raised questions of tribal consultation and free, prior, and informed consent. A part of all these discussions, of course, was the looming background of climate change, fueled by fossil fuels. Indigenous peoples are often famous for looking seven generations into the future; indigenous nations, too, however, have to make economic decisions within a capitalist market that favors short-term perspectives.

Apart from environmental impacts, energy booms in rural areas, especially in indigenous communities, very often create social issues beyond the control of local societies. An influx of relatively wealthy, most often single, young men into underdeveloped communities creates the need for entertainment. This often leads to problems with drugs and prostitution. At the same time, the presence of more money and more demand can lead to an inflation of prices for goods that are needed by indigenous communities. Some members of tribes may now receive royalties for their own leases; others, however, are not better off, yet need to deal with inflationary prices that affect everything from housing to groceries. As such, resource booms can lead to divisions in the community and undermine the social cohesion that often served as an economic safety net.

Environmental Values

How indigenous communities and individuals react to energy development depends on many factors, as does whether these communities can take advantage of the opportunities and avoid the risks. Control over one's own resources, education, previous experiences with booms, and perspectives on relations to the environment are all extremely important. In this context, it is important to realize that indigenous peoples live in the midst of modernity, and do not have an inborn, instinctual specific relationship with nature. As for anybody else, environmental values are cultural values, and as such they are learned and subject to change. With 80% of

Native people living off reservations in the United States, it should not come as a surprise that industrialization, alienation, and commodification affect indigenous peoples, too. And just like there are many non-Native people who have strong ties to their environments, so do many American Indians. Sometimes, Native and non-Native people work together to protect the environment, sometimes they work together to extract natural resources, and sometimes Native as well as non-Native peoples have internal discussions about which is more important. The answer might come down to how people react to a question that Frank T'Seleie asked of the developers of the proposed Mackenzie Valley pipeline in 1975:

> You are coming to destroy a people that have history of thirty thousand years. Why? For twenty years of gas? Are you really that insane? [...] You can destroy my nation, Mr. Blair, or you could be a great help to give us our freedom. Which choice do you make, Mr. Blair? Which choice do you make for your children and mine?

But the answer given by others has never been enough. Instead, Native peoples have always given their answers, too, and acted accordingly, as far as they were allowed to, and sometimes, when the stakes seemed high enough, without asking whether they were allowed to. They did and do not always agree on the answer, but it behooves others to listen.

Sources and Further Readings

Marjane Ambler. 1990. *Breaking the Iron Bonds. Indian Control of Energy Development.* Lawrence: University Press of Kansas.
James Robert Allison, III. 2015. *Sovereignty for Survival. American Energy Development and Indian Self-Determination.* New Haven: Yale University Press.
Elspeth Young. 1995. *Third World in the First. Development and Indigenous Peoples.* London: Routledge.
Sherry L. Smith and Brian Frehener (eds.). 2010. *Indians and Energy. Exploitation and Opportunity in the American Southwest.* Santa Fe: School for Advanced Research Press.
John C. Bodley. 2008. *Victims of Progress.* Fifth edition. Lanham: AltaMira Press.

Coal
Saleem H. Ali. 2003. *Mining, the Environment, and Indigenous Development Conflicts.* Tucson: University of Arizona Press.
U.S. General Accounting Office. 1986. *Surface Mining. Issues Associated with Indian Assumption of Regulatory Authority.* GAO/RCED-86-155.
Charles F. Wilkerson. 1996. "Home Dance, the Hopi, and Black Mesa Coal: COnquest and Endurance in the American Southwest." *BYU Law Review*, Vol. 2, pp. 449-482.

Uranium
Sandra E. Bregman and Gerald W. Cormick. 1982. "Uranium Mining on Indian Lands." *Environment: Science and Policy for Sustainable Development*, Vol. 24, no. 7, pp. 6-33.
Anita Moore-Nall. 2015. "The Legacy of Uranium Development on or Near Indian Reservations and Health Implications Rekindling Public Awareness." *Geosciences*, Vol. 5, pp. 15-29.

Doug Brugge. 2002. "The History of Uranium Mining and the Navajo People." *American Journal of Public Health*, Vol. 92, No. 9, pp. 1410-1419.

U.S. Government. 2014. *Federal Actions to Address Impacts of Uranium Contamination in the Navajo Nation*. https://www.epa.gov/sites/production/files/2016-06/documents/nn-five-year-plan-2014.pdf

U.S. Government. 2008. *Health and Environmental Impacts of Uranium Contamination in the Navajo Nation. Five-Year Plan*. https://www.epa.gov/sites/production/files/2016-06/documents/nn-5-year-plan-june-12.pdf

Timber

Thomas Davis. 2000. *Sustaining the Forest, the People, and the Spirit*. Albany: SUNY Press.

Susan Hood. 1972. "Termination of the Klamath Indian Tribe of Oregon." *Ethnohistory*, Vol. 19, No. 4, pp. 379-392.

NARF. 2002. "The Long Struggle Home: The Klamath Tribe's Fight to Restore Their Land, People and Economic Self-Sufficiency." *NARF Legal Review*, Vol. 27, No. 1, pp. 1-11.

Stephen J. Hertzberg. 1978. "The Menominee Indians: Termination to Restoration." *American Indian Law Review*, Vol. 6, No. 1, pp. 143-186.

Nancy Oestreich Lurie. 1972. "Menominee Termination: From Reservation to Colony." *Human Organization*, Vol. 31, No. 3, pp. 257-270.

Ronald L. Trosper. 2007. "Indigenous Influence on Forest Management on the Menominee Indian Reservation." *Forest Ecology and Management*, Vol. 248, pp. 134-139.

Water

Michael L. Lawson. 1982. *Dammed Indians. The Pick-Sloan Plan and the Missouri River Sioux, 1944-1980*. Norman: University of Oklahoma Press.

Mark W. T. Harvey. 1996. "North Dakota, the Northern Plains, and the Missouri Valley Authority" in Janet Daily Lysengen and Ann M. Rathke (eds.), *The Centennial Anthology of North Dakota History, Journal of the Northern Plains*. Bismarck: State Historical Society of North Dakota, pp. 376-389.

Franklin D. Roosevelt: "Remarks at Fort Peck Dam, Montana.," August 6, 1934. Online by Gerhard Peters and John T. Woolley, *The American Presidency Project*. http://www.presidency.ucsb.edu/ws/?pid=14735

Oil and Gas

Kathleen P. Chamberlain. 2000. *Under Sacred Ground. A History of Navajo Oil, 1922-1982*. Albuquerque: University of New Mexico Press.

Thomas R. Berger. 1988. *Northern Frontier, Northern Homeland*. Revised Edition. Vancouver: Douglas & McIntyre.

Mel Watkins (ed.). 1980. *Dene Nation. The Colony Within*. Toronto: University of Toronto Press.

Kent Demaret. 1979. "There's Fuel in Them Thar Hills, and Peter MacDonald's Indians May Now Get Theirs" *People* Magazine, September 3, 1979.

Health in American Indian Communities
Birgit Hans

Health issues in Indian country are as complex as the other aspects of American Indian life. There are Native people who believe exclusively in western medicine and would never consider seeking advice from a tribal healer, and then there are those who utilize both tribal practitioners and medical doctors for health care. In some cases, Native spirituality and western medicine work together successfully for the benefit of the patients.

Sacred Practitioners

All American Indian cultures recognize that there is sacred knowledge and honor those that are the guardians of this knowledge. While Christian churches have attempted to spread their sacred knowledge which is contained in the Bible and accessible to everyone, American Indian cultures consider some sacred knowledge restricted to sacred practitioners. Not even every member of the tribe has the right to access such knowledge. In some cases, the sacred knowledge is owned by an individual outright, and his or her disposal of that knowledge cannot be questioned.

Tribes have their own names for spiritually powerful people who also have the power to heal. The Dine refer to them as singers, the Lakota as medicine men, the Ojibway as Mide priests of the Grand Medicine Society, the Shawnee as dreamers, to name just a few. How these sacred practitioners acquire their ability to heal depends again on the tribe. In some tribes healers go through an apprenticeship, in others they have a vision that gives them their healing powers, and in still others the power to heal is transferred to them by someone else, etc.

In Dine culture, for example, there are a number of sacred specialists. An individual or a family will approach a diagnostician, who is either a hand trembler, a star gazer, or a crystal gazer, to find out what ceremony is needed to restore the patient to physical health and spiritual harmony. The diagnostician, in turn, recommends which of the multi-day chantways (ceremonies) must be performed. It is not clear how many chantways still exist today; some have not been handed on and some are no longer completely known to singers. Each chantway relates to an event in the oral tradition of the Dine and consists of songs, prayers, purification, and sandpaintings. In addition, the singer uses herbs, prayer plumes, bundles, and other sacred objects. Mistakes made by the singer affect the individual being treated as well as the entire community and, instead of curing the illness, may cause more illness and even death. The ceremonies last from five to nine days and should only be performed in the area between the sacred mountains which was specifically created for them by the Holy People. These chantways are costly, and the immediate and extended family will help to come up with the fee for a reputable singer and his helpers, the food necessary to feed the participants and visitors, and the gifts that are part of the giveaway.

The singer usually serves a long apprenticeship with a reputable singer or singers to learn all the songs, prayers, and the numerous complicated sandpaintings of each chantway. The fact that there are different versions is accepted by the Dine and does not devalue a ceremony. At the end of the apprenticeship, the apprentice will receive the necessary paraphernalia and will assemble his Mountain Earth bundle which contains earth from each sacred mountain as well as other objects.

Hosteen Klah (1867–1937) learned a number of different Navajo chantways throughout his life, but he only performed two, the Hail Chant and the Yeibechai/The Night Chant. In fact, he studied the Yeibechai for 26 years before he performed his first one by himself.[1] Frank Mitchell (1881–1967) learned the Blessingway from his father-in-law; he was known for his knowledge of every version of that particular chantway. In his autobiography, Frank Mitchell quoted the elders as saying about the importance of the ceremonies: "If you don't know any songs you have nothing to go by."[2] Being a sacred practitioner among the Dine requires great commitment and a sense of responsibility to the community at large. Contemporary singers continue to make it possible for the Dine to *walk in beauty*, i.e. to be in balance with the universe around them.

The medicine men of the northern Plains, on the other hand, acquire their healing powers through individual visions that are interpreted by elders and other medicine men, but they may also serve apprenticeships. The vision shows which spirit or spirits, animal or otherwise, will provide power to heal, how to heal, and what can be healed by this specific person. The objects shown in the vision are included in the medicine bundle that is part of the healing ceremony. The medicine men may also have helpers, for example in the Lakota Yuwipi ceremony the helper ties the medicine man up in a star quilt.

However, unlike among the Dine, the responsibility rests with the individual who had the vision. One of the most famous Lakota medicine men is probably Black Elk (c. 1863–1950) who received his vision at a young age and found that you cannot ignore such a vision and reject the responsibility to your people that comes with it. The needs of the community will always supersede the needs of your family. Joseph Eagle Elk (1931–1991), a contemporary Lakota medicine man who took many years to find the meaning of his vision, described how his obligations to any person asking for help almost destroyed his marriage and affected his own children. He also talks about the economic hardships that he and his family faced, since, unlike in Dine culture where a fee for the singer is agreed upon beforehand, there is no fixed fee for the services of the medicine man in Lakota culture. The healer is dependent on the gifts of his patients.[3]

Ceremonies

During the summer months, the tribes of the northern and southern Plains celebrate the Sun Dance[4] which was known by a variety of names before the second half of the nineteenth century. Even though Sun Dances take different forms, they all originally ensured the continuation of the buffalo and of the people who celebrate the ceremony. Today the dancers continue to pray to the creator for the well-being of the group and their people, even though they may also have individual reasons for participating in a Sun Dance, such as to give thanks for spiritual help that they received during difficult times, to ask for help, and to pray for someone's health. Spectators of Sun Dances add their prayers to those of the dancers as well, and during some Sun Dances, as for example in the Crow one, there are specific times for doctoring people. Everyone's prayers are needed and welcomed. Usually, dancers commit themselves to participate for a number of years, most often four years.

Sun Dances differ in many ways, but there are some broad commonalities. Each ceremony has a sponsor and is led by a spiritual leader who has the necessary sacred knowledge; the spiritual leader carries the responsibility for the Sun Dance. There is also a specific body of songs and specific rituals related to the Sun Dance; variations are tribally specific. Each Sun Dance uses a sacred tree that is centered in the circular arbor, and uses either a buffalo hide or skull or both to place in the sacred tree or at its base. While some Sun Dances permit the participation of women and or children, the majority of the dancers is still male. Some Sun Dances include piercing and dragging of buffalo skulls and some do not; piercing is part of some cultural traditions on the Plains and not of others. However, the sacredness of the ceremony demands a total spiritual commitment from the dancers and spectators, basically from everyone who is on the Sun Dance ground.

It is futile to speculate which American Indian culture on the Plains celebrated the Sun Dance first. Tribes all had some form of what came to be known as the Sun Dance in the second half of the nineteenth century, and elements of the sacred ceremony were exchanged between various tribes. Take the Crow Nation for example; their Sun Dance in the nineteenth century was sponsored by those who were seeking spiritual power to avenge themselves on their enemies. Therefore, this Sun Dance was not performed on an annual basis. In 1875, this original Crow Sun Dance was performed for the last time. For the next 66 years, the Crow did not celebrate the Sun Dance at all, until the Shoshoni Sun Dance was brought to the Crow Reservation from the Wind River Reservation in 1941. Since then the ceremony has been pledged every year. Thomas Yellowtail, the well-known Crow medicine man who was involved in returning the Sun Dance to his people, unequivocally states the importance of the ceremony to his people: "It is only through the strict observance that our tribe and the whole world can stay close to Acbadadea [Maker of All Things Above]. . . . It is only through prayer and the observance of the sacred rites that the world can continue."[5] For many tribes today, the annual Sun Dance is the most important single ceremony of the year. Like other ceremonies on the northern Plains, the Sun Dance is not a monolith but changes in accordance with the cultural needs of the people who celebrate it.

It is impossible to discuss American Indian spirituality and healing on the northern Plains without mentioning the sweatlodge, sacred bundles, and tobacco. The sweatlodge, a small dome-shaped structure, is used for purification purposes, and people usually enter the sweatlodge in preparation for a ceremony, but it can be used at any time that people feel a need to pray to the sacred beings and to purify themselves. It is often used to ward off evil and illness. There are a number of songs associated with the sweatlodge as well, and someone with the necessary spiritual knowledge will lead the prayers to the sacred beings. People leaving the sweatlodge feel reborn. Sage, sweatgrass, and cedar can also be used for purification purposes on the northern Plains.

Bundles are sacred objects of great spiritual power; people were and are usually instructed by visions on what the content of individual, family, clan, society, or tribal bundles should be, what the bundle's powers would be, what ceremonies they would be part of, and how they should be used. Bundles are considered living beings, and their spiritual powers demand respect. They are usually opened and spiritually renewed every year. How bundles are passed on varies from tribe to tribe. A vision will sometimes tell the owner of a bundle who is to be his successor, but sometimes bundles are purchased. There are tribal rules about passing on bundles.

And, finally, tobacco is used as an offering. In the form of smoke, it carries the peoples' prayers to the creator. However, its use also recognizes the interconnectedness of everything in the universe. Tobacco is offered, for example, to the spirit of a dead animal by a hunter to recognize the sacrifice it has made for humans; it appeases the water spirits before people set out to harvest wild rice; etc. Ceremonial tobacco is sacred.

American Indian spirituality is rich, complex, multi-faceted, and tribally specific. Even though there are sacred practitioners and ceremonies to ensure the well-being of the universe and the people that dwell in it, the individual is called upon to assume responsibility for the welfare of the people and the universe around him as well. This responsibility does not require a particular space, like a church building, or a particular context, like Sunday church services. However, it requires a constant commitment. It also mandates the acceptance of difference, i.e. of different religious ideas, since American Indian spiritualities do not advocate missionizing others, but merely ask for respect for their own belief systems.

Encounters with Non-Native Health Care

Early colonization is often associated with the spread of European diseases to which American Indians had no resistance. Smallpox, typhus, whooping cough, measles, influenza, and many others led to devastating losses in villages and camps. Entire tribes were wiped out by these pandemics. In recent years, there has been much discussion of whether these diseases were deliberately introduced as a means of biological warfare; however, there seems to be no conclusive evidence that that was the case.

The 1837 smallpox epidemic that greatly affected the northern Plains, particularly the Mandan, Hidatsa, and Arikara on the upper Missouri River, may serve as an example for how devastating these pandemics could be. Actually, the three tribes suffered devastating losses of human lives through several major smallpox epidemics; it is estimated that the Arikara were probably reduced by 75% in 1780 and that the 1837 smallpox epidemic almost wiped out the remaining Mandan. The Hidatsa fared slightly better than the other two tribes.[6] It is known that the smallpox arrived with the steamboat St. Peter, a vessel of the American Fur Company. The captain's decision to not quarantine the affected passengers and crew seems to have led to the spread of the disease when the steamboat landed at Fort Clark on the upper Missouri.

The horrifying loss of life on the upper Missouri River might have been prevented though. In 1832, Congress had passed the Indian Vaccination Act "to provide the means of extending the benefits of vaccination, as a preventative of smallpox, to the Indian tribes, and therefore, as far as possible, to save them from the destructive ravages of that disease."[7] The decision of what tribes were going to be vaccinated lay with Secretary of War Lewis Cass, and, according to federal documents, he excluded the Mandan, Hidatsa, Arikara, Assiniboins, Blackfeet, and Cree from the vaccination program. In fact, Cass used the Indian Vaccination Act as a way to further the economic and political goals of the United States frontier politics. The Mandan, Hidatsa, and Arikara had ceased to be important trading partners in the fur trade, and there had been incidents of hostility between the tribes and non-Natives. Even though all three tribes had signed treaties with the United States, the conflicts on the upper Missouri had been severe enough for Cass to label the tribes "aggressor nations." As Pearson points out:

> Most important, political processes and historical perceptions and problems exacerbated by the United States on the upper Missouri River were among the main contributors to Cass's decision to limit vaccinations to Lower Missouri River Indian nations. Another critical concept in Cass's decision making was his perception of the Upper Missouri River tribes as savage nations. In 1826, Cass claimed that these nations were beyond the pale of civilization, and in 1832 Cass undoubtedly felt that it was politically efficacious to avoid vaccination of the Upper Missouri River tribes.[8]

Consequently, he deliberately excluded them from the vaccination program, and the smallpox epidemic caused devastating losses on the northern Plains between 1837 and 1838.

Another early health issue that people tend to be familiar with is alcoholism. Alcohol was brought by early settlers and fur traders and used as a trade item early on. Many of the American Indian leaders objected to the practice, since they saw the devastation caused by alcohol, but the use of alcohol as a trade item continued through the centuries.

American Indians negotiated treaties with first the European settlers and later the Americans, but, contrary to popular belief, the treaties did not provide for American Indian health care. Some treaties may have provided for a doctor among the services guaranteed in the treaties, for example the services of a farmer and blacksmith, but these services were limited to a certain time period and could be revoked by the federal government. American Indian health services were established under the Snyder Act of 1921. It is not surprising that Congress never consulted with American Indian peoples as to their health care needs; they simply decided how tribal moneys held in trust by the federal government were to be spent, especially during this time of continuous westward expansion and assimilation.

The federal government made every effort between the 1880s and 1920s to suppress American Indian spirituality and healing on the reservations. Tribal healers and their patients were tried by the Courts of Indian Offenses for engaging in traditional practices. At the same time, health on the reservations was generally problematic. On the northern Plains, for example, the numbers of people affected by tuberculosis grew steadily as well as the number of people suffering from illnesses associated with malnutrition. Furthermore, reservations were swept by epidemics periodically. Despite an urgent need for health care on the reservations, the total number of physicians supported by the BIA on the reservations in 1880 was only 77.[9]

One example of such a physician was Charles Alexander Eastman, a Dakota Sioux, who had a medical degree from Boston University; he arrived on the Pine Ridge Reservation in South

Dakota in 1890. Eastman found his office empty of medical supplies and his patients surprised that he would examine them before handing out medicines; he describes his predecessor's office and medical treatments as follows: "My first official act was to close up the 'hole in the wall', like a ticket seller's window, through which my predecessor had been wont to deal out pills and potions to a crowd of patients standing in line, and put a sign outside the door telling them to come in."[10] It was to his advantage that he did not require an interpreter to communicate with the Lakota of the reservation as he had grown up speaking Dakota, but he also managed to establish a good relationship with them and some of the medicine men of the reservation:

> I had some interesting experiences with the Indian conjurers, or "medicine men," to use the names commonly given. I would rather say, mental healer or Christian scientist of our day, for the medicine man was all of that, and further he practiced massage or osteopathy, used the Turkish bath, and some useful vegetable remedies. But his main hold on the minds of the people was gained through his appeals to the spirits and his magnetic and hypnotic powers.
>
> I was warned that these men would seriously hamper my work, but I succeeded in avoiding antagonism by a policy of friendliness. Even when brought face to face with them in the homes of my patients, I preserved a professional and brotherly attitude. I recall one occasion when a misunderstanding between the parents of a sick child had resulted in a double call. The father, who was a policeman and a good friend of mine, urgently requested me to see his child; while the frantic mother sent for the most noted of the medicine men.
>
> "Brother," I said, when I found him already in attendance, "I am glad you got here first. I had a long way to come, and the children need immediate attention."
>
> "I think so too," he replied, "but now that you are here, I will withdraw."
>
> "Why so? Surely two doctors should be better than one," I retorted. "Let us consult together. In the first place, we must determine what ails the child.. Then we will decide upon the treatment." He seemed pleased, and I followed up the suggestion of a consultation by offering to enter with him the sweat bath he had prepared as a means of purification before beginning his work. After that, I had no difficulty in getting his consent to my treatment of the patient, and in time he became one of my warm friends. It was not unusual for him and other conjurers to call at my office to consult me, or "borrow" my medicine.[11]

Eastman's unusually respectful interactions with Lakota medicine men at a time when the federal government tried to assimilate the Lakota and the various Christian churches went so far as to destroy their sacred objects, such as sacred bundles and medicine pouches,[12] if they could, stem from his cultural understanding. He had grown up in Dakota ways and did not convert to Christianity until he became a student after the age of 17. Because of his growing up in traditional Dakota ways, he also understood the medicinal plants used by the Lakota medicine men had proven effective through the centuries. Vogel points out in *American Indian Medicine* that: "In the present work, confined to remedies used by both Indian and whites, more than 500 botanical drugs have been listed. Huron H. Smith listed more than 200 botanical remedies used by the Meskwaki tribe alone, of which very few are adventive plants."[13] The above quotation indicates that Eastman was at least willing to encourage the continued use of such remedies. Unfortunately, the majority of physicians who served on reservations did not have Eastman's insight.

Needless to say, the Sun Dances came under attack during the last decades of the nineteenth century. The piercing and suffering, the dancing and singing of the Sun Dance epitomized the "savage state" of American Indians to the Euroamerican observers, a re-affirmation that American Indian people on the northern Plains had to be civilized. The agents used Indian policemen, rations, and even jail in an attempt to stamp out Native spirituality. Consequently, the ceremonies, among them the Sun Dance, went underground and were performed in remote areas of the reservations at times when they were sure that there would be no interference. Of course, there were also those tribal members who converted to Christianity and gave up the old ways completely. If they possessed sacred knowledge and or sacred objects, the knowledge was not handed on and the objects were frequently disposed of and, while tribal members might not have approved of such decisions, they could not object to them. There were also those who converted to Christianity and still participated in the Sun Dance, since to them Christianity and Native spirituality had the same spiritual goals. A well-known example would be Black Elk, the famous Lakota medicine man, who gave up his healing under pressure from the Jesuit priests to become a Catholic catechist; however, at the end of his life, he managed to openly combine both belief systems to the dismay of the Jesuit priests.[14]

Early attempts to deal with the health issues American Indian peoples faced on the reservations were not very successful. "Congress passed the Snyder Act in 1921, providing explicit legislative authorization for federal health programs for Indians by mandating the expenditure of funds for 'the relief of distress and conservation of health . . . [and] for the employment of . . . physicians . . . for Indian tribes.' This provided the first formal authority for federal provision of health care services to members of all federally recognized tribes."[15] Subsequently, the Merriam Report of 1928 called attention to the pressing health issues on the reservations. For example, in the 1930s "Of 5,342 pupils, average 13 years, representing various tribes in 30 different localities in the Southwest, 74.1 per cent showed a positive tuber-culin test."[16] On the Pine Ridge Reservation in South Dakota approximately one third of the population suffered from tuberculosis at that time.[17] Finally, in 1954 health care for American Indian peoples became part of the Public Health Service. "The IHS [Indian Health Service] was established as an agency under the Public Health Service in 1955. As the IHS began to build and staff hospitals and health centers in or near AI/AN [American Indian/Alaska Native] communities, Indian health care began to improve. While the IHS has never been fully funded, its creation is one of the few termination era actions of the federal government that was helpful to Indian people."[18]

IHS is divided into 12 areas and serves the entire American Indian population both on reservations and in urban centers. In 2017, the IHS budget request was 6.6 billion dollars, up 402 million dollars from the previous year and 53% higher than in 2008.[19] This significant increase in the IHS budget is due in large part to President Obama's commitment to dealing with health disparities in American Indian communities. Despite the fact that more than half of the American Indian population lives in cities today, the funding for urban health care has always been extremely low, but the Urban Indian Health Program, which operates 34 programs in various cities with high Native populations, benefits from the Indian Health Care Improvement Act of 1976 and from line item increases of the IHS budget. These programs make health care available to American Indians who do not meet the eligibility criteria of IHS or live too far away from their reservations to seek medical help there.[20] Like the Native population on reservations, the urban American Indian population suffers from a number of health issues, among others diabetes, depression, alcoholism, and lack of health care for families.

Contemporary American Indian Health Issues

Diabetes has long been a major concern in Indian country. The statistics collected in 2014 speak for themselves: 15.0% of American Indians/Alaska Natives suffer from diabetes compared to 7.6% of whites, 9% Asian Americans, 12.8% Hispanics, and 13.2% Blacks.[21] In order to address this problem, the last three IHS budgets show line items (150 million dollars each) for programs on reservations and in urban centers to deal with the problem. While they have not lowered the diabetes rate, according to IHS statistics, they have significantly slowed the growth of diabetes numbers between 2006 and 2012: 15.2% to 15.9%. Some tribes suffer from higher diabetes rates than others. For instance, the Pima of Arizona have a diabetes rate of 38%, the highest in the United States.

Diabetes is difficult to combat with the high poverty rates on reservations; in 2014, American Indians and Alaska Natives had a poverty rate of 26% as compared to whites at 11% (Hispanics 25% and Blacks [28%]).[22] Diabetes programs, which can be found on every reservation today, are helpful, but high unemployment rates – 11.3% for American Indians in 2013 as compared to Whites at 6.9%[23] – prevent people from buying the kinds of foods that they should be eating, like fresh fruits and vegetables, lean meats, and whole-grain breads. In general, commodity programs on the reservations are trying to make better choices available to American Indians. However, Indian tacos remain a staple at least on the northern Plains; every household has the ingredients for them available among its staples, and they are cheap to make as well as tasty. Different reservations and regions have developed different comfort foods from the available rations and later commodity foods, but none of them seem very healthy. Keesic Douglas, an Ojibwa from Mnjikaning First Nation in Canada, who is a photographer, filmmaker and artist, developed four posters entitled "4 Reservation Food Groups." Each poster shows a stack, i.e. the same item stacked in four rows of threes. The items are Wonder Bread, Cheez Whiz, KAM (the Canadian version of spam), and Kool-Aid. Douglas says that these posters are based not only on his father's memories, but also that he got more than tired of eating spam as a child.[24] Nothing in the "4Reservation Food Groups" recommends it to a diabetic, but, if that is the only food available, diabetics and others will eat and drink it.

Tragically, diabetes still leads to loss of limbs, especially in Indian Country. For some American Indians who follow their traditional spirituality, surgery and other medical procedures cause contamination within their traditional world view. The Navajo people are one example for that. Their origin story states that a Navajo must face the Holy People as a complete person after death; he or she must physically be the same as when they were born. Therefore, amputations of limbs may resolve medical conditions, but the surgery itself and the disposal of a limb will cause spiritual problems. The same is true for transplants and other biomedical procedures. Donald Denetdeal, a traditional singer, explained this contamination in an interview in 2004:

> ***DD:*** The only thing that normally happens after part of the body had been removed is to seek a medicine man to have a ceremony done to correct some of those imbalances and to help them [surgical patients] mentally so that they can better accept whatever may have been done with them and also to . . . pray to the Holy People, pray to the gods or the divinities to help them heal. . . .
>
> ***MS:*** So, are you saying that having, like, your uterus or a limb removed creates an imbalance?
>
> ***DD:*** Yes, it does. . . . [I]n Navajo belief, any time that a foreigner cuts a body it needs to be corrected. And so Navajo, we believe that we should not be cut, or any kind of lacerations or operations or any kind of surgical procedures done to a Navajo body –
>
> ***MS:*** Any kind?
>
> ***DD:*** Any kind. . . . That would be considered a contamination with a foreigner.[25]

To deal with the spiritual contamination is even more important than the physical recovery from surgery for the Navajo. Some Navajo solve the problem by joining various Christian churches and the Native American Church which do not share the Navajo traditional ideas about the person after death.

The leading causes of death for adults (25–65 years) are unintentional injury, heart disease, diabetes, and cancer. Life expectancy is 4.4 years less than that of the general population, i.e. American Indians have a life expectancy of 73.7 years.[26] At the same time, 16.2% of American Indians are in fair or poor health.[27] The National Congress of American Indians points out on their demographics page that Native people die at higher rates than Americans from

- tuberculosis: 600% higher? Alcoholism: 510% higher? Diabetes: 189% higher
- vehicle crashes: 229% higher? Injuries: 152% higher? Suicide:625 higher[28]

The Indian Health Services may have seen an increased budget, but health disparities are obvious. Depression and high teenage suicide rates are a major part of the picture as well.

In the last decades, tribes have increasingly worked on health issues. The funding for the Indian Health Service has improved, but many needs of tribes remain unaddressed and health disparities remain. In order to solve some of them, the tribes need to develop some culturally appropriate programs, for example, to further curb alcoholism and to deal with the devastatingly high incidents of teenage suicides. However, health issues cannot be addressed in isolation; at the same time, tribes have to find ways to develop employment opportunities on the reservations and deal with some of the social issues, such as violence against women and the education gap.

Endnotes

1. Franc Johnson Newcomb. 1964. *Hosteen Klah: Navaho Medicine Man and Sand Painter*. Norman: University of Oklahoma Press.
2. Charlotte J. Frisbie and David P. McAllester, eds. 1980. *Navajo Blessingway Singer: The Autobiography of Frank Mitchell 1881-1967*. Tucson: University of Arizona Press. The quotation can be found on p. 193.
3. Gerald Mohatt and Joseph Eagle Elk. 2000. *The Price of a Gift: A Lakota Healer's Story*. Lincoln: University of Nebraska Press.
4. JoAllyn Archambault, "Sun Dance" in *Handbook of North American Indians*, Vol 13, Part 2. 2001. Washington: Smithsonian Institution, pp. 985-995 provides an excellent overview of the Sun Dance.
5. Michael Oren Fitzgerald (as told to). 1991. *Yellowtail: Crow Medicine Man and Sun Dance Chief*. Norman: University of Oklahoma Press, p. 103.
6. Mary Jane Schneider. 1994. *North Dakota Indians: An Introduction*. Dubuque, Iowa: Kendall/Hunt Publishers, p. 228.
7. J. Diane Pearson, "Lewis Cass and the Politics of Disease: The Indian Vaccination Act of 1832," *Wicazo Sa Review*, Vol. 18, No. 2 (Autumn 2003), p. 29 (footnote 1). My brief summary of the political dimensions of the smallpox epidemic is based on Pearson's article.
8. Pearson, "Lewis Cass and the Politics of Disease," p. 29.
9. The number of physicians stems from Shelton, "Legal and Historical Roots of Health Care . . .," p. 6.
10. Charles A. Eastman. 1977. *From Deep Woods to Civilization: Chapters in the Autobiography of an Indian*. Lincoln: University of Nebraska Press, pp.78-79.
11. Eastman, *From Deep Woods to Civilization*, p. 122.-123.
12. Mohatt and Eagle Elk, *The Price of a Gift*, pp. 9-11.
13. Virgil J. Vogel.1970. *American Indian Medicine*. Norman: University of Oklahoma Press, p.9.
14. Raymond J. DeMallie, ed. *The Sixth Grandfather: Black Elk's Teaching Given to John G. Neihardt*. Lincoln: University of Nebraska Press.
15. Shelton, "Legal and Historical Roots of Health Care . . .," p. 7.
16. Jason G. Townsend, "Disease and the Indian," *The Scientific Monthly*, December 1938, p. 487.
17. Gary C. Collins and Charles V. Mutschler. 2010. *A Doctor among the Oglala Sioux Tribe: The Letters of Robert H. Ruby, 1953-1954*. Lincoln: University of Nebraska Press, pp. lii-liii.
18. Shelton, "Legal and Historical Roots of Health Care . . .," p. 9.
19. www.hhs.gov/about budget/fy2017/budget-in-brief/ihs/index.html#overview
20. Indian Health Service (/index.cfm), www.ihs.gov/urban/aboutus
21. American Diabetes Association National Diabetes Statistics Report, 2014.
22. "One-in-four Native Americans and Alaska Natives are living in poverty," PewResearchCenter, www.pewresearch.org/fact-tank/2014/06/13/...
23. https://thinkprogress.org/the-unemployment-rate-for-native-americans-has-been-over-10-percent-for-five-years-8f9ef18flf18
24. Lisa Charleyboy and Mary Beth Leatherdale, eds. 2015. *Dreaming in Indian: Contemporary Native American Voices*. Toronto: annick press, pp. 16-17.
25. Maureen Trudelle Schwarz.2008. *"I Choose Life": Contemporary Medical and Religious Practices in the Navajo World*. Norman: University of Oklahoma Press, p.3.
26. Indian Health Service, www.ihs.gov/newsroom/factsheets/disparities/
27. www.cdc.gov/nchs/fastats/american-indian-health.htm
28. www.ncai.org/about-tribes/demographics

Gender in American Indian Communities
Birgit Hans

The national narrative of America is a gendered one; it is the story of the male explorer(s) or settler(s) on his or their inexorable way westward to create safe spaces for the females to follow, spaces where civilization can be established. Needless to say, their ideas of gender and gender roles were culturally learned and, therefore, reflected in most cases the Christian doctrine. They recognized highly rigid male and female gender roles; any variation to males acting within male gender roles and females acting within female gender roles was considered suspect and usually judged to be deviant and licentious. The colonists recorded such encounters and judged the individuals that did not fit into their cultural understanding of gender and gender roles as deviant anomalies. It was always the goal of the newcomers to stamp out these "unnatural" behaviors in American Indian cultures and to assimilate American Indians into American culture. Once American Indian peoples were confined to reservations and children went to schools, especially federal boarding schools, pressures increased on those outside the gender roles accepted by Euroamericans to conform. Conversions to Christianity also helped in making alternative gender roles increasingly invisible on the reservations and, finally, the establishment of the Courts of Indian Offenses in 1883 gave administrative and religious officials the legal authority and a framework to deal with so-called deviants.[1]

Many of the American Indian peoples that the Europeans and later the Euroamericans encountered during their expansion westward had a more complex understanding of gender and gender roles than those postulated by the white newcomers at the time of contact. As Roscoe points out: "The original peoples of North America, whose principles are just as ancient as those of Judeo-Christian culture, saw no threat in homosexuality or gender variance. Indeed they believed individuals with these traits made unique contributions to their communities."[2] In fact, the variations in gender roles were sometimes sanctioned in a tribe's origin story, and other tribes considered them sacred beings; different American Indian cultures had different ways of including people of alternative genders. For example, in the case of the Navajo the *nádleeh*, the non-childbearing twins, are responsible for technological advances – pottery making and wicker bottles. These twins were certainly treated with respect as important community members by others within the context of the emerging Navajo culture. Gender, therefore, "refers to culturally constructed social roles and identities in which sex is one defining element whose importance (and definition) varies."[3] In other words, alternative gender roles may include sexual relationships of people of the same gender or of different genders.

Sometimes the alternative genders were referred to as the third and fourth genders; some tribes might have had even more gender roles. The third gender usually included those males dressing as females and working in female gender roles, and the fourth was commonly made up of females dressing as males and doing male work. However, not everyone who occupied an alternative gender role actually cross-dressed. Tribes have their own terms to designate people of alternative genders, and most Two-Spirits prefer the tribally appropriate term, for example "agokwa" in Ojibwa, "winkte" in Lakota, "mih-dacha" in Mandan, and "t-coo-coo-a" in Fox-sauk.[4]

Until two decades ago, the term *berdache* was used to describe individuals identified as being part of an alternative gender. The term itself stems from the Indo-European language family and was associated with homosexuality in Europe and was in use there until the middle of the nineteenth century.[5] Today it is less acceptable to use the term, and the term *Two-Spirit* is the preferred one. As mentioned above, the complexities of the alternative genders mostly disappeared with the relentless pressures from the federal government and the various missionary societies. In his "Tribal Index of Alternative Gender Roles and Sexuality" Roscoe identifies 157 tribal groups from all across the United States as originally having had such alternative gender roles as well as the sources he used in his research.[6] His list is most likely incomplete though because, unless the information was recorded in the historic and anthropological record, it is unlikely to be retrieved today. It is likely that some Europeans and Euroamericans decided not to document information about alternative genders considering most non-Natives' attitudes toward gender fluidity.

While attempting to destroy gender roles that existed when they arrived on the shores of what is now the United States, Europeans also constructed gendered roles for American Indian peoples: the Noble Savage and the Princess on one side of the spectrum and the Savage Warrior and Squaw on the other. The Noble Savage is often the last of his tribe; he may lament the passing of his people, but he recognizes it as inevitable to make room for civilization. He may even support the white intruders against other tribes. Hollywood films like *Dances with Wolves* and *The Last of the Mohicans* support the stereotype of the Noble Savage. On the female side, the Indian Princess is probably the most prominent of the stereotypes, since Walt Disney made her world famous with the film "*Pocahontas*." The historic figure of *Pocahontas*, who is reputed to have saved Captain John Smith's life against her father Powhatan's will in Virginia in 1607, has little to do with the girl presented in the Disney version, except that in both versions of her life *Pocahontas* is said to have chosen to support the white man against her father's wishes. Unfortunately, there is no American Indian account of the event from that time. The image of the Indian Princess helping non-Native men against her own people has long been troublesome to American Indian women, since it implies that the Princess automatically recognizes the cultural superiority of the intruders and, therefore, chooses to ally herself with them. On the negative side of the stereotypes, the Savage Warrior and the Squaw share many characteristics. In westerns, for example, they are often associated with drunkenness, thievery, indiscriminate murder of Native and non-Native people alike as well as seduction and rape. Images of both men and women are highly sexualized today; even the Disney movie *Pocahontas* shows the heroine in a short, skimpy outfit that has little to do with traditional clothing and as the object of desire of both a Native and non-Native male.

These gendered stereotypes that continue to perpetuate themselves are especially troubling when considering the statistics about sexual violence suffered by American Indian women: one out of three Native women will experience sexual assault. Recently, Sashay Schettler, a member of The Three Affiliated Tribes, wrote the following in her analysis of the Princess stereotype in an alcohol advertisement:

> . . . images of "sexy squaws" are constantly presented in the media and in popular culture. These images perpetuate the image of Indian women as sex objects, which excuses sexual assault and manipulates the minds of the masses to adopt a "blame the victim" attitude. As a result of this external image, Indian women are then burdened and blamed for their own sexual assault. Scott Lyons remarks in his book *X-Marks: Native Signatures of Assent* that being "Indian was defined by deficiency," and therefore to [be] Indian is a bad thing. (Lyons 67) These images suggest to American Indian people and non-Indians that these stereotypes of deficiency represent Indians' full potential. If you are a female, then you are sexually promiscuous and available. If you are Native, then you immediately assume the role of an alcoholic. The danger here is that American Indians do not construct their own identity, but rather their identity is being constructed by outsiders, and then being broadcasted by cartoons and other forms of media with unhealthy consequences. Our education system and media do not illustrate that American Indians are productive and contributing members of society, but rather they are broadcasted as deficient, stereotypical images who are to blame for their own problems. This system of thought has insidious consequences for American Indian communities.[7]

Like Sashay Schettler, many American Indians feel that they are defined by non-Native people within this stereotypical framework. If people choose the Noble Savage/Savage Warrior route for their framework, they believe in male cultures devoid of women and children and in feather-bedecked Plains Indians on horses who are warriors forever. This male Indian culture is forever locked in physical conflict. The problem with these stereotypical portrayals is that it denies the contemporaneousness of American Indian cultures and, when issues like sports logo controversies and the Dakota Access Pipeline come up, the opinions of Native peoples are dismissed and too often they immediately become the enemy.

Traditional Gender Roles

In traditional American Indian cultures, the relationship of women and men were based on reciprocity, i.e. each gender recognized that the other contributed in essential and important ways to the survival of the family and the community. On the northern Plains, men provided important foodstuff by hunting, but so did the women by cultivating their gardens if that was their cultural tradition or by gathering foodstuff, such as prairie turnips and berries. The hide of the killed animals was important for shelter, clothing, and everyday items as well as sacred objects, but the hides needed to be tanned by the women and then turned into whatever was needed. Women and men needed to cooperate to survive. The division of labor was not absolute however.

Most of the property belonged in the women's sphere, as with the Hidatsa for instance. Women constructed and owned the earthlodges and tipis; women cultivated the gardens and decided what was to be done with the harvest, and the game that Hidatsa men killed belonged to the women once the men brought the meat into the village. Men owned the property that belonged to the men's sphere: their ceremonial objects, weapons, clothes, and horses, once horses became available on the northern Plains in the early 1700s. The Lakota did not garden, but the women owned their tipis and determined how the game that the men killed was to be distributed. The Dine (Navajo) of the Southwest, on the other hand, had a different concept of gendered spheres from cultures on the northern Plains. Among the Dine (Navajo), the women owned the sheep whose wool was important for weaving and as meat while both men and women worked in the corn fields. The hooghan, the traditional eight-sided log dwelling of the Dine, belonged to the women. Among their Hopi neighbors, the men worked the fields, but the corn was stored in the women's sphere of the pueblos and became part of their economic resources. The American Indian women's control over goods and foodstuff was very different from that of American women historically who gave up their right to own property individually on marriage. It was not until 1839 that the Married Women's Property Acts empowered American women to own property apart from their husbands; some states did not enact legislation in regard to women as property owners until the 1880s.[8]

In fact, in some cases American Indian women could become economically independent on the northern Plains by achieving special skills in the production of valued objects. In Hidatsa culture, young women would approach those with specialized knowledge of, for example, quillwork and ask to be taught the craft as well as the stories and other spiritual knowledge that were connected to quillwork. Whether the request would be granted depended on the need for another person with that specialized knowledge. The women recognized the importance of the imparted knowledge by giving gifts to the teacher. Women who had such specialized knowledge were sought after, and their knowledge and skill brought wealth and status to them as well as their families.[9]

While European and Euroamerican cultures are bilateral in reckoning descent, American Indian cultures can be either patrilineal, matrilineal, or bilateral. On the northern Plains, the Mandan and Hidatsa are matrilineal; the Plains Ojibwa, Arikara, Blackfeet, Cheyenne, and Crow are patrilineal. Other groups like the Lakota and Dakota are bilateral. The Sac and Fox Tribes of the Mississippi in Iowa are patrilineal. In some of the gardening tribes then, descent was reckoned through the mother rather than the father. The northern Plains are not unique in that regard, and there are a number of tribes throughout the United States that are matrilineal as well. One example would be the nations that make up the Iroquois Confederacy in the eastern United States: Onondaga, Oneida, Mohawk, Cayuga, Seneca, and Tuscarora. Even though many tribes are matrilineal and even matrilocal, there are traditionally no American Indian tribes, however, that are matriarchies.

Men conducted the sacred ceremonies and provided the tribes with healers. Depending on the culture, healers received their power through visions, through apprenticeships, or through transmission of power. Women supported them in matters of spirituality; they provided food for ceremonies, made the items for the giveaways, and often had knowledge of herbal medicines. Cecilia Hernandez Montgomery, a Lakota elder, described her grandmother's knowledge of herbs in the following way:

> Her Indian beliefs were strong, her medicine was good; she believed in all the herbs and roots and leaves and she used to come see my mother every now and then. She used to give her, they call them pejuta opahte, that's "medicine bag." She used to bring her these Bull

Durham sacks; she used to take those and bring a little bit of everything to my mother and tell her what each one was. That was good medicine, good leaves or herbs or some of it was ground real fine, some of it was put in little packages with little bone grease in it, where they used it for sores and things like that. That's how they used to doctor their own people in the olden days.[10]

Sometimes the spiritual and social success of a Native man required a close partnership with a woman. The "boss wife" of an important Southern Arapaho man, for example, would dedicate herself to the political and spiritual success of her husband and pass through the successive ceremonial lodges at his side and, consequently, might have decided not to have children.[11]

Traditionally, American Indian communities were governed in a number of different ways: the council of male elders, a council of chiefs, a village council, to name just a few. Decisions were based on consensus. Women did not officially participate in the governance of the group. That does not mean that they had no influence in the decision-making process though. Among the matrilineal Onondaga (Iroquois Confederacy), for instance, the clan mothers select the chief even today and also have the right to depose him.[12] On the northern Plains, women made their opinions known through their brothers, sons, and husbands, and they were heard because they controlled a number of important economic and spiritual resources.

Changing Lives on Early Reservations

By 1890, the last nomadic American Indian groups were settled on various reservations on the northern Plains. Men's roles underwent tremendous changes during the early reservation times. Being warriors and protectors of the people had always been of tremendous importance to men; that role basically came to an end with the Massacre of Wounded Knee (1890); the last armed conflict on the Plains. Their political autonomy was at an end, and their sovereignty was not acknowledged by the federal government until the Indian Reorganization Act (1934). They were denied the opportunity to take care of their families' economic needs when the agent denied their requests to hunt buffalo outside the reservation boundaries. Wage work was difficult to find and, if work was available, the stereotype of the "savage warrior" often prevented their being hired. There was an employment opportunity for relatively few males on the northern Plains though: the Wild West shows. The organizers of such shows preferred to hire Plains warriors, preferably Lakota; needless to say, the Indian agents did not approve of men joining the shows. Instead of donning civilized clothing and follow civilized pursuits, these men were encouraged to portray their past, a past that had little to recommend itself in the agents' eyes. Some American Indian people chose to join though, despite the Indian agents' disapproval; it gave them an opportunity to leave the poverty-stricken reservations and make money for their families, but it also gave them the opportunity to travel, even to Europe, and to celebrate their Native cultures rather than assimilate. For some communities, it also provided a market for their "crafts," since the Native performers marketed them when on tour in the United States or abroad.[13] On the reservations, even if they used their allotments, which they had received in the General Allotment Act (1887), to farm, they were as much victims of the weather and other obstacles as their non-Native neighbors. For example, after several successful season of farming, the Lakota of the Pine Ridge Reservation in South Dakota lost their crops in a severe drought and, shortly thereafter, their cattle to the Black Leg Disease. While their white neighbors could work cooperatively, the application of federal policies discouraged Native men from doing so and, ultimately, made them less successful. Men despaired and became increasingly dependent on rations.[14]

Once confined to reservations, large numbers of both male and female American Indians converted to Christianity. That did not mean, however, that traditional spiritualities disappeared as many people believe. The philosophical ideas of Lakota spirituality, for instance, do not contradict the Christian beliefs, and some Lakota have always participated in both ceremonial contexts. Because of the Courts of Indian Offenses (1883) and their charge to suppress American Indian spiritualities, Lakota spirituality went mostly underground in the late nineteenth century and, in general, did not become a public event again until the 1960s, the beginning of the American Indian civil rights struggle. However, ceremonies continued to be conducted more or less publicly; the Sun Dance, for example, continued through the years. Medicine men also continued to doctor people. Like today, there were Lakota on the early reservations who completely rejected any traditional spirituality and followed the Christian faith exclusively, then there were Lakota who followed only traditional spiritual ways, and then there were those who believed in both and followed both. Even during those difficult economic times during early reservation life and despite the pressures to assimilate, Lakota men fulfilled their spiritual obligations.

During these early reservation times those Native people who occupied alternative gender roles experienced a lot of pressure. Agents had a great deal of power and controlled many of the essential economic resources on reservations. They did not hesitate to use their resources to bring pressure to bear on alternative gender people; for instance, they were forced to wear gender appropriate clothing, do men's work, etc. Roscoe's description of the Crow *boté* Osh-Tish's life contains the following:

> Osh-Tish did not escape this campaign of morals. As Lowie reported, "Former agents have repeatedly tried to make him don male clothes, but the other Indians themselves protested against this, saying that it was against his nature." In 1982, tribal historian Joe Medicine Crow related these events to anthropologist Walter Williams:
>
> One agent in the late 1890s was named Briskow [Briscoe], or maybe it was Williamson. He did more crazy things here. He tried to interfere with Osh-Tish, who was the most respected *badé*. The agent incarcerated the *badés*, cut off their hair, made them wear men's clothing. He forced them to do manual labor, planting these trees that you see here on the BIA [Bureau of Indian Affairs] grounds. The people were so upset with this that Chief Pretty Eagle came into Crow Agency, and told Briskow to leave the reservation. It was a tragedy, trying to change them Briskow was crazy.[15]

In this particular Crow case, the Crow people were willing to defend Osh-Tish, who was a respected artist and also warrior and had supernatural powers. That was not always the case though, especially if people in alternative gender roles were being attacked by the missionaries. Converts to the new faith were less likely to deviate from the "moral law" postulated by the missionaries. Ultimately, Crow *boté* and other tribal people in alternative gender roles disappeared from the reservation life.

The roles of women did not change as drastically as those of other members of their communities. They still had to raise the children, they still had to cook for and feed their families, they still had many household chores to do, and they still had many things to manufacture for the survival of their families. They also found it easier to find wage work, especially once they became trained in the Euroamerican version of domesticity. In addition to taking care of their households and families, many women also were the ones who contributed most to the financial support of their families. In many cases, the pattern of women as breadwinners of families continues to this day.

One of the most important changes for American Indian women was their training to become "proper wives and mothers." Of course, American Indian women were skilled homemakers long before their confinement to reservations. However, the missionaries and their wives, the nuns, the teachers and housekeepers at day schools, and the field matrons engaged by the government to help with the assimilation process simply dismissed their knowledge and skills and insisted on training them to become homemakers in their own cultural, i.e. non-Native perception of what that should be. The Leech Lake Reservation in Minnesota may serve as an example:

> Ojibwe women as well as men discovered that, in seeking to adapt the Euro-American civilization program to their own ends, they needed to learn a daunting range of new skills and work roles. Susie Bonga Wright and her contemporaries began living in log or frame houses equipped with heavy furnishings in place of their mothers' easily cleaned and easily transported bark *wigiwams*. They ceased to manufacture basic household items such as storage containers, dishes, and other cooking and eating utensils from forest resources, relying instead on more-fragile crockery that had to be carefully cleaned and maintained. They began cooking on woodstoves instead of open-pit fires, and they had to learn to process and prepare a range of new foodstuffs. As the Ojibwe's began wearing Euro-American-style dress, women sought to learn to construct, clean, and maintain clothing and bedding made of wool and cotton instead of tanned animal skins. Ojibwe women evidently pursued knowledge of their half of the new agrarian lifestyle with an enthusiasm that initially gratified the Euro-American missionaries.[16]

On the northern Plains, women learned to sew and other handicrafts in the St. Mary's societies, the Catholic Church's women's society, and in sewing circles that were organized in the communities. Fabric was probably too expensive to purchase for the majority of women even if there were stores that carried it. However, they had access to some fabric through treaty provisions, although treaty promises were often not kept. The Fort Laramie Treaty of 1868, for example, promises in Article X a suit of clothing for every man and "For each female over twelve years of age, a flannel shirt, or the goods necessary to make it, a pair of woolen hose, twelve yards of calico, and twelve yards of cotton domestics." Boys and girls were also promised the "flannel and cotton goods as may be needed to make each a suit as aforesaid." Women, who had to make clothes as well as quilted bed covers, also had access to clothing donations that were sent from the east coast as charitable donations. Clothing was altered if it was suitable for life on the Plains; if it was not, it was cut into pieces for quilting.

In fact quilting has become an important tradition on the northern Plains. The eight-sided star, a mainstream quilt pattern called the Morning Star, has become a symbol of American Indian identity on the northern Plains. The pattern seems to have been particularly attractive to American Indian women because of the traditionally painted feathered circles that resemble the Morning Star somewhat. Many women manufacture star quilts in great numbers for all ceremonial occasions: yuwipi ceremony, giveaways, funerals, graduations, any honoring, etc.

Reservations could not support their populations by hunting; they quickly became over-hunted. Hunting also interfered with the goal outlined in the General Allotment Act (1887) to turn American Indian males into individual farmers. Therefore, one of the major adjustments that women had to deal with concerned the foodstuffs that were available to feed their families. The change in diet that this brought has ramifications even today. Originally, people on the northern Plains were meat eaters, buffalo meat in particular. The beef the federal government issued was much less healthy, and American Indians initially liked neither its smell nor its texture. In addition to beef, American Indian peoples were given sugar, syrup, and canned goods of all kinds. A diet that was originally high in fiber and protein became one that was high in fats and sugars.

Women faced with these new foodstuffs did not always know what to do with them. For example, the government issued raw coffee beans that had to be roasted before they could be pounded with a rock. The resulting brew was black and bitter. They were also issued flour; wheat was not indigenous to the United States, so women had to learn how to make bread and other baked goods. There are accounts of women simply dumping the flour over river banks and using the flour sacks to make shirts for children or for quilts.[17] They received canned meats, spam, salt pork, and other preserved meats that women had to learn how to prepare. American Indian women learned from extension workers and other white women what to do with the unfamiliar foods.

The federal government provides commodities today to low-income American Indian households that are located on the reservations or near them; they have replaced the rations. Until about 15 years ago, commodities consisted primarily of canned foods, preserved foods, flour, etc. Peanut butter and cheese have remained perennial favorites; the cookies and Mac & Cheese they make are excellent, mostly because they are so high in fat. Things have improved over the years, and those in charge of commodities try to offer healthier food choices. Low-fat meats are offered, fresh fruits and vegetables as well as better quality canned goods. People have also got more choices than they used to. However, the damage has been done and health problems such as diabetes, high blood pressure, heart disease, and obesity are common in Indian Country on the northern Plains, although these health problems are not entirely due to commodities. Other culprits are, to name just a few, salt, sodas, and Kool-Aid.

It is difficult to change eating habits. Women, faced with different staples than the ones they had used for hundreds of years, developed new dishes that have become the "traditional" fare of Indian Country. One example would be Indian Tacos; lettuce, tomatoes, fried hamburger, cheese, and onions are placed on a flat piece of fry bread. It is a cheap meal whose toppings can be modified to reflect the content of your cupboards. Since flour is part of the commodity program, almost every family has flour available. Considering unemployment and the financial situation in general, fry bread will remain popular. In a way, it has become the comfort food of Indian Country.

Finally, American Indian parents lost control, at least in part, of the educational process of their children who attended day schools, mission schools, or on- and off-reservation boarding schools. Every attempt was made to assimilate the children, to remove the children from the cultural knowledge of their parents. This process must have affected girls even more than boys. Their teachers would have emphasized their own understanding of gender roles, i.e. Euroamerican gender roles that postulated the husband as the head of the household and agrarian breadwinner whereas the wife was to be a housekeeper and his subservient helper. Housework has always been undervalued in mainstream culture. This model offered no room for either reciprocal gender relationships or gender fluidity and led to a decline in women's status. That many men internalized these teachings is reflected in the comments of some women who participated in the American Indian Movement in the 1970s; they felt that the colonized young American Indian men did not understand the traditional reciprocal gender relationships. Young women were potentially deprived of their traditional positions within the family units by the Euroamerican educational model; instead of reciprocal relationships, they would be taught patriarchal ones.

Early Reservation Times and Resistance

It seems likely that American Indian women used the sewing circles and the St. Mary's societies to circumvent the agents' intention to individualize them. In the name of furthering assimilation, they could meet and work together as they had done during pre-reservation times, except that they learned non-Native handicrafts. During those meetings, they also produced clothing, quilts, etc. that could be given to community members in need. The ministers and priests regarded this as Christian charity and encouraged it. However, it also followed Native guidelines of traditional generosity during pre-reservation times.

Sewing circles could also be used to continue political involvement, as the example of Susie Bonga Wright, an Ojibwe from the Leech Lake Reservation in Minnesota, illustrates. On the Leech Lake Reservation, the assimilation program was supervised by the Episcopalian Church. In the 1870s and 1880s, the Ojibwe hoped to use the new religious framework to maintain their own traditional values and some of their cultural traits, such as the decision-making processes and the involvement of women in the decision-making process. While Euroamericans saw Susie Bonga Wright as an exemplary homemaker, a true success of assimilation, the Ojibwa valued her for her wisdom and the adaptive strategies that made her a successful cultural broker. She used the sewing circle she established, which was based on the traditional working circles of Ojibwa women, for women to voice their political opinions and to provide an opportunity to follow traditional dictates of generosity. Initially, the Episcopalian Church's representatives approved whole-heartedly of the sewing circle as evidence of progressing domesticity; however, they disapproved when they realized that women continued to influence political decisions and that such input was valued by male Ojibwe leaders.[18] In all likelihood other women also used the sewing circles and other societies in the same way to maintain cultural continuity.

American Indian males also employed strategies of resistance. An example of using the new structures to perpetuate traditional values would be the Lakota medicine man Black Elk. He converted to Catholicism at the end of the nineteenth century and became a very successful catechist on the Pine Ridge Reservation in South Dakota. As a traditional Lakota leader, he had certain obligation toward the community, and his small monthly stipend permitted him to fulfill some of these obligations. In his case, the Catholic missionaries often complained that he was overly generous and certainly did not value the money he earned as he should have. As a catechist he also had access to, among other things, clothing donations and handed those out to his people; this used clothing was considered a valuable resource at the time. Other Native catechists did similar things to fulfill their obligations as leaders of their communities. Although the Catholic Church advocated charity, the clergy also emphasized the need for Native people to learn the importance of private property, and, in a way, people like Black Elk and other catechists were considered too generous by them. Again, the framework of a Christian denomination is used here to continue Lakota values and cultural traits that the Catholic Church did not approve of.[19]

Even though the above examples show resistance during early reservation time, American Indian peoples had shown the ability to adapt church structures for their own needs as early as the fur trade. In the eighteenth century, the Native women of the western Great Lakes area, for example, had used the Catholic Church to build new kinship ties. Traditionally, Native women who married non-Native fur traders helped to incorporate their husbands into their own kinship networks which their husbands found essential in their work. Women converted to Catholicism and found a similar opportunity to extend their own social networks. They became godmothers to the mixed-blood children of such unions and served as witnesses to marriages within fur trade society. Through this new network of Catholic relatives, they increased their access to furs, their wealth, and their power.[20]

In the 1960s and 1970s, there were a significant number of Native women among the members of the American Indian Movement (AIM). Most people are only aware of the male leaders, but there were women who lost their lives and the lives of their children in the struggle for American Indian civil rights: two examples are Tina Trudell and her children and Anna Mae Aquash. In addition, Jaimes estimates that at least 69 AIM members were killed on the Pine Ridge Reservation in South Dakota and that 21 of those were women. Some women were also prosecuted after the AIM members surrendered at Wounded Knee, but the federal government targeted the male members of the organization for long-term prison sentences. Madonna Thunderhawk, a Lakota member of AIM, summed up the importance of women in American Indian activism: "Indian women had *had* to be strong because of what this colonialist system has done to our men . . . alcohol, suicides, car wrecks, the whole thing. And after Wounded Knee, while all that persecution of the men was going on, we women had to keep things going."[21]

The activism of American Indian women has been ongoing. To give just one example, Cecilia Hernandez Montgomery, an urban Lakota grandmother from Rapid City, was instrumental in founding a citizen group that successfully advocated for running water for the so-called

Sioux Addition of the city. "Anyway, I was noted for my big mouth, I guess, for wherever there was something going and if it concerned us, our community, or our Indians, well, I was right there."[22] Today women also make their voices heard as tribal council members, as tribal chair women, and in many other capacities.

Meanwhile members of the gay Indian community began to establish their own identity in the 1980s. For many tribal people, the one-time existence of gender fluidity in their cultures was at best a dim memory, and the Christian moral code informed their thinking about people in alternative gender roles. As Gilley points out, gay Indians were usually closeted on the reservations and found it difficult to find a cultural identity. Their daily realities were often not much different from those of gay people outside their cultures. In the 1980s, they moved increasingly to urban centers, where they established communities and focused on dealing with the ever increasing threat of the HIV/AIDS epidemic and emphasized the "indigenous gay experience" which was marked by the use of the term Two-Spirit to describe themselves and their communities.[23] Gilley says about their emerging identity:

> The transition from being a "gay Indian" to "Two-Spirit" and the establishment of Two-Spirit societies created an alternative identity for many of the largely urban-oriented indigenous gay and lesbian people. However, the term Two-Spirit had another effect: it allowed individuals who were still living within the cultural and social sphere of their tribal communities a way of bringing together their sexual orientation and their Native identity. When we consider that only a handful of Native communities continue to have words for gender-different people in their language, and still fewer have social roles for alternative genders, we can see the benefit of Two-Spirit as a descriptive term and concept. This flexibility is in large part responsible for the seemingly overnight acceptance and use of the term by Native gays and lesbians. Also, giving a Native-oriented name to one's identity takes one's sexual orientation out of association with "white" ways and places it within the realm of Indian culture.[24]

Gilley implies here that the term Two-Spirit does not only cover homosexual relationships but also those of alternative gender roles that may not be related to sexuality but cultural identity.

In a 2012 interview Adrian Stimson, a Blackfoot artist from Alberta, Canada, mentions some of the ways in which he as a Two-Spirit contributes to his community. He has adopted a friend's children as his in the Blackfoot way and, in many ways, replaces their absentee father: ". . . I'm not lacking as a Two Spirited person. I have many children in my life who I nurture. I look at that and that's the traditional way back home."[25] There is a clear understanding that being Two-Spirit must not alienate you from your cultural heritage today and that Two-Spirits may slowly be finding a way back into reservation life.

At the same time, American Indian tribes have not always been welcoming to gay members, and many still have laws that state that only a male and a female can be married. Others of the federally recognized tribes explicitly permit same gender marriages while still others "explicitly prohibit same-sex marriage."[26] The Lumbee of North Carolina is one of the latter tribes, and Mary Ann Jacobs, an enrolled member and chair of the American Indian Studies Department at the University of North Carolina-Pembroke, points out that the Lumbee are primarily Baptist or Methodist: ". . . tribes internalized the harsh way Native Americans were assimilated into Christianity when European settlers first arrived. She said they've projected some of that oppression over time in their interpretation of religion."[27] Since the Lumbee were missionized very early, no knowledge of possible gender fluidity exists any more. The same is true for other tribes.

In a recent opinion, however, Todd Hembree, Attorney General of the Cherokee Nation, stated that the Cherokee Nation Marriage and Family Act of 2006, which does not permit same-sex marriages, violates the Cherokee Constitution. In addition to the legal argument, he offers a cultural argument as well: "Oral history also teaches that the Cherokee and Euroamerican worldviews differed dramatically regarding appropriate gender roles, marriage, sexuality, and spiritual beliefs. Indeed, while the majority of Cherokees subscribed to culturally defined gender roles, evidence suggests a tradition of homosexuality or alternative sexuality among a minority of Cherokees. Though such traditions are infrequently recorded, in his papers, John Howard Payne describes a ceremony that bonded two people of the same sex together for life. The relationship described in some respects would seem to parallel a modern day same-sex marriage in the depth of its commitment, its permanence, and its recognition by the other members of the tribe."[28]

Challenges of Contemporary Life

Many American Indian families in Indian Country and in urban areas are single-parent families, especially families with single mothers. Raising their children by themselves is a time consuming and difficult task; speaking about parenting under the best of circumstances, Celane Not Help Him, a Lakota elder, points out: "Grandpa told us, 'Being a parent, you have to be strong, wacin nitanka kte. You have to have patience and knowledge. And you have to be brave, cante nit'inzin kte, nahan fortitude. Wa'unsiyala kte [you must have mercy], wacante yagnakin kte [you must have compassion]. You have to have all these."[29] This innately difficult and challenging job is made even more difficult by the absence of the necessary physical resources.

Statistics show that the **average American Indian family** at 3.72 people is larger than the average family in the United States at 2.66 people.[30] These numbers presents unique challenges to the head of the household, especially when the **median income** of American Indian and Alaska Native households is $37,227 while the U.S median income in 2014 was $53,667. The overall American Indian and Alaska Native **poverty rate** is 27.3% as compared to 14.2% in the United States overall.[31] In North Dakota, the disparity is even more pronounced; 39.8%[32] of American Indians are below the poverty line whereas only 13% of the ND population overall is. At the same time, the **unemployment rate** in North Dakota ranges from 4.4% (Turtle Mountain) to 24.4% (Standing Rock) for American Indians and is 3.3% overall.[33] There are more people to feed with significant less money and very little prospect of finding a decent paying job.

The American Indian population is a young population. In 2017, the **median age** of the American Indian and Alaska Native population on reservations is 26 years, and the population overall showed a median age of 37; 32% of Native youths are under 18 years of age and 24% of the non-Native population.[34] The heads of American Indian households support a large number of dependents, and fewer people are available to contribute to the household income even if they could find jobs. In fact, the large number of dependents strains the available resources, such as schools, day care facilities, health-care facilities, and government programs for women and children (e.g. Women Infant Children). Because of the high unemployment rate, fathers find it impossible to support children, no matter whether they are actually a member of the household or not. However, there are also considerations beyond the lack of physical resources. Reservations offer few recreational opportunities for children and teenagers. They get bored and, consequently, often into trouble. It is not surprising then that many reservations face increasing problems with gangs. There is some concern that the decreasing number of elders will affect the continuity of tribal cultures because there will be fewer and fewer people to pass them on.

In pre-reservation times, grandparents and especially grandmothers were typically involved in raising the grandchildren. There has always been a strong connection between grandparents and their grandchildren. Celane Not Help Him, an elder herself, says that they have the wisdom and the values to raise you well: "It's good to have been raised by grandparents. Grandpa Beard never go to school but he's a smart man; he had a lot of patience with us, and Grandma's like that too, They know what's right and what's wrong; they got values and they set you straight."[35] Some grandmothers still choose to raise their grandchildren, especially if their children live off the reservation, and they want to ensure that the grandchildren develop a connection to and some knowledge of their tribal culture. Often they raised their own children in an urban environment and have experienced their children's disconnect from their tribal cultures first-hand.[36]

Today there are about twice as many women who reach elder status as there are men; this lack of male elders affects the younger men. Among other things, there are fewer males who can serve as role models, a lack that came up repeatedly in McKegney's interviews about indigenous masculinity. Janice C. Hill Kanonhsyonni, a member of the Mohawk Nation, said about her search for a role model for her younger son in 2010:

> It's very disheartening for me to know that I've been in my community the last year trying to find men who would commit to teaching him the things he needs to learn and our community is not that large and I'm having trouble. I'm struggling trying to find men to teach him what he needs to know. . . . I can teach him to be a good human being to the best of my abilities but I can't teach him how to be a man.[37]

The absence of men is at least in part due to risky behaviors at a young age: the consumption of alcohol and drugs, involvement in traffic accidents, terrifyingly high suicide rates, and others. The American Indian male suicide rates are three times higher than those of males in other ethnic groups; in the age group 15–25 years, 34.46 in 100,000 committed suicide from 1999 to 2003 as compared to 19.14 white males. Male suicide rates are five times higher than those for American Indian females in the same communities.[38] The reasons most often given for male suicide are historical trauma, depression, loss of cultural identity, etc. In a 2007 interview, Basil Johnston said: "Being healed – the healing has to come from inside, from ourselves. And some don't know it, unfortunately."[39]

While grandfathers are absent in many cases, many grandmothers find themselves raising their grandchildren for a variety of reasons. In some cases, children have been removed from alcoholic parents or drug addicts, parents leave children in their grandparents' care to find work off the reservation, parents are in ill health, or parents cannot handle their children. This development is by no means unique to reservations. All ethnic groups are observing a similar development.

Unfortunately, women in Indian Country are likely to become victims of violence. The statistics paint a dismal picture: one out of ten American Indians older than 12 years will be victim of a violent crime, in the age group of 25 to 34 "the rate of violent crime victimization was more than 2 ½ times the rate for all persons of the same age," "American Indians were more likely to be victims of assault and rape/sexual assault committed by a stranger or acquaintance rather than an intimate partner of family member," and 70% of the perpetrators are described as white. These statistics are absolutely abysmal and have not improved by much since the last time the statistics were updated.[40] Because of jurisdictional issues, i.e. tribal courts have no jurisdiction over non-Natives and members of other tribes, abusers know that they can probably get away with their crime. When the Violence against Women Act (VAWA) was re-authorized in 2013, it acknowledged for the first time the special situation of American Indian women as members of sovereign nations and attempted to take care of the problem. It now extends jurisdiction to non-tribal perpetrators under certain circumstances, but there are conditions that are too expensive for tribes on the northern Plains to put into place; for example, judges have to have special training, there needs to be a public defender system put in place, etc. Most of these crimes against women are not being investigated or prosecuted at this time. In fact, women often do not report sexual assault, because they know that the lack of law enforcement officers on the reservation prevents an investigation, some officials still blame the victims which is encouraged by the highly sexualized images of prevalent stereotypes about American Indian women, and, if the assailant happens to be a member of the community, women worry about repercussions within the family and the community. It is not surprising that women who have been victims of sexual violence turn to alcohol and drugs to help them cope, show some mental disorders, and suffer from Post Traumatic Stress Disorder.[41]

In addition to physical danger, American Indian women as well as men also face a number of health issues. Diabetes remains the number one health problem on the northern Plains. Frequently, the chronic underfunding of the Indian Health Service (IHS) prevents people from getting care. Furthermore, the isolation of the reservations on the northern Plains makes it difficult for people to access IHS clinics or to participate in the diabetes programs offered by the IHS. The economic situation causes additional hardship when lack of financial resources does not permit people to buy the foods that they need. In addition, diabetes is also responsible for triggering additional health problems, such as high blood pressure and cardio-vascular diseases.

One of the most long-standing health problems among American Indians is alcoholism. Dakota elder Stella Pretty Sounding Flute describes the destruction wrought by alcohol and, by extension other drugs, as follows:

> Our greatest enemy right now is alcohol and drugs and it's a silent massacre. Our grand-
> children are getting weak. There's no hope; they want to die. Our grandchildren are dying

by the hundreds. They are dying on the road and killing themselves; they pull a trigger and blow their brains out. They use alcohol more and commit crimes; the penitentiary is filled with the grandchildren. That's not the way. So this alcohol has taken a lot of lives. That's the only sadness I have. My hopes and dreams is that some day this alcohol and drugs will leave all the reservations.[42]

Alcoholism leads to liver disease and cirrhosis; many car accidents are also related to the excessive consumption of alcohol. If women consume alcohol during a pregnancy, children can be born with Fetal Alcohol Syndrome (FAS) or Fetal Alcohol Effect (FAE). Tribes have developed culturally specific programs to deal with alcoholism rather than depending on mainstream programs. However, progress in this area is slow, partly because the economic situation of reservations causes despair and depression, and many families have multigenerational histories of alcoholism, a cycle that is very difficult to break.

The gender roles have changed significantly in American Indian communities through the centuries. The reciprocal gender roles of pre-reservation times were changed by the patriarchal structures of the newcomers and their differing moral laws. However, in the face of the challenges presented to American Indian peoples in the second half of the twentieth and the beginning of the twenty-first centuries, women have a assumed a leading role in many cases; they have not only reclaimed the private sphere but are also a presence in tribal government and administration as well as other areas of the public sphere. At the same time, they are vulnerable because of the gendered stereotypes developed by the Europeans and perpetuated throughout the centuries. The physical and spiritual dangers that American Indian women face are present both on reservations and in urban centers and, in the long run, can profoundly affect their present roles.

Endnotes

1. Brian Joseph Gilley. 2006. *Becoming Two-Spirit: Gay Identity and Social Acceptance in Indian Country.* Lincoln: University of Nebraska Press, pp. 14-15.
2. Will Roscoe. 1998. *Changing Ones: Third and Fourth Genders in Native North America.* New York: St. Martin's Griffin, p. 4.
3. Roscoe, *Changing Ones*, p. 17.
4. Roscoe, *Changing Ones*, pp. 213-22.
5. Roscoe, *Changing Ones*, p. 7.
6. Roscoe, *Changing Ones,* pp. 223-247.
7. Sashay Schettler.2016. "Inebriated Indians and Sexy Squaws: Generations of Beset Indian Identities," paper for Indigenous Identities, Spring 2016. She is quoting from Scott Richard Lyons. 2010. *X-Marks: Signatures of Ascent.* University of Minnesota Press.
8. **coverture**. 2008. In *Encyclopedia Britannica*. Retrieved September 27, 2008, from Encyclopedia Britannica Online: http://www.britannica.com/EBchecked/141184/coverture as well as **Married Women's Property Acts**. (2008). In *Encyclopedia Britannica*. Retrieved September 27, 2008, from Encyclopedia Britannica Online: http://www.britannica.com/EBchecked/topic/366305/Married-Womens-Property-Acts

9. An excellent discussion of who had such skills and how they were transmitted can be found in Mary Jane Schneider. 1983. Women's Work: An Examination of Women's Roles in Plains Indian Arts and Crafts. In *The Hidden Half: Studies in Plains Indian Women, ed. Patricia Albers and Beatrice Medicine, 101-121.* New York: Lanham, 1983.

10. Sarah Penman, ed. 2000. *Honor the Grandmothers: Dakota and Lakota Women Tell Their Stories.* Minnesota Historical Society Press, pp. 87-88.

11. Loretta Fowler, *Wives and Husbands: . . .*

12. Sandy Johnson (as told to). 1994. *The Book of Elders: The Life Stories of Great American Indians.* HarperSan Francisco, pp. 72-73.

13. Bol, Marsha C. 1999."Defining Lakota Tourist Art, 1880-1915." In Ruth B. Phillips and Christopher B. Steiner, eds. *Unpacking Culture: Art and Commodity in Colonial and Postcolonial Worlds..* Berkeley: University of California Press, pp. 214-228.

14. Joe Starita. 1995. *The Dull Knifes of Pine Ridge: A Lakota Odyssey.* Lincoln: University of Nebraska Press, p. 93.

15. Roscoe, *Changing Ones*, p. 35.

16. Rebecca Kugel, and Lucy Eldersveld Murphy, eds. 2007. *Native Women's History in Eastern North America before 1900: A Guide to Research and Writing.* Lincoln: University of Nebraska Press,
p. 174.

17. Luther Standing Bear. 1975. *My People the Sioux.* Lincoln: University of Nebraska Press, 71-72 and Joe Starita. 1995. *The Dull Knifes of Pine Ridge: A Lakota Odyssey.* Lincoln: University of Nebraska Press, p. 89.

18. The information about Susie Bonga Wright comes from an article by Rebecca Kugel, Leadership within the Women's Community:Susie Bonga Wright of the Leech Lake Ojibwe. In Rebecca Kugel, & Lucy Eldersveld Murphy, eds. 2007. *Native Women's History in Eastern North America before 1900: A Guide to Research and Writing.* Lincoln: University of Nebraska Press, pp. 166-200.

19. A detailed account of Black Elk's life as a catechist can be found in Raymond DeMallie. (Ed.). 1984. *The Sixth Grandfather: Black Elk's Teaching Given to John G, Neihardt.* Lincoln: University of Nebraska Press.

20. My information is taken from an article by Susan Sleeper-Smith, Women, Kin, and Catholicism: New Perspectives on the Fur Trade. In Rebecca Kugel, Lucy Eldersveld Murphy, eds. 2007. *Native Women's History in Eastern North America before 1900: A Guide to Research and Writing.* Lincoln: University of Nebraska Press, pp. 234-274.

21. The information on women in AIM and the quotation can be found in an article by M.Annette Jaimes with Theresa Halsey, "American Indian Women at the Center of Indigenous Resistance in Contemporary North America. In M. Annette Jaimes, ed. 1992. *The State of Native America.* Boston, Massachusetts: South End Press, pp. 311-337.

22. Sarah Penman, ed. 2000. *Honor the Grandmothers: Dakota and Lakota Women Tell Their Stories.* Minnesota Historical Society Press, p. 99.

23. Brian Joseph Gilley 2006. *Becoming Two-Spirit: Gay Identity and Social Acceptance in Indian Country.* Lincoln: University of Nebraska Press, pp. 25-32.

24. Gilley, *Becoming Two-Spirit*, p. 32.

25. Sam McKegney. 2014. *MASCULINDIANS: Conversations about Indigenous Manhood.* East Lansing: Michigan State University Press, p. 154.

26. Kathleen Brown, 11 Native American Tribes Including the Two Largest, Prohibit Gay Marriage, CNSNews.com, June 8, 2015.

27. Hayley Fowler, Gay marriage discouraged within American Indian tribes, dailytarheel.com, August 18, 2015.

28. Todd Hembree, Opinion of the Cherokee Nation Attorney General, December 9, 2016, pp. 4-5.

29. Sarah Penman, ed. 2000. *Honor the Grandmothers: Dakota and Lakota Women Tell Their Stories.*

30. "2016 Average Household Size in the United States," arcgis.com

31. U.S. Department of Commerce, on the web page of the National Indian Child Welfare Association (NICWA), "American Indian Children and Families"

32. "North Dakota American Indian Health Profile," ndhealth.gov

33. "Growing North Dakota by Numbers," North Dakota Census Office, commerce.nd.gov

34. "Indian Country Demographics," National Congress of American Indians (NCAI), web page

35. Sarah Penman, ed. 2000. *Honor the Grandmothers: Dakota and Lakota Women Tell Their Stories.* Minnesota Historical Society Press, p. 24.

36. Joan Weibel-Orlando, Powwow Princess and Gospelettes: Cross-Generational Enculturation in American Indian Families. In Marjorie M. Schweitzer. 1999. *American Indian Grandmothers: Traditions and Transitions.* Albuquerque: University of New Mexico Press, pp. 181-202.

37. McKegney, *MASCULINDIANS*, p. 19.

38. Retrieved March 18, 2017: http://health and welfare.idaho.gov

39. McKegney, *MASCULINDIANS*, p. 43.

40. American Indians and Crime, 1992-2002, Bureau of Justice Statistics. Retrieved September 28, 2008: http://www.ojp.usdoj.gov/bjs/pub/pdf/aic02.pdf

41. Article in INDIAN COUNTRY TODAY.

42. Sarah Penman, ed. 2000. *Honor the Grandmothers: Dakota and Lakota Women Tell Their Stories.* Minnesota Historical Society Press, p. 74.

Case Studies

Native Communities: Three Case Studies
Sebastian F. Braun

Because of the fundamental differences between American Indian cultures, a historical or ethnographic overview of Native societies and their interactions with each other and with the different colonial powers as well as the United States lies beyond the page limitations and the intent of this book. There are too many contemporary Native societies to provide a meaningful description of all their cultures and histories. While the text thus remains consciously somewhat limited in its scope, it can well serve as a discussion of the most important historical and cultural developments in general. What should become apparent, at least implicitly from the examples discussed, is that Native America is not easily generalized. We hope to provide an impetus for the readers to not simply accept stereotypical depictions of American Indian societies as one culture, but instead to look for detailed and problematized descriptions of individual societies and their historical decisions and acts.

The authors encourage the reader to go on from here and continue the investigation of Native societies and histories. This further, detailed investigation is needed to truly understand the complex, sometimes contradictory historical and contemporary situations of Native American cultures: it is necessary to investigate other, connected areas and their societies; the settlement of the continent as a whole; the development of federal policies and American values through time and in different places; agriculture in the Southwest and Southeast; fishing and hunting on the Northwest Coast; trade between the Pacific, Atlantic, and the Gulf; the literature and images of American Indian peoples; etc. By looking at snapshots of history and culture, this text tries to show trends that can be used to think about a general, introductory analysis.

Native communities have different cultures; they also exist in their current forms because of different histories. To explore this a little further, three communities can serve as case studies for the various forms in which communities in their modern and legal forms were established. The three communities selected here are the Cheyenne River Sioux Reservation in South Dakota, the Turtle Mountain Band of Chippewa Reservation in North Dakota, and the Meskwaki Settlement in Iowa. They were established by treaty and land reduction, by proclamation, and by purchasing their own lands.

Treaty: Cheyenne River

The United States had signed treaties with Native nations since before becoming legally independent. Most treaties signed concerned land purchases from specific nations, but some were peace treaties, regulated intertribal disputes, or concerned other affairs. Treaty negotiations were complicated affairs, involving not simply two small delegations that sat around a table.

Instead, government delegations met with the various leaders of Native groups, and the negotiations were often a complex compromise between traditional political theater, involving public speeches and revocations of history, and strict military negotiations. Hundreds and thousands of people with their camps and horses would live around the negotiations, which could last for weeks. Often, the treaty negotiations took the place of traditional summer encampments, and ceremonies, horse races, games, courtship, and hunting expeditions created distractions on top of the requirements of daily lives. Traditionally, treaties between oral societies necessitated the recounting of their interactions by specialists and political leaders; these long speeches set the tone for the resulting agreements. A long list of leaders had to speak and be heard, and in the American understanding of negotiations, these speeches had to be translated, transcribed, and filed. Often, the American side did not understand that those speeches were the negotiating process and not simply a preamble, while Native leaders could not understand how the Americans wanted to hasten through this important process. Problems with translation were exacerbated by problems with cultural translations. Calling the President "father," for example, had very different connotations for Americans (who associated the role of a father with authority) than for indigenous peoples (who often thought of the role as having responsibility), and the issue of who had authority to sign a treaty and what kind of responsibility that involved for its enforcement was a constant cause for misunderstandings and conflict, as were different interpretations of concepts such as land ownership or legal provisions. Such treaty councils were even more complex when they involved more than one Native nation.

On the northern plains, the treaty of Fort Laramie of 1851 brought almost all the regional indigenous nations together in an attempt by the federal government to delineate their respective boundaries in order to create a lasting peace between them. This was one of a few treaties that did not involve the cessation of lands to the United States, and thus did not set up reservations. Instead, it attempted to initiate a controlled and peaceful situation by defining land claims between Native nations. The attempt was short-lived because the expanding Lakota had no intentions to halt their progressive conquest of Crow and Pawnee lands in the Powder River valley and in northwestern Nebraska. They could not afford to do so: their political economy demanded a continued expansion. In 1851, the government tried to create peaceful relations between these nations especially to protect the Oregon Trail. The United States payed them annuities, at that time a form of tribute for keeping the peace. The Oregon Trail created many disturbances and increasingly conflict because after the conquest of California from Mexico and the subsequent gold rush, more and more settlers used the trail. The increasingly volatile situation of direct competition over resources and territory between the Lakota and the United States did not yet result in full-fledged war. However, the Lakota experienced the American will to use military violence with their relatives. In 1862, the Dakota were driven from Minnesota, and the army pursued them to the West in the following years. In 1864, the Cheyenne became embroiled in a war with Colorado that led to the infamous massacre at Sand Creek. It was after the Civil War that the army turned its attention to the high plains: in the north, against the Cheyenne, Arapaho and Lakota, in the south, against the Kiowa, Comanche and Apache. Experiences of their neighbors warned plains nations of what might come. The Navajo and

Mescalero Apache, for example, had been forced to remove to Bosque Rodondo in 1862 and 1864. There, they were supposed to eke out an agricultural living from a small, dry and infertile territory. Finally, in 1868, the Navajo were allowed to return to their homelands.

When, in 1865, the federal government moved to build forts along the Bozeman Trail from Fort Laramie to the Montana goldfields, it supported the trail that cut right through the Powder River valley, a last refuge for the shrinking bison herds and newly conquered by the Lakota from the Crow. The Lakota and their Northern Cheyenne and Arapaho allies defeated the United States in the following war; the 1868 treaties were thus, at least in the eyes of the victorious Lakota, a negotiation for peace. Although large numbers of American Indian delegates had met with representatives of the federal government to negotiate the terms of the treaty, the final result followed a model treaty that included articles that had never been discussed. The same articles on land allotment, annuities and education appear in both the 1867 treaties for the southern plains and the 1868 treaties for the northern plains, for example. So does a clause stipulating that the only way for a change in the treaty was the agreement of three quarters of all adult male residents of the newly established reservations. This would lead to, on hand, the 1903 Supreme Court decision in *Lone Wolf v. Hitchcock*, and on the other hand to the Black Hills land claims case by the Lakota.

In the 1868 treaty, the Lakota retained the western half of South Dakota as their reservation, and the Powder River valley, between the Black Hills and the Big Horn Mountains, was declared unceded territory. In 1874, an expedition to the Black Hills found gold there, and that led to a gold rush. As the Black Hills were on the territory of the Great Sioux Reservation, this was illegal trespassing of the reservation. After the army tried to patrol the reservation boundaries and escort trespassers out, the government decided to try and buy the area from the Lakota. When these negotiations failed, in part because some of the Lakota did not want to sell, and others felt the price offered was far too low, President Grant decided that all Lakota had to live on the reservation. Because the traditional bands and their Cheyenne and Arapaho allies were already in the Powder River valley and refused to follow that order, the army was ordered to engage these "hostiles." This led to the battles of Rosebud and Little Big Horn in 1876, and then to the surrender or exile of these Lakota bands.

In 1877, under the Moneypenny Agreement, the Great Sioux Reservation was reduced by the western third, which included the Black Hills. This agreement did not follow the 1868 treaty and was therefore illegal. South Dakota was now faced with a situation where the state was divided by the remaining Great Sioux Reservation. The solution to this, for the state, was that in 1889 two transportation corridors were opened through the reservation. At the same time, the remaining reservation was divided into five small reservations. In that way, the Pine Ridge, Rosebud, Lower Brule, Standing Rock, and Cheyenne River reservations were created. Because both the 1877 and the 1889 diminishments were illegal – neither one followed the requirement that three quarters of male Lakota approve the change in borders – the Cheyenne River Lakota, together with their relatives from the other current reservations, still claim the whole Great Sioux reservation as their reservation territory. This is especially important in regards to the Black Hills, considered sacred by many Lakota. In 1980, United States Supreme Court came to the conclusion that

> the 1877 Act effected a taking of tribal property, property which had been set aside for the
> exclusive occupation of the Sioux by the Fort Laramie Treaty of 1868. That taking implied

an obligation on the part of the Government to make just compensation to the Sioux Nation, and that obligation, including an award of interest, must now, at last, be paid.

All Lakota tribal governments since, however, have refused to touch the moneys now accumulating for them because they know that once they take them, they will forfeit any land claims. Despite some law suits that have tried to force the tribal governments to take the money and pay it out to tribal members as per capita payments, none of the tribes have moved in that direction. One cautionary example for them might be the case of the Western Shoshone, who have seen their land claims to most of Nevada extinguished after the government paid out compensation to one faction of the tribe that was allowed to speak for the whole.

Proclamation: Turtle Mountain

After the 1867/68 treaties, the government signed agreements, but most of these were simply a matter of legitimizing policies, without leaving any role or space for negotiations. Most American Indians were not citizens of the United States. However, in order to solve the "Indian problem," the federal government increasingly saw their future, if they were allowed to have one at all, as integrated into the state and American society and not as separate, sovereign nations. Buried in an 1871 appropriations bill, Congress made clear that it no longer regarded American Indian nations as sovereign and ended treaty making:

> Provided, that hereafter no Indian nation or tribe within the territory of the United States shall be acknowledged or recognized as an independent nation, tribe, or power with whom the United States may contract by treaty. . . .

The powers to enlarge, diminish and establish reservations, Congress decided, would unilaterally rest with the president. Existing treaties, however, were not affected, and remained the law of the land. Even after 1871, the United States could not simply end or ignore the inherent sovereignty of indigenous societies. The so-called agreements that replaced the treaty process were often signed by Native people. However, there were no real negotiations, and the federal government often hand-picked American Indians to be appointed as leaders, who would then sign these agreements.

The Ojibwa or Chippewa lived in the northern woodlands of Wisconsin, Minnesota, western Ontario, and southeastern Manitoba in the early nineteenth century, but they were in a process of moving westwards. With the fur trade coming down from Hudson Bay to their relatives, the Cree, they expanded into central Manitoba, and some bands eventually started living on the plains. They adopted a plains lifestyle as temporarily nomadic buffalo hunters. Some of the Ojibwa and Cree women had also married French and Scot traders, and their families adopted a new culture, from European and Native influences. Those people became known as Metis. There are many different people who identify as Metis; here, the term is used exclusively for Red River Metis, so-called because they settled initially along the Red River. From there, however, they quickly moved west and north, into Montana and Alberta.

In the United States, so-called "mixed-bloods" were often not granted a Native identity by state and federal governments. This was especially true from the second half of the nineteenth century on. While before, some treaties had included the establishment of separate reservations for "mixed-bloods," when the Plains Ojibwe in Minnesota and North Dakota started to negotiate for treaties, their alleged status as Metis led to discussions over whether they actually should be considered for reservations. Also into this hesitancy played the fact that many Ojibwa groups on the northern Plains included not only Metis, but also Cree people. In disregard of the fact that these related groups had been living together for some time, and that national boundaries were a recent imposition on the landscape, the Cree were considered to be a Canadian group, with no rights in the United States.

In 1863, at negotiations for the Old Crossings Treaty in Minnesota, Metis claims to the Red River Valley were not recognized, although their claims to individual property were formalized. With wheat farming booming in Eastern North Dakota in the 1870s, some of the Ojibwa groups there, especially those referred to as the Pembina Band, resettled to the White Earth communities in Minnesota. Those who lived further west, though, petitioned for a reservation in the Turtle Mountains in 1876. In 1882, the federal government opened lands in the area for settlement, without having negotiated for their title first. Chippewa people who had made improvements to lands would receive title for their individual tracts, and in the same year, President Chester Arthur proclaimed the establishment of a reservation in the Turtle Mountains, a tract twenty-four by thirty-two miles large. Those Ojibwe without individual tracts would have to move onto the reservation. However, the government had ignored the Metis. It only planned to deal with the 300-400 "fullbloods," not the 1,000 Metis who were part of the Native population. The "fullbloods" preferred a smaller reservation, to be held in common; many of the Metis were experienced farmers and were looking to own their own tracts. In March 1884, the government reduced the area of the reservation from twenty-two townships to two townships by executive order:

> It is hereby ordered that the tract of country in the Territory of Dakota withdrawn from sale and settlement and set apart for the use and occupancy of the Turtle Mountain band of Chippewa Indians by Executive order dated December 21, 1882, except townships 162 and 163 north, range 71 west, be, and the same is hereby, restored to the mass of the public domain.

This reduction had also excluded most of the good farmlands from the reservation. The advice for Metis was that they should occupy public lands around the reduced reservations, if they wanted to stay in the area. However, in June of the same year, one of the two townships was exchanged for another one:

> The Executive order dated March 29, 1884, whereby certain lands in the Territory of Dakota previously set apart for the use and occupancy of the Turtle Mountain band of Chippewa Indians were, with the exception of townships 162 and 163 north, range 71 west, restored to the mass of the public domain, is hereby amended so as to substitute township 162 north, range 70 west, for township 163 north, range 71 west, the purpose and effect of such amendment

being to withdraw from sale and settlement and set apart for the use and occupancy of said Indians said township 162 north, range 70 west, in lieu of township 163 north, range 71 west, which last-mentioned township is thereby restored to the mass of the public domain.

The apparent arbitrary use of executive orders to establish, diminish, and move their reservation within two years surely did not establish too much trust by the Turtle Mountain Chippewa in the ability or willingness of their trustee to represent or act in their interests.

In addition, because the Chippewa felt that the entire establishment of the reservation ignored their established land claims in the area, many of those who settled outside the reservation boundaries did not file for title claims on their lands. They felt that doing so would be interpreted as agreeing with the abolishment of their larger claims. Many Metis and Ojibwe also still traveled away during the summer, mostly to western North Dakota and Montana, and were not in the area during open season for claim enrollment. Thus, American settlers often filed double-claims on their lands. With power relations as they were, Native people did not have a way to successfully challenge most of these claims. Government agents refused to provide rations to those they felt were not part of the community - mostly Metis who lived off the reservation as well as Metis and others who had come from Canada to live with their relatives. Finally, in 1890, the federal government sent a commission to try and settle the land claims, as well as to convince the fullbloods to move to Minnesota. This commission was utterly unsuccessful. The Tribal Council refused to consider relocating to Minnesota; Little Shell, a leader of the fullbloods, argued for an expansion of the reservation; and the government could not figure out who was to be classified as Chippewa and as Metis. Little Shell went to the Milk River area in Montana and asked for a reservation there, but the government was unwilling to establish another reservation. Instead, it formed another commission, which proceeded to establish an alternative Council. Finally, in 1904, the federal government accepted a settlement, which was accepted by the people on Turtle Mountain in 1905. While this settlement was essentially the same as one the commission had proposed in 1892, the situation had changed in the meantime. The settlement provided that the reservation would not be enlarged; that it would not be held in common, but allotted into individual tracts; that the government would pay not more than ten cents an acre for the lands ceded in this agreement; and that most of that money would be spent for supplies and services. In 1979, the Indian Claims Commission awarded the Turtle Mountain Band of Chippewas $52,527,338 as additional payment for the lands ceded in the agreement of 1904. Divided by enrolled members, that sum would have come to about $2,000 per person.

As it was not possible to provide land within the reservation boundaries to even those who were officially enrolled at the reservation, over half of the tribal members had to leave the reservation and take allotments on public lands elsewhere. Fifteen families filed for land on Graham's Island, close to Devils Lake; 390 families went to western North Dakota, around Trenton; some were allowed to stay on public lands within the original Turtle Mountain reservation; and around 150 people took lands in Montana, close to Great Falls and Lewistown. In those areas far from Turtle Mountain, non-Indians protested the allotment of trust lands because they would be exempt from local property taxes for at least 25 years. The Commissioner of

Indian Affairs proposed to pay money to the allottees and buy them out of their allotments, but the government never made those payments, and so the status of their allotments remained in limbo. After decades of trying to achieve federal recognition, the Little Shell Tribe is still trying to do so in 2017.

Buying Lands: Meskwaki

Some American Indian reservations in the United States were neither created by a treaty nor a proclamation, but by Native communities buying land for themselves. For example, in Washington State, the Jamestown S'Klallam Tribe bought 210 acres in 1874; after long struggles, the tribe finally received federal recognition in 1981. When Native peoples bought lands themselves, they often faced difficulties in meeting expectations of outsiders as to how American Indians should live, partially because they had successfully created a space that was not under the control of the federal government. One of the most prominent cases for this are the Meskwaki in Iowa.

Officially, the Meskwaki Nation is called the Sac and Fox Tribe of the Mississippi in Iowa. The name already alerts to the fact that the Meskwaki have been seen as a part of the "Sac and Fox" tribe. The Meskwaki had moved south from Wisconsin into Illinois in the early eighteenth century, with the Sac, their relatives. They lived on the west banks of the Mississippi until after the Black Hawk war. Although the Meskwaki did not get involved in the fighting between the Sac under Black Hawk and the federal government, which claimed that the Sac had ceded their lands in Illinois, they were punished together with their relatives. To punish tribes or factions of tribes clearly not involved in conflicts with the United States was an established practice by the government by the 1830s. The Meskwaki had to move further west into Iowa. Like other tribes, they, or their headmen, became indebted to traders, and in 1842, they had to cede their lands in Iowa. The treaty called for a removal of Meskwaki to a joint reservation with the Sac in Kansas. Not all Meskwaki left, and of those who initially moved to Kansas, many came back to their old lands. The federal government tried to round up Native people in Iowa every year and evicted them back to Kansas. This was a spectacle not approved of by many white settlers. In 1856, the Iowa governor and the legislature, petitioned by settlers in the state, approved of the Meskwaki being allowed to stay. The next year, the Meskwaki used money from their annuities to buy 80 acres of land and set up a village there. The accounts of the migration back differ. As Richard Brown put it in his 1964 MA thesis:

> The Iowa Mesquakie could raise only $15 in cash but they offered to give up some of their ponies to make up the $250 difference. In the meantime, the sympathizing white settlers continued to use their influence on the Iowa legislators. On July 15, 1856, the Iowa Assembly passed an act permitting the tribe to reside in Iowa. There was one legal snag, however. The Mesquakie were not citizens of the United States; therefore, they could not own land. Knowing this, those settlers favorable to the Mesquakie's cause once again prevailed on the Governor of Iowa, James W. Grimes, to hold the newly purchased land in trust for the Indians. After much deliberation, the governor agreed to the trust, and on July 13, 1857, he signed the deed in the names of the five Mesquakie from Kansas. Thus, for $1,000 the

Mesquakie Nation acquired possession of eighty acres of land west of the present towns of Tama-Toledo, in Tama County, Iowa.

William Hagan insists that the "reason for this completely unprecedented attitude by whites [i.e., sympathy for Indians] must have been the government payments. As the tribesmen had once enriched men like Davenport by their hunting, now their $51,000 annuity attracted exploiters." However, this ignores the fact that the federal government refused to pay the annuities in Iowa, and is a rather simplistic generalization of both American and Meskwaki realities. John Zielinski wrote that:

> Governor Grimes took $735 in gold from the Indians and paid $1,000 in gold to the Butler family to obtain the first parcel of what is today's settlement at Tama. Nothing is stated about where the extra $265 came from, whether from state funds or the governor's own pocket.

Regardless of how the land was acquired, whether the state or the governor pitched in, or whether the Meskwaki sold some of their ponies, the arrangement was not so much unprecedented because some Americans were sympathetic to Native people, but because a state was moved to actively interfere on behalf of an Indian tribe, against the wishes of the federal government. While the state of Iowa agreed to the Meskwaki settling in Iowa, and Iowans actively lobbied for that, however, as a result, the federal government was not happy at all. It did not like that Native people would become private, though communal, landowners of property that was outside their direct control. The government thus did not recognize the Meskwaki as an Indian tribe.

Although the state asked the federal government to deliver the annuities due to them in Iowa, the federal government refused, and actually refused to recognize the Meskwaki in Iowa as a separate tribe. The government held up the fiction that all Sac and Fox lived on their reservation in Kansas and therefore paid the annuities for both to the people there. Annuities were finally delivered to Iowa starting in 1867; however, the Meskwaki in the settlement were not recognized in their own right, but only as a band of the larger Sac and Fox. Despite obstacles, the tribe was successful in buying more land. In 1915, it reached 3253 acres. Because the Meskwaki lands were not held in trust by the federal government but by the state of Iowa, the Meskwaki were paying property taxes to the state and obeyed state laws. However, as private land owners, they avoided allotment so that the Settlement's land is still held in common. The state of Iowa often acted as benevolent, if paternalistic, intermediary when the federal government tried to impose federal policies on the Settlement. The Meskwaki organized themselves, and were able to continue many of their traditional lifeways during some of the most oppressive years of federal policy. In 1878, the state of Iowa almost terminated its relationship with the tribe, which would have meant removal to Kansas. Upon petitions from neighbors, the state legislature stayed course, and the resolution for removal failed in the U.S. Senate.

However, growing assimilationist sentiments among Iowans meant that pressures continued to mount for the state to relinquish its laissez-faire attitude. In 1896, the state transferred the land trust to the federal government, which was seen as the stricter parent, perhaps. Along with that came jurisdiction. Thus, the Meskwaki lands acquired the same status as other Indian reservations. Although the Meskwaki and legal questions delayed this action, in 1908 all Meskwaki lands became held in trust by the federal government. In 1928, some Meskwaki petitioned the Commissioner of Indian Affairs to remove trust status for their lands; he responded that the condition for this would be full allotment, and the tribe refused. The relationship between the tribe and the federal government remained contentious; the issue of whether the government was responsible to provide schools, for example, would linger long into the twentieth century. In 1948, Congress passed a law that simply declared that "jurisdiction is hereby conferred on the State of Iowa over offenses committed by or against Indians on the Sac and Fox Indian Reservation in that State to the same extent as its courts have jurisdiction generally over offenses committed within said State outside of any Indian reservation." Although their lands were held in trust by the United States, however, the tribe continued to pay property taxes to the state of Iowa until 1976, when the federal government declared full reservation status for the Settlement. The Meskwaki continue to refer to their lands as a "settlement" and not as a "reservation" to make the point that theirs is a history of lands bought for themselves by themselves. Their relationship with both federal and state governments is continuously evolving. Iowa called on Congress to repeal the 1948 law in 2015, and in 2016, the Iowa Senate passed a bill that would cede the state's criminal jurisdiction.

Different Histories

These different Native nations all experienced different ways to hold on to or gain rights over their current lands. There are as many Native histories as there are recognized and unrecognized American Indian tribes; what should be clear is that none of these nations were simply dictated to. Rather than following the whims of federal policies as helpless victims, they all responded to these policies as sovereign nations, exploring their own paths. As much as possible, they continued to search for ways in which to pursue their own interests according to their own values. Sometimes they were not successful in doing so. However, the sovereignty of Native nations, never extinguished, continues to be exercised by people well aware of their own histories and cultures, and exploring and finding solutions for their communities.

Sources and Further Readings

Cheyenne River:
Raymond J. DeMallie. 2009. "Community in Native America: Continuity and Change among the Sioux." *Journal de la Societe des Americanistes,* Vol. 95, No. 1, pp. 185-205.
Sebastian F. Braun. 2008. *Buffalo Inc. American Indians and Economic Development.* Norman: University of Oklahoma Press.
Roxanne Dunbar Ortiz, (ed.) 1977. *The Great Sioux Nation. Sitting in Judgment on America.* New York: American Indian Traty Council Information Center/San Francisco: Moon Books.
Robert M. Utley. 1963. *The Last Days of the Sioux Nation.* New Haven: Yale University Press.

Turtle Mountain:
Gerhard J. Ens. 1996. *Homeland to Hinterland. The Changing Worlds of the Red River Metis in the Nineteenth Century.* Toronto: University of Toronto Press.

Stanley N. Murray. 1996. "The Turtle Mountain Chippewa, 1882-1905" in Janet Daley Lysengen and Ann M. Rathle (eds.) *The Centennial Anthology of North Dakota History, Journal of the Northern Plains*. Bismarck: State Historical Society of North Dakota, pp. 83-109.

John S. Milloy. 1990. *The Plains Cree. Trade, Diplomacy and War, 1790 to 1870*. Winnipeg: University of Manitoba Press.

David G. Mandelbaum. 1979. *The Plains Cree. An Ethnographic, Historical, and Comparative Study*. Regina: Canadian Plains Research Center, University of Regina.

Elwyn B. Robinson. 1966. *History of North Dakota*. Lincoln: University of Nebraska Press.

Meskwaki Settlement:

Eric Steven Zimmer. 2014. "Settlement Sovereignty: The Meskwaki Fight for Self-Governance, 1856–1937." *The Annals of Iowa*, Vol. 73, No. 4, pp. 311-347.

Richard Frank Brown. 1964. *A social history of the Mesquakie Indians, 1800–1963*. MA Thesis in History, Iowa State University.

John M. Zielinski. 1976. *Mesquakie and Proud of It*. Kalona: Photo-Art Gallery Publications.

William T Hagan. 1958. *The Sac and Fox Indians*. Norman: University of Oklahoma Press.

Case Study: The Indian Child Welfare Act
Mississippi Band of Choctaw Indians v. Holyfield, 430 U.S. 30 (1989)
Grant Christensen

Among the most important recent federal laws involving Indians, the Indian Child Welfare Act (ICWA) touches every Indian family regardless of whether they live on the reservation. ICWA even applies to Indian children who are not actually enrolled in their tribe but only eligible for enrollment. Essentially, whenever any court (state or tribal) is making a custody decision for a child who could be enrolled in a federally recognized Indian tribe the requirements of ICWA attach to that decision. For this reason an understanding of ICWA is important for tribal employees, for social workers, for persons working in the criminal justice system, for family and child advocates, and even for health care professions.

This case study presents the first situation under ICWA to reach the United States Supreme Court and thus it includes a preliminary discussion of the statute and Congress' intent and purpose in enacting it into law. This context will give students who are new to ICWA some important background information and provide a foundation upon which to understand the purpose of Congressional intervention on behalf of Indian children.

This case presented to the Supreme Court a question of tribal power to control the actions of its citizens. The facts are these: a young couple, both enrolled members of the Mississippi Band of Choctaw Indians and living on the reservation, decided to leave the reservation for the purpose of giving birth. The Indian couple had identified a non-Indian adoptive couple from Ohio and wanted to give up their parental rights to allow the non-Indian couple to adopt their twins. After giving birth in Mississippi and consenting to the adoption, the Indian couple returned to the reservation. The state courts in Mississippi promptly effectuated the tribal couple's choice and awarded custody to the non-Indian Holyfield family.

Under ordinary law in Mississippi the adoption would have been perfectly legal. However, because the twins were the children of tribal members, and thus eligible for enrollment, the Mississippi Band of Choctaw Indians contested the adoption. ICWA has a couple provisions dealing with the appropriate court to handle custody decisions. Under ICWA if an Indian child is domiciled on the reservation *ONLY* the tribal court can legally adjudicate the adoption. (Domicile simply means the individual's legal residence.) Furthermore, even if the Indian child is domiciled off the reservation, ICWA requires that the tribe be notified of the adoption proceedings and given an opportunity to request the case be transferred to tribal court. State courts are obligated to transfer the case unless the party opposing the transfer can show 'good cause' to deny the transfer. None of these procedures were followed by the state of Mississippi.

Accordingly the Mississippi Band of Choctaw Indians argued that the adoption that was completed by the state court of Mississippi was in fact unlawful. The tribe demanded the return of the twins away from their non-Indian adoptive family so that the tribal court could decide where to place them. The Holyfield's fought to maintain custody of their children. The resulting legal battle was ultimately resolved by the Supreme Court in a contentiously divided 6-3 opinion.

As you read the case consider the various perspectives. The Holyfield family does not want to lose custody of the twin children they have parented literally since birth. They are less concerned with the development of the law and more concerned with having the Court affirm them as the legal parents of their adoptive children. The biological parents went to some lengths to try to avoid the law. Even though they had limited resources they journeyed hundreds of miles away from the reservation to be sure to give birth in the state of Mississippi, believing this would allow them to choose the Holyfields as the adoptive parents. Should the Court take into account the biological parent's intent to have the children adopted in Mississippi instead of by the tribal court? Should ICWA have an exception that protects the intent of the biological parents? Finally the Mississippi Band of Choctaw Indians is concerned with upholding ICWA and ensuring that states cannot avoid complying with the law no matter how sympathetic the facts. The tribe may be less concerned with these particular children but is very worried about creating a legal precedent which recognizes the tribal court's authority to make decisions regarding its own children. The tribe does not want the state to be able to control the custody of its children.

The Supreme Court had to balance each of these considerations when interpreting the law. Do you like the outcome it ultimately reaches?

....

MISSISSIPPI BAND OF CHOCTAW INDIANS V. HOLYFIELD
Supreme Court of the United States 430 U.S. 30 (1989)

JUSTICE BRENNAN Delivered the Opinion of the Court

This appeal requires us to construe the provisions of the Indian Child Welfare Act that establish exclusive tribal jurisdiction over child custody proceedings involving Indian children domiciled on the tribe's reservation.

A

The Indian Child Welfare Act of 1978 (ICWA), 25 U. S. C. §§ 1901-1963, was the product of rising concern in the mid-1970's over the consequences to Indian children, Indian families, and Indian tribes of abusive child welfare practices that resulted in the separation of large numbers of Indian children from their families and tribes through adoption or foster care placement, usually in non-Indian homes. Senate oversight hearings in 1974 yielded numerous examples, statistical data, and expert testimony documenting what one witness called "[t]he wholesale removal of Indian children from their homes,... the most tragic aspect of Indian life today." Studies undertaken by the Association on American Indian Affairs in 1969 and 1974, and presented in the Senate hearings, showed that 25 to 35% of all Indian children had been separated from their families and placed in adoptive families, foster care, or institutions. Adoptive placements counted significantly in this total: in the State of Minnesota, for example, one in eight Indian children under the age of 18 was in an adoptive home, and during the year 1971-1972 nearly one in every four infants under one year of age was placed for adoption. The adoption rate of Indian children was eight times that of non-Indian children. Approximately 90% of the Indian placements were in non-Indian homes. A number of witnesses also testified to the serious adjustment problems encountered by such children during adolescence, as well as the impact of the adoptions on Indian parents and the tribes themselves.

Further hearings, covering much the same ground, were held during 1977 and 1978 on the bill that became the ICWA. While much of the testimony again focused on the harm to Indian parents and their children who were involuntarily separated by decisions of local welfare authorities, there was also considerable emphasis on the impact on the tribes themselves of the massive removal of their children. For example, Mr. Calvin Isaac, Tribal Chief of the Mississippi Band of Choctaw Indians and representative of the National Tribal Chairmen's Association, testified as follows:

> "Culturally, the chances of Indian survival are significantly reduced if our children, the only real means for the transmission of the tribal heritage, are to be raised in non-Indian homes and denied exposure to the ways of their People. Furthermore, these practices seriously undercut the tribes' ability to continue as self-governing communities. Probably in no area is it more important that tribal sovereignty be respected than in an area as socially and culturally determinative as family relationships."

Chief Isaac also summarized succinctly what numerous witnesses saw as the principal reason for the high rates of removal of Indian children:

> "One of the most serious failings of the present system is that Indian children are removed from the custody of their natural parents by nontribal government authorities who have no basis for intelligently evaluating the cultural and social premises underlying Indian home life and childrearing. Many of the individuals who decide the fate of our children are at best ignorant of our cultural values, and at worst contemptful of the Indian way and convinced that removal, usually to a non-Indian household or institution, can only benefit an Indian child."

The congressional findings that were incorporated into the ICWA reflect these sentiments. The Congress found:

> "(3) that there is no resource that is more vital to the continued existence and integrity of Indian tribes than their children...;

"(4) that an alarmingly high percentage of Indian families are broken up by the removal, often unwarranted, of their children from them by nontribal public and private agencies and that an alarmingly high percentage of such children are placed in non-Indian foster and adoptive homes and institutions; and

"(5) that the States, exercising their recognized jurisdiction over Indian child custody proceedings through administrative and judicial bodies, have often failed to recognize the essential tribal relations of Indian people and the cultural and social standards prevailing in Indian communities and families." 25 U. S. C. § 1901.

At the heart of the ICWA are its provisions concerning jurisdiction over Indian child custody proceedings. Section 1911 lays out a dual jurisdictional scheme. Section 1911(a) establishes exclusive jurisdiction in the tribal courts for proceedings concerning an Indian child "who resides or is domiciled within the reservation of such tribe," as well as for wards of tribal courts regardless of domicile. Section 1911(b), on the other hand, creates concurrent but presumptively tribal jurisdiction in the case of children not domiciled on the reservation: on petition of either parent or the tribe, state-court proceedings for foster care placement or termination of parental rights are to be transferred to the tribal court, except in cases of "good cause," objection by either parent, or declination of jurisdiction by the tribal court.

Various other provisions of ICWA Title I set procedural and substantive standards for those child custody proceedings that do take place in state court. The procedural safeguards include requirements concerning notice and appointment of counsel; parental and tribal rights of intervention and petition for invalidation of illegal proceedings; procedures governing voluntary consent to termination of parental rights; and a full faith and credit obligation in respect to tribal court decisions. The most important substantive requirement imposed on state courts is that of § 1915(a), which, absent "good cause" to the contrary, mandates that adoptive placements be made preferentially with (1) members of the child's extended family, (2) other members of the same tribe, or (3) other Indian families.

The ICWA thus, in the words of the House Report accompanying it, "seeks to protect the rights of the Indian child as an Indian and the rights of the Indian community and tribe in retaining its children in its society." It does so by establishing "a Federal policy that, where possible, an Indian child should remain in the Indian community," and by making sure that Indian child welfare determinations are not based on "a white, middle-class standard which, in many cases, forecloses placement with [an] Indian family."

B

This case involves the status of twin babies, known for our purposes as B. B. and G. B., who were born out of wedlock on December 29, 1985. Their mother, J. B., and father, W. J., were both enrolled members of appellant Mississippi Band of Choctaw Indians (Tribe), and were residents and domiciliaries of the Choctaw Reservation in Neshoba County, Mississippi. J. B. gave birth to the twins in Gulfport, Harrison County, Mississippi, some 200 miles from the reservation. On January 10, 1986, J. B. executed a consent-to-adoption form before the Chancery Court of Harrison County. W. J. signed a similar form. On January 16, appellees Orrey and Vivian Holyfield filed a petition for adoption in the same court, and the chancellor issued a Final Decree of Adoption on January 28. Despite the court's apparent awareness of the ICWA, the adoption decree contained no reference to it, nor to the infants' Indian background.

* * * The Supreme Court of Mississippi [] rejected the Tribe's arguments that the state court lacked jurisdiction and that it, in any event, had not applied the standards laid out in the ICWA. The court recognized that the jurisdictional question turned on whether the twins were domiciled on the Choctaw Reservation. It answered that question as follows:

> "At no point in time can it be said the twins resided on or were domiciled within the territory set aside for the reservation. Appellant's argument that living within the womb of their mother qualifies the children's residency on the reservation may be lauded for its creativity; however, apparently it is unsupported by any law within this state, and will not be addressed at this time due to the far-reaching legal ramifications that would occur were we to follow such a complicated tangential course."

* * * It noted that "the Indian twins... were voluntarily surrendered and legally abandoned by the natural parents to the adoptive parents, and it is undisputed that the parents went to some efforts to prevent the children from being placed on the reservation as the mother arranged for their birth and adoption in Gulfport Memorial Hospital, Harrison County, Mississippi." Therefore, the court said, the twins' domicile was in Harrison County and the state court properly exercised jurisdiction over the adoption proceedings. Indeed, the court appears to have concluded that, for this reason, *none* of the provisions of the ICWA was applicable. * * *

Because of the centrality of the exclusive tribal jurisdiction provision to the overall scheme of the ICWA, as well as the conflict between this decision of the Mississippi Supreme Court and those of several other state courts, we granted plenary review. We now reverse.

II

* * * The state-court proceeding at issue here was a "child custody proceeding." That term is defined to include any "'adoptive placement' which shall mean the permanent placement of an Indian child for adoption, including any action resulting in a final decree of adoption." Moreover, the twins were "Indian children."

The sole issue in this case is, as the Supreme Court of Mississippi recognized, whether the twins were "domiciled" on the reservation.

* * *

It remains to give content to the term "domicile" in the circumstances of the present case. The holding of the Supreme Court of Mississippi that the twin babies were not domiciled on the Choctaw Reservation appears to have rested on two findings of fact by the trial court: (1) that they had never been physically present there, and (2) that they were "voluntarily surrendered" by their parents. The question before us, therefore, is whether under the ICWA definition of "domicile" such facts suffice to render the twins nondomiciliaries of the reservation. * * *

"Domicile" is, of course, a concept widely used in both federal and state courts for jurisdiction and conflict-of-laws purposes, and its meaning is generally uncontroverted. * * * For adults, domicile is established by physical presence in a place in connection with a certain state of mind concerning one's intent to remain there. One acquires a "domicile of origin" at birth, and that domicile continues until a new one (a "domicile of choice") is acquired. Since most minors are legally incapable of forming the requisite intent to establish a domicile, their domicile is determined by that of their parents. In the case of an illegitimate child, that has traditionally meant the domicile of its mother. Under these principles, it is entirely logical that "[o]n occasion, a child's domicile of origin will be in a place where the child has never been."

It is undisputed in this case that the domicile of the mother (as well as the father) has been, at all relevant times, on the Choctaw Reservation. Thus, it is clear that at their birth the twin babies were also domiciled on the reservation, even though they themselves had never been there. The statement of the Supreme Court of Mississippi that "[a]t no point in time can it be said the twins... were domiciled within the territory set aside for the reservation," may be a correct statement of that State's law of domicile, but it is inconsistent with generally accepted doctrine in this country and cannot be what Congress had in mind when it used the term in the ICWA.

Nor can the result be any different simply because the twins were "voluntarily surrendered" by their mother. Tribal jurisdiction under § 1911(a) was not meant to be defeated by the actions of individual members of the tribe, for Congress was concerned not solely about the interests of Indian children and families, but also about the impact on the tribes themselves of the large numbers of Indian children adopted by non-Indians. * * *

In addition, it is clear that Congress' concern over the placement of Indian children in non-Indian homes was based in part on evidence of the detrimental impact on the children themselves of such placements outside their culture. Congress determined to subject such placements to the ICWA's jurisdictional and other provisions, even in cases where the parents consented to an adoption, because of concerns going beyond the wishes of individual parents. As the 1977 Final Report of the congressionally established American Indian Policy Review Commission stated, in summarizing these two concerns, "[r]emoval of Indian children from their cultural setting seriously impacts a long-term tribal survival and has damaging social and psychological impact on many individual Indian children."

These congressional objectives make clear that a rule of domicile that would permit individual Indian parents to defeat the ICWA's jurisdictional scheme is inconsistent with what Congress intended. The appellees in this case argue strenuously that the twins' mother went to great lengths to give birth off the reservation so that her children could be adopted by the Holyfields. But that was precisely part of Congress' concern. Permitting individual members of the tribe to avoid tribal exclusive jurisdiction by the simple expedient of giving birth off the reservation would, to a large extent, nullify the purpose the ICWA was intended to accomplish. * * *

[. . .T]he law of domicile Congress used in the ICWA cannot be one that permits individual reservation-domiciled tribal members to defeat the tribe's exclusive jurisdiction by the simple expedient of giving birth and placing the child for adoption off the reservation. Since, for purposes of the ICWA, the twin babies in this case were domiciled on the reservation when adoption proceedings were begun, the Choctaw tribal court possessed exclusive jurisdiction pursuant to 25 U. S. C. § 1911(a). The Chancery Court of Harrison County was, accordingly, without jurisdiction to enter a decree of adoption; under ICWA, its decree of January 28, 1986, must be vacated.

III

We are not unaware that over three years have passed since the twin babies were born and placed in the Holyfield home, and that a court deciding their fate today is not writing on a blank slate in the same way it would have in January 1986. Three years' development of family ties cannot be undone, and a separation at this point would doubtless cause considerable pain.

Whatever feelings we might have as to where the twins should live, however, it is not for us to decide that question. We have been asked to decide the legal question of *who* should make the custody determination concerning these children -- not what the outcome of that determination should be. The law places that decision in the hands of the Choctaw tribal court. Had the mandate of the ICWA been followed in 1986, of course, much potential anguish might have been avoided, and in any case the law cannot be applied so as automatically to "reward those who obtain custody, whether lawfully or otherwise, and maintain it during any ensuing (and protracted) litigation." It is not ours to say whether the trauma that might result from removing these children from their adoptive family should outweigh the interest of the Tribe -- and perhaps the children themselves -- in having them raised as part of the Choctaw community. Rather, "we must defer to the experience, wisdom, and compassion of the [Choctaw] tribal courts to fashion an appropriate remedy."

The judgment of the Supreme Court of Mississippi is reversed, and the case is remanded for further proceedings not inconsistent with this opinion.

It is so ordered.

JUSTICE STEVENS, with Whom THE CHIEF JUSTICE and JUSTICE KENNEDY Join, Dissenting

The parents of these twin babies unquestionably expressed their intention to have the state court exercise jurisdiction over them. J. B. gave birth to the twins at a hospital 200 miles from the reservation, even though a closer hospital was available. Both parents gave their written advance consent to the adoption and, when the adoption was later challenged by the Tribe, they reaffirmed their desire that the Holyfields adopt the two children. As the Mississippi Supreme Court found, "the parents went to some efforts to prevent the children from being placed on the reservation as the mother arranged for their birth and adoption in Gulfport Memorial Hospital, Harrison County, Mississippi." Indeed, Appellee Vivian Holyfield appears before us today, urging that she be allowed to retain custody of B. B. and G. B.

Because J. B.'s domicile is on the reservation and the children are eligible for membership in the Tribe, the Court today closes the state courthouse door to her. I agree with the Court that Congress intended a uniform federal law of domicile for the Indian Child Welfare Act of 1978 (ICWA) * * * I cannot agree, however, with the cramped definition the Court gives that term. To preclude parents domiciled on a reservation from deliberately invoking the adoption procedures of state court, the Court gives "domicile" a meaning that Congress could not have intended and distorts the delicate balance between individual rights and group rights recognized by the ICWA.

The ICWA was passed in 1978 in response to congressional findings that "an alarmingly high percentage of Indian families are broken up by the *removal*, often unwarranted, of their children from them by nontribal public and private agencies," and that "the States, exercising their recognized jurisdiction over Indian child custody proceedings through administrative and judicial bodies, have often failed to recognize the essential tribal relations of Indian people and the cultural and social standards prevailing in Indian communities and families." 25 U. S. C. §§ 1901(4), (5) (emphasis added). The Act is thus primarily addressed to the unjustified removal of Indian children from their families through the application of standards that inadequately recognized the distinct Indian culture.

* * *

Although parents of Indian children are shielded from the exercise of state jurisdiction when they are temporarily off the reservation, the Act also reflects a recognition that allowing the tribe to defeat the parents' deliberate choice of jurisdiction would be conducive neither to the best interests of the child nor to the stability and security of Indian tribes and families. Section 1911(b), providing for the exercise of concurrent jurisdiction by state and tribal courts when the Indian child is not domiciled on the reservation, gives the Indian parents a veto to prevent the transfer of a state-court action to tribal court. "By allowing the Indian parents to 'choose' the forum that will decide whether to sever the parent-child relationship, Congress promotes the security of Indian families by allowing the Indian parents to defend in the court system that most reflects the parents' familial standards." As Mr. Calvin Isaac, Tribal Chief of the Mississippi Band of Choctaw Indians, stated in testimony to the House Subcommittee on Indian Affairs and Public Lands with respect to a different provision:

> "The ultimate responsibility for child welfare rests with the parents and we would not support legislation which interfered with that basic relationship."

If J. B. and W. J. had established a domicile off the reservation, the state courts would have been required to give effect to their choice of jurisdiction; there should not be a different result when the parents have not changed their own domicile, but have expressed an unequivocal intent to establish a domicile for their children off the reservation. * * *

The interpretation of domicile adopted by the Court requires the custodian of an Indian child who is off the reservation to haul the child to a potentially distant tribal court unfamiliar with the child's present living conditions and best interests. Moreover, it renders any custody decision made by a state court forever suspect, susceptible to challenge at any time as void for having been entered in the absence of jurisdiction. Finally, it forces parents of Indian children who desire to invoke state-court jurisdiction to establish a domicile off the reservation. Only if the custodial parent has the wealth and ability to establish a domicile off the reservation will the parent be able to use the processes of state court. I fail to see how such a requirement serves the paramount congressional purpose of "promot[ing] the stability and security of Indian tribes and families."

The Court concludes its opinion with the observation that whatever anguish is suffered by the Indian children, their natural parents, and their adoptive parents because of its decision today is a result of their failure to initially follow the provisions of the ICWA. By holding that parents who are domiciled on the reservation cannot voluntarily avail themselves of the adoption procedures of state court and that all such proceedings will be void for lack of jurisdiction, however, the Court establishes a rule of law that is virtually certain to ensure that similar anguish will be suffered by other families in the future. Because that result is not mandated by the language of the ICWA and is contrary to its purposes, I respectfully dissent.

....

The *Holyfield* case illustrates the difficult tensions that underlie federal Indian policy. Congress never defined the term 'domicile' in the statute itself. Accordingly the Supreme Court had to try to determine the intent of Congress and what interpretation would make sense given the history of federal Indian policy in the area of children and families. Notice the tension between the majority and the dissent on these questions related to the power of the tribe versus the power of individual tribal parent to decide on the placement of an Indian child. Are you more persuaded by the majority or the dissent?

When the majority looks at ICWA, it sees a statute enacted by Congress to protect tribes from losing their children. The majority emphasized the fact-finding Congress engaged in prior to enacting ICWA showing the tremendous dangers tribal governments faced given the loss of a generation of tribal children. Against this history the majority decided that Congress must have intended to prevent Indian parents from leaving the reservation in order to circumvent the rules of ICWA. The majority firmly places the control of Indian children under the tribal government, a decision which has given tribes a great deal of autonomy and authority when it comes to the placement of their minor members. This power exists even if opposed by the individual Indian parent.

The dissent has a very different understanding of the statute. It argues that ICWA is intended to protect the tribe only in instances where the adoption may be involuntary. The dissent would distinguish this case, where the Indian parents intentionally left the reservation to control the adoption of their children, from other cases where Indian children were abandoned or removed from their parents for cause. The dissent would thus give effect to the choice of the Indian parent in this case, leaving the tribe to control the custody or placement of Indian children who were surrendered involuntarily or who were actually born on the reservation itself.

Holyfield has an interesting post-script. The Supreme Court held that only the tribal court has jurisdiction over the adoption of Indian children domiciled on the reservation and that, despite being born outside the reservation, Indian children take on the domicile of their parents at birth. Since the biological parents did not permanently leave the reservation, the Indian twins were domiciled on the reservation and thus the adoption attempted by the state of Mississippi was invalid. The question of the custody of the twins was transferred to the Choctaw tribal court which had the power under ICWA to make a final decision on the adoption of tribal members. The tribal court examined all the facts and decided that it would be in the best interest of the tribe and the Indian children if they remained with the Holyfields, the non-Indian adoptive family. The Holyfield's adoption was thus confirmed and effectuated by the tribal court.

In the end, while the Holyfield's lost the legal argument at the Supreme Court, they were able to keep custody of their twins as legally recognized adoptive parents. The recognition was conferred not by the state of Mississippi but by the Choctaw tribal court.

Appendix: Treaties with the Sioux
Grant Christensen

The following materials are provided as just one representation of the federal government's dealings with Indian tribes. Any number of original treaty materials could have been included in this section. As textbook authors we have included the Sioux materials because they are a particularly good teaching resource representing changes in federal Indian policy over the course of four successive decades; The Fort Laramie Treaty of 1851, The Fort Laramie Treaty of 1868, The Agreement of 1877, and The Agreement of 1889.

As you read the materials remember the historical context in which they were signed. The first is an 1851 treaty during the pre-civil war era when most of the country was convinced the western plains remained mostly unfit for agriculture and the government's goal was to minimize conflict on the frontier. Then an 1868 treaty in the post-civil war era where the government was now interested in finding new land for settlers and had an army capable of taking land by force that was no longer distracted by the war between the states.

In 1871 the House of Representatives passed a law that denied federal funds for the negotiation of treaties with Indians and thereafter legally binding 'agreements' were approved by both branches of Congress before being signed by the President (treaties need only to be ratified by the Senate). This prohibition on Indian treaty making continues today. The Sioux's subsequent dealings with the United States took the form of 'agreements' which in practice were often not sincerely agreed to by a majority of tribal members.

In 1877, following the Battle of Little Big Horn in 1876, a new 'agreement' was forced upon the Sioux by the government redefining reservation boundaries and ceding away the Black Hills along with other valuable lands. Finally in 1889 North and South Dakota were negotiating their statehood with the United States. As part of those negotiations the federal government entered into a new 'agreement' with the Sioux, over a great deal of opposition particularly from the Dakota and Lakota, which further reduced the reservation territory in order to secure additional land for the new states. This final agreement broke up the great Sioux nation into six smaller fragments resulting in the loss of an additional 9 million acres of land.

Taken together these four documents tell the changing story of Indian policy. They reflect a history that is not unique to the Sioux, but which befell many Indian tribes. Throughout the latter parts of the nineteenth century Indian commissioners continued to seek tribal land cession to increasingly erode the tribal land base. As you review the treaties and agreements that follow remember that were enacted in consecutive decades. Can you identify how these four documents, taken together, resulted in the erosion of tribal lands? In exchange for the loss of their land what does the United States offer in return? What promises does the United States make in each one? How do these promises change over time?

Sioux Treaty 1851

Articles of a treaty made and concluded at Fort Laramie, in the Indian Territory, between D. D. Mitchell, superintendent of Indian affairs, and Thomas Fitzpatrick, Indian agent, commissioners specially appointed and authorized by the President of the United States, of the first part, and the chiefs, headmen, and braves of the following Indian nations, residing south of the Missouri River, east of the Rocky Mountains, and north of the lines of Texas and New Mexico, viz, the Sioux or Dahcotahs, Cheyennes, Arrapahoes, Crows. Assinaboines, Gros- Ventre Mandans, and Arrickaras, parties of the second part, on the seventeenth day of September, A. D. one thousand eight hundred and fifty-one.[1]

Sept. 17, 1851.
11 Stats., p. 749.

ARTICLE 1. The aforesaid nations, parties to this treaty, having assembled for the purpose of establishing and confirming peaceful relations amongst themselves, do hereby covenant and agree to abstain in future from all hostilities whatever against each other, to maintain good faith and friendship in all their mutual intercourse, and to make an effective and lasting peace.

Peace to be observed.

ARTICLE 2. The aforesaid nations do hereby recognize the right of the United States Government to establish roads, military and other posts, within their respective territories.

Roads may be established.

ARTICLE 3. In consideration of the rights and privileges acknowledged in the preceding article, the United States bind themselves to protect the aforesaid Indian nations against the commission of all depredations by the people of the said United States, after the ratification of this treaty.

Indians to be protected.

ARTICLE 4. The aforesaid Indian nations do hereby agree and bind themselves to make restitution or satisfaction for any wrongs committed, after the

Depredations on whites to be satisfied.

---

[1] This treaty as signed was ratified by the Senate with an amendment changing the annuity in Article 7 from fifty to ten years, subject to acceptance by the tribes. Assent of all tribes except the Crows was procured (see Upper Platte C., 570, 1853, Indian Office, and in subsequent agreements this treaty has been recognized as in force (see post p. 776).

ratification of this treaty, by any band or individual of their people, on the people of the United States, whilst lawfully residing in or passing through their respective territories.

Boundaries of lands.

ARTICLE 5. The aforesaid Indian nations do hereby recognize and acknowledge the following tracts of country, included within the metes and boundaries hereinafter designated, as their respective territories, viz:

Sioux.

The territory of the Sioux or Dahcotah Nation, commencing the mouth of the White Earth River, on the Missouri River; thence in a south westerly direction to the forks of the Platte River; thence up the north fork of the Platte River to a point known as the Red Bute, or where the road leaves the river; thence along the range of mountains known as the Black Hills, to the head-waters of Heart River; thence down Heart River to its mouth; and thence down the Missouri River to the place of beginning.

Groaventre, etc.

The territory of the Gros Ventre, Mandans, and Arrickaras Nations, commencing at the mouth of Heart River; thence up the Missouri River to the mouth of the Yellowstone River; thence up the Yellowstone River to the mouth of Powder River in a southeasterly direction, to the head-waters of the Little Missouri River; thence along the Black Hills to the head of Heart River, and thence down Heart River to the place of beginning.

Assinaboin

The territory of the Assinaboin Nation, commencing at the mouth of Yellowstone River; thence up the Missouri River to the mouth of the Muscle-shell River; thence from the mouth of the Muscle-shell River in a southeasterly direction until it strikes the head-waters of Big Dry Creek; thence down that creek to where it empties into the Yellowstone River, nearly opposite the mouth of Powder River, and thence down the Yellowstone River to the place of beginning.

Blackfoot.

The territory of the Blackfoot Nation, commencing at the mouth of Muscle-shell River; thence up the Missouri River to its source; thence along the main range of the Rocky Mountains, in a southerly direction, to the head-waters of the northern source of the Yellowstone River; thence down the Yellowstone River to the mouth of Twenty-five Yard Creek; thence across to the head-waters of the Muscle-shell River, and thence down the Muscle-shell River to the place of beginning.

Crow.

The territory of the Crow Nation, commencing at the mouth of Powder River on the Yellowstone; thence up Powder River to its source; thence along the main range of the Black Hills and Wind River Mountains to the head-waters of the Yellowstone River; thence down the Yellowstone River to the mouth of Twenty-five Yard Creek; thence to the head waters of the Muscle-shell River; thence down the Muscle-shell River to its mouth; thence to the head-waters of Big Dry Creek, and thence to its mouth.

Cheyenne and Arapaho.

The territory of the Cheyennes and Arrapahoes, commencing at the Red Bute, or the place where the road leaves the north fork of the Platte River; thence up the north fork of the Platte River to its source; thence along the main range of the Rocky Mountains to the head-waters of the Arkansas River; thence down the Arkansas River to the crossing of the Santa Fé road; thence in a northwesterly direction to the forks of the Platte River, and thence up the Platte River to the place of beginning.

It is, however, understood that, in making this recognition and acknowledgement, the aforesaid Indian nations do not hereby a bandon or prejudice any rights or claims they may have to other lands; and further, that they do not surrender the privilege of hunting, fishing, or passing over any of the tracts of country heretofore described. *Rights in other lands.*

ARTICLE 6. The parties to the second part of this treaty having selected principals or head-chiefs for their respective nations, through whom all national business will hereafter be conducted, do hereby bind themselves to sustain said chiefs and their successors during good behavior. *Head chiefs of said tribes.*

ARTICLE 7. In consideration of the treaty stipulations, and for the damages which have or may occur by reason thereof to the Indian nations, parties hereto, and for their maintenance and the improvement of their moral and social customs, the United States bind themselves to deliver to the said Indian nations the sum of fifty thousand dollars per annum for the term of ten years, with the right to continue the same at the discretion of the President of the United States for a period not exceeding five years thereafter, in provisions, merchandise, domestic animals, and agricultural implements, in such proportions as may be deemed best adapted to their condition by the President of the United States, to be distributed in proportion to the population of the aforesaid Indian nations. *Annuities.*

ARTICLE 8. It is understood and agreed that should any of the Indian nations, parties to this treaty, violate any of the provisions thereof, the United States may withhold the whole or a portion of the annuities mentioned in the preceding article from the nation so offending, until, in the opinion of the President of the United States, proper satisfaction shall have been made. *Annuities suspended by violation of treaty.*

In testimony whereof the said D. D. Mitchell and Thomas Fitzpatrick commissioners as aforesaid, and the chiefs, headmen, and braves, parties hereto, have set their hands and affixed their marks, on the day and at the place first above written.

D. D. Mitchell
Thomas Fitzpatrick
Commissioners.

Sioux:

Mah-toe-wha-you-whey, his x mark.
Mah-kah-toe-zah-zah, his x mark.
Bel-o-ton-kah-tan-ga, his x mark.
Nah-ka-pah-gi-gi, his x mark.
Mak-toe-sah-bi-chis, his x mark.
Meh-wha-tah-ni-hans-kah, his x mark.

Cheyennes:

Wah-ha-nis-satta, his x mark.
Voist-ti-toe-vetz, his x mark.
Nahk-ko-me-ien, his x mark.
Koh-kah-y-wh-cum-est, his
    x mark.

Arrapahoes:

Bè-ah-té-a-qui-sah, his x mark.
Neb-ni-bah-seh-it, his x mark.
Beh-kah-jay-beth-sah-es, his
    x mark.

Crows:

Arra-tu-ri-sash, his x mark.
Doh-chepit-seh-chi-es, his x mark.

Assinaboines:

Mah-toe-wit-ko, his x mark.
Toe-tah-ki-eh-nan, his x mark.

Mandans and Gros Ventres:

Nochk-pit-shi-toe-pish, his x mark.
She-oh-mant-ho, his x mark.

Arickarees:

Koun-hei-ti-shan, his x mark.
Bi-atch-tah-wetch, his x mark.

In the presence of—

A. B. Chambers, secretary.
S. Cooper, colonel, U. S. Army.
R. H. Chilton, captain, First Drags.
Thomas Duncan, captain, Mounted
    Riflemen.
Thos. G. Rhett, brevet captain R. M. R.
W. L. Elliott, first lieutenant R. M. R.
C. Campbell, interpreter for Sioux.
John S. Smith, interpreter for Cheyennes.
Robert Meldrum, interpreter for the
    Crows.
H. Culbertson, interpreter for Assiniboines
    and Gros Ventres.
Francois L'Etalie, interpreter for Arickarees.
John Pizelle, interpreter for the Arrapahoes.
B. Gratz Brown.
Robert Campbell.
Edmond F. Chouteau.

Sioux Treaty 1868

Treaty between the United States of America and different Tribes of Sioux Indians; Concluded April 29 et seq., 1868; Ratification advised February 16, 1869; Proclaimed February 24, 1869.

Andrew Johnson,
President of the United States of America,

TO ALL AND SINGULAR TO WHOM THESE PRESENTS SHALL COME, GREETING:

WHEREAS a treaty was made and concluded at Fort Laramie, in the Territory of Dakota, [now in the Territory of Wyoming,] on the twenty-ninth day of April, and afterwards, in the year of our Lord one thousand eight hundred and sixty-eight, by and between Nathaniel G. Taylor, William T. Sherman, William S. Harney, John B. Sanborn, S. F. Tappan, C. C. Augur, and Alfred H. Terry, commissioners, on the part of the United States, and Ma-za-pon-kaska, Tah-shun-ka-co-qui-pah, Heh-won-ge-chat, Mah-to-non-pah, Little Chief, Makh-pi-ah-lu-tah, Co-cam-i-ya-ya, Con-te-pe-ta, Ma-wa-tau-ni-hav-ska, He-na-pin-wa-ni-ca, Wah-pah-shaw, and other chiefs and headmen of different tribes of Sioux Indians, on the part of said Indians, and duly authorized thereto by them, which treaty is in the words and figures following, to wit:

> Articles of a treaty made and concluded by and between Lieutenant-General William T. Sherman, General William S. Harney, General Alfred H. Terry, General C. C. Augur, J. B. Henderson, Nathaniel G. Taylor, John B. Sanborn, and Samuel F. Tappan, duly appointed commissioners on the part of the United States, and the different bands of the Sioux Nation of Indians, by their chiefs and headmen, whose names are hereto subscribed, they being duly authorized to act in the premises.

ARTICLE I. From this day forward all war between the parties to this agreement shall forever cease. The government of the United States desires peace, and its honor is hereby pledged to keep it. The Indians desire peace, and they now pledge their honor to maintain it.

April 29 1868.
Preamble.

Contracting parties.

War to cease and peace to be kept.

Offenders against the Indians to be arrested, &c.

If bad men among the whites, or among other people subject to the authority of the United States, shall commit any wrong upon the person or property of the Indians, the United States will, upon proof made to the agent and forwarded to the Commissioner of Indian Affairs at Washington city, proceed at once to cause the offender to be arrested and punished according to the laws of the United States, and also reimburse the injured person for the loss sustained.

Wrong-doer against the whites to be punished.

Damages.

If bad men among the Indians shall commit a wrong or depredation upon the person or property of any one, white, black, or Indian, subject to the authority of the United States, and at peace therewith, the Indians herein named solemnly agree that they will, upon proof made to their agent and notice by him, deliver up the wrong-doer to the United States, to be tried and punished according to its laws; and in case they wilfully refuse so to do, the person injured shall be reimbursed for his loss from the annuities or other moneys due or to become due to them under this or other treaties made with the United States. And the President, on advising with the Commissioner of Indian Affairs, shall prescribe such rules and regulations for ascertaining damages under the provisions of this article as in his judgment may be proper. But no one sustaining loss while violating the provisions of this treaty or the laws of the United States shall be reimbursed therefor.

Reservation.

Boundaries.

ARTICLE II. The United States agrees that the following district of country, to wit, viz: commencing on the east bank of the Missouri river where the forty-sixth parallel of north latitude crosses the same, thence along low-water mark down said east bank to a point opposite where the northern line of the State of Nebraska strikes the river, thence west across said river, and along the northern line of Nebraska to the one hundred and fourth degree of longitude west from Greenwich, thence north on said meridian to a point where the forty-sixth parallel of north latitude intercepts the same, thence due east along said parallel to the place of beginning; and in addition thereto, all existing reservations on the east bank of said river shall be, and the same is, set apart for the absolute and undisturbed use and occupation of the Indians herein named, and for such other friendly tribes or individual Indians as from time to time they may be willing, with the consent of the United States, to admit amongst them; and the United States now solemnly agrees that no persons except those herein designated and authorized so to do, and except such officers, agents, and employés of the government as may be authorized to enter upon Indian reservations in discharge of duties enjoined by law, shall ever be permitted to pass over, settle upon, or reside in the territory described in this article, or in such territory as may be added to this reservation for the use of said Indians, and henceforth they will and do hereby relinquish all claims or right in and to any portion of the United States or Territories, except such as is embraced within the limits aforesaid, and except as hereinafter provided.

Certain persons not to enter or reside thereon.

ARTICLE III. If it should appear from actual survey or other satisfactory examination of said tract of land that it contains less than one hundred and sixty acres of tillable land for each person who, at the time, may be authorized to reside on it under the provisions of this treaty, and a very considerable number of such persons shall be disposed to commence cultivating the soil as farmers, the United States agrees to set apart, for the use of said Indians, as herein provided, such additional quantity of arable land, adjoining to said reservation, or as near to the same as it can be obtained, as may be required to provide the necessary amount.

Additional arable land to be added, if, &c.

ARTICLE IV. The United States agrees, at its own proper expense, to construct at some place on the Missouri river, near the centre of said reservation, where timber and water may be convenient, the following buildings, to wit: a warehouse, a storeroom for the use of the agent in storing goods belonging to the Indians, to cost not less than twenty-five hundred dollars; an agency building for the residence of the agent, to cost not exceeding three thousand dollars; a residence for the physician, to cost not more than three thousand dollars; and five other buildings, for a carpenter, farmer, blacksmith, miller, and engineer, each to cost not exceeding two thousand dollars; also a school-house or mission building, so soon as a sufficient number of children can be induced by the agent to attend school, which shall not cost exceeding five thousand dollars.

Buildings on reservation.

The United States agrees further to cause to be erected on said reservation, near the other buildings herein authorized, a good steam circular saw-mill, with a grist-mill and shingle machine attached to the same, to cost not exceeding eight thousand dollars.

ARTICLE V. The United States agrees that the agent for said Indians shall in the future make his home at the agency building; that he shall reside among them, and keep an office open at all times for the purpose of prompt and diligent inquiry into such matters of complaint by and against the Indians as may be presented for investigation under the provisions of their treaty stipulations, as also for the faithful discharge other duties enjoined on him by law. In all cases of depredation person or property he shall cause the evidence to be taken in writing forwarded, together with his findings, to the Commissioner of Indian Affairs, whose decision, subject to the revision of the Secretary of the Interior, shall be binding on the parties to this treaty.

Agent's residence, office, and duties.

ARTICLE VI. If any individual belonging to said tribes of Indians, or legally incorporated with them, being the head of a family, shall desire to commence farming, he shall have the privilege to select, in the presence and with the assistance of the agent then in charge, a tract of land within said reservation, not exceeding three hundred and twenty acres in extent, which tract when so selected, certified, and recorded in the "land book," as herein directed, shall

Heads of families may select land for farming.

cease to be held in common, but the same may be occupied and held in the exclusive possession of the person selecting it, and of his family, so long as he or they may continue to cultivate it.

Others may select land for cultivation. Any person over eighteen years of age, not being the head of a family, may in like manner select and cause to be certified to him or her, for purposes of cultivation, a quantity of land not exceeding eighty acres in extent, and thereupon be entitled to the exclusive possession of the same as above directed.

Certiflcate. For each tract of land so selected a certificate, containing a description thereof, and the name of the person selecting it, with a certificate endorsed thereon that the same has been recorded, shall be delivered to the party entitled to it, by the agent, after the same shall have been recorded' by him in a book to be kept in his office, subject to inspection, which said book shall be known as the " Sioux Land Book."

Surveys. The President may, at any time, order a survey of the reservation, and, when so surveyed, Congress shall provide for protecting the rights of said settlers in their improvements, and may fix the character of the title held by each. The United States may pass such laws on the subject of alienation **Alienation and descent of property.** and descent of property between the Indians and their descendants as may be thought proper. And it is further stipulated that any male Indians over eighteen years of age, of any band or tribe that is or shall hereafter become a party to this treaty, who now is or who shall hereafter become a resident or occupant of any reservation or territory not included in the tract of country designated and described in this treaty for the permanent home of the Indians, which is not mineral land, nor reserved by the United States for special purposes other than Indian occupation, and who shall have made improvements thereon of the value of two hundred dollars or more, and **Certain Indians may receive patents for one hundred and sixty acres of land.** continuously occupied the same as a homestead for the term of three years, shall be entitled to receive from the United States a patent for one hundred and sixty acres of land including his said improvements, the same to be in the form of the legal subdivisions of the surveys of the public lands. Upon application in writing, sustained by the proof of two disinterested witnesses, made to the register of the local land office when the land sought to be entered is within a land district, and when the tract sought to be entered is not in any land district, then upon said application and proof being made to the commissioner of the general land office, and the right of such Indian or Indians to enter such tract or tracts of land shall accrue and be perfect from the date of his first improvements thereon, and shall continue as long as he **Such Indians receiving patents to become citizens of the United States.** continues his residence and improvements, and no longer. And any Indian or Indians receiving a patent for land under the foregoing provisions, shall thereby and from thenceforth become and be a citizen of the United States, and be entitled to all the privileges and immunities of such citizens, and shall, at the same time, retain all his rights to benefits accruing to Indians under this treaty.

ARTICLE VII. In order to insure the civilization of the Indians entering into this treaty, the necessity of education is admitted, especially of such of them as are or may be settled on said agricultural reservations, and they therefore pledge themselves to compel their children, male and female, between the ages of six and sixteen years, to attend school; and it is hereby made the duty of the agent for said Indians to see that this stipulation is strictly complied with; and the United States agrees that for every thirty children between said ages who can be induced or compelled to attend school, a house shall be provided and a teacher competent to teach the elementary branches of an English education shall be furnished, who will reside among said Indians, and faithfully discharge his or her duties as a teacher. The provisions of this article to continue for not less than twenty years.

Education.

Children to attend school.

School-houses and teachers.

ARTICLE VIII. When the head of a family or lodge shall have selected lands and received his certificate as above directed, and,the agent shall be satisfied that he intends in good faith to commence cultivating the soil for a living, he shall be entitled to receive seeds and agricultural implements for the first year, not exceeding in value one hundred dollars, and for each succeeding year he shall continue to farm, for a period of three years more, he shall be entitled to receive seeds and implements as aforesaid, not exceeding in value twenty-five dollars.

Seeds and agricultural implements.

And it is further stipulated that such. persons as commence farming shall receive instruction from the farmer herein provided for, and whenever more than one hundred persons shall enter upon the cultivation of the soil, a second blacksmith shall be provided, with such iron, steel, and other material as may be needed.

Instruction in farming.
Second black-smith.

ARTICLE IX. At any time after ten years from the making of this treaty, the United States shall have the privilege of withdrawing the physician, farmer, blacksmith, carpenter, engineer, and miller herein provided for, but in case of such withdrawal, an additional sum thereafter of ten thousand dollars per annum shall be devoted to the education of said Indians, and the Commissioner of Indian Affairs shall, upon careful inquiry into their condition, make such rules and regulations for the expenditure of said sum as will best promote the educational and moral improvement of said tribes.

Physician, farmer, &c. may be withdrawn. Additional appropriation in such case.

ARTICLE X. In lieu of all sums of money or other annuities provided to be paid to the Indians herein named, under any treaty or treaties heretofore made, the United States agrees to deliver at the agency house on the reservation herein named, on [or before[2]] the first day of August of each year, for thirty years, the following articles, to wit:

Delivery of goods in lieu of money or other annuities.

[2] The words "or before" are inserted with black pencil.

Clothing.

For each male person over fourteen years of age, a suit of good substantial woollen clothing, consisting of coat, pantaloons, flannel shirt, hat, and a pair of home-made socks.

For each female over twelve years of age, a flannel skirt, or the goods necessary to make it, a pair of woollen hose, twelve yards of calico, and twelve yards of cotton domestics.

For the boys and girls under the ages named, such flannel and cotton goods as may be needed to make each a suit as aforesaid, together with a pair of woollen hose for each.

Census.

And in order that the Commissioner of Indian Affairs may be able to estimate properly for the articles herein named, it shall be the duty of the agent each year to forward to him a full and exact census of the Indians, on which the estimate from year to year can be based.

Other necessary articles.

And in addition to the clothing herein named, the sum of ten dollars for each person entitled to the beneficial effects of this treaty shall be annually appropriated for a period of thirty years, while such persons roam and hunt, and twenty dollars for each person who engages in farming, to be used by the Secretary of the Interior in the purchase of such articles as from time to time the condition and necessities of the Indians may indicate to be proper. And if

Appropriation to continue for thirty years.

within the thirty years, at any time, it shall appear that the amount of money needed for clothing under this article can be appropriated to better uses for the Indians named herein, Congress may, by law, change the appropriation to other purposes; but in no event shall the amount of this appropriation be withdrawn or discontinued for the period named. And the President shall annually detail an officer of the army to be. present and attest the delivery of

Army officer to attend the delivery.

all the goods herein named to the Indians, and he shall inspect and report on the quantity and quality of the goods and the manner of their delivery. And it is hereby expressly stipulated that each Indian over the age of four years, who shall have removed to and settled permanently upon said reservation and complied with the stipulations of this treaty, shall be eutitled to receive from the United States, for the period of four years after he shall have settled

Meal and flour.

upon said reservation, one pound of meat and one pound of flour per day, provided the Indians cannot furnish their own subsistence at an earlier date. And it is further stipulated that the United States will furnish and deliver to each lodge of Indians or family of persons legally incorporated with them, who shall remove to the reservation herein described and commence farm-

Cows and oxen.

ing, one good American cow, and one good well-broken pair of American oxen within sixty days after such lodge or family shall have so settled upon said reservation.

ARTICLE XI. In consideration of the advantages and benefits conferred by this treaty and the many pledges of friendship by the United States, the tribes who are parties to this agreement hereby stipulate that they will relinquish all right to occupy permanently the territory outside their reservation as herein defined, but yet reserve the right to hunt on any lands north of North Platte, and on the Republican Fork of the Smoky Hill river, so long as the buffalo may range thereon in such numbers as to justify the chase. And they, the said Indians, further expressly agree:

1st. That they will withdraw all opposition to the construction of the railroads now being built on the plains.

2d. That they will permit the peaceful construction of any railroad not passing over their reservation as herein defined.

3d. That they will not attack any persons at home, or travelling, nor molest or disturb any wagon trains, coaches, mules, or cattle belonging to the people of the United States, or to persons friendly therewith.

4th. They will never capture, or carry off from the settlements, white women or children.

5th. They will never kill or scalp white men, nor attempt to do them harm.

6th. They withdraw all pretence of opposition to the construction of the railroad now being built along the Platte river and westward to the Pacific ocean, and they will not in future object to the construction of railroads, wagon roads, mail stations, or other works of utility or necessity, which may be ordered or permitted by the laws of the United States. But should such roads or other works be constructed on the lands of their reservation, the government will pay the tribe whatever amount of damage may be assessed by three disinterested commissioners to be appointed by the President for that purpose, one of said commissioners to be a chief or headman of the tribe.

7th. They agree to withdraw all opposition to the military posts or roads now established south of the North Platte river, or that may be established, not in violation of treaties heretofore made or hereafter to be made with any of the Indian tribes.

ARTICLE XII. No treaty for the cession of any portion or part of the reservation herein described which may be held in common shall be of any validity or force as against the said Indians, unless executed and signed by at least three fourths of all the adult male Indians, occupying or interested in the same; and no cession by the tribe shall be understood or construed in such manner as to deprive, without his consent, any individual member of the tribe of his rights to any tract of land selected by him, as provided in Article VI. of this treaty.

ARTICLE XIII. The United States hereby agrees to furnish annually to the Indians the physician, teachers, carpenter, miller, engineer, farmer, and blacksmiths, as herein contemplated, and that such appropriations shall be made from time to time, on the estimates of the Secretary of the Interior, as will be sufficient to employ such persons.

Presents for best crops.

ARTICLE XIV. It is agreed that the sum of five hundred dollars annually, for three years from date, shall be expended in presents to the ten persons of said tribe who in the judgment of the agent may grow the most valuable crops for the respective year.

Reservation to be permanent home of tribes.

ARTICLE XV. The Indians herein named agree that when the agency house and other buildings shall be constructed on the reservation named, they will regard said reservation their permanent home, and they will make no permanent settlement elsewhere; but they shall have the right, subject to the conditions and modifications of this treaty, to hunt, as stipulated in Article XI. hereof.

Unceded Indian territory.

Not to be occupied by whites, &c.

ARTICLE XVI. The United States hereby agrees and stipulates that the country north of the North Platte river and east of the summits of the Big Horn mountains shall be held and considered to be unceded Indian territory, and also stipulates and agrees that no white person or persons shall be permitted to settle upon or occupy any portion of the same; or without the consent of the Indians, first had and obtained, to pass through the same; and it is further agreed by the United States, that within ninety days after the conclusion of peace with all the bands of the Sioux nation, the military posts now established in the territory in this article named shall be abandoned, and that the road leading to them and by them to the settlements in the Territory of Montana shall be closed.

Effect of this treaty upon former treaties.

ARTICLE XVII. It is hereby expressly understood and agreed by and between the respective parties to this treaty that the execution of this treaty and its ratification by the United States Senate shall have the effect, and shall be construed as abrogating and annulling all treaties and agreements heretofore entered into between the respective parties hereto, so far as such treaties and agreements obligate the United States to furnish and provide money, clothing, or other articles of property to such Indians and bands of Indians as become parties to this treaty, but no further.

In testimony of all which, we, the said commissioners, and we, the chiefs and headmen of the Brulé band of the Sioux nation, have hereun to set our hands and seals at Fort Laramie, Dakota Territory, this twenty-ninth day of April, in the year one thousand eight hundred and sixty-eight.

Execution by the Brulé band.

N. G. TAYLOR,   [SEAL.]
W. T. SHERMAN,   [SEAL.]
Lt. Genl.
WM. S. HARNEY,   [SEAL.]
Bvt. Maj. Gen. U. S. A.
JOHN B. SANBORN,   [SEAL.]
S. F. TAPPAN,   [SEAL.]
C. C. AUGUR,   [SEAL.]

Bvt. Maj. Genl.
ALFRED H. TERRY,   [SEAL.]
Bvt. M. Gen. U. S. A.

Attest:

A. S. H. WHITE, *Secretary.*

Executed on the part of the Brulé band of Sioux by the chiefs and head-men whose names are hereto annexed, they being thereunto duly authorized, at Fort Laramie, D. T., the twenty-ninth day of April, in the year A. D. 1868.

MA-ZA-PON-KASKA, his x mark, Iron Shell.   [SEAL.]
WAH-PAT-SHAH, his x mark, Red Leaf.   [SEAL.]
HAH-SAH-PAH, his x mark, Black Horn.   [SEAL.]
ZIN-TAH-GAH-LAT-SKAH, his x mark, Spotted Tail.   [SEAL.]
ZIN-TAH-SKAH, his x mark, White Tail.   [SEAL.]
ME-WAH-TAH-NE-HO-SKAH, his x mark, Tall Mandas.   [SEAL.]
SHE-CHA-CHAT-KAH, his x mark, Bad Left Hand.   [SEAL.]
NO-MAH-NO-PAH, his x mark, Two and Two.   [SEAL.]
TAH-TONKA-SKAH, his x mark, White Bull.   [SEAL.]
CON-RA-WASHTA, his x mark, Pretty Coon.   [SEAL.]
HA-CAH-CAH-SHE-CHAH, his x mark, Bad Elk.   [SEAL.]
WA-HA-KA-ZAH-ISH-TAH, his x mark, Eye Lance.   [SEAL.]
MA-TO-HA-KE-TAH, his x mark, Bear that looks behind. [SEAL.]
BELLA-TONKA-TONKA, his x mark, Big Partisan.   [SEAL.]
MAH-TO-HO-HONKA, his x mark, Swift Bear.   [SEAL.]
TO-WIS-NE, his x mark, Cold Place.   [SEAL.]
ISH-TAH-SKAH, his x mark, White Eyes.   [SEAL.]
MA-TA-LOO-ZAH, his x mark, Fast Bear.   [SEAL.]
AS-HAH-KAH-NAH-ZHE, his x mark, Standing Elk.   [SEAL.]
CAN-TE-TE-KI-YA, his x mark, The Brave Heart.   [SEAL.]
SHUNKA-SHATON, his x mark, Day Hawk.   [SEAL.]
TATANKA-WAKON, his x mark, Sacred Bull.   [SEAL.]
MAPIA SHATON, his x mark, Hawk Cloud.   [SEAL.]
MA-SHA-A-OW, his x mark, Stands and Comes.   [SEAL.]
SHON-KA-TON-KA, his x mark, Big Dog.   [SEAL.]

Attest:

ASUTON S. H. WHITE, *Secretary of Commission.*
GEORGE B. WITHS, *Phonographer to Commission.*
GEO. H. HOLTZMAN.
JOUN D. HOWLAND.
JAMES C. O'CONNOR.
CHAS. E. GUERN, *Interpreter.*
LEON F. PALLARDY, *Interpreter.*

Nicholas Janis, *Interpreter.*

Executed on the part of the Ogallalah band of Sioux by the chiefs and headmen whose names are hereto subscribed, they being thereunto duly authorized, at Fort Laramie, the twenty-fifth day of May, in the year A. D. 1868.

Execution by the Ogallalah band.

TAH-SHUN-KA-CO-QUI-PAH, his x mark, Man-afraid-of-his-horses.   [SEAL.]
SHA-TON-SKAH, his x mark, White Hawk.   [SEAL.]
SHA-TON-SAPAH, his x mark, Black Hawk.   [SEAL.]
E-GA-MON-TON-KA-SAPAH, his x mark, Black Tiger.   [SEAL.]
OH-WAH-SHE-CHA, his x mark, Bad Wound.   [SEAL.]
PAH-GEE, his x mark, Grass.   [SEAL.]
WAH-NON-REH-CHE-GEH, his x mark, Ghost Heart.   [SEAL.]
CON-REEH, his x mark, Crow.   [SEAL.]
OH-HE-TE-KAH, his x mark, The Brave.   [SEAL.]
TAH-TON-KAH-HE-YO-TA-KAH, his x mark, Sitting Bull. [SEAL.]
SHON-KA-OH-WAH-MON-YE, his x mark, Whirlwind Dog.   [SEAL.]
HA-HAH-KAH-TAH-MIECH, his x mark, Poor Elk.   [SEAL.]
WAM-BU-LEE-WAH-KON, his x mark, Medicine Eagle.   [SEAL.]

VOL. XV. TREAT. — 41

CHON-GAH-MA-HE-TO-HANS-KA, his x mark,
High Wolf.   [SEAL.]
WAH-SE-CHUN-TA-SHUN-KAH, his x mark,
American. Horse.   [SEAL.]
MAH-HAH-MAH-HA-MAK-NEAR, his x mark, Man
that walks under the ground.   [SEAL.]
MAH-TO-TOW-PAH, his x mark, Four Bears.   [SEAL.]
MA-TO-WEE-SHA-KTA, his x mark, One that
kills the bear.   [SEAL.]
OH-TAH-KEE-TOKA-WEE-CHAKTA, his x mark,
One that kills in a hard place.   [SEAL.]
TAH-TON-KAH-TA-MIECH, his x mark, The poor Bull.   [SEAL.]
OH-HUNS-EE-GA-NON-SKEN, his x mark, Mad Shade.   [SEAL.]
SHAH-TON-OH-NAH-OM-MINNE-NE-OH-MINNE,
his x mark, Whirling Hawk.   [SEAL.]
MAH-TO-CHUN-KA-OH, his x mark, Bear's Back.   [SEAL.]
CHE-TON-WEE-KOH, his x mark, Fool Hawk.   [SEAL.]
WAH-HOH-KE-ZA-AH-HAH, his x mark,
One that has the lance.   [SEAL.]
SHON-GAH-MANNI-TOH-TAN-KA-SEH,
his x mark, Big Wolf Foot.   [SEAL.]
EH-TON-KAH, his x mark, Big Mouth.   [SEAL.]

MA-PAH-CHE-TAH, his x mark, Bad Hand.   [SEAL.]
WAH-KE-YUN-SHAH, his x mark, Red Thunder.   [SEAL.]
WAK-SAH, his x mark, One that Cuts Off.   [SEAL.]
CHAM-NOM-QUI-YAH, his x mark, One that
Presents the Pipe.   [SEAL.]
WAH-KE-KE-YAN-PUH-TAH, his x mark, Fire Thunder. [SEAL.]
MAH-TO-NONK-PAH-ZE, his x mark,
Bear with Yellow Ears.   [SEAL.]
CON-REE-TEH-KA, his x mark, The Little Crow.   [SEAL.]
HE-HUP-PAH-TOH, his x mark, The Blue War Club.   [SEAL.]
SHON-KEE-TOH, his x mark, The Blue Horse.   [SEAL.]
WAM-BALLA-OH-CONQUO, his x mark, Quick Eagle. [SEAL.]
TA-TONKA-SUPPA, his x mark, Black Bull.   [SEAL.]
MOH-TO-HA-SHE-NA, his x mark, The Bear Hide.   [SEAL.]

Attest:
S. E. WARD.
JAS. C. O'CONNOR.
J. M. SHERWOOD.
W. C. SLICER.
SAM DEON.
H. M. MATTHEWS.
JOSEPH BISSONETTE, *Interpreter.*
NICHOLAS JANIS, *Interpreter.*
LEFROY JOTT, *Interpreter.*
ANTOINE JANIS, *Interpreter.*

Executed on the part of the Minneconjon band of Sioux by the chiefs and headmen whose names are hereto subscribed, they being thereunto duly authorized.

Execution by the Minneconjon band.

At Fort Laramie, D. T., HEH-WON-GE-CHAT,
his x mark, One Horn.   [SEAL.]
May 26, '68, 13 names.
OH-PON-AH-TAH-E-MANNE, his x mark,
The Elk that bellows Walking.   [SEAL.]
At Fort Laramie, D. T., May 25, '68, 2 names. HEH-HO-
LAH-REH-CHA-SKAH, his x mark, Young White Bull. [SEAL.]
WAH-CHAH-CHUM-KAH-COH-KEE-PAH, his x mark,
One that is afraid of Shield.   [SEAL.]
HE-HON-NE-SHAKTA, his x mark, The Old Owl.   [SEAL.]
MOC-PE-A-TOH, his x mark, Blue Cloud.   [SEAL.]
OH-PONG-GE-LE-SKAH, his x mark, Spotted Elk.   [SEAL.]
TAH-TONK-KA-HON-KE-SCHNE, his x mark, Slow Bull. [SEAL.]

SHONK-A-NEE-SHAH-SHAH-A-TAH-PE, his x mark,
The Dog Chief.   [SEAL.]
MA-TO-TAH-TA-TONK-KA, his x mark, Bull Bear.   [SEAL.]
WOM-BEH-LE-TON-KAH, his x mark, The Big Eagle.   [SEAL.]
MA-TOH-EH-SCHNE-LAH, his x mark, The Lone Bear.   [SEAL.]
MAH-TOH-KE-SU-YAH, his x mark,
The One who Remembers the Bear.   [SEAL.]
MA-TOH-OH-HE-TO-KEH, his x mark, The Brave Bear.   [SEAL.]
EH-CHE-MA-HEH, his x mark, The Runner.   [SEAL.]
TI-KI-YA, his x mark, The Hard.   [SEAL.]
HE-MA-ZA, his x mark, Iron Horn.   [SEAL.]

Attest:

JAS. C. O'CONNOR.
WM. H. BROWN.
NICHOLAS JANIS, *Interpreter.*
ANTOINE JANIS, *Interpreter.*

Executed on the part of the Yanctonais band of Sioux by the chiefs and head-men whose names are hereto subscribed, they being thereunto duly authorized:

Execution by the Yanctonais band.

MAH-TO-NON-PAH, his x mark, Two Bears.   [SEAL.]
MA-TO-HNA-SKIN-YA, his x mark, Mad Bear.   [SEAL.]
HE-O-PU-ZA, his x mark, Louzy.   [SEAL.]
AH-KE-CHE-TAH-CHE-CA-DAN, his x mark, Little Soldier. [SEAL.]
MAH-TO-E-TAN-CHAN, his x mark; Chief Bear.   [SEAL.]
CU-WI-H-WIN, his x mark, Rotten Stomach.   [SEAL.]
SKUN-KA-WE-TKO, his x mark, Fool Dog.   [SEAL.]
ISH-TA-SAP-PAH, his x mark, Black Eye.   [SEAL.]
IH-TAN-CHAN, his x mark, The Chief.   [SEAL.]
I-A-WI-CA-KA, his x mark, The one who Tells the Truth.   [SEAL.]
AH-KE-CHE-TAH, his x mark, The Soldier.   [SEAL.]
TA-SHI-NA-GI, his x mark, Yellow Robe.   [SEAL.]
NAH-PE-TON-KA, his x mark, Big Hand.   [SEAL.]
CHAN-TEE-WE-KTO, his x mark, Fool Heart.   [SEAL.]
HOH-GAN-SAH-PA, his x mark, Black Catfish.   [SEAL.]
MAH-TO-WAH-KAN, his x mark, Medicine Bear.   [SEAL.]
SHUN-KA-KAN-SHA, his x mark, Red Horse.   [SEAL.]
WAN-RODE, his x mark, The Eagle.   [SEAL.]
CAN-HPI-SA-PA, his x mark, Black Tomahawk.   [SEAL.]
WAR-HE-LE-RE, his x mark, Yellow Eagle.   [SEAL.]
CHA-TON-CHE-CA, his x mark, Small Hawk, or Long Fare. [SEAL.]
SHU-GER-MON-E-TOO-HA-SKA, his x mark, Tall Wolf.   [SEAL.]
MA-TO-U-TAH-KAH, his x mark, Sitting Bear.   [SEAL.]

HI-HA-CAH-GE-NA-SKENE, his x mark, Mad Elk.   [SEAL.]

LITTLE CHIEF, his x mark.   [SEAL.]   *Arapahoes.*

TALL BEAR, his x mark.   [SEAL.]

TOP MAN, his x mark.   [SEAL.]

NEVA, his x mark.   [SEAL.]

THE WOUNDED BEAR, his x mark.   [SEAL.]

THIRLWIND, his x mark.   [SEAL.]

THE FOX, his x mark.   [SEAL.]

THE DOG BIG MOUTH, his x mark.   [SEAL.]

SPOTTED WOLF, his x mark.   [SEAL.]

SORREL HORSE, his x mark.   [SEAL.]

BLACK COAL, his x mark.   [SEAL.]

BIG WOLF, his x mark.   [SEAL.]

KNOCK-KNEE, his x mark.   [SEAL.]

BLACK CROW, his x mark.   [SEAL.]

THE LONE OLD MAN, his x mark.   [SEAL.]

PAUL, his x mark.   [SEAL.]

BLACK BULL, his x mark.   [SEAL.]

BIG TRACK, his x mark.   [SEAL.]

THE FOOT, his x mark.   [SEAL.]

BLACK WHITE, his x mark.   [SEAL.]

YELLOW HAIR, his x mark.   [SEAL.]

LITTLE SHIELD, his x mark.   [SEAL.]

BLACK BEAR, his x mark.   [SEAL.]

WOLF MOCASSIN, his x mark.   [SEAL.]

BIG ROBE, his x mark.   [SEAL.]

WOLF CHIEF, his x mark.   [SEAL.]

Witnesses:

ROBT. P. McKIBBIN,
    Capt. 4 Inf. Bvt. Lt. Col. U. S. A. Comdg. Ft. Laramie.

WM. H. POWELL, *But. Maj. Capt. 4th Inf.*

HENRY W. PATTERSON, *Capt. 4th Infy.*

THEO. E. TRUE, *2d Lieut. 4th Inf.*

W. G. BULLOCK.

CHAS. E. GUERN,
    Special Indian Interpreter for the Peace Commission.

                FORT LARAMIE, WG. T., *Nov.* 6, 1868.

MAKH-PI-AH-LU-TAH, his x mark, Red Cloud.   [SEAL.]

WA-KI-AH-WE-CHA-SHAH, his x mark, Thunder Man.   [SEAL.]

MA-ZAH-ZAH-GEH, his x mark. Iron Cane.   [SEAL.]

WA-UMBLE-WHY-WA-KA-TUYAH, his x mark,
High Eagle.   [SEAL.]

KO-KE-PAH, his x mark. Man Afraid.   [SEAL.]
WA-KI-AH-WA-KOU-AH, his x mark,
Thunder Flying Running.   [SEAL.]

Witnesses:

    W. McE. DYE, *Bvt. Col. U. S. A. Comg.*
    A. B. CAIN, *Capt. 4 Inf. Bt. Maj. U. S. A.*
    ROBT. P. McKIBBIN, *Capt. 4 Inf. Bvt. Lt. Col. U. S. A.*
    JNO. MILLER, *Capt. 4th Inf.*
    G. L. LUHN, *1st Lieut. 4th Inf. Bvt. Capt. U. S. A.*
    H. C. SLOAN, *2d Lt. 4th Inf.*
    WHITTINGHAM COX, *1st. Lieut. 4th Infy.*
    A. W. VOGDES, *1st Lt. 4th Infy.*
    BUTLER D. PRICE, *2d Lt. 4th Inf.*

HEADQRS., FORT LARAMIE, *Novr.* 6, '68.

Executed by the above on this date.

All of the Indians are Ogallalahs excepting Thunder Man and Thunder Flying Running, who are Brulés.

WM. McE. DYE,
Maj. 4th Infy. and Bvt. Col. U. S. A. Comg.

Attest:

    JAS. C. O'CONNOR.
    NICHOLAS JANIS, *Interpreter.*
    FRANC. LA FRAMBOISE, *Interpreter.*
    P. J. DE SMET, S. J., *Missionary among the Indians.*
    SAML. D. HINMAN, B. D., *Missionary.*

Executed on the part of the Uncpapa band of Sioux, by the chiefs and headmen whose names are hereto subscribed, they being thereunto duly authorized.

Execution by the Unepapa band.

CO-KAM-I-YA-YA, his x mark, The Man that
Goes in the Middle.   [SEAL.]
MA-TO-CA-WA-WEKSA, his x mark, Bear Rib.   [SEAL.]
TA-TO-KA-IN-YAN-KE, his x mark, Running Antelope. [SEAL.]
KAN-GI-WA-KI-TA, his x mark, Looking Crow.   [SEAL.]
A-KI-CI-TA-HAN-SKA, his x mark, Long Soldier.   [SEAL.]
WA-KU-TE-MA-NI, his x mark, The One who Shoots
Walking.   [SEAL.]
UN-KCA-KI-KA, his x mark, The Magpie.   [SEAL.]
KAN-GI-O-TA, his x mark, Plenty Crow.   [SEAL.]
HE-MA-ZA, his x mark, Iron Horn.   [SEAL.]
SHUN-KA-I-NA-PIN, his x mark, Wolf Necklace.   [SEAL.]
I-WE-HI-YU, his x mark, The Man who Bleeds
from the Mouth.   [SEAL.]

HE-HA-KA-PA, his x mark, Elk Head. [SEAL.]
I-ZU-ZA, his x mark, Grind Stone. [SEAL.]
SHUN-KA-WI-TKO, his x mark, Fool Dog. [SEAL.]
MA-KPI-YA-PO, his x mark, Blue Cloud. [SEAL.]
WA-MLN-PI-LU-TA, his x mark, Red Eagle. [SEAL.]
MA-TO-CAN-TE, his x mark, Bear's Heart. [SEAL.]
A-KI-CI-TA-I-TAU-CAN, his x mark, Chief Soldier. [SEAL.]

Attest:

Jas. C. O'Connor.
Nicholas Janis, *Interpreter.*
Franc. La Frambois[e], *Interpreter.*
P. J. De Smet, S. J., *Missy. among the Indians.*
Saml. D. Hinman, *Missionary.*

Executed on the part of the Blackfeet band of Sioux by the chiefs and head-men whose names are hereto subscribed, they being thereunto duly authorized. *by the Blackfeet band.*

CAN-TE-PE-TA, his x mark, Fire Heart. [SEAL.]
WAN-MDI-KTE, his x mark, The One who Kills Eagle. [SEAL.]
SHO-TA, his x mark, Smoke. [SEAL.]
WAN-MDI-MA-NI, his x mark, Walking Eagle. [SEAL.]
WA-SHI-CUN-YA-TA-PI, his x mark, Chief White Man. [SEAL.]
KAN-GI-I-YO-TAN-KE, his x mark, Sitting Crow. [SEAL.]
PE-JI, his x mark, The Grass. [SEAL.]
KDA-MA-NI, his x mark, The One that Rattles as he Walks. [SEAL.]
WAH-HAN-KA-SA-PA, his x mark, Black Shield. [SEAL.]
CAN-TE-NON-PA, his x mark, Two Hearts. [SEAL.]

Attest:

Jas. C. O'Connor.
Nicholas Janis, *Interpreter.*
Franc. La Framboise, *Interpreter.*
P. J. De Smet, S. J., *Missy. among the Indians.*
Saml. D. Hinman, *Missionary.*

Executed on the part of the Cutheads band of Sioux by the chiefs and headmen whose names are hereto subscribed, they being thereunto duly authorized. *Execution by the Cutheads band.*

TO-KA-IN-YAN-KA, his x mark,
The One who Goes Ahead Running. [SEAL.]
TA-TAN-KA-WA-KIN-YAN, his x mark, Thunder Bull. [SEAL.]
SIN-TO-MIN-SA-PA, his x mark, All over Black. [SEAL.]
CAN-I-CA, his x mark, The One who Took the Stick. [SEAL.]
PA-TAN-KA, his x mark, Big Head. [SEAL.]

Attest:

    Jas. C. O'Connor.

    Nicholas Janis, *Interpreter.*

    Franc. La Frambois[e], *Interpreter.*

    P. J. De Smet, S. J., *Missy. among the Indians.*

    Saml. D. Hinman, *Missionary.*

by the Two Kettle band;

Executed on the part of the Two Kettle band of Sioux by the chiefs and headmen whose names are hereto subscribed, they being thereunto duly authorized.

    MA-WA-TAN-NI-HAN-SKA, his x mark, Long Mandan.   [SEAL.]

    CAN-KPE-DU-TA, his x mark, Red War Club.   [SEAL.]

    CAN-KA-GA, his x mark, The Log.   [SEAL.]

Attest:

    Jas. C. O'Connor.

    Nicholas Janis, *Interpreter.*

    Franc. La Framboise, *Interpreter.*

    P. J. De Smet, S. J., *Missy. among the Indians.*

    Saml. D. Hinman, *Missionary to the Dakotas.*

by the Sans Arch band.

Executed on the part of the Sans Arch band of Sioux by the chiefs and headmen whose names are hereto annexed, they being thereunto duly authorized.

    HE-NA-PIN-WA-NI-CA, his x mark, The One that has

    Neither Horn.   [SEAL.]

    WA-INLU-PI-LU-TA, his x mark, Red Plume.   [SEAL.]

    CI-TAN-GI, his x mark, Yellow Hawk.   [SEAL.]

    HE-NA-PIN-WA-NI-CA, his x mark, No Horn.   [SEAL.]

Attest:

    Jas. C. O'Connor.

    Nicholas Janis, *Interpreter.*

    Franc. La Frambois[e], *Interpreter.*

    P. J. De Smet, S. J., *Missy. among the Indians.*

    Saml. D. Hinman, *Missionary.*

Execution by the Santee band.

Executed on the part of the Santee band of Sioux by the chiefs and headmen whose names are hereto subscribed, they being thereunto duly authorized.

    WA-PAH-SHAW, his x mark, Red Ensign.   [SEAL.]

    WAH-KOD-TAY, his x mark, Shooter.   [SEAL.]

    HOO-SHA-SHA, his x mark, Red Legs.   [SEAL.]

    O-WAN-CHA-DU-TA, his x mark, Scarlet all over.   [SEAL.]

    WAU-MACE-TAN-KA, his mark x, Big Eagle.   [SEAL.]

    CHO-TAN-KA-E-NA-PE, his x mark, Flute-player.   [SEAL.]

    TA-SHUN-KE-MO-ZA, his x mark, His Iron Dog.   [SEAL.]

Attest:

    SAML. D. HINMAN, B. D., *Missionary.*
    J. N. CHICKERING, *2d Lt. 22d Infy., Bvt. Capt. U. S. A.*
    P. J. DE SMET, S. J.
    NICHOLAS JANIS, *Interpreter.*
    FRANC. LA FRAMBOISE, *Interpreter.*

And whereas, the said treaty having been submitted to the Senate of the United States for its constitutional action thereon, the Senate did, on the sixteenth day of February, one thousand eight hundred and sixty-nine, advise and consent to the ratification of the same, by a resolution in the words and figures following, to wit: Ratification.

IN EXECUTIVE SESSION, SENATE OF THE UNITED STATES,

                                         February 16, 1869.

Resolved (two thirds of the senators present concurring), That the Senate advise and consent to the ratification of the treaty between the United States and the different bands of the, Sioux nation of Indians, made and concluded the 29th April, 1868.

Attest:

                              GEO. C. GORHAM,

                                    Secretary.

Now, therefore, be it known that I, ANDREW JOHNSON, President of the United States of America, do, in pursuance of the advice and consent of the Senate, as expressed in its resolution of the sixteenth of February, one thousand eight hundred and sixty-nine, accept, ratify, and confirm the said treaty.   Proclamation.

In testimony whereof I have hereto signed my name, and caused the seal of the United States to be affixed.

Done at the city of Washington, this twenty-fourth day of February, in the year of our Lord one thousand eight hundred and sixty-nine, and of the Independence of the United States of America, the ninety-third.

    [SEAL.]

                              ANDREW JOHNSON.

By the President:

    WILLIAM H. SEWARD, *Secretary of State.*

Agreement of 1877

An act to ratify an agreement with certain bands of the Sioux Nation of Indiana and also with the Northern Arapaho and Cheyenne Indians.

Be it enacted by the Senate and House of Representatives of the United States of America in Congress assembled, That a certain agreement made by George W. Manypenny, Henry B. Whipple, Jared W. Daniels, Albert G. Boone, Henry C. Bulis, Newton Edmunds, and Augustine S. Gaylord, commissioners on the part of the United States, with the different bands of the Sioux Nation of Indians, and also the Northern Arapaho and Cheyenne Indians, be, and the same is hereby, ratified and confirmed: *Provided,* That nothing in this act shall be construed to authorize the removal of the Sioux Indians to the Indian Territory and the President of the United States is hereby directed to prohibit the removal of any portion of the Sioux Indians to the Indian Territory until the same shall be authorized by an act of Congress hereafter enacted, except article four, except also the following portion of article six: "And if said Indians shall remove to said Indian Territory as hereinbefore provided, the Government shall erect for each of the principal chiefs a good and comfortable dwelling-house" said article not having been agreed to by the Sioux Nation; said agreement is in words and figures following, namely: "Articles of agreement made pursuant to the provisions of an act of Congress entitled "An act making appropriations for the current and contingent expenses of the Indian Department, and for fulfilling treaty stipulations with various Indian tribes, for the year ending June thirtieth, eighteen hundred and seventy-seven, and for other purposes," approved August 15, 1876, by and between George W. Manypenny, Henry B. Whipple, Jared W. Daniels, Albert G. Boone, Henry C. Bulis, Newton Edmunds, and Augustine S. Gaylord, commissioners on the part of the United States, and the different bands of the Sioux Nation of Indians, and also the Northern Arapahoes and Cheyennes, by their chiefs and headmen, whose names are hereto subscribed, they being duly authorized to act in the premises.

Agreement with Sioux Indians and Northern Arapaho and Cheyenue Indians confirmed, except, etc.

Sioux not to be removed.

"ARTICLE 1. The said parties hereby agree that the northern and western boundaries of the reservation defined by article 2 of the treaty between the United States and different tribes of Sioux Indians, concluded April 29, 1868, and proclaimed February 24, 1869, shall be as follows: The western boundaries shall commence at the intersection of the one hundred and third meridian of longitude with the northern boundary of the State of Nebraska; thence north along said meridian to its intersection with the South Fork of the Cheyenne River; thence down said stream to its junction with the North Fork; thence up the North Fork of said Cheyenne River to the said one hundred and third meridian; thence north along said meridian to the South Branch of Cannon Ball River or Cedar Creek; and the northern boundary of their said reservation shall follow the said South Branch to its intersection with the main Cannon Ball River, and thence down the said main Cannon Ball River to the Missouri River; and the said Indians do hereby relinquish and cede to the United States all the territory lying outside the said reservation, as herein modified and described, including all privileges of hunting; and article 16 of said treaty is hereby abrogated.

"ARTICLE 2 The said Indians also agree and consent that wagon and other roads, not exceeding three in number, may be constructed and maintained, from convenient and accessible points on the Missouri River, through said reservation, to the country lying immediately west thereof, upon such routes as shall be designated by the President of the United States; and they also consent and agree to the free navigation of the Missouri River.

"ARTICLE 3. The said Indians also agree that they will hereafter receive all annuities provided by the said treaty of 1868, and all subsistence and supplies which may be provided for them under the present or any future act of Congress, at such points and places on the said reservation, and in the vicinity of the Missouri River, as the President of the United States shall designate.

"ARTICLE 4. The Government of the United States and the said Indians, being mutually desirous that the latter shall be located in a country where they may eventually become self-supporting and acquire the arts of civilized life, it is therefore agreed that the said Indians shall select a delegation of five or more chiefs and principal men from each band, who shall, without delay, visit the Indian Territory under the guidance and protection of suitable persons, to be appointed for that purpose by the Department of the Interior, with a view to selecting therein a permanent home for the said Indians. If such delegation shall make a selection which shall be satisfactory to them-selves, the people whom they represent, and to the United States, then the said Indians agree that they will remove to the country so selected within one year from this date. And the said Indians do further agree in all things to submit themselves to such beneficent plans as the Government may provide

Boundaries of reservation.

Roads through reservation.

Annuities, where received.

Delegation to select home in Indian Territory.

Removal within one year.

for them in the selection of a country suitable for a permanent home, where they may live like white men.

"ARTICLE 5. In consideration of the foregoing cession of territory and rights, and upon full compliance with each and every obligation assumed by the said Indians, the United States does agree to provide all necessary aid to assist the said Indians in the work of civilization; to furnish to them schools and instruction in mechanical and agricultural arts, as provided for by the treaty of 1868. Also to provide the said Indians with subsistence consisting of a ration for each individual of a pound and a half of beef, (or in lieu thereof, one half pound of bacon,) one-half pound of flour, and one-half pound of corn; and for every one hundred rations, four pounds of coffee, eight pounds of sugar, and three pounds of beans, or in lieu of said articles the equivalent thereof, in the discretion of the Commissioner of Indian Affairs. Such rations, or so much thereof as may be necessary, shall be continued until the Indians are able to support themselves. Rations shall, in all cases, be issued to the head of each separate family; and whenever schools shall have been provided by the Government for said Indians, no rations shall be issued for children between the ages of six and fourteen years (the sick and infirm excepted) unless such children shall regularly attend school. Whenever the said Indians shall be located upon lands which are suitable for cultivation, rations shall be issued only to the persons and families of those persons who labor, (the aged, sick, and infirm excepted;) and as an incentive to industrious habits the Commissioner of Indian Affairs may provide that such persons be furnished in payment for their labor such other necessary articles as are requisite for civilized life. The Government will aid said Indians as far as possible in finding a market for their surplus productions, and in finding employment, and will purchase such surplus, as far as may be required, for supplying food to those Indians, parties to this agreement, who are unable to sustain themselves; and will also employ Indians, so far as practicable, in the performance of Government work upon their reservation.

Assistance, schools, rations, purchase of surplus, employment.

"ARTICLE 6 Whenever the head of a family shall, in good faith, select an allotment of land upon such reservation and engage in the cultivation thereof, the Government shall, with his aid, erect a comfortable house on such allotment; and if said Indians shall remove to said Indian Territory as herein before provided, the Government shall erect for each of the principal chiefs a good and comfortable dwelling-house.

Erection of houses.

"ARTICLE 7. To improve the morals and industrious habits of said Indians, it is agreed that the agent, trader, farmer, carpenter, blacksmith, and other artisans employed or permitted to reside within the reservation belonging to the Indians, parties to this agreement, shall be lawfully married and living with their respective families on the reservation; and no person other than an Indian of full blood, whose fitness, morally or otherwise, is not, in the opinion of

Artisans to be married, etc.

Unfit persons to receive no benefits.

the Commissioner of Indiar. Affairs, conducive to the welfare of said Indians, shall receive any benefit from this agreement or former treaties, and may be expelled from the reservation.

Treaty of 1868, 15 Stat., 655.
In force.
Subject to laws of United States.

"ARTICLE 8. The provisions of the said treaty of 1868, except as herein modified, shall continue in full force, and, with the provisions of this agreement, shall apply to any country which may hereafter be occupied by the said Indians as a home; and Congress shall, by appropriate legislation, secure to them an orderly government; they shall be subject to the laws of the United States, and each individual shall be protected in his rights of property, person, and life.

Indians pledged to this agreement.

"ARTICLE 9. The Indians, parties to this agreement, do hereby solemnly pledge themselves, individually and collectively, to observe each and all of the stipulations herein contained, to select allotments of laud as soon as possible after their removal to their permanent home, and to use their best efforts to learn to cultivate the same. And they do solemnly pledge themselves that they will at all times maintain peace with the citizens and Government of the United States; that they will observe the laws thereof and loyally endeavor to fulfill all the obligations assumed by them under the treaty of 1868 and the present agreement, and to this end will, whenever requested by the President of the United States, select so many suitable men from each band to co-operate with him in maintaining order and peace on the reservation as the President may deem necessary, who shall receive such compensation for their services as Congress may provide.

Annual census.

"ARTICLE 10. In order that the Government may faithfully fulfill the stipulations contained in this agreement, it is mutually agreed that a census of all Indians affected hereby shall be taken in the month of December of each year, and the names of each head of family and adult person registered; said census to be taken in such manner as the Commissioner of Indian Affairs may provide.

Term "reservation."

"ARTICLE 11. It is understood that the term reservation herein contained shall be held to apply to any country which shall be selected under the authority of the United States as the future home of said Indians.

Agreement subject to approval.

"This agreement shall not be binding upon either party until it shall have received the approval of the President and Congress of the United States.

"Dated and signed at Red Cloud agency, Nebraska, September 26, 1876.

"GEORGE W. MANYPENNY.	[SEAL.]
"HENRY B. WHIPPLE.	[SEAL.]
"J. W. DANIELS.	[SEAL.]
"ALBERT G. BOONE.	[SEAL.]
"H. C. BULIS.	[SEAL.]
"NEWTON EDMUNDS.	[SEAL.]
"A. S. GAYLORD.	[SEAL.]

"Attest:

"CHARLES M. HENDLEY,
          "*Secretary.*

"OGALLALLA SIOUX—CHIEFS AND HEADMEN.

"Marpiya-luta, (Red Cloud,) his x mark, seal.
"Taxunke-kokipe, (Afraid-of-his-Horse,) his x mark, seal.
"Xunka-luta, (Red Dog,) his x mark, seal.
"Taopi-cikala, (Little Wound,) his x mark, seal.
"Waxicun-taxunke, (American Horse,) his x mark, seal.
"Mato-kokipa, (Afraid of-the-Bear,) his x mark, seal.
"Mato-yamni, (Three Bears,) his x mark, seal.
"Wakinyan-peta, (Fire-Thunder,) his x mark, seal.
"Mato-luza, (Fast Bear,) his x, mark, seal.
"Kangi-ho-waxte, (Crow-with-a-good-voice,) his x mark, seal
"Mato-ayuwi, (Turning Bear,) his x mark, seal.
"Itunkassan-waumli, (Weasel-Eagle,) his x mark, seal.
"Warpe-xa, (Red Leaf,) his x mark, seal.
"Ixta-peta, (Fire Eyes, or White Bull,) his x mark, seal.
"Pte-san-wicaxa, (Man White Cow,) his x mark, seal.
"Kangi-tanka, (Big Crow,) his x mark, seal.
"Tatanka-waxte, (Good Bull,) his x mark, seal.
"Xunkikyuha, (Sorrel Horse,) his x mark seal.
"Itunkasan-mato, (Weasel-Bear,) his x mark, seal.
"Wahukeza-nonpa, (Two-Lance,) his x mark, seal.
"Owe-xica, (Bad Wound,) his x mark, seal.
"Mato-wankantu, (High Bear,) his x mark, seal.
"Tokicu, (He-Takes-the-Enemy,) his x mark, seal.
"Akicita, (Soldier,) his x mark, seal.
"Ite-glega, (Stupid Face, or Slow Bull,) his x mark, seal.
"Xunmanito-wankantu, (High Wolf,) his x mark, seal.
"Si-tanka, (Big Foot,) his x mark, seal.
XIX——17
"Wakinyan-ska, (White Thunder,) his x mark, seal.
"Xunki-to (Blue Horse,) his x mark, seal.

                    "ARAPAHOES
"Black Coal, his x mark, seal.
"Crazy Bull, his x mark, seal.
"Little Wolf, his x mark, seal.
"Sharp Nose, his x mark, seal.
"Six Feathers, his x mark, seal.
"White Horse, his x mark, seal.
                    "CHEYENNES

Signatures.
Orgallalla Sioux.

Arapahoes.

Cheyennes.

"Living Bear, his x mark, seal.
"Spotted Elk, his x mark, seal.
"Black Bear, his x mark, seal.
"Turkey Legs, his x mark, seal.
"Calfskin Shirt, his x mark, seal.

"Dated and signed at Spotted Tail agency, Nebraska, September 23, 1876.
"BRULE SIOUX

Brule Sioux.

"Sinta gleska, (Spotted Tail,) his x mark, seal.
"Mato-luza, (Swift Bear,) his x mark, seal.
"Nom-karpa, (Two Strike,) his x mark, seal.
"Wakinyan-ska, (White Thunder,) his x mark, seal.
"Heraka-najou, (Standing Elk,) his x mark, seal.
"Hi toto, (Blue Teeth,) his x mark, seal.
"Baptiste Good, his x mark, seal.
"Kangi-sapa, (Black Crow,) his x mark, seal.
"Taxunke-wakita, (Looking Horse,) his x mark, seal.
"Mato-ocin-xica, (Wicked Bear,) his x mark, seal.
"Wamli-cikala, (Little Eagle,) his x mark, seal.
"Xunka-luta, (Red Dog,) his x mark, seal.
"Tacampi-to, (Blue Tomahawk,) his x mark, seal.
"Xunka-luza, (Fast Dog,) his x mark, seal.
"Miwatani-banska, (Tall Mandan,) his x mark, seal.
"Hitunkasan-luta, (Red Weasel,) his x mark, seal.
"Mato-wakan, (Sacred Bear,) his x mark, seal.
"Muggins, his x mark, seal.
"Ixnalawica, (Only Male,) his x mark, seal.
"Mato-can-wegna-iyaye, (Bear-in-the-wood,) his x mark, seal.
"Hobu, (Coarse Voice,) his x mark, seal.
"No Flesh, (Conica-wanica,) his x mark, seal.
"Mato-wankantu, (High Bear,) his x mark, seal.
"Wicampi-tanka, (Big-Star,) his x mark, seal.
"Akan-ka-kte, (Killed-on-horseback,) his x mark, seal.
"Ixta-ska-ska, (White Eyes,) his x mark, seal.
"Wamnionmi-akicita, (Whirlwind Soldier,) his x mark, seal.
"Wakinyan-cangleska, (Ring Thunder,) his x mark, seal.
"Wakingan-wamli, (Thunder Eagle,) his x mark, seal.
"Xkeca-guaxkingan, (Crazy Mink,) his x mark, seal.
"Ho-waxte, (Good Voice,) his x mark, seal.
"Ta-kudankokipexni, (Afraid-of-nothing,) his x mark, seal.
"Cante-peta, (Fire heart,) his x mark, seal.
"Wapaswapi, (Roast,) his x mark, seal.
"Itecantku-ze, (Yellow Breast,) his x mark, seal.

"Maza-wanapinya, (Iron Necklace,) his x mark, seal.
"Sinte-gleska-holkxila, (Young Spotted Tail,) his x mark, seal.
"Mato-wanagi, (Bear Ghost,) his x mark, seal.
"Xunka-ixlala, (Lone Dog,) his x mark, seal.
"Pte-sanwicaxa, (White Buffalo man,) his x mark, seal.
"Maz-ixta, (Iron Eyes,) his x mark, seal.
"Asanpi, (Milk,) his x mark, seal.
"Cetanwamli, (Eagle Hawk,) his x mark, seal.

"I certify that the foregoing treaty was read and explained by me, and   Certificate.
was fully understood by the above named Indians, before signing, and
that the same was executed by the above Ogallalla Sioux, Cheyennes,
and Arapahoes, at Red Cloud agency, on the 20th day of September, A.
D. 1876, and by the Brule Sioux at Spotted Tail agency on the 28d day of
September, A. D. 1876

                              "SAML. D. HINMAN,
                                        "*Official Interpreter.*

"Attest:
       "Louis Bordeaux,
           "William Garnett,
           "William Roland,
           "Henry C. Clifford,
                   "*Interpreters.*

"The foregoing articles of agreement having been fully explained to us in   Consent of Sioux at
open council, we, the undersigned chiefs and headmen of the various bands   Standing Rock.
of Sioux Indians receiving rations and annuities at the Standing Rock agency,
in the Territory of Dakota, do hereby consent and agree to all the stipulations
therein contained, with the exception of so much of article four of said agreement as relates to our visit and removal to the Indian Territory; in all other
respects the said article remaining in full force and effect.
    "Witness our bands and seals at Standing Rock agency, Territory of Dakota,
this 11th day of October, A. D. 1876.

                    "Lower Yanotonais.   Lower Yanctonais.

"Mato-nonpa, (Two Bears,) his x mark, seal.
"Tashunka-kokipapi, (He-fears-his-horse,) his x mark, seal.
"Waha, (Cotton Wood,) his x mark, seal.
"Hogan-duta, (Red Fish,) his x mark, seal.
"Mato-Guashkinyan, (Mad Bear,) his x mark, seal.
"Cokamti, (Camp in Middle,) his x mark, seal.
"Tatanka-wanagi, (Bull's Ghost,) his x mark, seal.
"Waonzoege, (Pantaloons,) his x mark, seal.

"Mato chitika, (Brave Bear,) his x mark, seal.
"Can-Icu, (Drag Wood,) his x mark, seal.
"Iyayog-manni, (Walk out of the way,) his x mark, seal.
"Igmu-sapa, (Black Wild Cat,) his x mark, seal.
"Akicita cikala, (Little Soldier,) his x mark, seal.
"Canhpi-sapa, (Black Tomahawk,) his x mark, seal.
"Hahaka-maza, (Iron Elk,) his x mark, seal.
"Inyang-mani, (Running Walker,) his x mark, seal.
"Tashunka-witko, (Fool Dog,) his x mark, seal.
"Wanmli-napin, (Eagle Necklace,) his x mark, seal.

Upper Yanctonais.

"UPPER YANCTONAIS

"Nasulan-tanka, (Big Head,) his x mark, seal.
"Shunkaha-napin, (Wolf Necklace,) his x mark, seal.
"Ishta-sapa, (Black Eye,) his x mark, seal.
"Tahinca-ska, (White Dear,) his x mark, seal.
"Tatanka-luta, (Red Bull,) his x mark, seal.
"Maga, (Goose,) his x mark, seal.
"Tacanonpa, (His Pipe,) his x mark, seal.
"Cante-witko, (Fool Heart,) his x mark, seal.
"Mato-wakantuya, (High Bear,) his x mark, seal.
"Tatanka-pa, (Bull Head,) his x mark, seal.
"Shunka-wanjila, (Lone Dog,) his x mark, seal
"Nape-tanka, (Big Hand,) his x mark, seal.

Uncpapas.

"UNCPAPAS.

"Cetan-wakinyan, (Thunder Hawk,) his x mark, seal.
"Mato-cuwiyuksa, (Bear Rib,) his x mark, seal.
"Tatoke-inyanke, (Running Antelope,) his x mark, seal.
"He-maza, (Iron Horn,) his x mark, seal.
"Wakute-mani, (Walking Shooter,) his x mark, seal.
"Akicita-hauska, (Long Soldier,) his x mark, seal.
"Wicasha-wakan, (Medicine Mau,) his x mark, seal.
"Ishta-ska, (White Eye,) his x mark, seal.
"Zitkala-sapa, (Black Bird,) his x mark, seal.
"Nape-shica, (Bad Hand,) his x mark, seal.
"Wahukeza-luta, (Scarlet Lance,) his x mark, seal.

Blackfeet.

"BLACKFEET

"Peji, (John Grass,) his x mark, seal.
"Kangi-iyotanka, (Sitting Crow,) his x mark, seal.
"Cante-peta, (Fire Heart,) his x mark, seal.

"Zitkala-wankantuya, (High Bird,) his x mark, seal.
"Nata-opi, (Wounded-Head,) his x mark, seal.
"Tashunka-luta, (Red Horse,) his x mark, seal.
"Cetan-luta, (Red Hawk,) his x mark, seal.

"Attest:
  "R. E. JOHNSTON
    "Captain First Infantry, Bvt. Lieut. Col.,
        "U. S. A., Acting Indian Agent.
  "W. D. WOLVERTON,
    "Surgeon U. S. A.

"I certify that the foregoing agreement was read and explained by me, and **Certificate** was fully understood by the above named Sioux Indians before signing, and that the same was executed by said Sioux Indians at Standing Rock agency, Dak, on the 11th day of October, A. D. 1876.

                          "SAML D. HINMAN,
                                "Official Interpreter.

"Attest:
  "LOUIS AGARD,
  "WILLIAM HALSEY,
  "E. H. ALLISON,
    "Interpreters."

"The foregoing articles of agreement having been fully explained to us **Assent of Sioux at** in open council, we, the chiefs and headmen of the various bands of Sioux **Cheyenne River.** Indians, receiving rations and annuities at the Cheyenne River agency, in the Territory of Dakota, do hereby consent and agree to all the stipulations therein contained, with the exception of so much of article 4 of said agreement as relates to our visit and removal to the Indian Territory; in all other respects the said article remaining in full force and effect.

"Witness our hands and seals at Cheyenne River agency, Territory of Dakota, this 16th day of October, A. D. 1876.

                    "SANS ARC.   Sans Arc.

"Kangi-wiyaka, (Crow Feather,) his x mark, seal.
"Waanatan, (The Charger,) his x mark, seal.
"Cetan-gi, (Yellow Hawk,) his x mark, seal.
"Taku-kokipa-xni, (Fearless,) his x mark, seal.
"Wiyaka-luta, (Red Feather,) his x mark, seal.
"Ho-waxte, (Good Voice,) his x mark, seal.
"Ite-xujahan, (Scare the Hawk,) his x mark, seal.
"Waiglu-xica, (Man that Hurts Himself,) his x mark, seal.

"Tatanka-ska, (White Bull,) his x mark, seal.
"Pehin-xaxa, (Red Hair,) his x mark, seal.

Blackfeet.   "BLACKFEET

"Mato-ayuwi, (Turning Bear,) his x mark, seal.
"Wakinyan-ska, (White Thunder,) his x mark, seal.
"Ixto-xakiya, (Red Arm,) his x mark, seal.
"Hehloga, (Yearling,) his x mark, seal.
"Pa-hoton, (Sounding Head,) his x mark, seal.
"Mahpiya-gleglega, (Striped Cloud,) his x mark, seal.
"Itoye-psunpsunla, (Awkward Face,) his x mark, seal.
"Maza-napin, (Iron Necklace,) his x mark, seal.

Two Kettle.   "TWO KETTLE.

"Mato-topa, (Four Bears,) his x mark, seal.
"Cuwi-hla-mani, (Rattling Ribs,) his x mark, seal.
"Mawatani-hanska-hokxila, (Long Mandan's Son,) his x mark, seal.
"Can-haba, (The Log,) his x mark, seal.
"Tacanhpi-luta, (Red Tomahawk,) his x mark, seal.
"Wokaye, (Brings the Food,) his x mark, seal.
"Mato-waaktonsya, (Forgetful Bear,) his x mark, seal.
"Xung-gleska-sapa, (Black Spotted Horse,) his x mark, seal.
"Xunka-wanjila, (The Lone Dog,) his x mark, seal.
"Hehaka-ska, (White Elk,) his x mark, seal.
"Mato-gleska, (Spotted Bear,) his x mark, seal.
"Ptesan-wanmli, (White Cow Eagle,) his x mark, seal.
"Mato wanmli, (Bear Eagle,) his x mark, seal.
"Mato-tanka, (Big Bear,) his x mark, seal.
"Cetan-luzahan, (Swift Hawk,) his x mark, seal.
"Wamniomni-luzahan, (Swift Whirlwind,) his x mark, seal.
"Taxunke-kokipapi, (Afraid-of-his-horse,) his x mark, seal.
"Hebola-nonpa, (Good Thunder,) his x mark, seal.
"Peji-to, (Green Grass,) his x mark, seal.
"Zitkala-kinyan, (Flying Bird,) his x mark, seal.
"Taxunka-maza, (Iron Horse,) his x mark, seal.
"Ptesan-wicaxa, (White Cow Man,) his x mark, seal.
"Sinte-nonpa, (Two Tails,) his x mark, seal.
"Kinyan-axapi, (Flying Laughing,) his x mark, seal.
"Inyan-hanksa, (Long Stone,) his x mark, seal.
"Natala, (Head,) his x mark, seal.
"Xungleska, (Spotted Horse,) his x mark, seal.
"Xiyo-sapa, (Black Prairie Chicken,) his x mark, seal.
"Wakuwa-mani, (Walking Hunter,) his x mark, seal.

"MINNECONJOU   minneconjou.

"Magaska, (Swan,) his x mark, seal.
"Magakxica, (The Duck,) his x mark, seal.
"Cante-wanica, (No Heart,) his x mark, seal.
"Cante-wanica-wicahca, (Old Man No Heart,) his x mark, seal.
"Mahaka, (Standing Bear,) his x mark, seal.
"Ixnawasanica, (The Half,) his x mark, seal.
"Xina-ska, (White Robe,) his x mark, seal.
"Canhpi-sapa, (Black Tomahawk,) his x mark, seal.
"Mato-wankantuya, (High Bear,) his x mark, seal.
"Winkte-nonpa, (The Keg,) his x mark, seal.
"Kankaca-luta, (Red Plume,) his x mark, seal.
"Hchanskaska, (Long Horn,) his x mark, seal.
"Mato-waxte, (Good Bear,) his x mark, seal.
"Tatanka-pahakan-najin, (Bull on the Hill,) his x mark, seal.
"Xiyo-hanska, (Tall Prairie Chicken,) his x mark, seal.
"Cetan-gleska, (Spotted Hawk,) his mark, seal.
"Inyan-boslahan, (Standing Rock,) his x mark, seal.

"Attest:

"CHARLES A. WICKOFF,
"Capt Eleventh Infantry.
"LESLIE SMITH
"Capt. First Infantry, Bvt. Major, U. S. Army.

"WM. FIELDER,
"MARK WELLS,
"Interpreters.

"I certify that the foregoing agreement was read and explained by me, and   Certificate.
was fully understood by the above named Sioux Indians before signing; and
that the same was executed by said Sioux Indians at Cheyenne River agency,
Dakota, on the 16th day of October, A. D. 1876.

"SAML. D. HINMAN,
"Official Interpreter.

"The foregoing articles of agreement having been fully explained to us   Consent of Sioux at
in open council, we, the undersigned chiefs and headmen of the Sioux Indi-   Crow Creek.
ans, receiving rations and annuities at Crow Creek agency, in the Territory of
Dakota, do hereby consent and agree to all the stipulations therein contained,
with the exception of so much of article 4 of said agreement as relates to our
visit and removal to the Indian Territory; in all other respects the said article
remaining in full force and effect.

"Witness our hands and seals at Crow Creek agency, Territory of Dakota,
this 21st day of October. A. D. 1876.

Lower Yanctonais.

"LOWER YANOTONAIS

"Wanigi-ska, (White Ghost,) his x mark. seal.
"Wanmdi-sapa, (Black Eagle,) his x mark, seal.
"Wizi, (Old Lodge,) his x mark, seal.
"Najinyan-upi, (Surrounded,) his x mark, seal.
"Mato-watakpe, (Attacking Bear,) his x mark. seal.
"Mato-wakuwa-wicarca, (Old Man Running Bear,) his x mark, seal.
"Mato-wakuwa-hokxina, (Young Man Running Bear,) his x mark, seal.
"Katayapi, (Killed,) his x mark, seal.
"Mato-wakokipe-xni, (Fearless Bear,) his x mark, seal.
"Mato ska, (White Bear,) his x mark, seal.
"Waksuyemani, (Returns from War,) his x mark, seal.
"Kasde, (Splits,) his x mark, seal.
"Cagu-ska, (White Lungs or Bear Ghost,) his x mark, seal.
"Wanmdi-wicaxa, (Eagle Man,) his x mark, seal.
"Mato-cekiyapi, (They Worship the Bear,) his x mark, seal.
"Kangi-iawakan, (Sacred Talking Crow,) his x mark, seal.
"Cetan-koyagmani, (Walks With a Hawk,) his x mark, seal.
"Maga-bobdu, (Stormy Goose,) his x mark, seal.
"Wage-hunka, (Yellow Man,) his x mark, seal.
"Nakpa-wanjina, (One Ear,) his x mark, seal.
"Onspexni, (He Don't Know,) his x mark, seal.
"Attest:

"HENRY F. LIVINGSTON.
"FRANKLIN J. DE WITT.

"EDWD ASHLEY,
"H BURT,
"ANTOINE LE CLARE,
    "*Interpreters.*

Certificate.

"I certify that the foregoing agreement was read and explained by me, and was fully understood by the above-named Sioux Indians before signing; and that the same was executed by said Sioux Indians at Crow Creek agency, Dakota, on the 21st day of October, A. D. 1876.

"SAML D. HINMAN.
"*Official Interpreter.*

Consent of Sioux at Lower Brule.

"The foregoing articles of agreement having been folly explained to us in open council, we, the undersigned chiefs and headmen of the Sioux Indians, receiving rations and annuities at Lower Brule agency, in the Territory of Dakota, do hereby consent and agree to all the stipulations therein contained, with the exception of so much of article 4 of said agreement as relates to our visit and removal to the Indian Territory; in all other respects the said article remaining in full force and effect.

Witness our hands and seals at Lower Brule agency, Territory of Dakota, this 24th day of October, A. D. 1876.

"LOWER BRULES.

Lower Brules.

"Maza-oyate, (Iron Nation,) his x mark, seal.
"Tatanka-wakan, (Medicine Bull,) his x mark, seal.
"Ptesan-wicakte, (White Buffalo Cow,) his x mark, seal.
"Xiyocikala, (Little Pheasant,) his x mark, seal.
"Tatanka-pa, (Buffalo Head,) his x mark, seal.
"Marpiya-inajin, (Standing Cloud,) his x mark, seal.
"Cante-wicuwa, (Useful Heart,) his x mark, seal.
"Mato-xake-hanska, (Long Bear Claws,) his x mark, seal.
"Ixna-wica, (Only Man,) his x mark, seal.
"Attest

"HENRY E. GREGORY,
"I. D. DE RUSSY,
"Captain Second Infantry, U. S. A.

"ZEPHIR RENCOUNTRE,
"H BURT,
"Interpreters.

"I certify that the foregoing agreement was read and explained by me, and was fully understood by the above named Sioux Indians before signing; and that the same was executed by said Sioux Indians at Lower Brule agency, Dakota, on the 24th day of October, A. D. 1876.

Certificate.

"SAML. D. HINMAN,
"Official Interpreter.

"The foregoing articles of agreement having been fully explained to us in open council, we, the undersigned chiefs and headmen of the Sioux Indians, receiving rations and annuities at the Santee reservation, in Knox County, in the State of Nebraska, do hereby consent and agree to all the stipulations therein contained, saving, reserving, and excepting all our rights, both collective and individual, in and to the said Santee reservation, in said Knox County and State of Nebraska, upon which we, the undersigned, and our people are now residing.

Consent of Sioux at
Santee reservation.

"Witness our hands and seals at Santee agency, county of Knox, State of Nebraska, this 27th day of October, A. D. 1876.

"SANTEE

Santees.

"Joseph Wabashaw, seal.
"Hake-waxte, his x mark, seal.

"Wakute, (The Shooter,) his x mark, seal
"Huxaxa, (Red Legs,) his x mark, seal.
"Marpiya-duta, (Red Cloud,) his x mark, seal.
"Wakaninihanku, his x, mark, seal.
"Wamanonsa, (The Thief,) his x, mark, seal.
"Star Frazier, his x mark, seal.
"Pepe, (Sharp,) his x mark, seal.
"Hehaka-masa, (Iron Elk,) his x mark, seal.
"Tunkanwaxtexte, (The Good Stone God,) his x mark, seal.
"Daniel W. Hemans, seal.
"Eli Abraham, seal.
"Geo. Paypay, seal.
"Artemas Ehuamani, his x mark, seal.
"James Paypay, seal.

"Attest:

"CHAS. H. SEARING.
"JOSEPH W. COOK.

"CHARLES MITOHELL,
"ALFRED L. RIGGS,
        "*Interpreters.*

Certificate.

"I certify that the foregoing agreement was read and explained by me, and was fully understood by the above named Sioux Indians, before signing, and that the same was executed by said Sioux Indians at Santee agency, county of Knox, and State of Nebraska, on the 27th day of October, A. D. 1876.

"SAML. D. HINMAN,

"*Official Interpreter.*"

Approved, February 28, 1877.

Agreement of 1889

An act to divide a portion of the reservation of the Sioux Nation of Indians in Dakota into separate reservations and to secure the relinquishment of the Indian title to the remainder, and for other purposes.

Be it enacted by the Senate and House of Representatives of the United States of America in Congress assembled, That the following tract of land, being a part of the Great Reservation of the Sioux Nation, in the Territory of Dakota, is hereby set apart for a permanent reservation for the Indians receiving rations and annuities at the Pine Ridge Agency, in the Territory of Dakota, namely: Beginning at the intersection of the one hundred and third meridian of longitude with the northern boundry of the State of Nebraska; thence north along said meridian to the South Fork of Cheyenne River, and down said stream to the mouth of Battle Creek; thence due east to White River; thence down White River to the mouth of Black Pipe Creek on White River; thence due south to said north line of the State of Nebraska; thence west on said north line to the place of beginning. Also, the following tract of land situate in the State of Nebraska, namely: Beginning at a point on the boundary-line between the State of Nebraska and the Territory of Dakota where the range line between ranges forty-four and forty-five west of the sixth principal meridian, in the Territory of Dakota, intersects said boundary-line; thence east along said boundary-line, five miles; thence due south five miles; thence due west ten miles; thence due north to said boundary-line; thence due east along said boundary-line to the place of beginning: *Provided,* That the said tract of land in the State of Nebraska shall be reserved, by Executive order, only so long as it may be needed for the use and protection of the Indians receiving rations and annuities at the Pine Ridge Agency.

SEC. 2. That the following tract of land, being a part of the said Great Reservation of the Sioux Nation, in the Territory of Dakota, is hereby set apart for a permanent reservation for the Indians receiving rations and annuities at the Rosebud Agency, in said Territory of Dakota, namely: Commencing in the middle of the main channel of the Missouri River at the intersection of the south line of Brule County; thence down said middle of the main channel of said river, to

March 2, 1889.

Sioux Indian Rsservation Dakota. Subdivision of Ante, p.94

Pine Ridge Reservation Boundaries. Dakota.

Nebraska.

Proviso, Nebraska lands.

Rosebud Reservation. Boundaries.

237

the intersection of, the ninety-ninth degree of west longitude from Greenwich; thence due south to the forty-third parallel of latitude; thence west along said parallel to a point due south from the mouth of Black Pipe Creek; thence due north to the mouth of Black Pike Creek; thence down White River to a point intersecting the west line of Gregory County extended north; thence south on said extended west line of Gregory County to the intersection of the south line of Brule County extended west; thence due east on said south line of Brule County extended to the point of beginning in the Missouri River, including entirely within said reservation all islands, if any, in said river.

Standing Rock
Reservation.
Boundaries.

SEC. 3. That the following tract of land, being a part of the said Great Reservation of the Sioux Nation, in the Territory of Dakota, is hereby set apart for a permanent reservation for the Indians receiving rations and annuities at the Standing Rock Agency, in the said Territory of Dakota, namely: Beginning at a point in the center of the main channel of the Missouri River, opposite the mouth of Cannon Ball River; thence down said center of the main channel to a point ten miles north of the mouth of the Moreau River, including also within said reservation all island, if any, in said river; thence due west to the one hundred and second degree of west longitude from Greenwich; thence north along said meridian to its intersection with the South Branch of Cannon Ball River, also known as Cedar Creek; thence down said South Branch of Cannon Ball River to its intersection with the main Cannon Ball River, and down said main Cannon Ball River to the center of the main channel of the Missouri River at the place of beginning.

Cheyenne River
Reservation.
Boundaries.

SEC. 4. That the following tract of land, being a part of the said Great Reservation of the Sioux Nation, in the Territory of Dakota, is hereby set apart for a permanent reservation for the Indians receiving rations and annuities at the Cheyenne River Agency, in the said Territory of Dakota, namely: Beginning at a point in the center of the main channel of the Missouri River, ten miles north of the mouth of the Moreau River, said point being the southeastern corner of the Standing Rock Reservation;, thence down said center of the main channel of the Missouri River, including also entirely within said reservation all islands, if any, in said river, to a point opposite the mouth of the Cheyenne River; thence west to said Cheyenne River, and up the same to its intersection with the one hundred and second meridian of longitude; thence north along said meridian to its intersection with a line due west from a point in the Missouri River ten miles north of the mouth of the Moreau River; thence due east to the place of beginning.

Lower Brule
Reservation.
Boundaries.

SEC. 5. That the following tract of land, being a part of the said Great Reservation of the Sioux Nation, in the Territory, of Dakota, is hereby set apart for a permanent reservation for the Indians receiving rations and annuities at the Lower Brule Agency, in said Territory of Dakota, namely: Beginning on the Missouri River at Old Fort George; thence running due west to the western boundary of Presho County; thence running south on said western boundary to the fourty-fourth degree of latitude; thence on said forty-fourth degree of latitude to western boundary of township number seventy-two; thence south on said township western line to an intersecting line running due west from Fort Lookout; thence eastwardly on said line to the center of the main channel of the Missouri River at Fort Lookout; thence north in the center of the main channel of the said river to the original starting point.

SEC. 6. That the following tract of land, being a part of the Great Reservation of the Sioux Nation, in the Territory of Dakota, is hereby set apart for a permanent reservation for the Indians receiving rations and annuities at the Crow Creek Agency, in said Territory of Dakota, namely: The whole of township one hundred and six, range seventy; township one hundred and seven, range seventy-one; township one hundred and eight, range seventy-one; township one hundred and eight, range seventy-two; township one hundred and nine, range seventy-two, and the south half of township one hundred and nine, range seventy-one, and all except sections one, two, three, four, nine, ten, eleven, and twelve of township one hundred and seven, range seventy, and such parts as lie on the east or left bank of the Missouri River, of the following townships, namely: Township one hundred and six, range seventy-one; township one hundred and seven, range seventy two; township one hundred and eight, range seventy-three; township one hundred and eight, range seventy-four; township one hundred and eight, range seventy-five; township one hundred and eight, range seventy-six; township one hundred and nine, range seventy-three; township one hundred and nine, range seventy-four; south half of township one hundred and nine, range seventy-five, and township one hundred and seven, range seventy-three; also the west half of township one hundred and six, range sixty-nine, and sections sixteen, seventeen, eighteen, nineteen, twenty, twenty-one, twenty-eight, twenty-nine, thirty, thirty-one, thirty-two, and thirty-three, of township one hundred and seven, range sixty-nine.

Crow Creek Reservation. Boundaries.

SEC. 7. That each member of the Santee Sioux tribe of Indians now occupying a reservation in the State of Nebraska not having already taken allotments shall be entitled to allotments upon said reserve in Nebraska as follows: To each head of a family, one-quarter of a section; to each single person over eighteen years of age, one-eighth of a section; to each orphan child under eighteen years, one-eighth of a section; to each other person under eighteen years of age now living, one-sixteenth of a section; with title thereto, in accordance with the provisions of article six of the treaty concluded April twenty-ninth, eighteen hundred and sixty-eight, and the agreement with said Santee Sioux approved February twenty-eighth, eighteen hundred and seventy-seven, and rights under the same in all other respects conforming to this act. And said Santee Sioux shall be entitled to all other benefits under this act in the same manner and with the same conditions as if they were residents upon said Sioux

Santee Sioux in Nebraska. Allotment of lands to. Vol. 12, p. 637. Proviso. Former allotments confirmed.

Reservation, receiving rations at one of the agencies herein named: *Provided,* That all allotments heretofore made to said Santee Sioux in Nebraska are hereby ratified and confirmed; and each member of the Flandreau band of Sioux Indians is hereby authorized to take allotments on the Great Sioux Reservation, or in lieu therefor shall be paid at the rate of one dollar per acre for the land to which they would be entitled, to be paid out of the proceeds of lands relinquished under this act, which shall be used under the direction of the Secretary of the Interior; and said Flandreau band of Sioux Indians is in all other respects entitled to the benefits of this act the same as if receiving rations and annuities at any of the agencies aforesaid.

Indians to receive lands in severaity when civilized. Allotment. Increased. *Proviso.* Grazing lands.

SEC. 8. That the President is hereby authorized and required, whenever in his opinion any reservation of such Indians, or any part thereof, is advantageous for agricultural or grazing purposes, and the progress in civilization of the Indians receiving rations on either or any of said reservations shall be such as to encourage the belief that an allotment in severalty to such Indians, or any of them, would be for the best interest of said Indians, to cause said reservation, or so much thereof as is necessary, to be surveyed, or re-surveyed, and to allot the lands in said reservation in severalty to the Indians located thereon as aforesaid, in quantities as follows: To each head of a family, three hundred and twenty acres; to each single person over eighteen years of age, one-fourth of a section; to each orphan child under eighteen, years of age, one-fourth of a section; and to each other person under eighteen years now living, or who may be born prior to the date of the order of the President directing an allotment of the lands embraced in any reservation, one-eighth of a section. In case there is not sufficient land in either of said reservations to allot lands to each individual of the classes above named in quantities as above provided, the lands embraced in such reservation or reservations, shall be allotted to each individual of each of said classes pro rata in accordance with the provisions of this act: *Provided,* That where the lands on any reservation are mainly valuable for grazing purposes, an additional allotment of such grazing lands, in quantities as above provided, shall be made to each individual; or in case any two or more Indians who may be entitled to allotments shall so agree, the President may assign the grazing lands to which they may be entitled to them in one tract, and to be held and used in common.

Selections to be made by Indians. *Provisos.* Selections to be made within five years. Not compulsory.

SEC. 9. That all allotments set apart under the provisions of this act shall be selected by the Indians, heads of families selecting for their minor children, and the agents shall select for each orphan child, and in such manner as to embrace the improvements of the Indians making the selection. Where the improvements of two or more Indians have been made on the same legal subdivision of land, unless they shall otherwise agree, a provisional line may be run dividing said lands between them, and the amount to which each is entitled shall be equalized in the assignment of the remainder of the land to which they are entitled under this act: *Provided,* That if any one entitled to an allotment shall fail to make a selection within five years after the President shall direct that allotments may be made on a particular reservation, the Secretary of the Interior may direct the agent of such tribe or band, if such there be, and if there be no agent, then a special agent appointed for that purpose, to make a selection for such Indian, which selection shall be allotted as in cases where selections are made by the Indians, and patents shall issue in like manner: *Provided,* That these sections as to the allotments shall not be compulsory without the consent of the majority of the adult members of the tribe, except that the allotments shall be made as provided for the orphans.

SEC. 10. That the allotments provided for in this act shall be made by special agents appointed by the President for such purpose, and the agents in charge of the respective reservations on which the allotments are directed to be made, under such rules and regulations as the Secretary of the Interior may from time to time prescribe, and shall be certified by such agents to the Commissioner of Indian Affairs, in duplicate, one copy to be retained in the Indian Office and the other to be transmitted to the Secretary of the Interior for his action, and to be deposited in the General Land Office.

> Special agents to make allotments.

SEC. 11. That upon the approval of the allotments provided for in this act by the Secretary of the Interior, he shall cause patents to issue therefor in the name of the allottees, which patents shall be of the legal effect, and declare that the United States does and will hold the lands thus allotted for the period of twenty-five years, in trust for the sole use and benefit of the Indian to whom such allotment shall have been made, or, in case of his decease, of his heirs according to the laws of the State or Territory where such land is located, and that at the expiration of said period the United States will convey the same by patent to said Indian, or his heirs, as aforesaid, in fee, discharged of said trust and free of all charge or incumbrance whatsoever, and patents shall issue accordingly. And each and every allottee under this act shall be entitled to all the rights and privileges and be subject to all the provisions of section six of the act approved February eighth, eighteen hundred and eighty-seven, entitled "An act to provide for the allotment of lands in severalty to Indians on the various reservations, and to extend the protection of the laws of the United States and the Territories over the Indians and for other purposes." *Provided,* That the President of the United States may in any case, in his discretion, extend the period by a term not exceeding ten years; and if any lease or conveyance shall be made of the lands set apart and allotted as herein provided, or any contract made touching the same, before the expiration of the time above mentioned, such lease or conveyance or contract shall be absolutely null and void: *Provided further,* That the law of descent and partition in force in the State or Territory where the lands may be situated shall apply thereto after patents therefor have been executed and delivered. Each of the patents aforesaid shall be recorded

> Patents to issue.
> Lands held in trust for twenty-five years.
> Citizenship, etc.
> Vol. 24, p. 390.
> *Provisos.*
> Extending trust period.
> State or Territory law to regulate descent, etc.

in the General Land Office, and afterward delivered, free of charge, to the allottee entitled thereto.

Purchase of lands not allotted.
Proviso.
To be held for actual settlers.
Homestead patents.
Purchase money.
Record of patents.

Sec. 12. That at any time after lands have been allotted to all the Indians of any tribe as herein provided, or sooner, if in the opinion of the President it shall be for the best interests of said tribe, it shall be lawful for the Secretary of the Interior to negotiate with such Indian tribe for the purchase and release by said tribe, in conformity with the treaty or statute under which such reservation is held of such portions of its reservation not allotted as such tribe shall, from time to time, consent to sell, on such terms and conditions as shall be considered just and equitable between the United States and said tribe of Indians, which purchase shall not be complete until ratified by Congress: *Provided, however,* That all lands adapted to agriculture, with or without irrigation, so sold or released to the United States by any Indian tribe shall be held by the United States for the sole purpose of securing homes to actual settlers, and shall be disposed of by the United States to actual and bona-fide settlers only in tracts not exceeding one hundred and sixty acres to any one person, on such terms as Congress shall prescribe, subject to grants which Congress may make in aid of education: *And provided further,* That no patents shall issue therefor except to the person so taking the same as and for a homestead, or his heirs, and after the expiration of five years' occupancy thereof as such homestead; and any conveyance of said lands so taken as a homestead, or any contract touching the same, or lien thereon, created prior to the date of such patent shall be null and void. And the sums agreed to be paid by the United States as purchase money for any portion of any such reservation shall be held in the Treasury of the United States for the sole use of the tribe or tribes of Indians to whom such reservation belonged; and the same, with interest thereon at five per centum per annum, shall be at all times subject to appropriation by Congress for the education and civilization of such tribe or tribes of Indians, or the members thereof. The patents aforesaid shall be recorded in the General Land Office, and afterward, delivered, free of charge, to the allottee entitled thereto.

Indian not residing on new reservations.
Allotment to Poncas.
Increased.
Ante, p. 99.
Lands in Nebraska.
Vol. 22, p. 36.

Sec. 13. That any Indian receiving and entitled to rations and annuities at either of the agencies mentioned in this act at the time the same shall take effect, but residing upon any portion of said Great Reservation not included in either of the separate reservations herein established, may, at his option, within one year from the time when this act shall take effect, and within one year after he has been notified of his said right of option in such manner as the Secretary of the Interior shall direct by recording his election with the proper agent at the agency to which he belongs, have the allotment to which he would be otherwise entitled on one of said separate reservations upon the land where such Indian may then reside, such allotment in all other respects to conform to the allotments hereinbefore provided. Each member of the Ponca tribe of Indians now occupying a part of the old Ponca Reservation, within the limits of the said Great Sioux Reservation, shall be entitled to allotments upon said old Ponca Reservation as follows: To each head of a family, three hundred and twenty acres; to each single person over eighteen years of age, one-fourth of a section; to each orphan child under eighteen years of age, one-fourth of a section; and to each other person under eighteen years of age now living, one-eighth of a section, with title thereto and rights under the same in all other respects conforming to this act. And said Poncas shall be entitled to all other benefits under this act in the same manner and with the same conditions as if they were a part of the Sioux Nation receiving rations at one of the agencies herein named. When allotments to the Ponca tribe of Indians and to such other Indians as allotments are provided for by this act shall have been made upon that portion of said reservation which is described in the act entitled "An act to extend the northern boundary of the State of Nebraska," approved March twenty-eighth, eighteen hundred and eighty-two, the President shall, in pursuance of said act, declare that the Indian title is extinguished to all lands described in said act not so allotted hereunder, and thereupon all of said land not so allotted and included in said act of March twenty-eighth, eighteen hundred and eighty-two, shall be open to settlement as provided in this act: *Provided,* That the allotments to Ponca and other Indians authorized by this act to be made upon the land described in the said act entitled "An act to extend the northern boundary of the State of Nebraska," shall be made within six months from the time this act shall take effect.

SEC. 14. That in cases where the use of water for irrigation is necessary to render the lands within any Indian reservation created by this act available for agricultural purposes, the Secretary of the Interior be, and he is hereby, authorized to prescribe such rules and regulations as he may deem necessary to secure a just and equal distribution thereof among the Indians residing upon any such Indian reservation created by this act; and no other appropriation or grant of water by any riparian proprietor shall be authorized or permitted to the damage of any other riparian proprietor.

Irrigation.

SEC. 15. That if any Indian has, under and in conformity with the provisions of the treaty with the Great Sioux Nation concluded April twenty-ninth, eighteen hundred and sixty-eight, and proclaimed by the President February twenty-fourth, eighteen hundred and sixty-nine, or any existing law, taken allotments of land within or without the limits of any of the separate reservations established by this act, such allotments are hereby ratified and made valid, and such Indian is entitled to a patent therefor in conformity with the provisions of said treaty and existing law and of the provisions of this act in relation to patents for individual allotments.

Ratification of prior allotments.
Vol. 15, p. 635.

SEC 16. That the acceptance of this act by the Indians in manner and form as required by the said treaty concluded between the different bands of the Sioux Nation of Indians and the United States, April twenty-ninth, eighteen hundred

Acceptance of this act to release Indian titles.

Titles of individual
Indians unaffected.
Rights of way.
Provisos.
Payments by rail-
road companies.
To be used for rail-
way purposes only.
Payments.
Locations to be
made in nine
months.
Construction and
completion of road.
Forfeiture.

and sixty-eight, and proclaimed by the President February twenty fourth, eighteen hundred and sixty-nine, as hereinafter provided, shall be taken and held to be a release of all title on the part of the Indians receiving rations and annuities on each of the said separate reservations, to the lands described in each of the other separate reservations so created, and shall be held to confirm in the Indians entitled to receive rations at each of said separate reservations, respectively, to their separate and exclusive use and benefit, all the title and interest of every name and nature secured therein to the different bands of the Sioux Nation by said treaty of April twenty-ninth, eighteen hundred and sixty eight. This release shall not affect the title of any individual Indian to his separate allotment on land not included in any of said separate reservations provided for in this act, which title is hereby confirmed, nor any agreement heretofore made with the Chicago, Milwaukee and Saint Paul Railroad Company or the Dakota Central Railroad Company for a right of way through said reservation; and for any lands acquired by any such agreement to be used in connection therewith, except as hereinafter provided; but the Chicago, Milwaukee and Saint Paul Railway Company and the Dakota Central Railroad Company shall, respectively, have the right to take and use, prior to any white person, and to any corporation, the right of way provided for in said agreements, with not to exceed twenty acres of land in addition to the right of way, for stations for every ten miles of road; and said companies shall also, respectively, have the right to take and use for right of way, side-track, depot and station privileges, machine-shop, freight-house, round house, and yard facilities, prior to any white person, and to any corporation or association, so much of the two separate sections of land embraced in said agreements; also, the former company so much of the one hundred and eighty-eight acres, and the latter company so much of the seventy five acres, on the east side of the Missouri River, likewise embraced in said agreements, as the Secretary of the Interior shall decide to have been agreed upon and paid for by said railroad, and to be reasonably necessary upon each side of said river for approaches to the bridge of each of said companies to be constructed across the river, for right of way, side-track, depot and station privileges, machine-shop, freight house, round-house, and yard facilities, and no more: *Provided,* That the said railway companies shall have made the payments according to the terms of said agreements for each mile of right of way and each acre of land for railway purposes, which said companies take and use under the provisions of this act, and shall satisfy the Secretary of the Interior to that effect: *Provided further,* That no part of the lands herein authorized to be taken shall be sold or conveyed except by way of sale of, or mortgage of the railway itself. Nor shall any of said lands be used directly or indirectly for town site purposes, it being the intention hereof that said lands shall be held for general railway uses and purposes only, including stock yards, warehouses, elevators, terminal and other facilities of and for said railways: but nothing herein contained shall be construed to prevent any such railroad company from building upon such lands houses for the accommodation or residence of their employees, or leasing grounds contiguous to its tracks for warehouse or elevator purposes connected with said railways: *And provided further,* That said payments shall be made and said conditions performed within six month after this act shall take effect: *And provided further,* That said railway companies and each of them shall, within nine months after this act takes effect, definitely locate their respective lines of road, including all station grounds and terminals across and upon the lands of said reservation designated in said agreements, and shall also, within the said period of nine months, file with the Secretary of the Interior a map of such definite location, specifying clearly the line of road the several station grounds and the amount of land required for railway purposes, as herein specified, of the said separate sections of land and said tracts of one hundred and eighty-eight acres and seventy five acres, and the Secretary of the Interior shall, within three months after the filing of such map, designate the particular portions of said sections and of said tracts of land which the said railway companies respectively may take and hold under the provisions of this act for railway purposes. And the said railway companies, and each of them, shall, within three years after this act takes effect, construct, complete, and put in operation their said lines of road; and in case the said lines of road are not definitely located and maps of location filed within the periods hereinbefore provided, or in case the said lines of road are not constructed, completed, and put in operation within the time herein provided, then, and in either case, the lands granted for right of way, station grounds, or other railway purposes, as in this act provided, shall, without any further act or ceremony be declared by proclamation of the President forfeited, and shall, without enty or further action on the part of the United States, revert to the United States and be subject to entry under the other provisions of this act; and whenever such forfeiture occurs the Secretary of the Interior shall ascertain the fact and give due notice thereof to the local land officers, and thereupon the lands so forfeited shall be open to homestead entry under the provisions of this act.

SEC. 17. That it is hereby enacted that the seventh article of the said treaty of April twenty-ninth, eighteen hundred and sixty-eight, securing to said Indians the benefits of education, subject to such modifications as Congress shall deem most effective to secure to said Indians equivalent benefits of such education, shall continue in force for twenty years from and after the time this act shall take effect: and the Secretary of the Interior is hereby authorized and directed to purchase, from time to time, for the use of said Indians, such and so many American breeding cows of good quality, not exceeding twenty-five thousand in number, and bulls of like quality, not exceeding one thousand in number, as in his judgment can be under regulations furnished by him, cared

Schools, etc.
Vol. 15, p. 638.

for and preserved, with their increase, by said Indians: *Provided,* That each head of family or single person over the age of eighteen years, who shall have or may hereafter take his or her allotment of land in severalty, shall be provided with two milch cows, one pair of oxens, with yoke and chain, or two mares and one set of harness in lieu of said oxen, yoke and chain, as the Secretary of the Interior may deem advisable, and they shall also receive one plow, one wagon, one harrow, one hoe, one axe, and one pitchfork, all suitable to the work they may have to do, and also fifty dollars in cash; to be expended under the direction of the Secretary of the Interior in aiding such Indians to erect a house and other buildings suitable for residence or the improvement of his allotment; no sales, barters or bargains shall be made by any person other than said Indians with each.other, of any of the personal property hereinbefore provided for, and any violation of this provision shall be deemed a misdemeanor and punished by fine not exceeding one hundred dollars, or imprisonment not exceeding one year or both in the discretion of the court; That for two years the necessary seeds shall be provided to plant five acres of ground into different crops, if so much can be used, and provided that in the purchase of such seed preference shall be given to Indians who may have raised the same for sale, and so much money as shall be necessary for this purpose is hereby appropriated out of any money in the Treasury not otherwise appropriated; and in addition thereto there shall be set apart, out of any money in the Treasury not otherwise appropriated, the sum of three millions of dollars, which said sum shall be deposited in the Treasury of the United States to the credit of the Sioux Nation of Indians as a permanent fund, the interest of which, at five per centum per annum, shall be appropriated, under the direction of the Secretary of the Interior, to the use of the Indians receiving rations and annuities upon the reservations created by this act, in proportion to the numbers that shall so receive rations and annuities at the time this act takes effect, as follows: One-half of said interest shall be so expended for the promotion of industrial and other suitable education among said Indians, and the other half thereof in such manner and for such purposes, including reasonable cash payments per capita as, in the judgment of said Secretary, shall, from time to time, most contribute to the advancement of said Indians in civilization and self-support; and the Santee Sioux, the Flandreau Sioux, and the Ponca Indians shall be included in the benefits of said permanent fund, as provided in sections seven and thirteen of this act: *Provided,* That after the Government has been reimbursed for the money expended for said Indians under the provisions of this act, the Secretary of the Interior may, in his discretion, expend, in addition to the interest of the permanent fund, not to exceed ten per centum per annum of the principal of said fund in the employment of farmers and in the purchase of agricultural implements, teams, seeds, including reasonable cash payments per capita, and other articles necessary to assist them in agricultural pursuits, and he shall report to Congress in detail each year his doings hereunder. And at the end of fifty years from the passage of this act, said fund shall be expended for the purpose of promoting education, civilization, and self-support among said Indians, or otherwise distributed among them as Congress shall from time to time thereafter determine.

SEC. 18. That if any land in said Great Sioux Reservation is now occupied and used by any religious society for the purpose of missionary or educational work among said Indians, whether situate

50–2———18

outside of or within the lines of any reservation constituted by this act, or if any such land is so occupied upon the Santee Sioux Reservation, in Nebraska, the exclusive occupation and use of said land, not exceeding one hundred and sixty acres in any one tract, is hereby, with the approval of the Secretary of the Interior, granted to any such society so long as the same shall be occupied and used by such society for educational and missionary work among said Indians; and the Secretary of the Interior is hereby authorized and directed to give to such religious society patent of such tract of land to the legal effect aforesaid; and for the purpose of such educational or missionary work any such society may purchase, upon any of the reservations herein created, any land not exceeding in any one tract one hundred and sixty acres, not interfering with the title in severalty of any Indian, and with the approval of and upon such terms, not exceeding one dollar and twenty-five cents an acre, as shall be prescribed by the Secretary of the Interior. And the Santee Normal Training School may, in like manner, purchase for such educational or missionary work on the Santee Reservation, in addition to the foregoing, in such location and quantity, not exceeding three hundred and twenty acres, as shall be approved by the Secretary of the Interior.

SEC. 19. That all the provisions of the said treaty with the different bands of the Sioux Nation of Indians concluded April twentyninth, eighteen hundred and sixty-eight, and the agreement with the same approved February twenty-eighth, eighteen hundred and seventy-seven, not in conflict with the provisions and requirements of this act, are hereby continued in force according to their tenor and limitation, anything in this act to the contrary notwithstanding.

SEC. 20. That the Secretary of the Interior shall cause to be erected not less than thirty school-houses, and more, if found necessary, on the different reservations, at such points as he shall think for the best interest of the Indians, but at such distance only as will enable as many as possible attending schools to return home nights, as white children do attending district schools: *And provided,* That any white children residing in the neighborhood are entitled to attend the said school on such terms as the Secretary of the Interior may prescribe.

Marginal notes:

Lands occupied for religious purposes.

Santee Normal Training School.

Treaty provisions not conflicting continued.
Vol. 15, p. 635

School-houses.
Proviso.
White children.

Lands outside of
separate reserva-
tions restored to
public domain.
Exceptions.
R. S., sec. 2301,
p.421.
Proviso.
Price increased.
Soldiers
homesteads.
R. S., secs. 2304,
2305, p. 422.
Lands unsold to
be bought by
Government.

Highways, etc.

American Island
donoted to Cham-
berlain Dark, for a
public park.

Farm Island do-
nated to Plerre,
Dark, for a public
park.

SEC. 21. That all the lands in the Great Sioux Reservation outside of the separate reservations herein described are hereby restored to the public domain, except American Island, Farm Island, and Niobrara Island, and shall be disposed of by the United States to actual settlers only, under the provisions of the homestead law (except section two thousand three hundred and one thereof) and under the law relating to town-sites: *Provided,* That each settler, under and in accordance with the provisions of said homestead acts, shall pay to the United States, for the land so taken by him, in addition to the fees provided by law, the sum of one dollar and twenty-five cents per acre for all lands disposed of within the first three years after the taking effect of this act, and the sum of seventy-five cents per acre for all lands disposed of within the next two years following thereafter, and fifty cents per acre for the residue of the lands then undisposed of, and shall be entitled to a patent therefor according to said homestead laws, and after the full payment of said sums: but the rights of honorably discharged Union soldiers and sailors in the late civil war as defined and described in sections twenty-three hundred and four and twenty-three hundred and five of the Revised Statutes of the United States, shall not be abridged, except as to said sums: *Provided,* That all lands herein opened to settlement under this act remaining undisposed of at the end of ten years from the taking effect of this act shall be taken and accepted by the United States and paid for by said United States at fifty cents per acre, which amount shall be added to and credited to said Indians as part of their permanent fund, and said lands shall thereafter be part of the public domain of the United States, to be disposed of under the homestead laws of the United States, and the provisions of this act; and any conveyance of said lands so taken as a homestead, or any contract touching the same, or lien thereon, created prior to the date of final entry, shall be null and void: *Provided,* That there shall be reserved public highways four rods wide around every section of land allotted, or opened to settlement by this act, the section lines being the center of said highways; but no deduction shall be made in the amount to be paid for each quarter-section of land by reason of such reservation. But if the said highway shall be vacated by any competent authority the title to the respective strips shall inure to the then owner of the tract of which it formed a part by the original survey. *And provided further,* That nothing in this act contained shall be so construed as to affect the right of Congress or of the government of Dakota to establish public highways, or to grant to railroad companies the right of way through said lands, or to exclude the said lands, or any thereof, from the operation of the general laws of the United States now in force granting to railway companies the right of way and depot grounds over and upon the public lands, American Island, an island in the Missouri River, near Chamberlain, in the Territory of Dakota, and now a part of the Sioux Reservation, is hereby donated to the said city of Chamberlain: *Provided further,* That said city of Chamberlain shall formally accept the same within one year from the passage of this act, upon the express condition that the same shall be preserved and used for all time entire as a public park, and for no other purpose, to which all persons shall have free access; and said city shall have authority to adopt all proper rules and regulations for the improvement and care of said park; and upon the failure of any of said conditions the said island shall revert to the United States, to be disposed of by future legislation only. Farm Island, an island in the Missouri River near Pierre, in the Territory of Dakota, and now a part of the Sioux Reservation, is hereby donated to the said city of Pierre: *Provided further,* That said city of Pierre shall formally accept the same within one year from the passage of this act, upon the express condition that the same shall be preserved and used for all time entire as a public park, and for no other purpose, to which all persons shall have free access; and said city shall have authority to adopt all proper rules and regulations for the improvement and care of said park; and upon the failure of any of said conditions the said island shall revert to the United States, to be disposed of by future legislation only. Niobrara Island, an island in the Niobrara River, near Niobrara, and now a part of the Sioux Reservation, is hereby donated to the said city of Niobrara: *Provided further,* That the said city of Niobrara, shall formally accept the same within one year from the passage of this act, upon the express condition that the same shall be preserved and used for all time entire as a public park, and for no other purpose, to which all persons shall have free access; and said city shall have authority to adopt all proper rules and regulations for the improvement and care of said park: and upon the failure of any of said conditions the said island shall revert to the United States, to be disposed of by future legislation only: *And provided further,* That if any full or mixed blood Indian, of the Sioux Nation shall have located upon Farm Island American Island, or Niobrara Island before the date of the passage of this act, it shall be the duty of the Secretary of the Interior, within three months from the time this act shall have taken effect, to cause all improvements made by any such Indian so located upon either of said islands, and all damage that may accrue to him by a removal therefrom, to be appraised, and upon the payment of the sum so determined, within six months after notice thereof by the city to which the island is herein donated to such Indian, said Indian shall be required to remove from said island, and shall be entitled to select instead of such location his allotment according to the provisions of this act upon any of the reservations herein established, or upon any land opened to settlement by this act not already located upon.

Niobrara Island donated to Niobrara, Nebr., for a public park.

Removal of Indains from islands.

STAT L—VOL XXV————57

SEC. 22. That all money accruing from the disposal of lands in conformity with this act shall be paid into the Treasury of the United States and be applied solely as follows: First, to the reimbursement of the United States for all necessary actual expenditures contemplated and provided for under the

Disposition of proceeds of saies.

provisions of this act, and the creation of the permanent fund hereinbefore provided; and after such reimbursement to the increase of said permanent fund for the purposes hereinbefore provided.

SEC. 23. That all persons who, between the twenty-seventh day of February, eighteen hundred and eighty-five, and the seventeenth day of April, eighteen hundred and eighty-five, in good faith, entered upon or made settlements with intent to enter the same under the homestead or pre-emption laws of the United States upon any part of the Great Sioux Reservation lying east of the Missouri River, and known as the Crow Creek and Winnebago Reservation, which, by the President's proclamation of date February twenty-seventh, eighteen hundred and eighty-five, was declared to be open to settlement, and not included in the new reservation established by section six of this act, and who, being otherwise legally entitled to make such entries, located or attempted to locate thereon homestead, pre-emption, or town site claims, by actual settlement and improvement of any portion of such lands, shall, for a period of ninety days after the proclamation of the President required to be made by this act, have a right to re-enter upon said claims and procure title thereto under the homestead or pre-emption laws of the United States, and complete the same as required therein, and their said claims shall, for such time, have a preference over later entries; and when they shall have in other respects shown themselves entitled and shall have complied with the law regulating such entries, and, as to homesteads, with the special provisions of this act, they shall be entitled to have said lands, and patents therefor shall be issued as in like cases: *Provided,* That pre-emption claimants shall reside on their lands the same length of time before procuring title as homestead claimants under this act. The price to be paid for town-site entries shall be such as is required by law in other cases, and shall be paid into the general fund provided for by this act.

SEC. 24. That sections sixteen and thirty-six of each township of the lands open to settlement under the provisions of this act, whether surveyed or unsurveyed, are hereby reserved for the use and benefit of the public schools, as provided by the act organizing the Territory of Dakota; and whether surveyed or unsurveyed said sections shall not be subject to claim, settlement, or entry under the provision of this act or any of the land laws of the United States: *Provided, however,* That the United States shall pay to said Indians, out of any moneys in the Treasury not otherwise appropriated, the sum of one dollar and twenty-five cents per acre for all lands reserved under the provisions of this section.

SEC. 25. That there is hereby appropriated the sum of one hundred thousand dollars, out of any money in the Treasury not otherwise appropriated, or so much thereof as may be necessary, to be applied and used towards surveying the lands herein described as being opened for settlement, said sum to be immediately available; which sum shall not be deducted from the proceeds of lands disposed of under this act.

Sec. 26. That all expenses for the surveying, platting, and disposal of the lands opened to settlement under this act shall be borne by the United States, and not deducted from the proceeds of said lands.

Sec. 27. That the sum of twenty-eight thousand two hundred dollars, or so much thereof as may be necessary, be, and hereby is, appropriated out of any money in the Treasury not otherwise appropriated, to enable the Secretary of the Interior to pay to such individual Indians of the Red Cloud and Red Leaf bands of Sioux as he shall ascertain to have been deprived by the authority of the United States of ponies in the year eighteen hundred and seventy-six, at the rate of forty dollars for each pony; and he is hereby authorized to employ such agent or agents as he may deem necessary in ascertaining such facts as will enable him to carry out this provision, and to pay them therefor such sums as shall be deemed by him fair and just compensation: *Provided,* That the sum paid to each individual Indian under this provision shall be taken and accepted by such Indian in full compensation for all loss sustained by such Indian in consequence of the taking from him of ponies as aforesaid: *And provided further,* That if any Indian entitled to such compensation shall have deceased, the sum to which such Indian would be entitled shall be paid to his heirs-at-law, according to the laws of the Territory of Dakota.

Payment of ponies, Red Cloud and Red Leaf bands.

Provisos. To be accepted in full.

Sec. 28. That this act shall take effect, only, upon the acceptance thereof and consent thereto by the different bands of the Sioux Nation of Indians, in manner and form prescribed by the twelfth article of the treaty between the United States and said Sioux Indians concluded April twenty-ninth, eighteen hundred and sixty-eight, which said acceptance and consent, shall be made known by proclamation by the President of the United States, upon satisfactory proof presented to him, that the same has been obtained in the manner and form required, by said twelfth article of said treaty; which proof shall be presented to him within one year from the passage of this act; and upon failure of such proof and proclamation this act becomes of no effect and null and void

Acceptance by Indians. Proclamation.

Sec. 29. That there is hereby appropriated, out of any money in the Treasury not otherwise appropriated, the sum of twenty-five thousand dollars, or so much thereof as may be necessary which sum shall be expended, under the direction of the Secretary of the Interior, for procuring the assent of the Sioux Indians, to this act provided in section twenty-seven.

Appropriation.

Sec. 30. That all acts and parts of acts inconsistent with the provisions of this act are hereby repealed.

Repeal.

Approved, March 2, 1889.